INTRODUCTION

KT-156-797

The confidence man —likable rogue, disturbing everyman, exemplar of modern, derationated man— has a distinguished literary pedigree: Dickens' *Martin Chuzzlewit*, Mann's *Felix Krull*, Ibsen's *Peer Gynt*, and, most conspicuously, Melville's singular masterpiece *The Confidence Man*.

But *Nightmare Alley* is quintessentially American, vaguely disreputable, a product of 1930s and '40s hard-boiled, pulp, and noir fiction; William Lindsay Gresham is as far from Dickens or Mann as comic books are from opera.

Nightmare Alley belongs to that rarefied literary species of undervalued genre novels that have acquired cult status among aficionados. It depicts a persistently bleak view of humanity, described by one critic as "a tough, relentless, colorful novel that exposes the private world of the freaks in order to comment on a sick, degrading society."

The novel traces the rise and fall of a con man with the improbably aristocratic name of Stanton Carlisle (later, in his guise as a bogus spiritualist, "The Great Stanton") and begins and ends in the sordid milieu of the carnival where hustling chumps —and each other— is a way of life.

Its reputation has probably been enhanced if not virtually monopolized by the 1947 film adaptation. Published in 1946, the novel's movie rights were quickly purchased by the actor Tyrone Power, who, wanting to discard —or at least expand upon— his narrow image as a romantic swashbuckler and, coming off the enormous success of *The Razor's Edge*, talked the studio into allowing him to star in the role of the irredeemably unsavory lead. It turned out to be one of Powers' most powerful performances and one of the most unnerving roles by a leading man (at least until Robert Mitchum played Max Cady in *Cape Fear*).

The film was directed by Edmund Goulding, a workhorse screenwriter/director whom Andrew Sarris gently described as "discreet and tasteful." Goulding was versatile and amazingly prolific, whose directorial assignments ranged from "women's" films —sort of a low-rent George Cukor, he was called in to direct several of Bette Davis' better '40s vehicles— to the charming romantic comedy *Riptide* to *Grand Hotel* to *Nightmare Alley*. He was aided by Lee Garmes, an artful cinematographer whose expressionistic lighting beautifully and faithfully transposed Gresham's noirish descriptive passages to the screen.

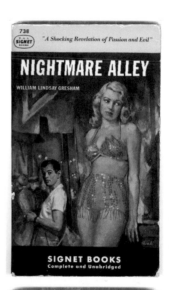

738

"A Shocking Revelation of Passion and Evil"

NIGHTMARE ALLEY

WILLIAM LINDSAY GRESHAM

SIGNET BOOKS
Complete and Unabridged

"I'm a hustler, damn it—

I'm on the make. Nothing matters in this damned lunatic asylum of a world but dough... When you get that you're the boss. If you don't have it you're the end man on the daisy chain."

That was Stan Carlisle, carnival spieler; The Great Stanton, night-club mentalist; Reverend Stanton Carlisle, spiritualist adviser to wealthy widows and lecherous businessmen. From warm-bodied Zeena he took the tricks of his trade. From lovely Molly he took virginity and desperate love. From Dr. Lilith Ritter he sought salvation and crowning success—but got neither. Instead there was sudden downfall, and an ugly finish to a career of deceit and evil.

William Lindsay Gresham was born in Baltimore, the descendant of a family that settled in Maryland in 1641. He moved to New York in 1917 and after graduating from high school began working at a varied succession of jobs—salesman, magician, copywriter, magazine editor, etc. *Nightmare Alley*, his first novel, was published by Rinehart in 1946.

PHOTO: LEJA GORSKA

Published by the New American Library

Gresham was not remote from his subject matter. He was born on August 20, 1909. According to Paul Duncan's *Noir Fiction: Dark Highways*, a young Gresham visited the freak show at Coney Island and was "fascinated by a sharply dressed, suave-looking Italian man, who had a small headless body hanging out of his stomach. The small body was also impeccably dressed." Gresham later sang folk music in a bohemian nightspot in Greenwich Village, and in 1936 joined the Communist Party under the name William Rafferty. In November 1937, he joined the Abraham Lincoln Brigade and fought on the side of the Republicans in the Spanish Civil War. It was there that he met a medic, Joseph Daniel 'Doc' Halliday, who reminisced about life in a carnival. "It was from him that Gresham learned all about the carny culture, the habits, the mentality, the language. And it was there that he first came across the word geek. It referred to the lowest of the low — an alcoholic or drug addict who was out of his head all the time. He could be prodded, cajoled and led into working for more drink or drugs. His job? To sit and crawl in his own excrement, as the wild man of Borneo, and occasionally bite the heads off chickens and snakes. Immediately, a story idea entered into Gresham's head, about the rise of a carny conman and his subsequent descent into geekdom."

Gresham returned to New York and eventually began work on *Nightmare Alley*, hanging out at the Dixie Hotel, where the carnival workers did their drinking. It met with immediate commercial success upon publication, and Gresham sold the movie rights for $60,000.

Gresham's private life was tumultuous, including an abusive relationship with his wife and children (who eventually moved away from him to England). "Reflecting on his life, Gresham told a fellow veteran from Spain, 'I sometimes think that if I have any real talent it is not literary but is a sheer talent for survival. I have survived three busted marriages, losing my boys, war, tuberculosis, Marxism, alcoholism, neurosis and years of freelance writing. Just too mean and ornery to kill, I guess."

Discovering that he had cancer of the tongue, a fatal disease, he checked into the Dixie Hotel on September 14, 1962 and took his own life.

Gresham's other works include the novel *Limbo Tower* (1949), about death, depression, disease, and tuberculosis in a hospital, a non-fiction book about freak shows and carnivals, *Monster Midway* (1953), and a biography of Harry Houdini, *Houdini: the Man Who Walked Through Walls* (1959). He also contributed short stories and articles to *Ellery Queen's Mystery Magazine*, *Esquire* and other publications.

In 1991, Bob Callahan entered into a partnership with Art Spiegelman to package for Avon Books a series of graphic novels adapted from some of the darkest noir novels throughout the century. Callahan was a writer, poet, and independent publisher who had recently contracted for several books for larger corporate publishers and had also become interested in comics, editing a collection of George McManus's *Bringing Up Father* (1985) and *The New Comics Anthology* (1990). Spiegelman is the author of *Maus* and a regular contributor to *The New Yorker*. According to Callahan, he and Spiegelman embarked on a "continuous dialogue" discussing adapting novels into comics. Callahan liked the idea of adapting crime novels because he felt that crime novels was a genre that resided somewhere between mainstream novels and comics, which had a history, particularly throughout the '50s, of exploiting the crime genre.

Avon Books eventually accepted their proposal, and released two graphic novels in the series — *City of Glass* (originally by Paul Auster, adapted by Paul Karasik and David Mazzucchelli) and *Perdita Durango* (originally by Barry Gifford, adapted by Callahan and Paul Gillis). *Nightmare Alley* was to be the third.

Callahan commissioned a script for *Nightmare Alley* by Tom DeHaven, a novelist and essayist well-known in comics circles for his series of Derby Dugan novels based on comics history (the latest of which is *Dugan Underground*). The commercial illustrator and occasional comics artist Mark Zingarelli had started drawing the book from DeHaven's script when a personal tragedy cut his involvement abruptly short. Callahan then approached Spain Rodriguez, the underground cartoonist best known for his Marxist character Trashman and his blue-collar autobiographical stories set in Buffalo, New York, who thought the novel was "riveting" and immediately agreed to do it. He preferred to adapt the story entirely himself, and the DeHaven script was set aside.

Spain had finished most of the book by the time Avon pulled the plug on the series in approximately 1996 and the book's been in limbo ever since. As soon as Fantagraphics Books, who published two of Spain's collections in the '90s (*Trashman* and *My True Story*, as well as his short stories in the anthology *Blab!*) picked the book up in 2001, Spain set down and finished the book, the longest single work of his career. All told, Spain spent seven years working on it, on and off. All told, more artists have worked on *Nightmare Alley*, adapting it into more media, than just about any other piece of fiction.

"Twenty years of research went into the book, plus two years of plotting and eight months of actual writing," Gresham once said of *Nightmare Alley*. "It put the word 'geek' into common language. It is nice to know that someone remembers it."

—Gary Groth
Seattle, December 22, 2003

I am indebted to Paul Duncan's *Noir Fiction: Dark Highways*, which had by far the most comprehensive biographical sketch of William Lindsay Gresham that I found. Thanks to Alex Henzel for supplying us with a copy of the original *Nightmare Alley* paperback.

NIGHTMARE ALLEY

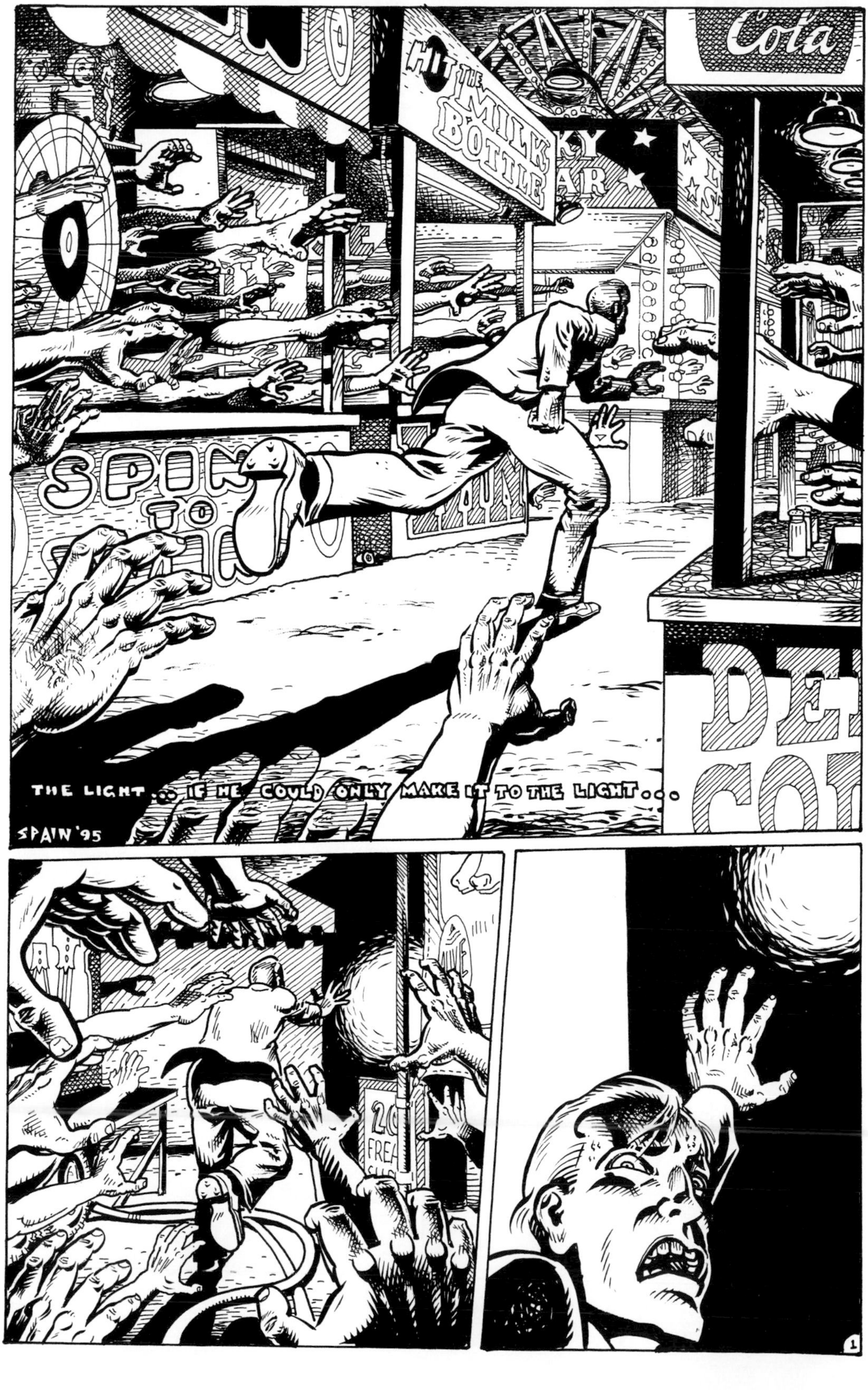
Cola
HIT THE MILKY BOTTLE
SPIN TO WIN
THE LIGHT... IF HE COULD ONLY MAKE IT TO THE LIGHT...
SPAIN '95
20¢
FREA

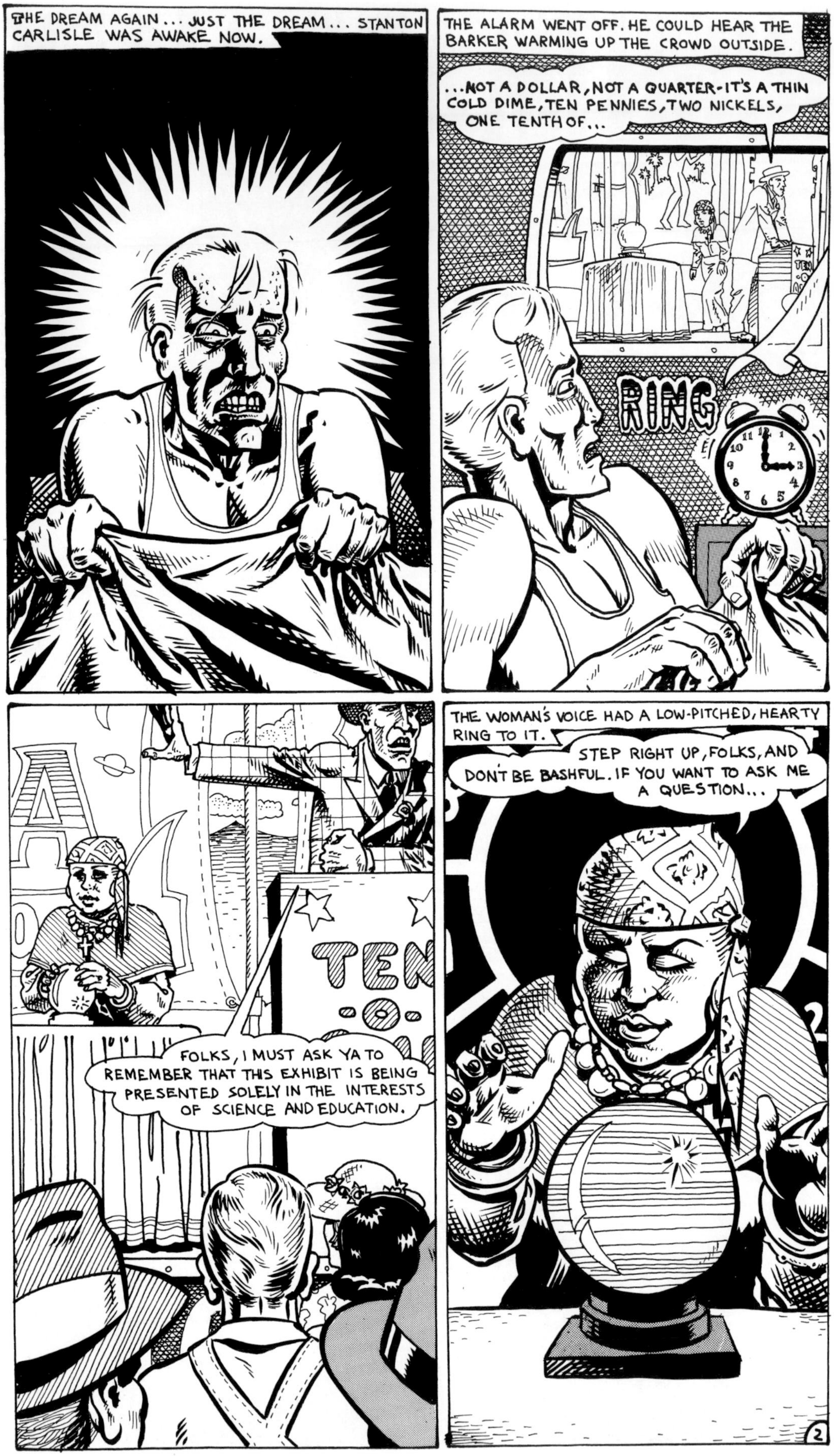
THE DREAM AGAIN... JUST THE DREAM... STANTON CARLISLE WAS AWAKE NOW.
THE ALARM WENT OFF. HE COULD HEAR THE BARKER WARMING UP THE CROWD OUTSIDE.
...NOT A DOLLAR, NOT A QUARTER-IT'S A THIN COLD DIME, TEN PENNIES, TWO NICKELS, ONE TENTH OF...
RING
FOLKS, I MUST ASK YA TO REMEMBER THAT THIS EXHIBIT IS BEING PRESENTED SOLELY IN THE INTERESTS OF SCIENCE AND EDUCATION.
THE WOMAN'S VOICE HAD A LOW-PITCHED, HEARTY RING TO IT.
STEP RIGHT UP, FOLKS, AND DON'T BE BASHFUL. IF YOU WANT TO ASK ME A QUESTION...

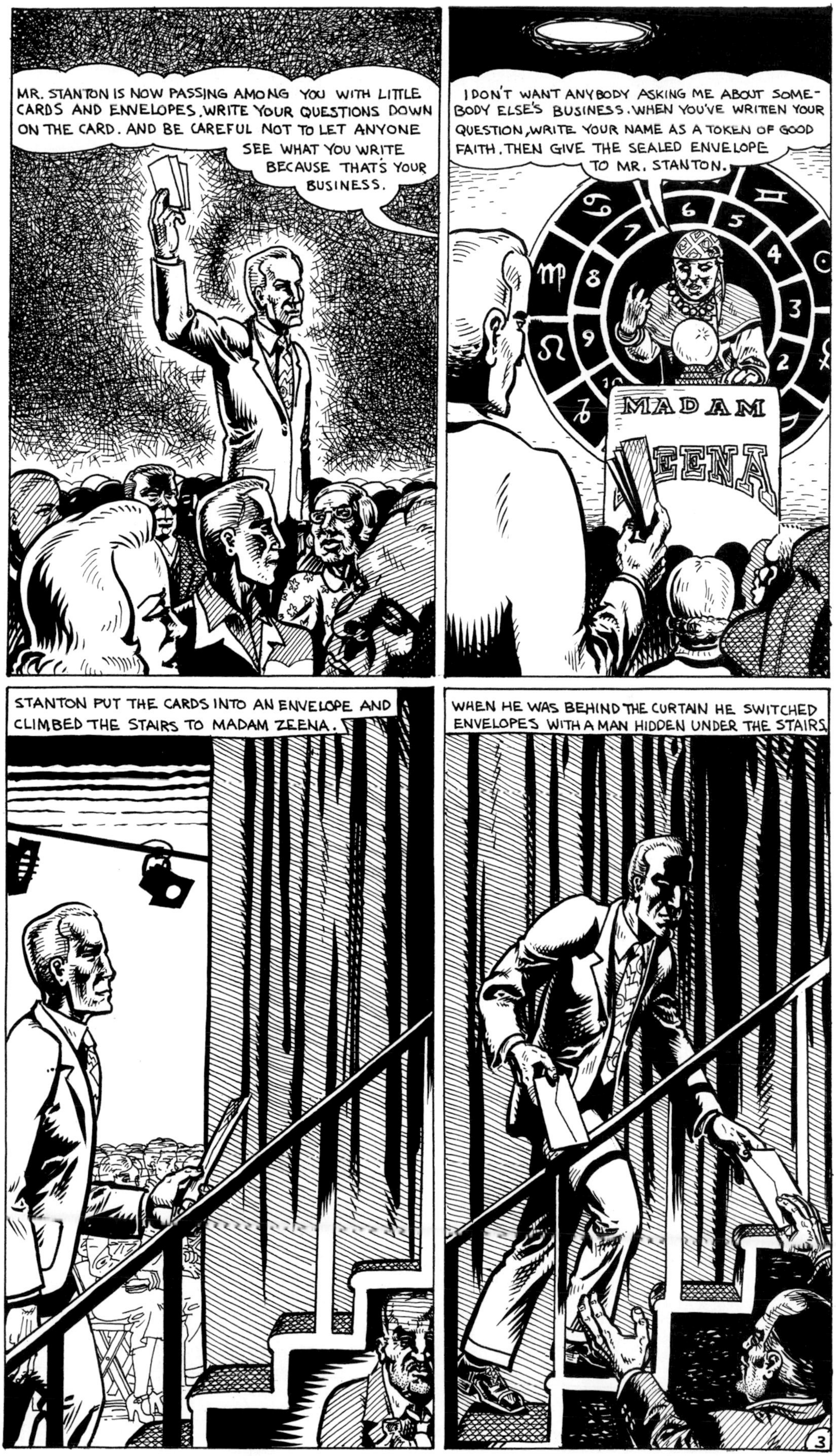

MR. STANTON IS NOW PASSING AMONG YOU WITH LITTLE CARDS AND ENVELOPES. WRITE YOUR QUESTIONS DOWN ON THE CARD. AND BE CAREFUL NOT TO LET ANYONE SEE WHAT YOU WRITE BECAUSE THAT'S YOUR BUSINESS.
I DON'T WANT ANYBODY ASKING ME ABOUT SOMEBODY ELSE'S BUSINESS. WHEN YOU'VE WRITTEN YOUR QUESTION, WRITE YOUR NAME AS A TOKEN OF GOOD FAITH. THEN GIVE THE SEALED ENVELOPE TO MR. STANTON.
MADAM
ZEENA
STANTON PUT THE CARDS INTO AN ENVELOPE AND CLIMBED THE STAIRS TO MADAM ZEENA.
WHEN HE WAS BEHIND THE CURTAIN HE SWITCHED ENVELOPES WITH A MAN HIDDEN UNDER THE STAIRS.

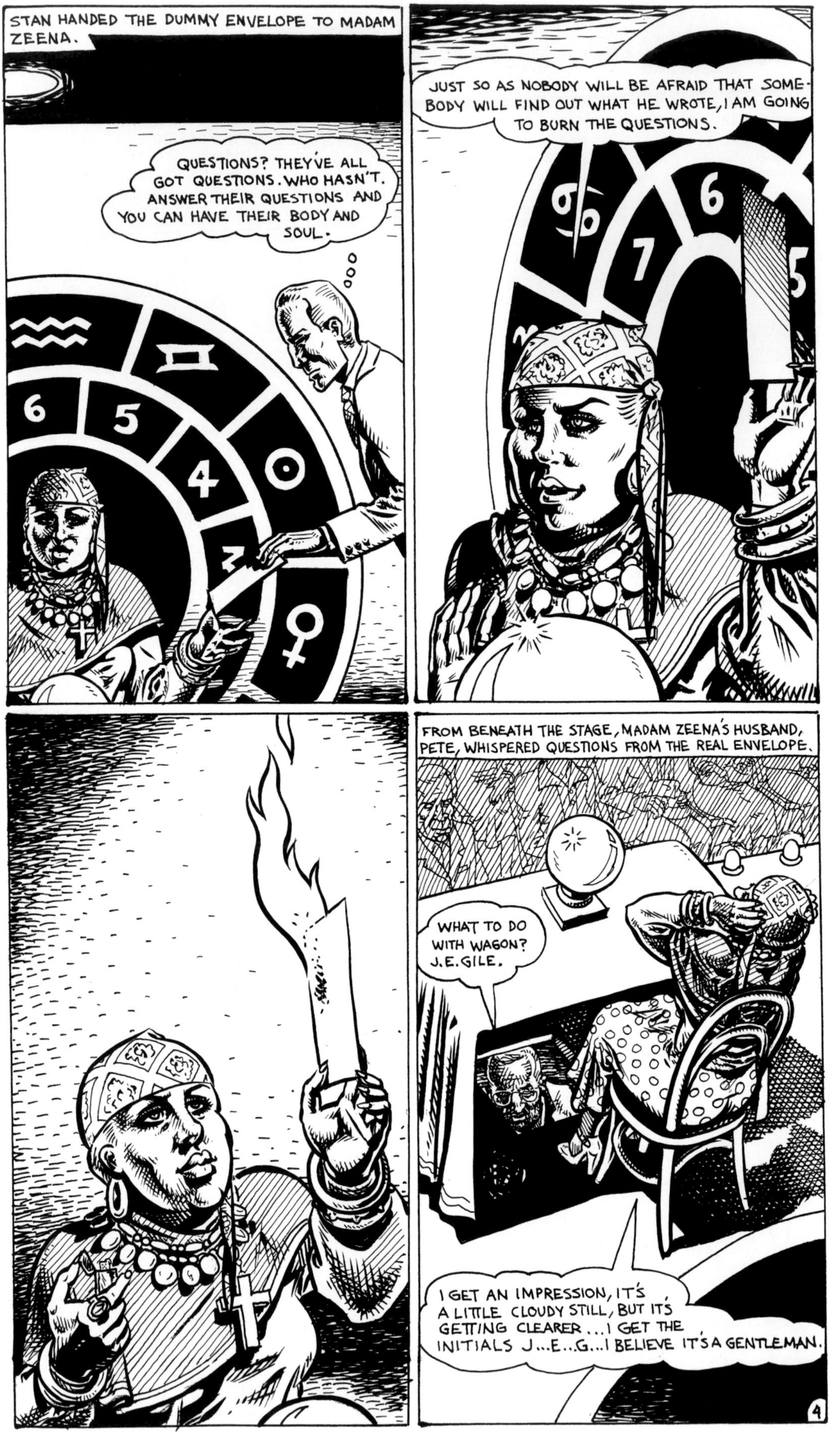
STAN HANDED THE DUMMY ENVELOPE TO MADAM ZEENA.
QUESTIONS? THEY'VE ALL GOT QUESTIONS. WHO HASN'T. ANSWER THEIR QUESTIONS AND YOU CAN HAVE THEIR BODY AND SOUL.
JUST SO AS NOBODY WILL BE AFRAID THAT SOMEBODY WILL FIND OUT WHAT HE WROTE, I AM GOING TO BURN THE QUESTIONS.
FROM BENEATH THE STAGE, MADAM ZEENA'S HUSBAND, PETE, WHISPERED QUESTIONS FROM THE REAL ENVELOPE.
WHAT TO DO WITH WAGON? J.E.GILE.
I GET AN IMPRESSION, IT'S A LITTLE CLOUDY STILL, BUT IT'S GETTING CLEARER ... I GET THE INITIALS J...E...G...I BELIEVE IT'S A GENTLEMAN.

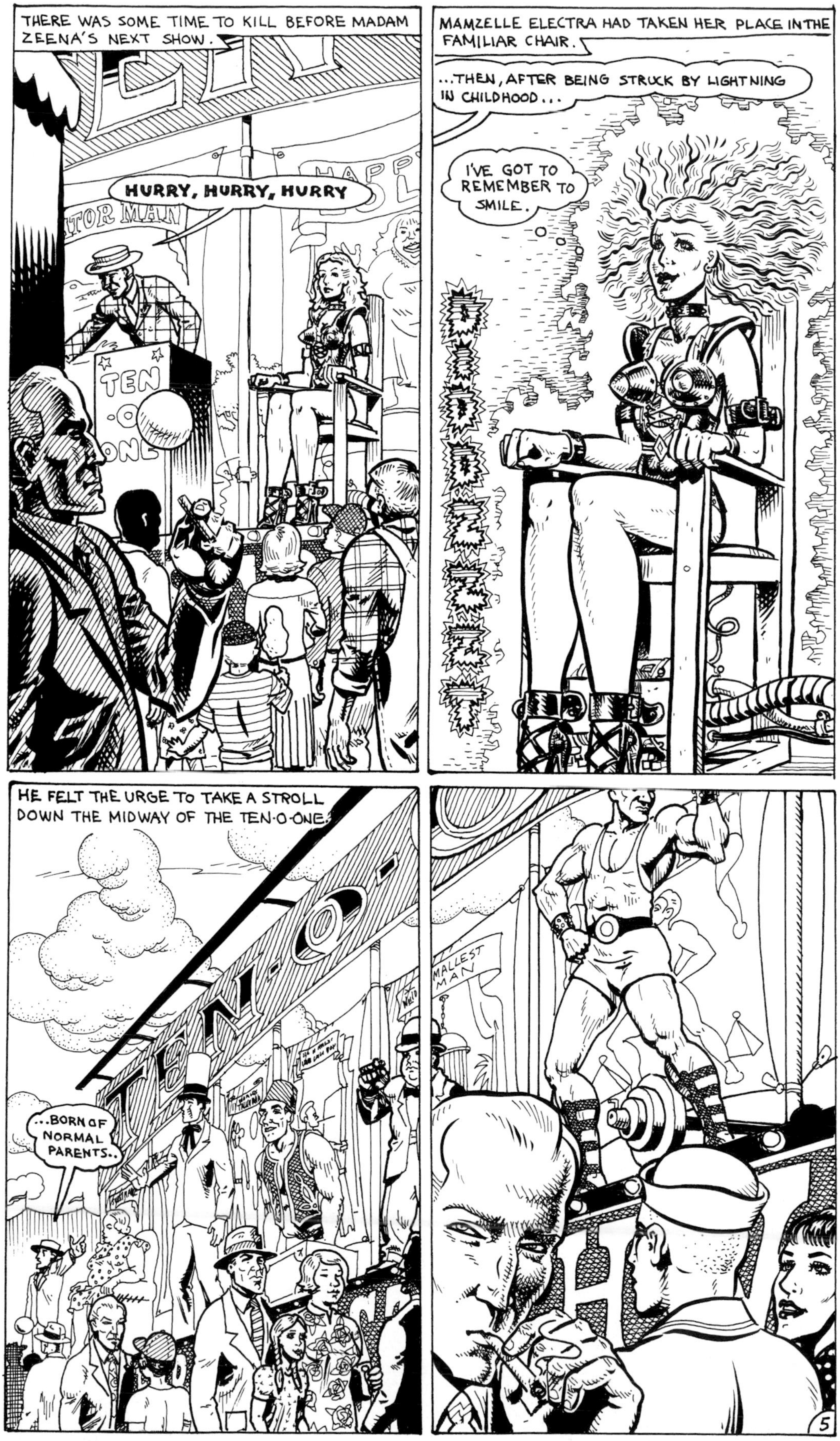
THERE WAS SOME TIME TO KILL BEFORE MADAM ZEENA'S NEXT SHOW.
HURRY, HURRY, HURRY
TEN -O- ONE
MAMZELLE ELECTRA HAD TAKEN HER PLACE IN THE FAMILIAR CHAIR.
...THEN, AFTER BEING STRUCK BY LIGHTNING IN CHILDHOOD...
I'VE GOT TO REMEMBER TO SMILE.
HE FELT THE URGE TO TAKE A STROLL DOWN THE MIDWAY OF THE TEN-O-ONE.
...BORN OF NORMAL PARENTS..
MALLEST MAN

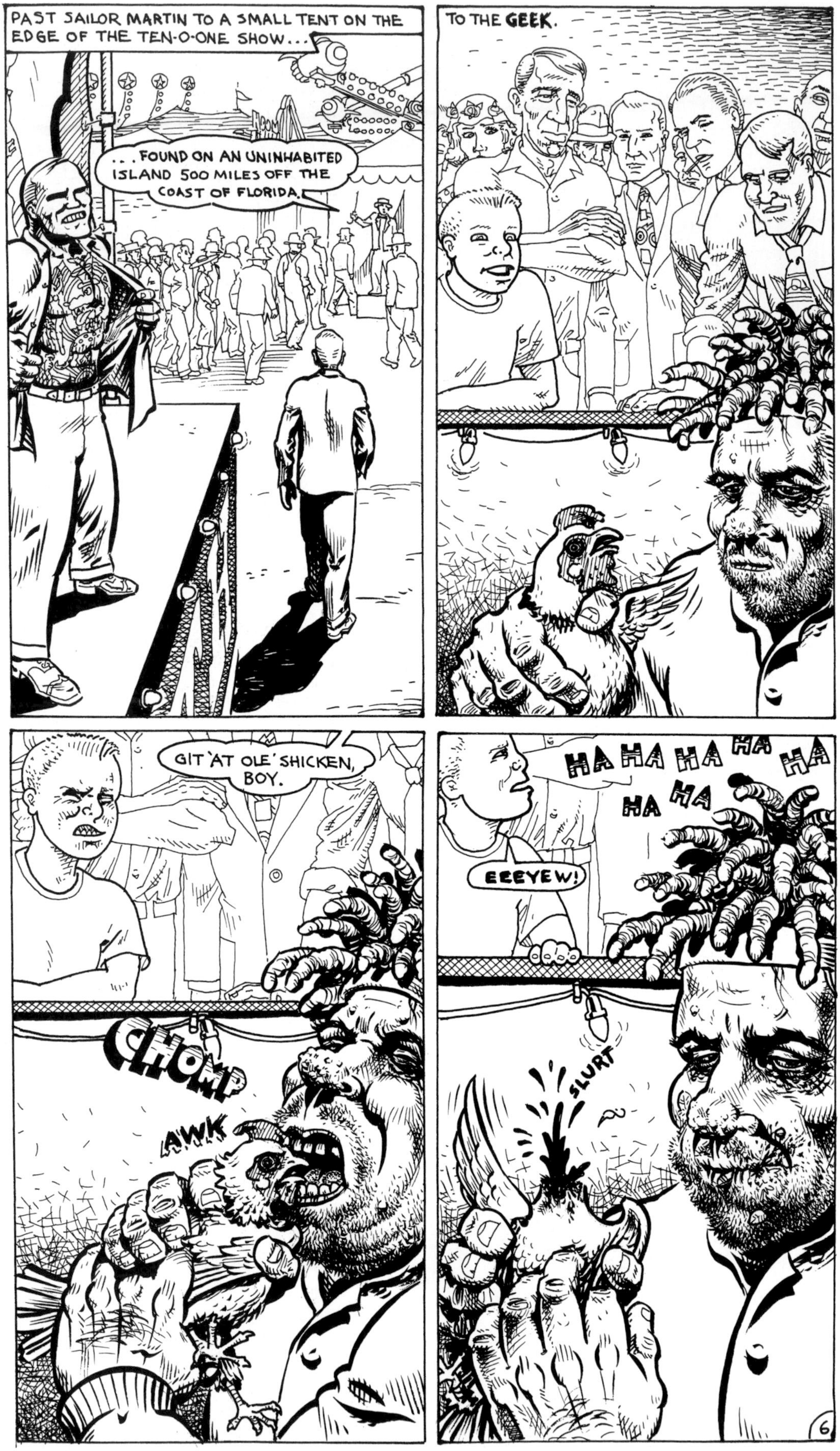
PAST SAILOR MARTIN TO A SMALL TENT ON THE EDGE OF THE TEN-O-ONE SHOW...
...FOUND ON AN UNINHABITED ISLAND 500 MILES OFF THE COAST OF FLORIDA.
TO THE GEEK.
GIT 'AT OLE' SHICKEN, BOY.
CHOMP
AWK
HA HA HA HA HA HA HA
EEEYEW!
SLURT

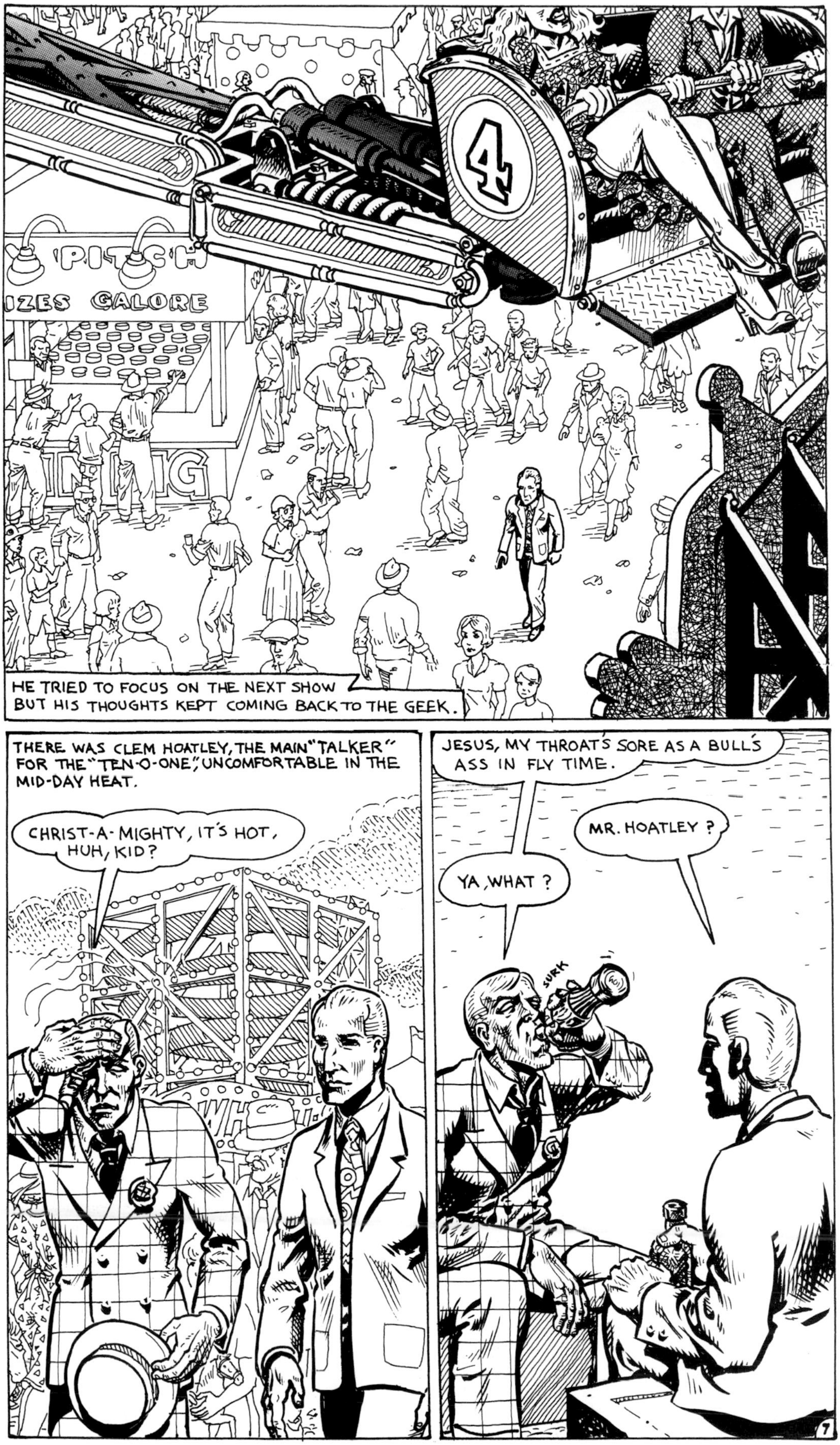
PITCH
IZES GALORE
HE TRIED TO FOCUS ON THE NEXT SHOW BUT HIS THOUGHTS KEPT COMING BACK TO THE GEEK.
THERE WAS CLEM HOATLEY, THE MAIN "TALKER" FOR THE "TEN-O-ONE", UNCOMFORTABLE IN THE MID-DAY HEAT.
CHRIST-A-MIGHTY, IT'S HOT, HUH, KID?
JESUS, MY THROAT'S SORE AS A BULL'S ASS IN FLY TIME.
MR. HOATLEY ?
YA, WHAT ?
SURK

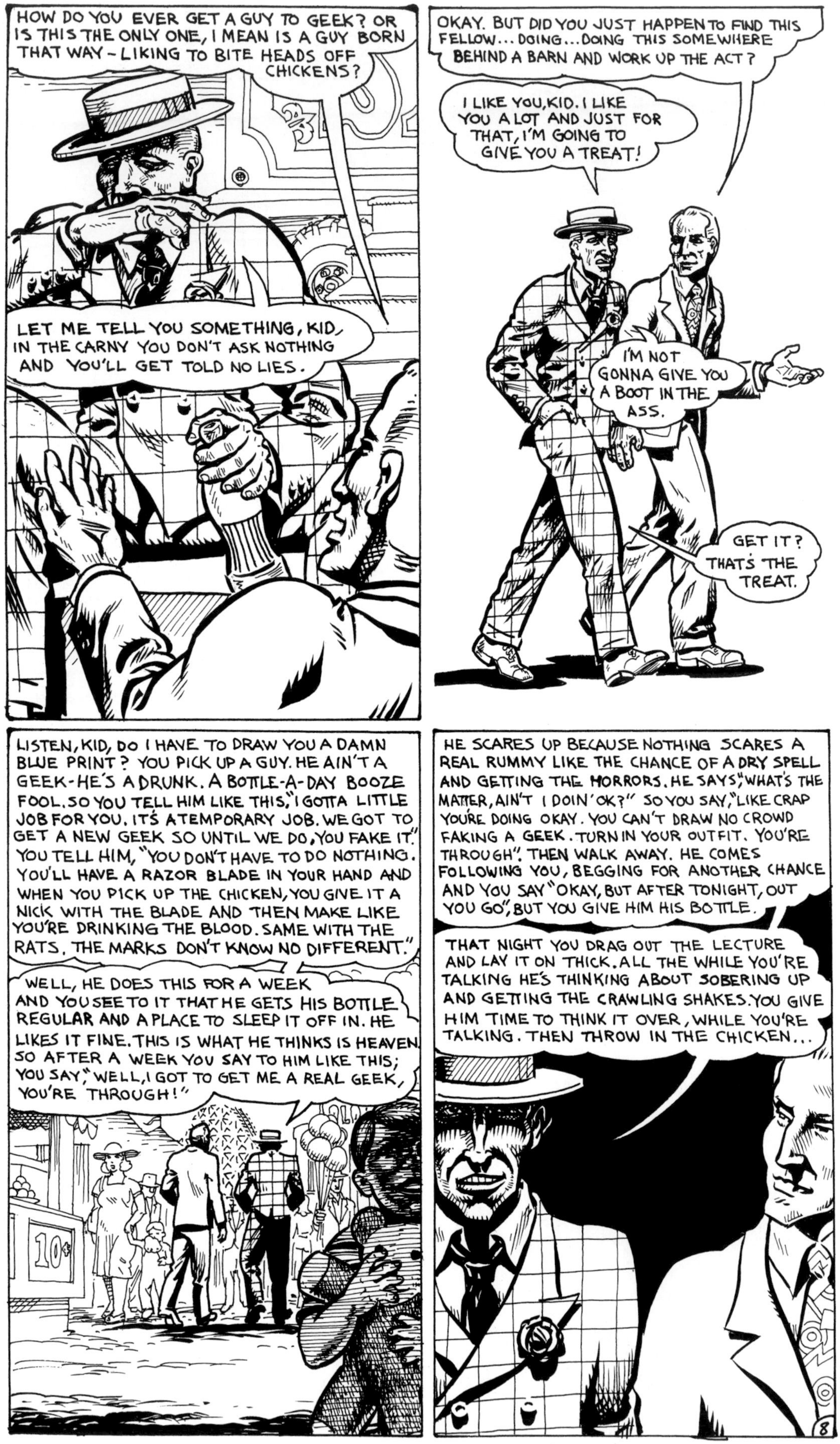
HOW DO YOU EVER GET A GUY TO GEEK? OR IS THIS THE ONLY ONE, I MEAN IS A GUY BORN THAT WAY - LIKING TO BITE HEADS OFF CHICKENS?
LET ME TELL YOU SOMETHING, KID, IN THE CARNY YOU DON'T ASK NOTHING AND YOU'LL GET TOLD NO LIES.
OKAY. BUT DID YOU JUST HAPPEN TO FIND THIS FELLOW... DOING... DOING THIS SOMEWHERE BEHIND A BARN AND WORK UP THE ACT?
I LIKE YOU, KID. I LIKE YOU A LOT AND JUST FOR THAT, I'M GOING TO GIVE YOU A TREAT!
I'M NOT GONNA GIVE YOU A BOOT IN THE ASS.
GET IT? THAT'S THE TREAT.
LISTEN, KID, DO I HAVE TO DRAW YOU A DAMN BLUE PRINT? YOU PICK UP A GUY. HE AIN'T A GEEK-HE'S A DRUNK. A BOTTLE-A-DAY BOOZE FOOL. SO YOU TELL HIM LIKE THIS, "I GOTTA LITTLE JOB FOR YOU. IT'S A TEMPORARY JOB. WE GOT TO GET A NEW GEEK SO UNTIL WE DO, YOU FAKE IT." YOU TELL HIM, "YOU DON'T HAVE TO DO NOTHING. YOU'LL HAVE A RAZOR BLADE IN YOUR HAND AND WHEN YOU PICK UP THE CHICKEN, YOU GIVE IT A NICK WITH THE BLADE AND THEN MAKE LIKE YOU'RE DRINKING THE BLOOD. SAME WITH THE RATS. THE MARKS DON'T KNOW NO DIFFERENT."
WELL, HE DOES THIS FOR A WEEK AND YOU SEE TO IT THAT HE GETS HIS BOTTLE REGULAR AND A PLACE TO SLEEP IT OFF IN. HE LIKES IT FINE. THIS IS WHAT HE THINKS IS HEAVEN. SO AFTER A WEEK YOU SAY TO HIM LIKE THIS; YOU SAY, "WELL, I GOT TO GET ME A REAL GEEK, YOU'RE THROUGH!"
10¢
HE SCARES UP BECAUSE NOTHING SCARES A REAL RUMMY LIKE THE CHANCE OF A DRY SPELL AND GETTING THE HORRORS. HE SAYS, "WHAT'S THE MATTER, AIN'T I DOIN' OK?" SO YOU SAY, "LIKE CRAP YOU'RE DOING OKAY. YOU CAN'T DRAW NO CROWD FAKING A GEEK. TURN IN YOUR OUTFIT. YOU'RE THROUGH". THEN WALK AWAY. HE COMES FOLLOWING YOU, BEGGING FOR ANOTHER CHANCE AND YOU SAY "OKAY, BUT AFTER TONIGHT, OUT YOU GO", BUT YOU GIVE HIM HIS BOTTLE.
THAT NIGHT YOU DRAG OUT THE LECTURE AND LAY IT ON THICK. ALL THE WHILE YOU'RE TALKING HE'S THINKING ABOUT SOBERING UP AND GETTING THE CRAWLING SHAKES. YOU GIVE HIM TIME TO THINK IT OVER, WHILE YOU'RE TALKING. THEN THROW IN THE CHICKEN...
8

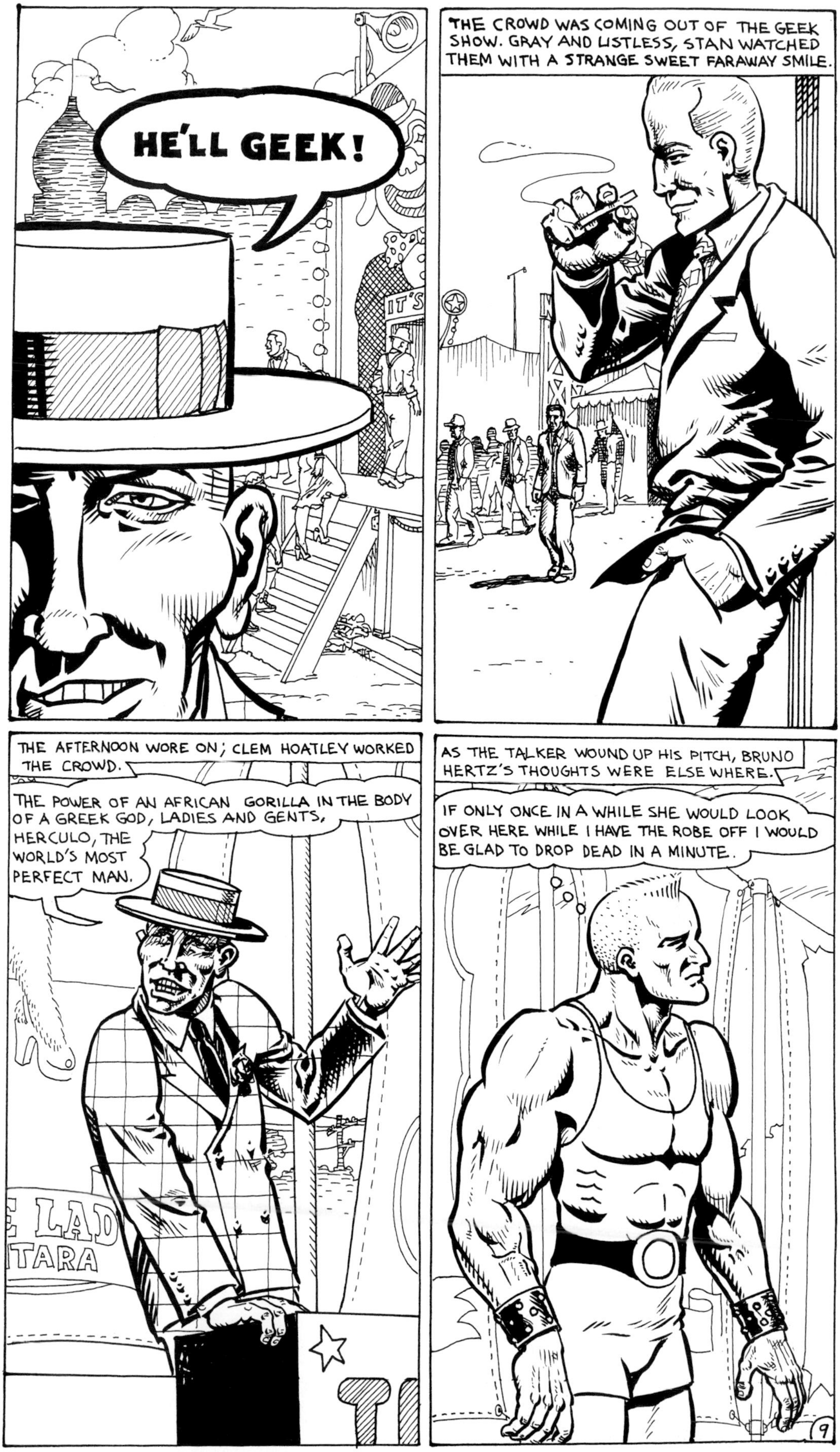
HE'LL GEEK!
IT'S
THE CROWD WAS COMING OUT OF THE GEEK SHOW. GRAY AND LISTLESS, STAN WATCHED THEM WITH A STRANGE SWEET FARAWAY SMILE.
THE AFTERNOON WORE ON; CLEM HOATLEY WORKED THE CROWD.
THE POWER OF AN AFRICAN GORILLA IN THE BODY OF A GREEK GOD, LADIES AND GENTS,
HERCULO, THE WORLD'S MOST PERFECT MAN.
E LAD
TARA
AS THE TALKER WOUND UP HIS PITCH, BRUNO HERTZ'S THOUGHTS WERE ELSEWHERE.
IF ONLY ONCE IN A WHILE SHE WOULD LOOK OVER HERE WHILE I HAVE THE ROBE OFF I WOULD BE GLAD TO DROP DEAD IN A MINUTE.
9

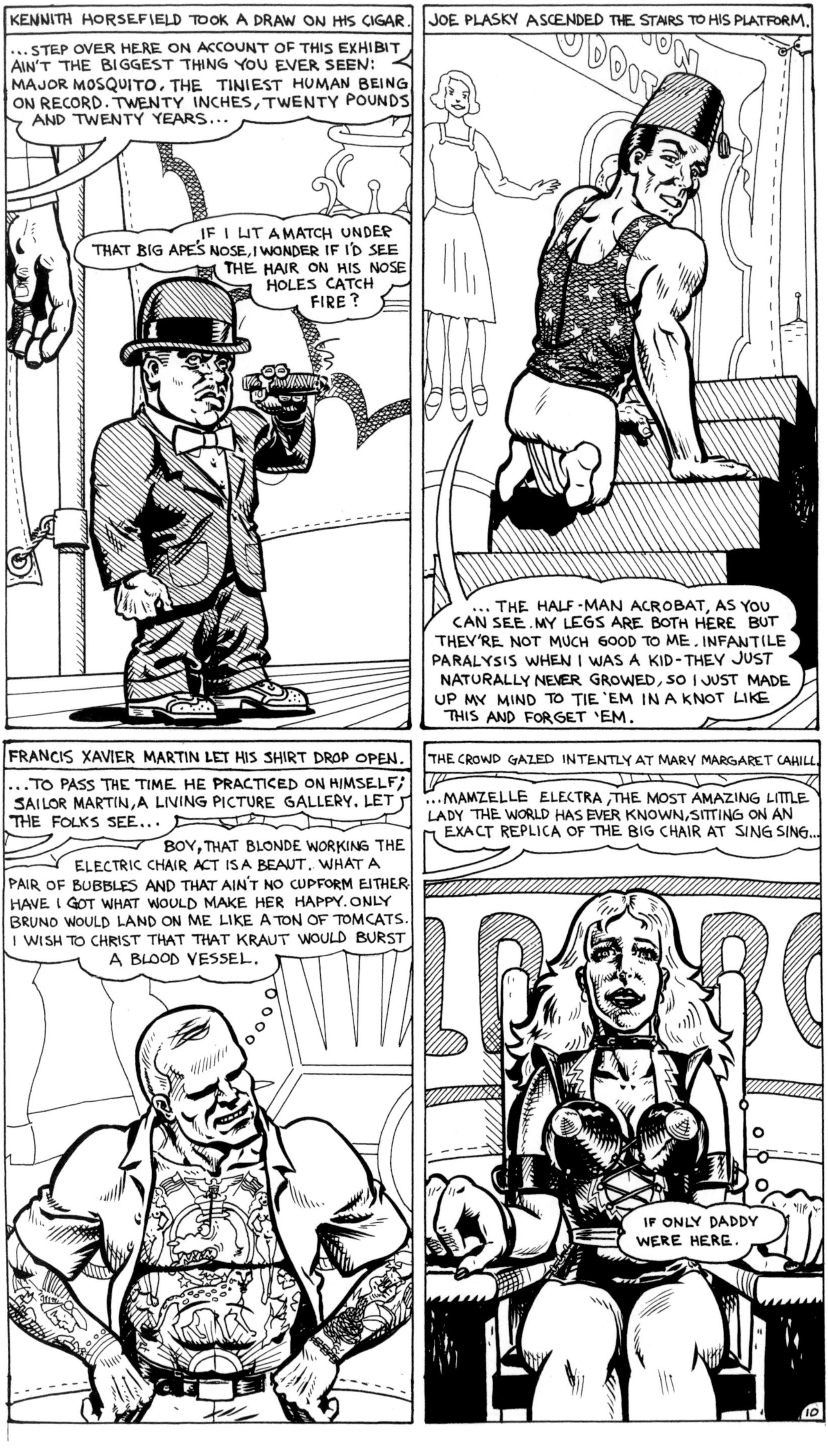
KENNITH HORSEFIELD TOOK A DRAW ON HIS CIGAR.
...STEP OVER HERE ON ACCOUNT OF THIS EXHIBIT AIN'T THE BIGGEST THING YOU EVER SEEN: MAJOR MOSQUITO, THE TINIEST HUMAN BEING ON RECORD. TWENTY INCHES, TWENTY POUNDS AND TWENTY YEARS...
IF I LIT A MATCH UNDER THAT BIG APE'S NOSE, I WONDER IF I'D SEE THE HAIR ON HIS NOSE HOLES CATCH FIRE?
JOE PLASKY ASCENDED THE STAIRS TO HIS PLATFORM.
...THE HALF-MAN ACROBAT, AS YOU CAN SEE. MY LEGS ARE BOTH HERE BUT THEY'RE NOT MUCH GOOD TO ME. INFANTILE PARALYSIS WHEN I WAS A KID-THEY JUST NATURALLY NEVER GROWED, SO I JUST MADE UP MY MIND TO TIE 'EM IN A KNOT LIKE THIS AND FORGET 'EM.
FRANCIS XAVIER MARTIN LET HIS SHIRT DROP OPEN.
...TO PASS THE TIME HE PRACTICED ON HIMSELF; SAILOR MARTIN, A LIVING PICTURE GALLERY. LET THE FOLKS SEE...
BOY, THAT BLONDE WORKING THE ELECTRIC CHAIR ACT IS A BEAUT. WHAT A PAIR OF BUBBLES AND THAT AIN'T NO CUPFORM EITHER. HAVE I GOT WHAT WOULD MAKE HER HAPPY. ONLY BRUNO WOULD LAND ON ME LIKE A TON OF TOMCATS. I WISH TO CHRIST THAT THAT KRAUT WOULD BURST A BLOOD VESSEL.
THE CROWD GAZED INTENTLY AT MARY MARGARET CAHILL.
...MAMZELLE ELECTRA, THE MOST AMAZING LITTLE LADY THE WORLD HAS EVER KNOWN, SITTING ON AN EXACT REPLICA OF THE BIG CHAIR AT SING SING...
IF ONLY DADDY WERE HERE.
10

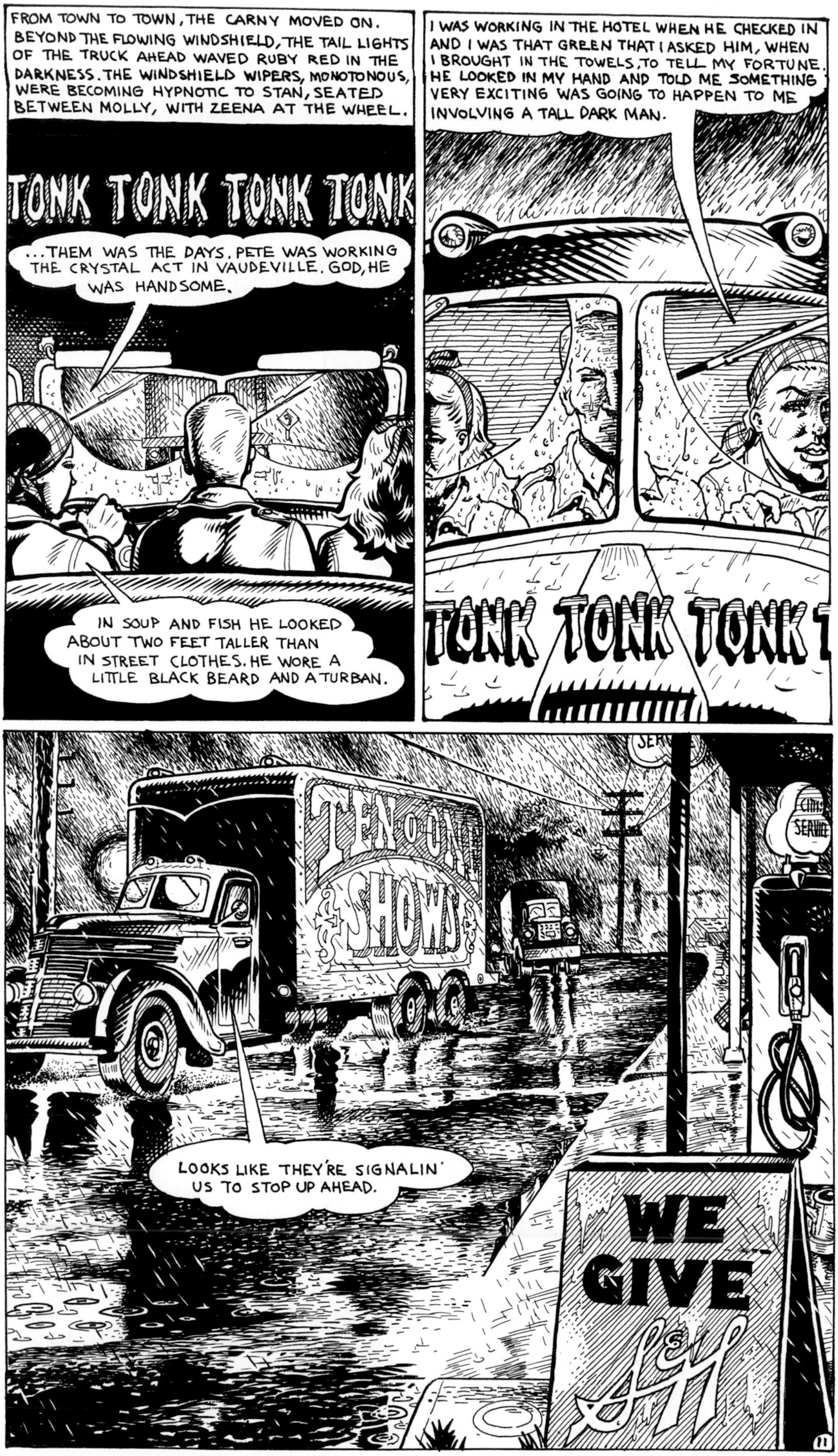
FROM TOWN TO TOWN, THE CARNY MOVED ON. BEYOND THE FLOWING WINDSHIELD, THE TAIL LIGHTS OF THE TRUCK AHEAD WAVED RUBY RED IN THE DARKNESS. THE WINDSHIELD WIPERS, MONOTONOUS, WERE BECOMING HYPNOTIC TO STAN, SEATED BETWEEN MOLLY, WITH ZEENA AT THE WHEEL.
TONK TONK TONK TONK
...THEM WAS THE DAYS. PETE WAS WORKING THE CRYSTAL ACT IN VAUDEVILLE. GOD, HE WAS HANDSOME.
IN SOUP AND FISH HE LOOKED ABOUT TWO FEET TALLER THAN IN STREET CLOTHES. HE WORE A LITTLE BLACK BEARD AND A TURBAN.
I WAS WORKING IN THE HOTEL WHEN HE CHECKED IN AND I WAS THAT GREEN THAT I ASKED HIM, WHEN I BROUGHT IN THE TOWELS, TO TELL MY FORTUNE. HE LOOKED IN MY HAND AND TOLD ME SOMETHING VERY EXCITING WAS GOING TO HAPPEN TO ME INVOLVING A TALL DARK MAN.
TONK TONK TONK
TEN-O-ONE SHOWS
CITIES SERVICE
LOOKS LIKE THEY'RE SIGNALIN' US TO STOP UP AHEAD.
WE GIVE S&H
11

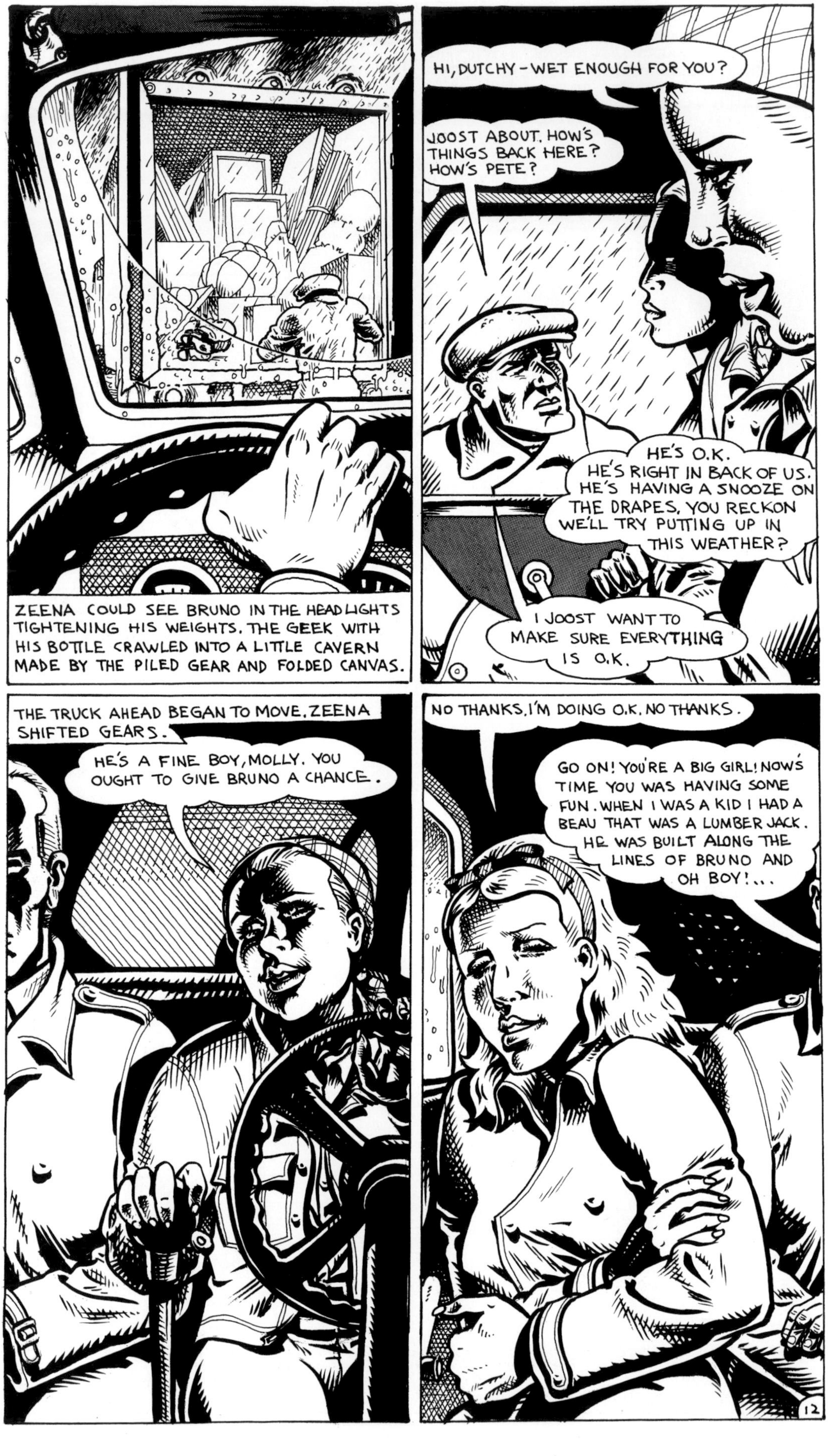
ZEENA COULD SEE BRUNO IN THE HEADLIGHTS TIGHTENING HIS WEIGHTS. THE GEEK WITH HIS BOTTLE CRAWLED INTO A LITTLE CAVERN MADE BY THE PILED GEAR AND FOLDED CANVAS.
HI, DUTCHY - WET ENOUGH FOR YOU?
JOOST ABOUT. HOW'S THINGS BACK HERE? HOW'S PETE?
HE'S O.K. HE'S RIGHT IN BACK OF US. HE'S HAVING A SNOOZE ON THE DRAPES. YOU RECKON WE'LL TRY PUTTING UP IN THIS WEATHER?
I JOOST WANT TO MAKE SURE EVERYTHING IS O.K.
THE TRUCK AHEAD BEGAN TO MOVE. ZEENA SHIFTED GEARS.
HE'S A FINE BOY, MOLLY. YOU OUGHT TO GIVE BRUNO A CHANCE.
NO THANKS. I'M DOING O.K. NO THANKS.
GO ON! YOU'RE A BIG GIRL! NOW'S TIME YOU WAS HAVING SOME FUN. WHEN I WAS A KID I HAD A BEAU THAT WAS A LUMBER JACK. HE WAS BUILT ALONG THE LINES OF BRUNO AND OH BOY!...

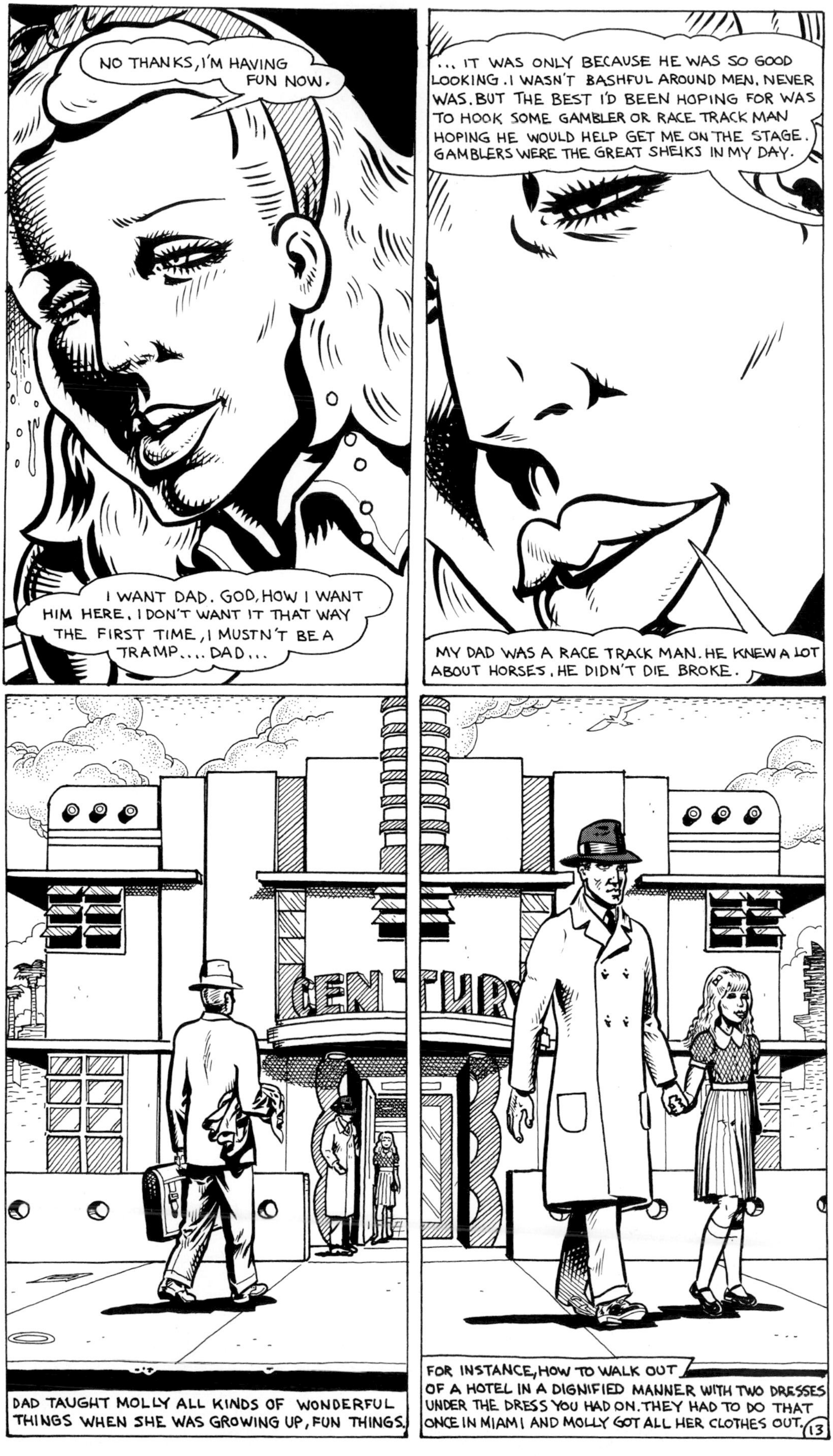
NO THANKS, I'M HAVING FUN NOW.
I WANT DAD. GOD, HOW I WANT HIM HERE. I DON'T WANT IT THAT WAY THE FIRST TIME, I MUSTN'T BE A TRAMP.... DAD...
... IT WAS ONLY BECAUSE HE WAS SO GOOD LOOKING. I WASN'T BASHFUL AROUND MEN. NEVER WAS. BUT THE BEST I'D BEEN HOPING FOR WAS TO HOOK SOME GAMBLER OR RACE TRACK MAN HOPING HE WOULD HELP GET ME ON THE STAGE. GAMBLERS WERE THE GREAT SHEIKS IN MY DAY.
MY DAD WAS A RACE TRACK MAN. HE KNEW A LOT ABOUT HORSES, HE DIDN'T DIE BROKE.
CENTURY
DAD TAUGHT MOLLY ALL KINDS OF WONDERFUL THINGS WHEN SHE WAS GROWING UP, FUN THINGS.
FOR INSTANCE, HOW TO WALK OUT OF A HOTEL IN A DIGNIFIED MANNER WITH TWO DRESSES UNDER THE DRESS YOU HAD ON. THEY HAD TO DO THAT ONCE IN MIAMI AND MOLLY GOT ALL HER CLOTHES OUT.

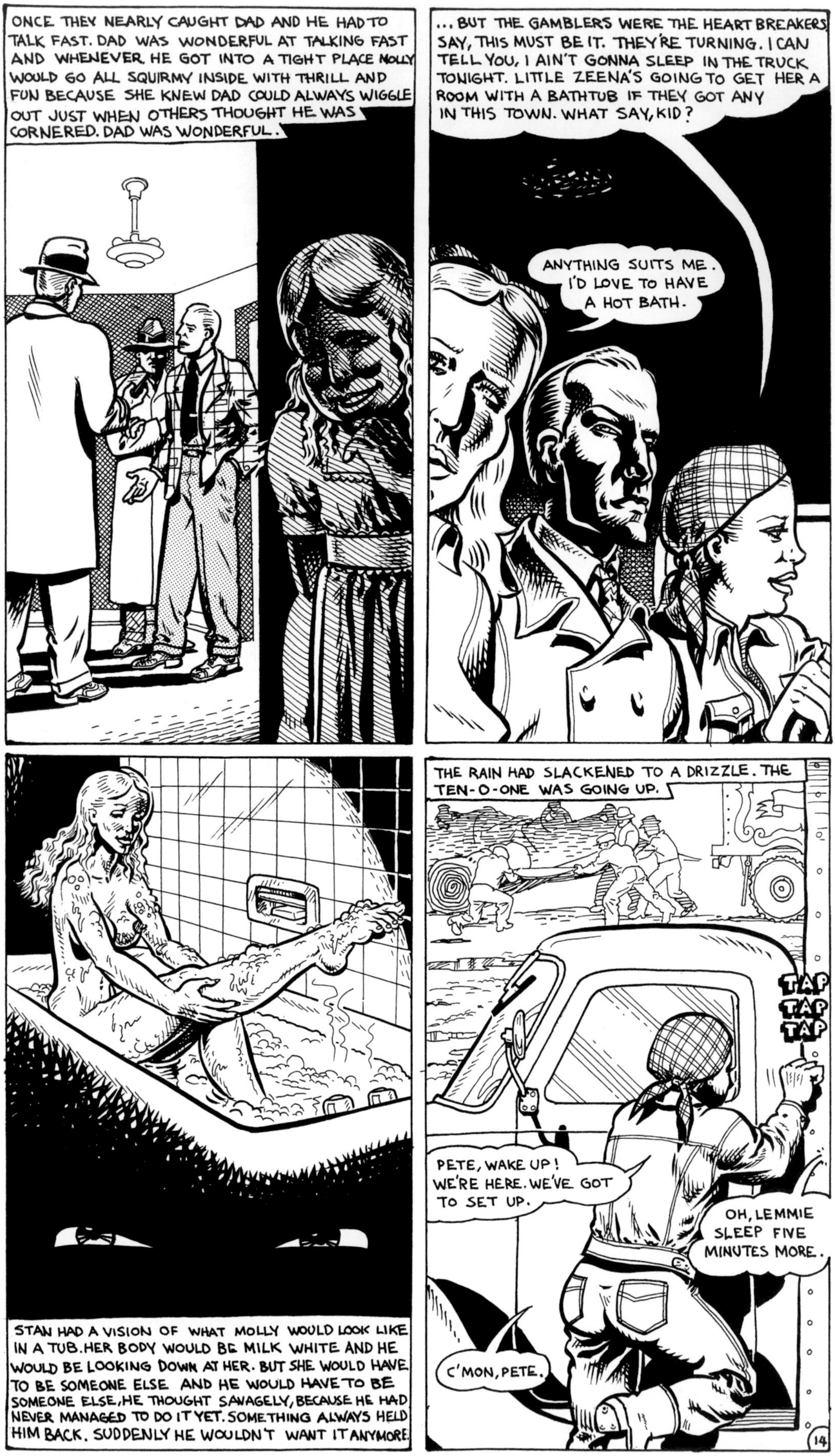
ONCE THEY NEARLY CAUGHT DAD AND HE HAD TO TALK FAST. DAD WAS WONDERFUL AT TALKING FAST AND WHENEVER HE GOT INTO A TIGHT PLACE MOLLY WOULD GO ALL SQUIRMY INSIDE WITH THRILL AND FUN BECAUSE SHE KNEW DAD COULD ALWAYS WIGGLE OUT JUST WHEN OTHERS THOUGHT HE WAS CORNERED. DAD WAS WONDERFUL.
... BUT THE GAMBLERS WERE THE HEART BREAKERS.
SAY, THIS MUST BE IT. THEY'RE TURNING. I CAN TELL YOU, I AIN'T GONNA SLEEP IN THE TRUCK TONIGHT. LITTLE ZEENA'S GOING TO GET HER A ROOM WITH A BATHTUB IF THEY GOT ANY IN THIS TOWN. WHAT SAY, KID?
ANYTHING SUITS ME. I'D LOVE TO HAVE A HOT BATH.
STAN HAD A VISION OF WHAT MOLLY WOULD LOOK LIKE IN A TUB. HER BODY WOULD BE MILK WHITE AND HE WOULD BE LOOKING DOWN AT HER. BUT SHE WOULD HAVE TO BE SOMEONE ELSE AND HE WOULD HAVE TO BE SOMEONE ELSE, HE THOUGHT SAVAGELY, BECAUSE HE HAD NEVER MANAGED TO DO IT YET. SOMETHING ALWAYS HELD HIM BACK. SUDDENLY HE WOULDN'T WANT IT ANYMORE.
THE RAIN HAD SLACKENED TO A DRIZZLE. THE TEN-O-ONE WAS GOING UP.
TAP TAP TAP
PETE, WAKE UP! WE'RE HERE. WE'VE GOT TO SET UP.
OH, LEMMIE SLEEP FIVE MINUTES MORE.
C'MON, PETE.

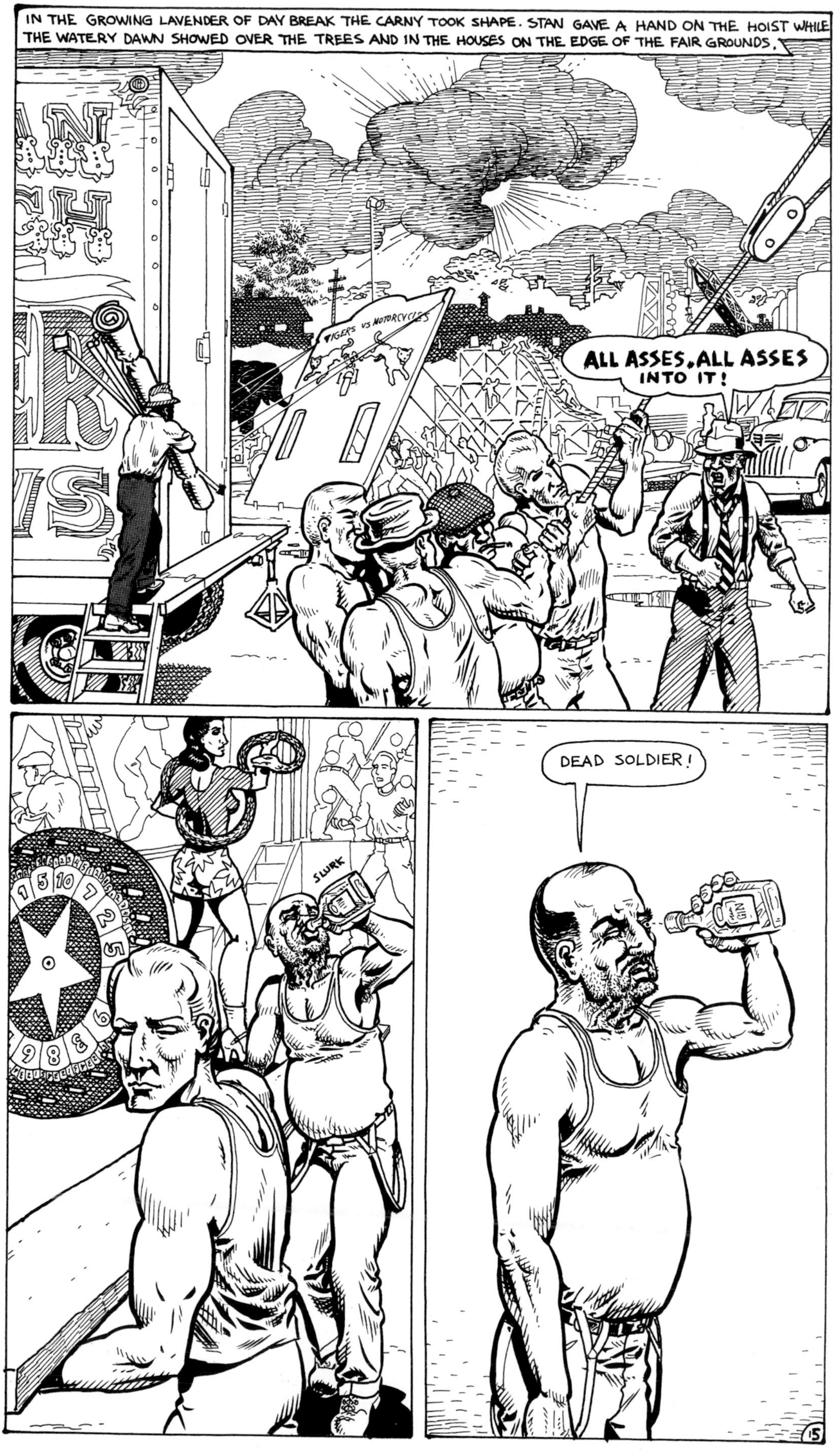
IN THE GROWING LAVENDER OF DAY BREAK THE CARNY TOOK SHAPE. STAN GAVE A HAND ON THE HOIST WHILE THE WATERY DAWN SHOWED OVER THE TREES AND IN THE HOUSES ON THE EDGE OF THE FAIR GROUNDS.
TIGERS VS MOTORCYCLES
ALL ASSES, ALL ASSES INTO IT!
SLURK
DEAD SOLDIER!

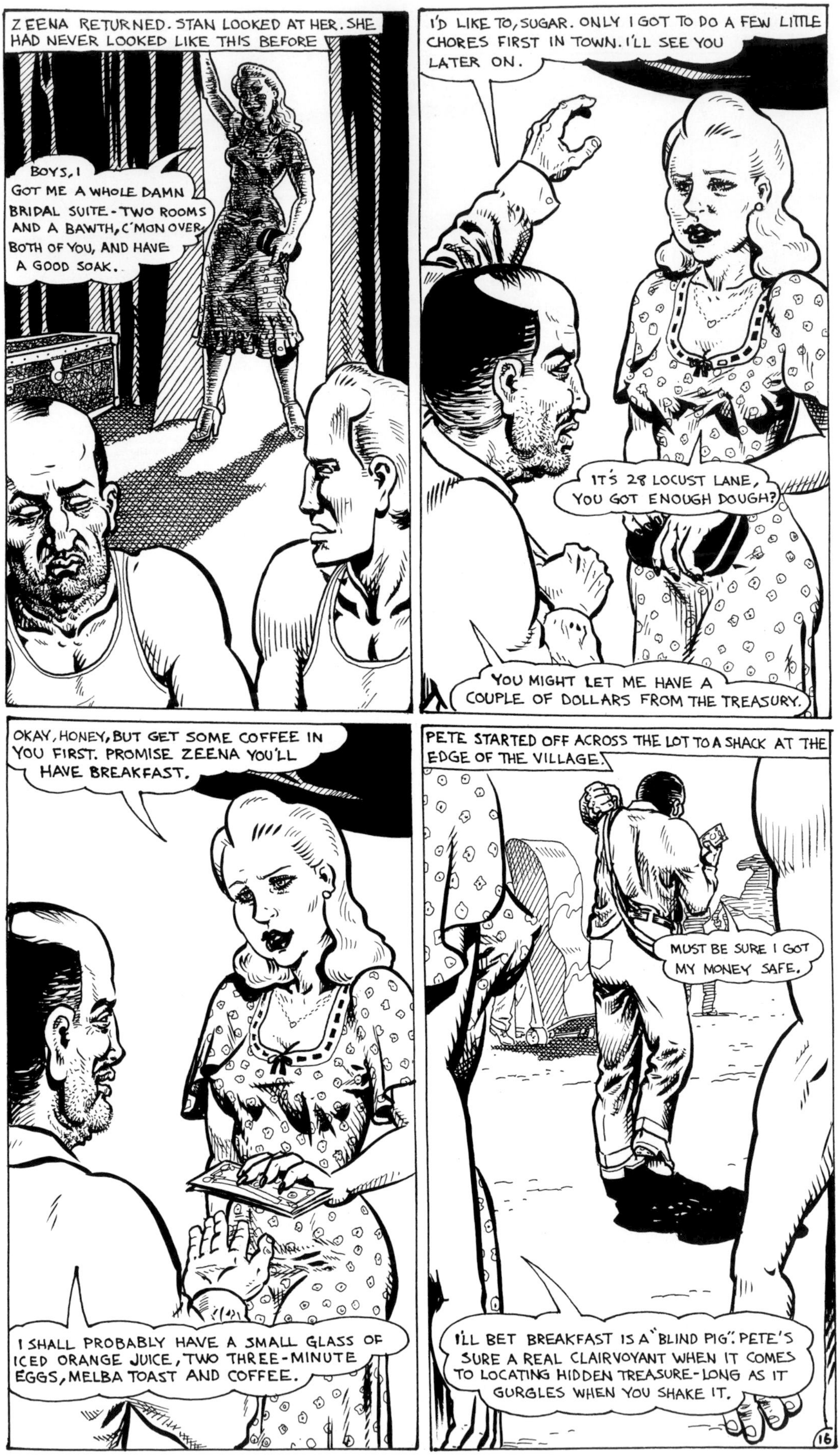
ZEENA RETURNED. STAN LOOKED AT HER. SHE HAD NEVER LOOKED LIKE THIS BEFORE
BOYS, I GOT ME A WHOLE DAMN BRIDAL SUITE - TWO ROOMS AND A BAWTH, C'MON OVER. BOTH OF YOU, AND HAVE A GOOD SOAK.
I'D LIKE TO, SUGAR. ONLY I GOT TO DO A FEW LITTLE CHORES FIRST IN TOWN. I'LL SEE YOU LATER ON.
IT'S 28 LOCUST LANE, YOU GOT ENOUGH DOUGH?
YOU MIGHT LET ME HAVE A COUPLE OF DOLLARS FROM THE TREASURY.
OKAY, HONEY, BUT GET SOME COFFEE IN YOU FIRST. PROMISE ZEENA YOU'LL HAVE BREAKFAST.
I SHALL PROBABLY HAVE A SMALL GLASS OF ICED ORANGE JUICE, TWO THREE-MINUTE EGGS, MELBA TOAST AND COFFEE.
PETE STARTED OFF ACROSS THE LOT TO A SHACK AT THE EDGE OF THE VILLAGE.
MUST BE SURE I GOT MY MONEY SAFE.
I'LL BET BREAKFAST IS A "BLIND PIG". PETE'S SURE A REAL CLAIRVOYANT WHEN IT COMES TO LOCATING HIDDEN TREASURE - LONG AS IT GURGLES WHEN YOU SHAKE IT.

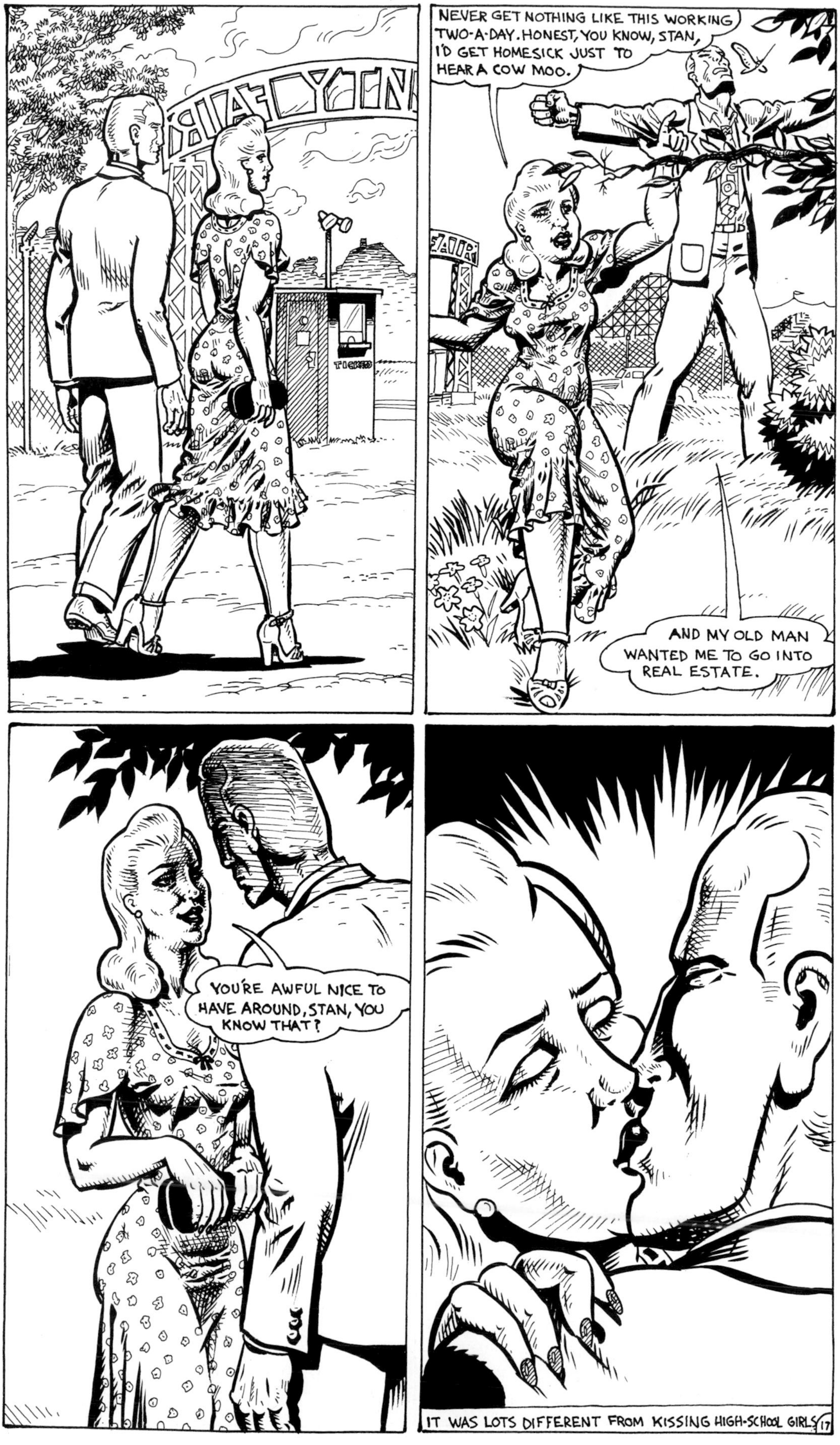

NEVER GET NOTHING LIKE THIS WORKING TWO-A-DAY. HONEST, YOU KNOW, STAN, I'D GET HOMESICK JUST TO HEAR A COW MOO.
AND MY OLD MAN WANTED ME TO GO INTO REAL ESTATE.
YOU'RE AWFUL NICE TO HAVE AROUND, STAN, YOU KNOW THAT?
IT WAS LOTS DIFFERENT FROM KISSING HIGH-SCHOOL GIRLS

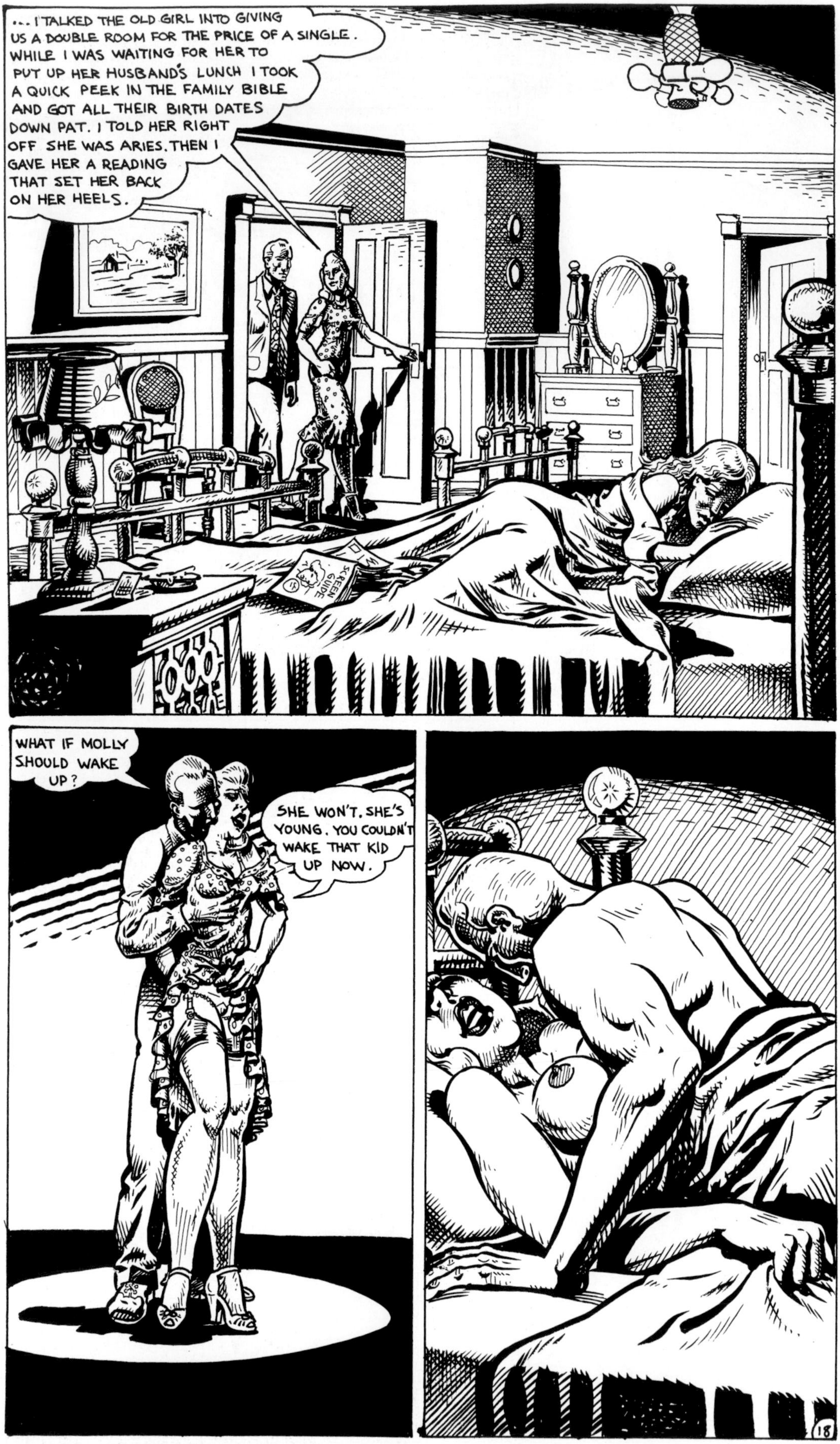

... I TALKED THE OLD GIRL INTO GIVING US A DOUBLE ROOM FOR THE PRICE OF A SINGLE. WHILE I WAS WAITING FOR HER TO PUT UP HER HUSBAND'S LUNCH I TOOK A QUICK PEEK IN THE FAMILY BIBLE AND GOT ALL THEIR BIRTH DATES DOWN PAT. I TOLD HER RIGHT OFF SHE WAS ARIES. THEN I GAVE HER A READING THAT SET HER BACK ON HER HEELS.
SCREEN GUIDE
WHAT IF MOLLY SHOULD WAKE UP?
SHE WON'T. SHE'S YOUNG. YOU COULDN'T WAKE THAT KID UP NOW.

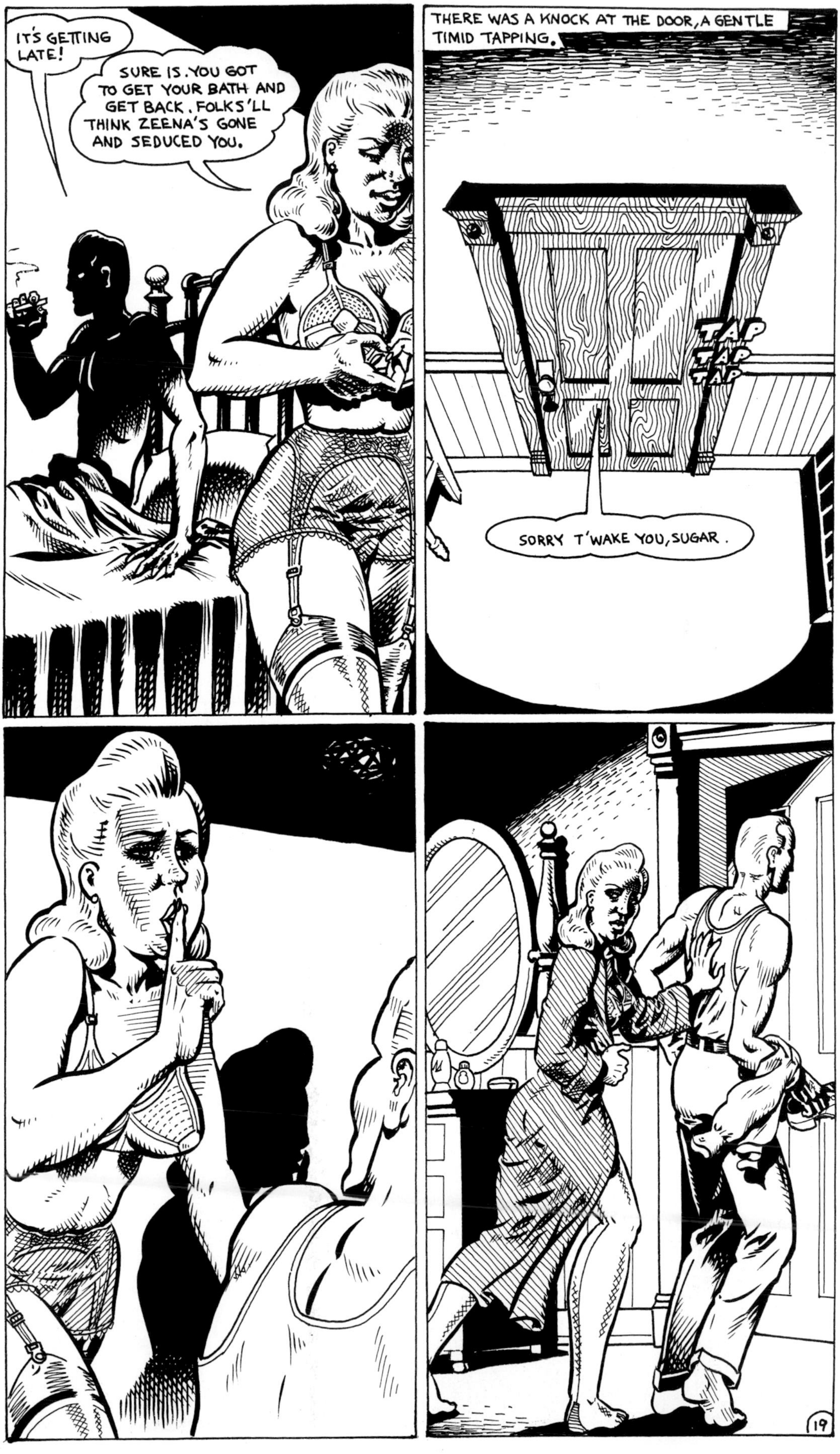
IT'S GETTING LATE!
SURE IS. YOU GOT TO GET YOUR BATH AND GET BACK. FOLKS'LL THINK ZEENA'S GONE AND SEDUCED YOU.
THERE WAS A KNOCK AT THE DOOR, A GENTLE TIMID TAPPING.
TAP TAP TAP
SORRY T'WAKE YOU, SUGAR.

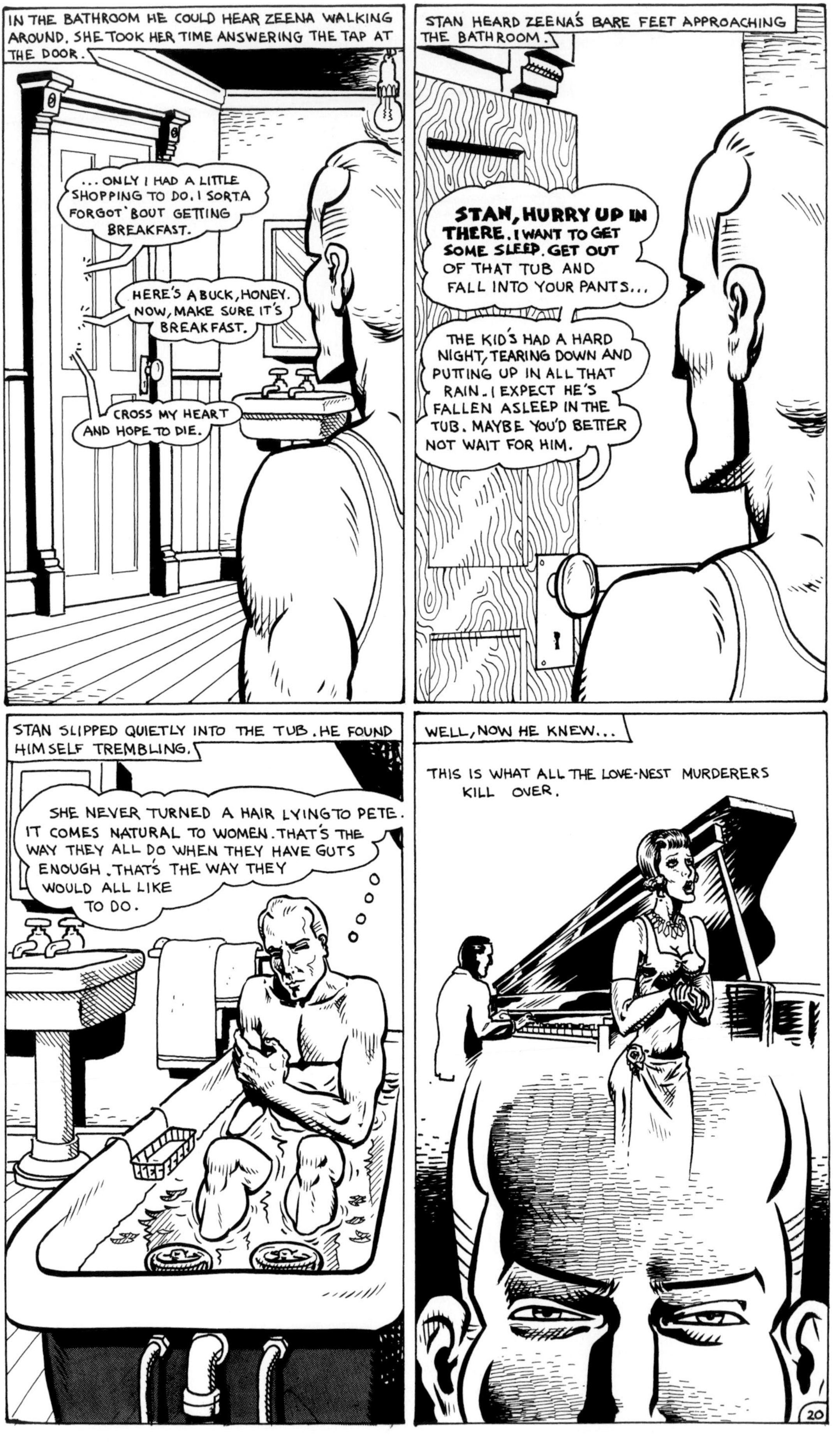
IN THE BATHROOM HE COULD HEAR ZEENA WALKING AROUND. SHE TOOK HER TIME ANSWERING THE TAP AT THE DOOR.
...ONLY I HAD A LITTLE SHOPPING TO DO. I SORTA FORGOT 'BOUT GETTING BREAKFAST.
HERE'S A BUCK, HONEY. NOW, MAKE SURE IT'S BREAKFAST.
CROSS MY HEART AND HOPE TO DIE.
STAN HEARD ZEENA'S BARE FEET APPROACHING THE BATHROOM.
STAN, HURRY UP IN THERE. I WANT TO GET SOME SLEEP. GET OUT OF THAT TUB AND FALL INTO YOUR PANTS...
THE KID'S HAD A HARD NIGHT, TEARING DOWN AND PUTTING UP IN ALL THAT RAIN. I EXPECT HE'S FALLEN ASLEEP IN THE TUB. MAYBE YOU'D BETTER NOT WAIT FOR HIM.
STAN SLIPPED QUIETLY INTO THE TUB. HE FOUND HIMSELF TREMBLING.
SHE NEVER TURNED A HAIR LYING TO PETE. IT COMES NATURAL TO WOMEN. THAT'S THE WAY THEY ALL DO WHEN THEY HAVE GUTS ENOUGH. THAT'S THE WAY THEY WOULD ALL LIKE TO DO.
WELL, NOW HE KNEW...
THIS IS WHAT ALL THE LOVE-NEST MURDERERS KILL OVER.
20

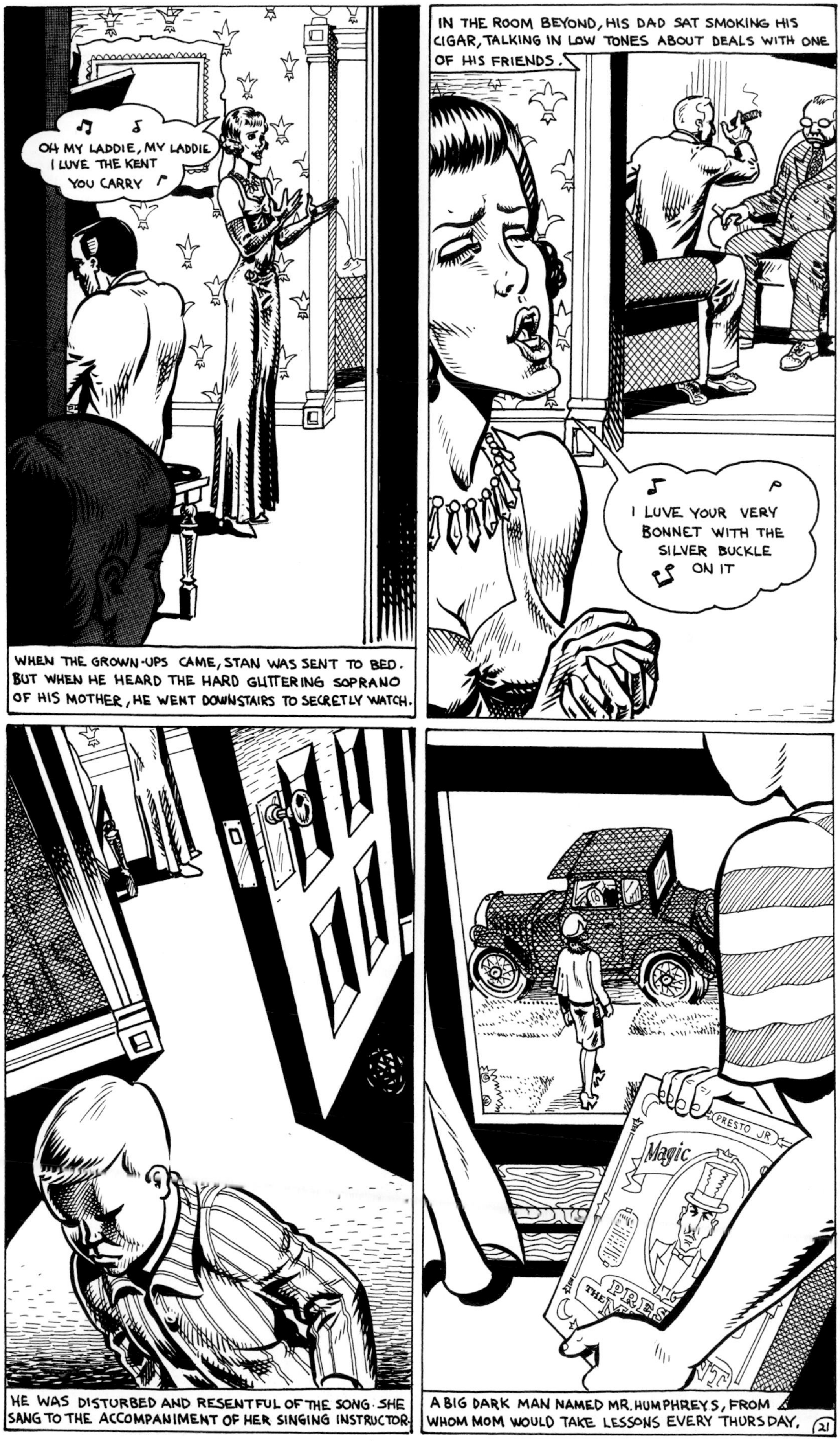
OH MY LADDIE, MY LADDIE
I LUVE THE KENT
YOU CARRY
WHEN THE GROWN-UPS CAME, STAN WAS SENT TO BED. BUT WHEN HE HEARD THE HARD GLITTERING SOPRANO OF HIS MOTHER, HE WENT DOWNSTAIRS TO SECRETLY WATCH.
IN THE ROOM BEYOND, HIS DAD SAT SMOKING HIS CIGAR, TALKING IN LOW TONES ABOUT DEALS WITH ONE OF HIS FRIENDS.
I LUVE YOUR VERY BONNET WITH THE SILVER BUCKLE ON IT
HE WAS DISTURBED AND RESENTFUL OF THE SONG. SHE SANG TO THE ACCOMPANIMENT OF HER SINGING INSTRUCTOR-
PRESTO JR
Magic
A BIG DARK MAN NAMED MR. HUMPHREYS, FROM WHOM MOM WOULD TAKE LESSONS EVERY THURSDAY.

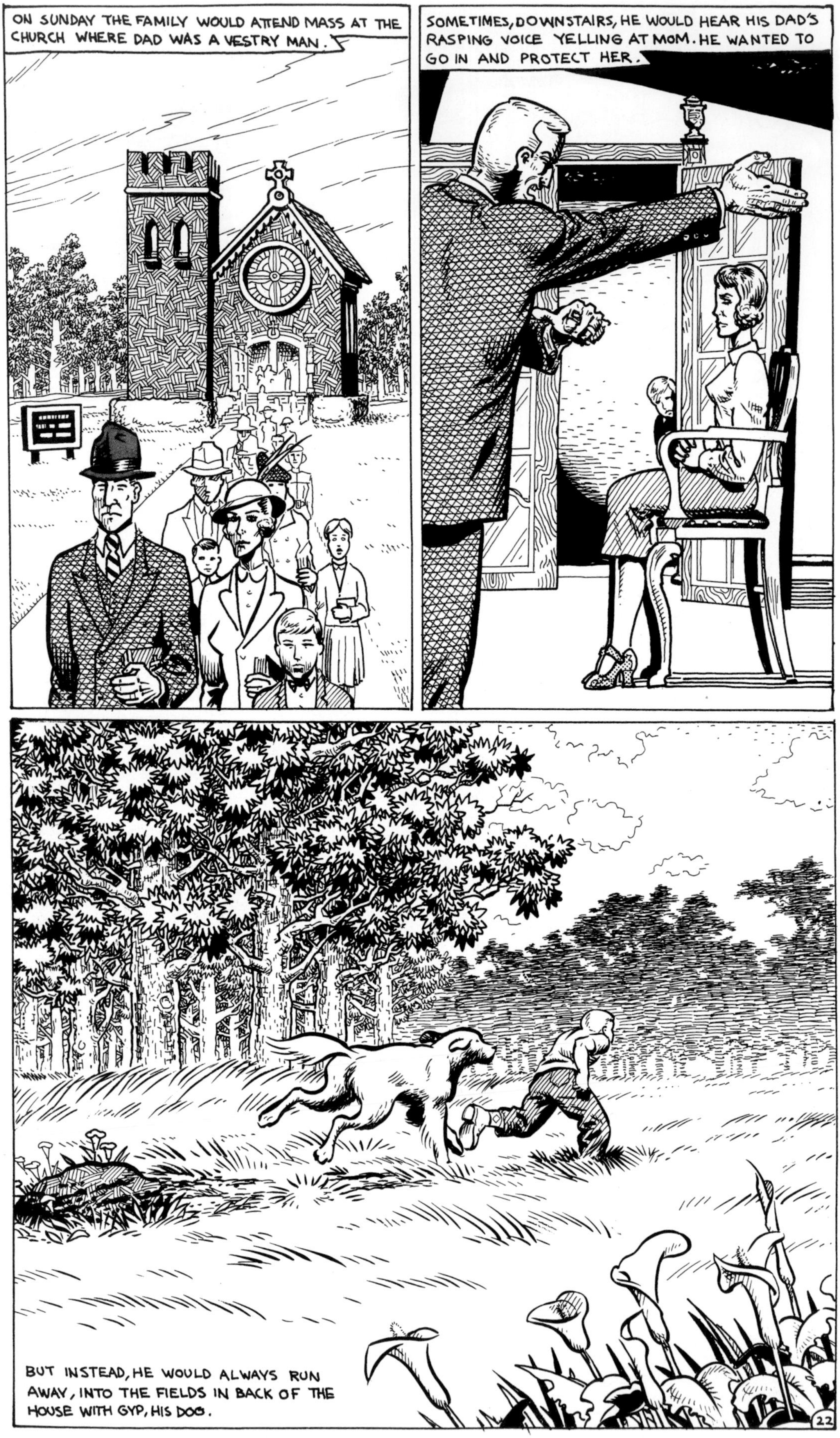
ON SUNDAY THE FAMILY WOULD ATTEND MASS AT THE CHURCH WHERE DAD WAS A VESTRY MAN.
SOMETIMES, DOWNSTAIRS, HE WOULD HEAR HIS DAD'S RASPING VOICE YELLING AT MOM. HE WANTED TO GO IN AND PROTECT HER.
BUT INSTEAD, HE WOULD ALWAYS RUN AWAY, INTO THE FIELDS IN BACK OF THE HOUSE WITH GYP, HIS DOG.

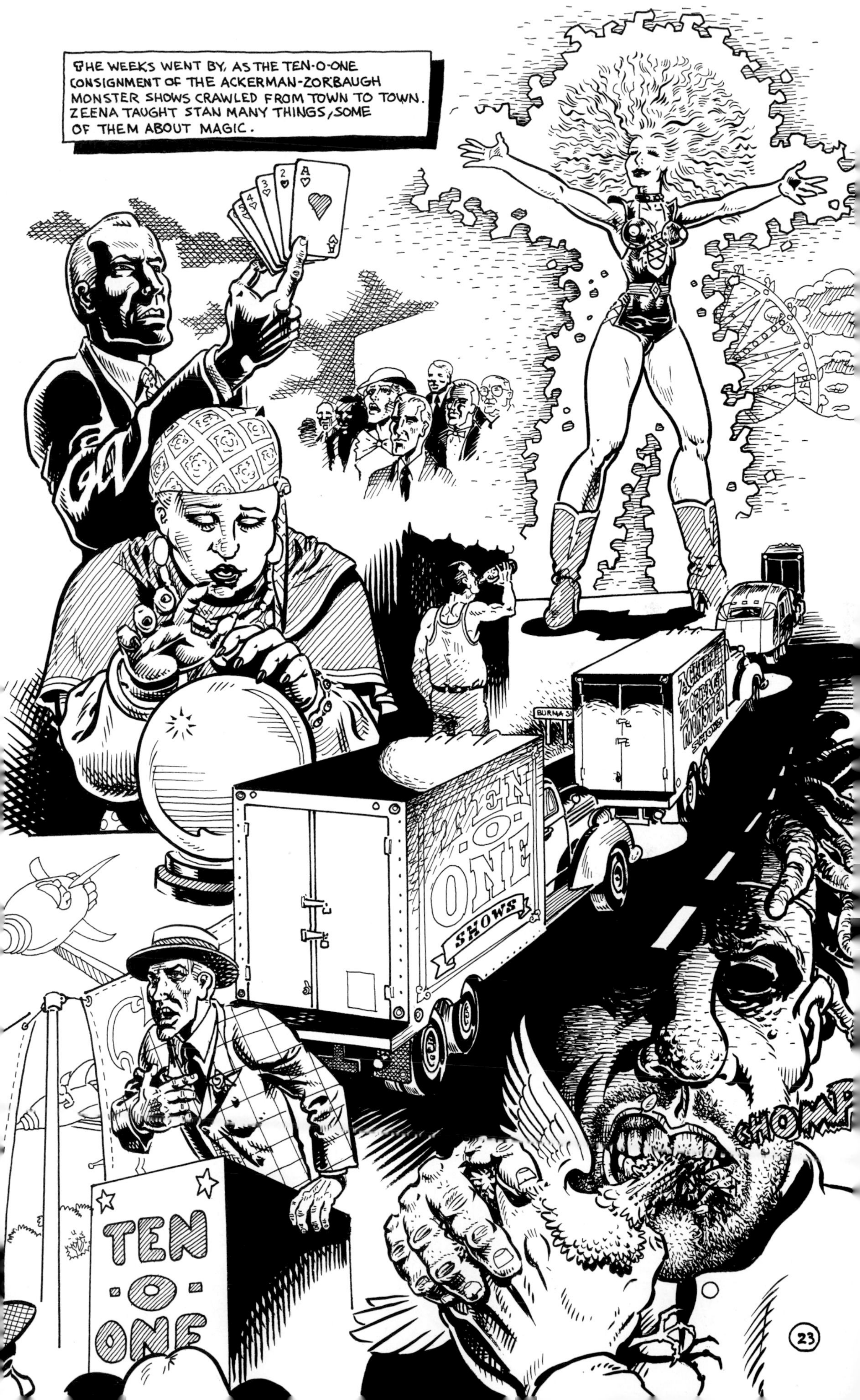
THE WEEKS WENT BY, AS THE TEN-O-ONE CONSIGNMENT OF THE ACKERMAN-ZORBAUGH MONSTER SHOWS CRAWLED FROM TOWN TO TOWN. ZEENA TAUGHT STAN MANY THINGS, SOME OF THEM ABOUT MAGIC.
ACKERMAN ZORBAUGH MONSTER SHOWS
TEN -O- ONE SHOWS
TEN -O- ONE

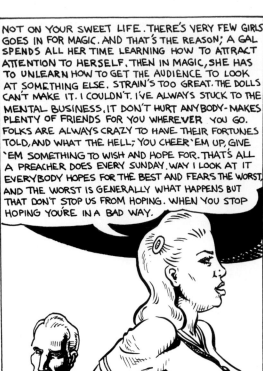

MISDIRECTION IS THE WHOLE WORKS, HONEY. YOU DON'T NEED NO FANCY PRODUCTION BOXES, TRAP DOORS AND TRICK TABLES. I'VE ALWAYS LET ON THAT A MAN THAT WILL SPEND HIS TIME LEARNING MISDIRECTION CAN JUST REACH IN HIS POCKET AND PUT SOMETHING IN A HAT AND THEN GO AHEAD AND TAKE IT OUT AGAIN AND EVERYBODY WILL SIT BACK AND GASP, WONDERING WHERE IT CAME FROM.

DID YOU EVER DO MAGIC?

NOT ON YOUR SWEET LIFE. THERE'S VERY FEW GIRLS GOES IN FOR MAGIC. AND THAT'S THE REASON; A GAL SPENDS ALL HER TIME LEARNING HOW TO ATTRACT ATTENTION TO HERSELF. THEN IN MAGIC, SHE HAS TO UNLEARN HOW TO GET THE AUDIENCE TO LOOK AT SOMETHING ELSE. STRAIN'S TOO GREAT. THE DOLLS CAN'T MAKE IT. I COULDN'T. I'VE ALWAYS STUCK TO THE MENTAL BUSINESS. IT DON'T HURT ANYBODY-MAKES PLENTY OF FRIENDS FOR YOU WHEREVER YOU GO. FOLKS ARE ALWAYS CRAZY TO HAVE THEIR FORTUNES TOLD, AND WHAT THE HELL; YOU CHEER 'EM UP, GIVE 'EM SOMETHING TO WISH AND HOPE FOR. THAT'S ALL A PREACHER DOES EVERY SUNDAY. WAY I LOOK AT IT EVERYBODY HOPES FOR THE BEST AND FEARS THE WORST, AND THE WORST IS GENERALLY WHAT HAPPENS BUT THAT DON'T STOP US FROM HOPING. WHEN YOU STOP HOPING YOU'RE IN A BAD WAY.

HAS PETE STOPPED HOPING?

ZEENA WAS SILENT FOR A TIME.

...SOMETIMES I THINK HE HAS. PETE'S SCARED OF SOMETHING, I THINK HE GOT GOOD AND SCARED OF HIMSELF A LONG TIME AGO. THAT'S WHAT MADE HIM SUCH A WIZ AS A CRYSTAL READER ...FOR A FEW YEARS.

HE WISHED LIKE ALL GET OUT THAT HE COULD REALLY READ THE FUTURE IN THE BALL. AND WHEN HE WAS THERE IN FRONT OF THEM HE REALLY BELIEVED HE WAS DOING IT. AND THEN ALL OF A SUDDEN HE BEGAN TO SEE THAT THERE WAS NO MAGIC ANYWHERE TO LEAN ON AND HE HAD NOBODY TO LEAN ON IN THE END BUT HIMSELF -NOT ME, NOT HIS FRIENDS, NOT LADY LUCK - JUST HIMSELF, AND HE WAS SCARED HE WOULD LET HIMSELF DOWN.

SO, HE DID?

YEAH, HE DID.

WHAT'S GOING TO HAPPEN TO HIM?

NOTHING'S GOING TO HAPPEN TO HIM. HE'S A SWEET MAN DOWN DEEP. LONG AS HE LASTS I'LL STICK TO HIM. IF IT HADN'T BEEN FOR PETE I'D OF PROBABLY ENDED UP IN A CRIB HOUSE. NOW I GOT A NICE TRADE THAT'LL ALWAYS BE IN DEMAND AS LONG AS THERE'S A SOUL IN THE WORLD WORRIED ABOUT WHERE NEXT MONTH'S RENT IS COMING FROM. I CAN ALWAYS GET ALONG AND TAKE PETE RIGHT ALONG WITH ME.

ZEENA AND STAN WATCHED AS, ACROSS FROM THE TENT, CLEM HOATLEY MOUNTED THE PLATFORM OF MAJOR MOSQUITO.

THE TOWNS CHANGE BUT IT'S ALWAYS THE SAME CROWD.

THE MAJOR DREW BACK A TINY FOOT AND AIMED A KICK WITH DEADLY ACCURACY AT HOATLEY'S SHIN.

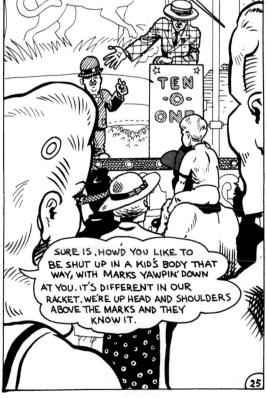

IT MADE THE TALKER STAMMER FOR A MOMENT.

THE MAJOR'S A NASTY LITTLE GUY.

SURE IS. HOW'D YOU LIKE TO BE SHUT UP IN A KID'S BODY THAT WAY, WITH MARKS YAWPIN' DOWN AT YOU. IT'S DIFFERENT IN OUR RACKET. WE'RE UP HEAD AND SHOULDERS ABOVE THE MARKS AND THEY KNOW IT.

25

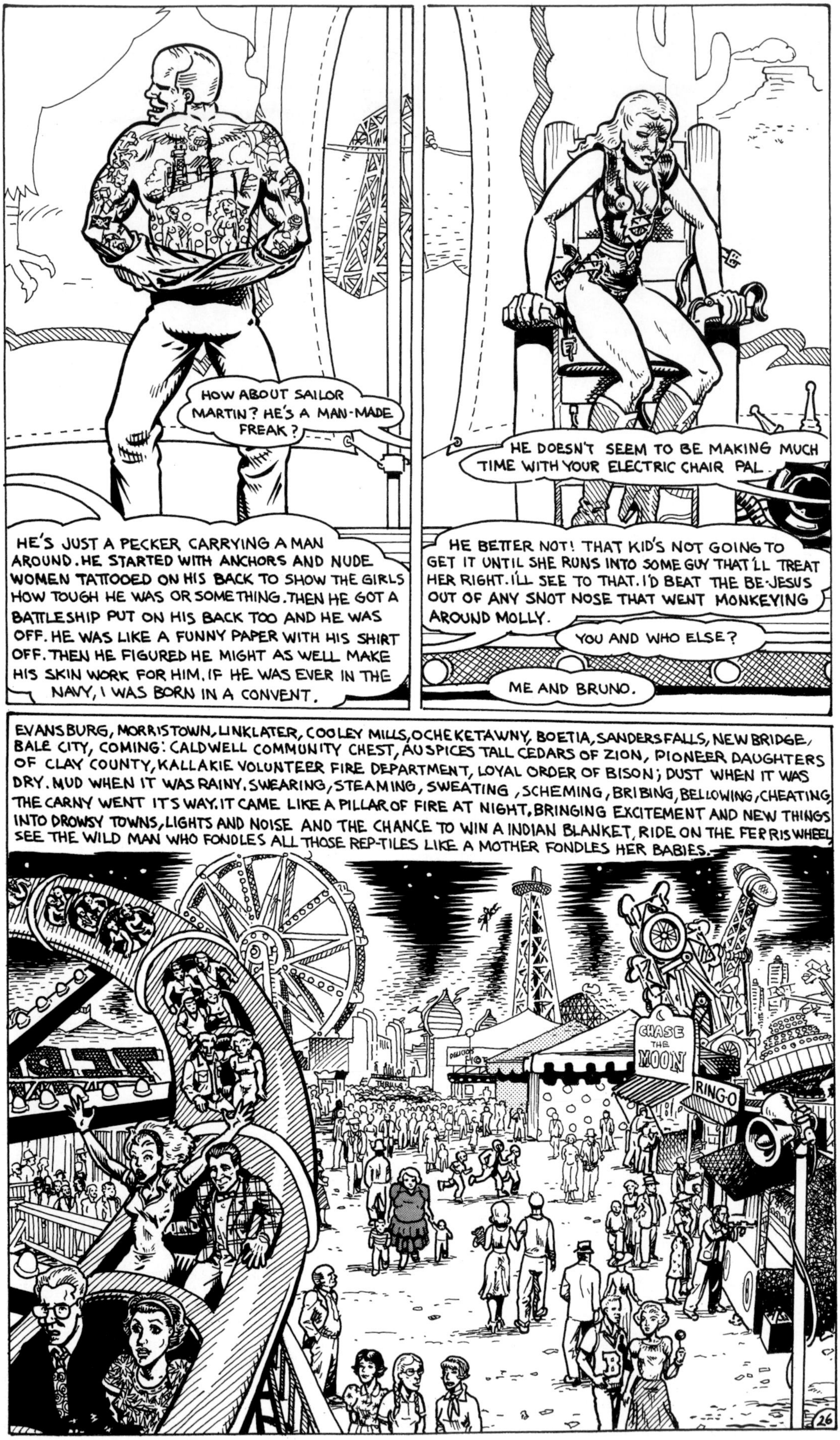

HOW ABOUT SAILOR MARTIN? HE'S A MAN-MADE FREAK?
HE DOESN'T SEEM TO BE MAKING MUCH TIME WITH YOUR ELECTRIC CHAIR PAL.
HE'S JUST A PECKER CARRYING A MAN AROUND. HE STARTED WITH ANCHORS AND NUDE WOMEN TATTOOED ON HIS BACK TO SHOW THE GIRLS HOW TOUGH HE WAS OR SOMETHING. THEN HE GOT A BATTLESHIP PUT ON HIS BACK TOO AND HE WAS OFF. HE WAS LIKE A FUNNY PAPER WITH HIS SHIRT OFF. THEN HE FIGURED HE MIGHT AS WELL MAKE HIS SKIN WORK FOR HIM. IF HE WAS EVER IN THE NAVY, I WAS BORN IN A CONVENT.
HE BETTER NOT! THAT KID'S NOT GOING TO GET IT UNTIL SHE RUNS INTO SOME GUY THAT'LL TREAT HER RIGHT. I'LL SEE TO THAT. I'D BEAT THE BE-JESUS OUT OF ANY SNOT NOSE THAT WENT MONKEYING AROUND MOLLY.
YOU AND WHO ELSE?
ME AND BRUNO.
EVANSBURG, MORRISTOWN, LINKLATER, COOLEY MILLS, OCHEKETAWNY, BOETIA, SANDERS FALLS, NEW BRIDGE, BALE CITY, COMING: CALDWELL COMMUNITY CHEST, AUSPICES TALL CEDARS OF ZION, PIONEER DAUGHTERS OF CLAY COUNTY, KALLAKIE VOLUNTEER FIRE DEPARTMENT, LOYAL ORDER OF BISON; DUST WHEN IT WAS DRY. MUD WHEN IT WAS RAINY. SWEARING, STEAMING, SWEATING, SCHEMING, BRIBING, BELLOWING, CHEATING, THE CARNY WENT IT'S WAY. IT CAME LIKE A PILLAR OF FIRE AT NIGHT, BRINGING EXCITEMENT AND NEW THINGS INTO DROWSY TOWNS, LIGHTS AND NOISE AND THE CHANCE TO WIN A INDIAN BLANKET, RIDE ON THE FERRIS WHEEL SEE THE WILD MAN WHO FONDLES ALL THOSE REP-TILES LIKE A MOTHER FONDLES HER BABIES.
CHASE THE MOON
RING-O
THRILLS

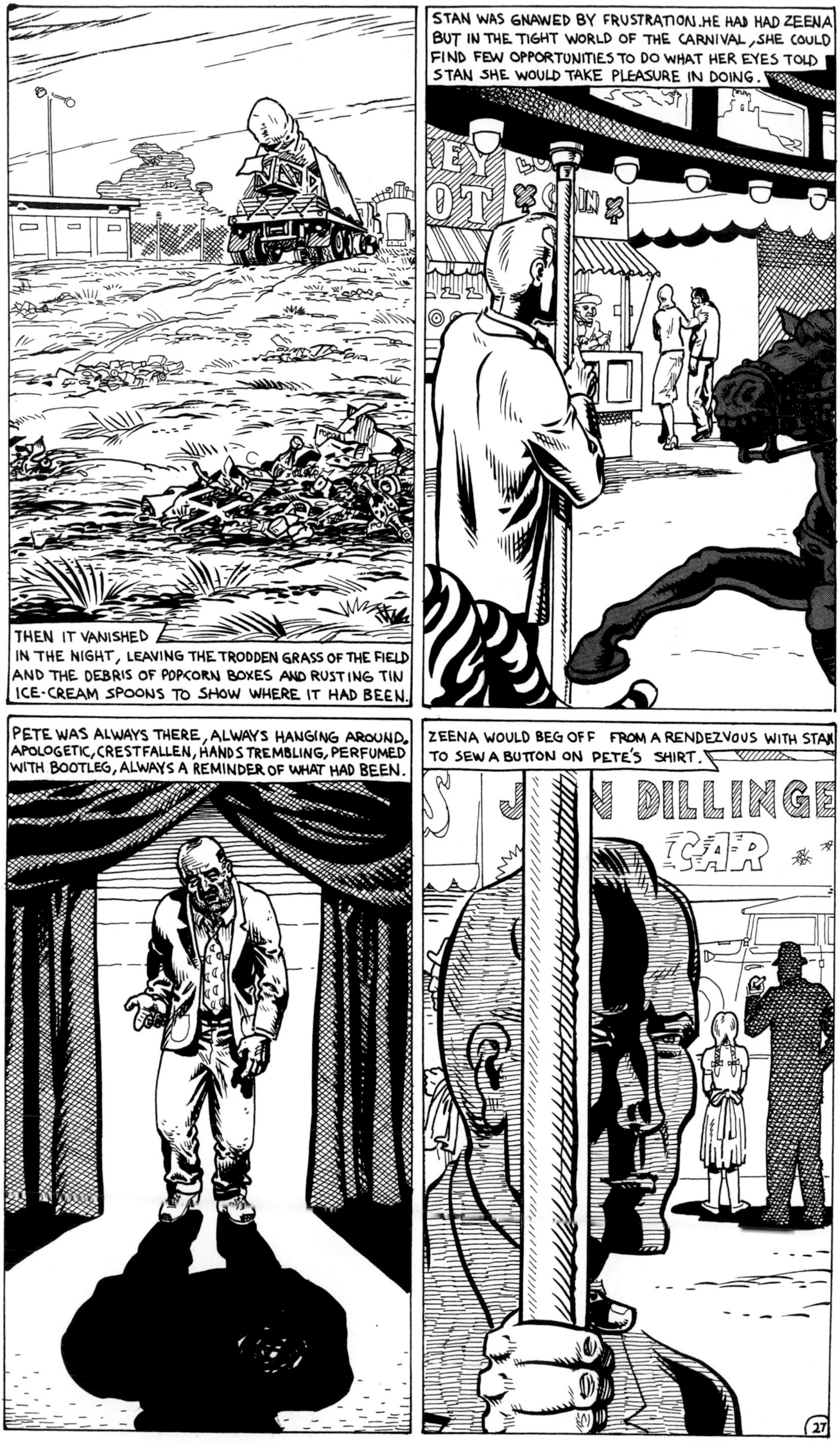
THEN IT VANISHED IN THE NIGHT, LEAVING THE TRODDEN GRASS OF THE FIELD AND THE DEBRIS OF POPCORN BOXES AND RUSTING TIN ICE-CREAM SPOONS TO SHOW WHERE IT HAD BEEN.
STAN WAS GNAWED BY FRUSTRATION. HE HAD HAD ZEENA BUT IN THE TIGHT WORLD OF THE CARNIVAL, SHE COULD FIND FEW OPPORTUNITIES TO DO WHAT HER EYES TOLD STAN SHE WOULD TAKE PLEASURE IN DOING.
PETE WAS ALWAYS THERE, ALWAYS HANGING AROUND, APOLOGETIC, CRESTFALLEN, HANDS TREMBLING, PERFUMED WITH BOOTLEG, ALWAYS A REMINDER OF WHAT HAD BEEN.
ZEENA WOULD BEG OFF FROM A RENDEZVOUS WITH STAN TO SEW A BUTTON ON PETE'S SHIRT.
CAR

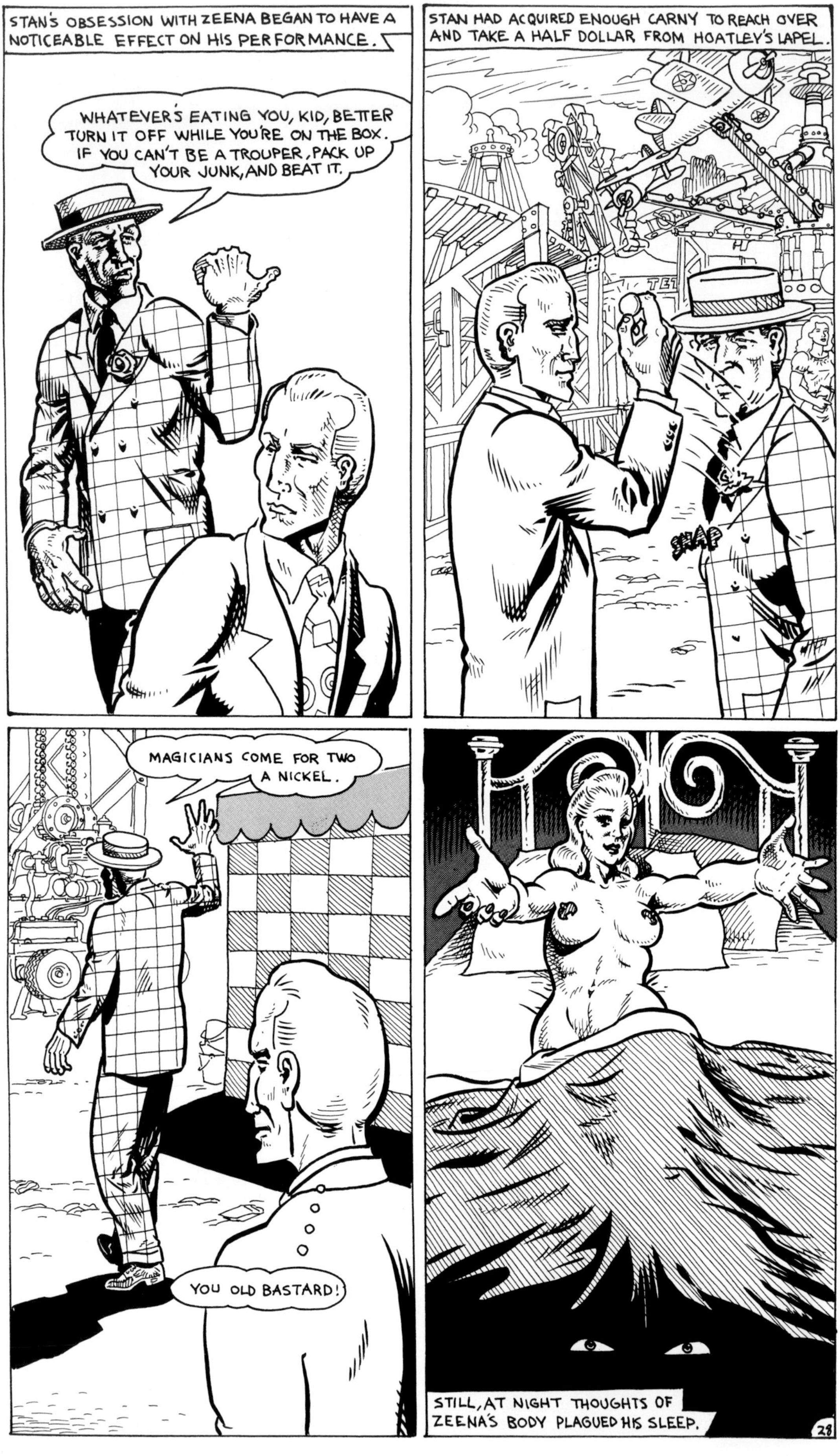
STAN'S OBSESSION WITH ZEENA BEGAN TO HAVE A NOTICEABLE EFFECT ON HIS PERFORMANCE.
WHATEVER'S EATING YOU, KID, BETTER TURN IT OFF WHILE YOU'RE ON THE BOX. IF YOU CAN'T BE A TROUPER, PACK UP YOUR JUNK, AND BEAT IT.
STAN HAD ACQUIRED ENOUGH CARNY TO REACH OVER AND TAKE A HALF DOLLAR FROM HOATLEY'S LAPEL.
SNAP
MAGICIANS COME FOR TWO A NICKEL.
YOU OLD BASTARD!
STILL, AT NIGHT THOUGHTS OF ZEENA'S BODY PLAGUED HIS SLEEP.

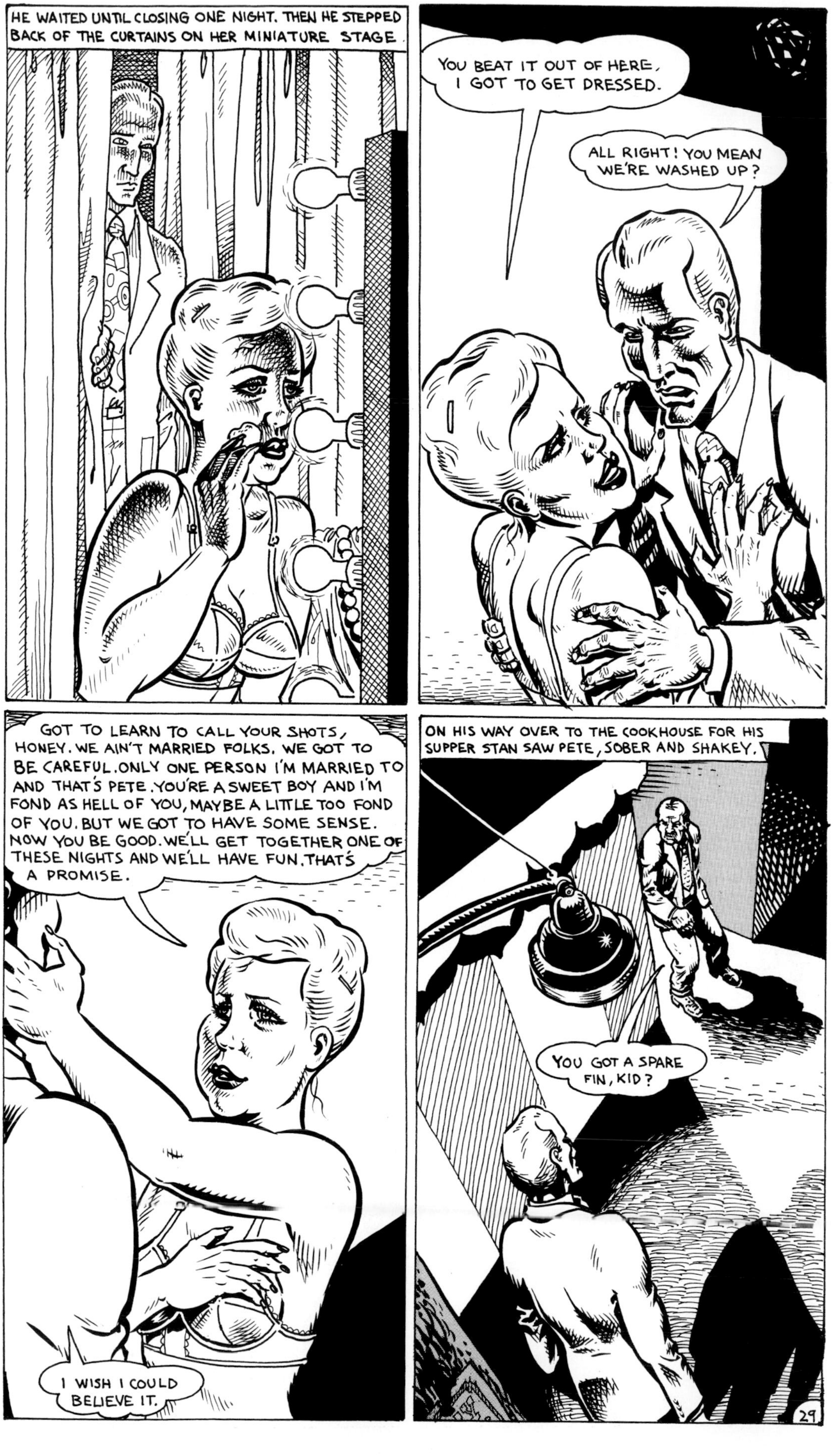
HE WAITED UNTIL CLOSING ONE NIGHT. THEN HE STEPPED BACK OF THE CURTAINS ON HER MINIATURE STAGE.
YOU BEAT IT OUT OF HERE, I GOT TO GET DRESSED.
ALL RIGHT! YOU MEAN WE'RE WASHED UP?
GOT TO LEARN TO CALL YOUR SHOTS, HONEY. WE AIN'T MARRIED FOLKS. WE GOT TO BE CAREFUL. ONLY ONE PERSON I'M MARRIED TO AND THAT'S PETE. YOU'RE A SWEET BOY AND I'M FOND AS HELL OF YOU, MAYBE A LITTLE TOO FOND OF YOU. BUT WE GOT TO HAVE SOME SENSE. NOW YOU BE GOOD. WE'LL GET TOGETHER ONE OF THESE NIGHTS AND WE'LL HAVE FUN. THAT'S A PROMISE.
I WISH I COULD BELIEVE IT.
ON HIS WAY OVER TO THE COOKHOUSE FOR HIS SUPPER STAN SAW PETE, SOBER AND SHAKEY.
YOU GOT A SPARE FIN, KID?

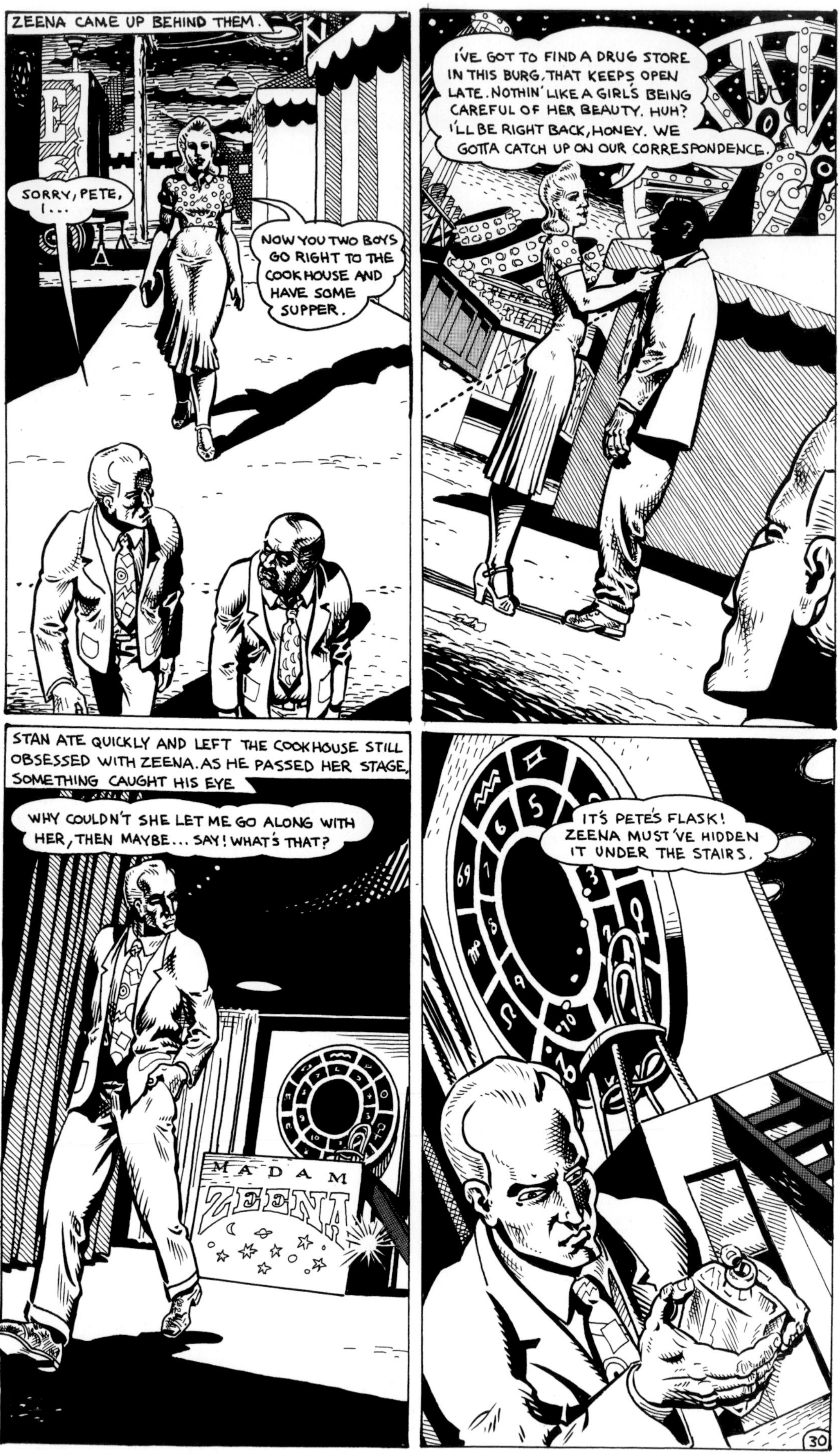
ZEENA CAME UP BEHIND THEM.
SORRY, PETE, I...
NOW YOU TWO BOYS GO RIGHT TO THE COOKHOUSE AND HAVE SOME SUPPER.
I'VE GOT TO FIND A DRUG STORE IN THIS BURG, THAT KEEPS OPEN LATE. NOTHIN' LIKE A GIRL'S BEING CAREFUL OF HER BEAUTY, HUH? I'LL BE RIGHT BACK, HONEY. WE GOTTA CATCH UP ON OUR CORRESPONDENCE.
STAN ATE QUICKLY AND LEFT THE COOKHOUSE STILL OBSESSED WITH ZEENA. AS HE PASSED HER STAGE, SOMETHING CAUGHT HIS EYE
WHY COULDN'T SHE LET ME GO ALONG WITH HER, THEN MAYBE... SAY! WHAT'S THAT?
MADAM ZEENA
IT'S PETE'S FLASK! ZEENA MUST'VE HIDDEN IT UNDER THE STAIRS.

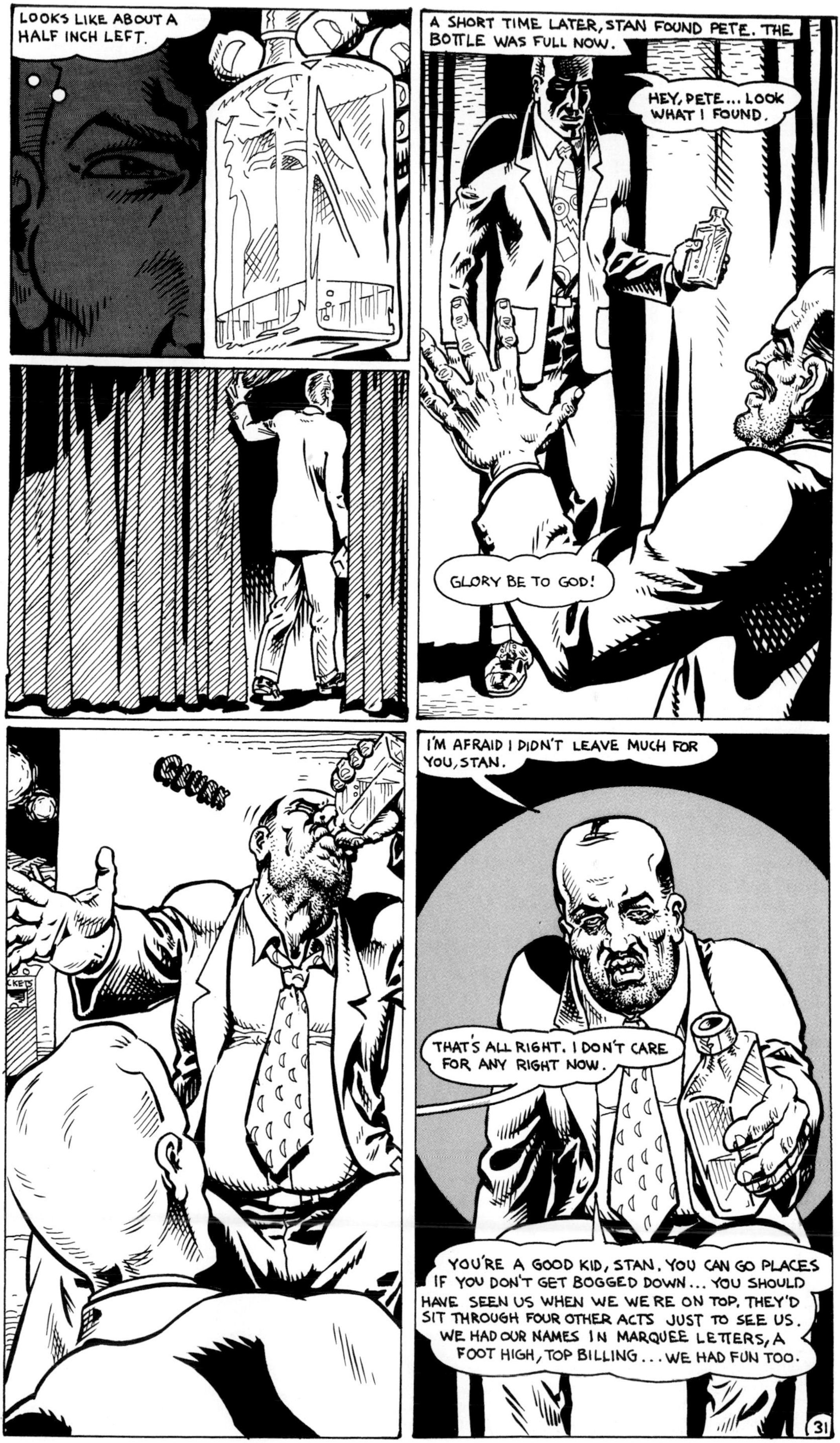
LOOKS LIKE ABOUT A HALF INCH LEFT.
A SHORT TIME LATER, STAN FOUND PETE. THE BOTTLE WAS FULL NOW.
HEY, PETE... LOOK WHAT I FOUND.
GLORY BE TO GOD!
I'M AFRAID I DIDN'T LEAVE MUCH FOR YOU, STAN.
THAT'S ALL RIGHT. I DON'T CARE FOR ANY RIGHT NOW.
YOU'RE A GOOD KID, STAN. YOU CAN GO PLACES IF YOU DON'T GET BOGGED DOWN... YOU SHOULD HAVE SEEN US WHEN WE WERE ON TOP. THEY'D SIT THROUGH FOUR OTHER ACTS JUST TO SEE US. WE HAD OUR NAMES IN MARQUEE LETTERS, A FOOT HIGH, TOP BILLING... WE HAD FUN TOO.

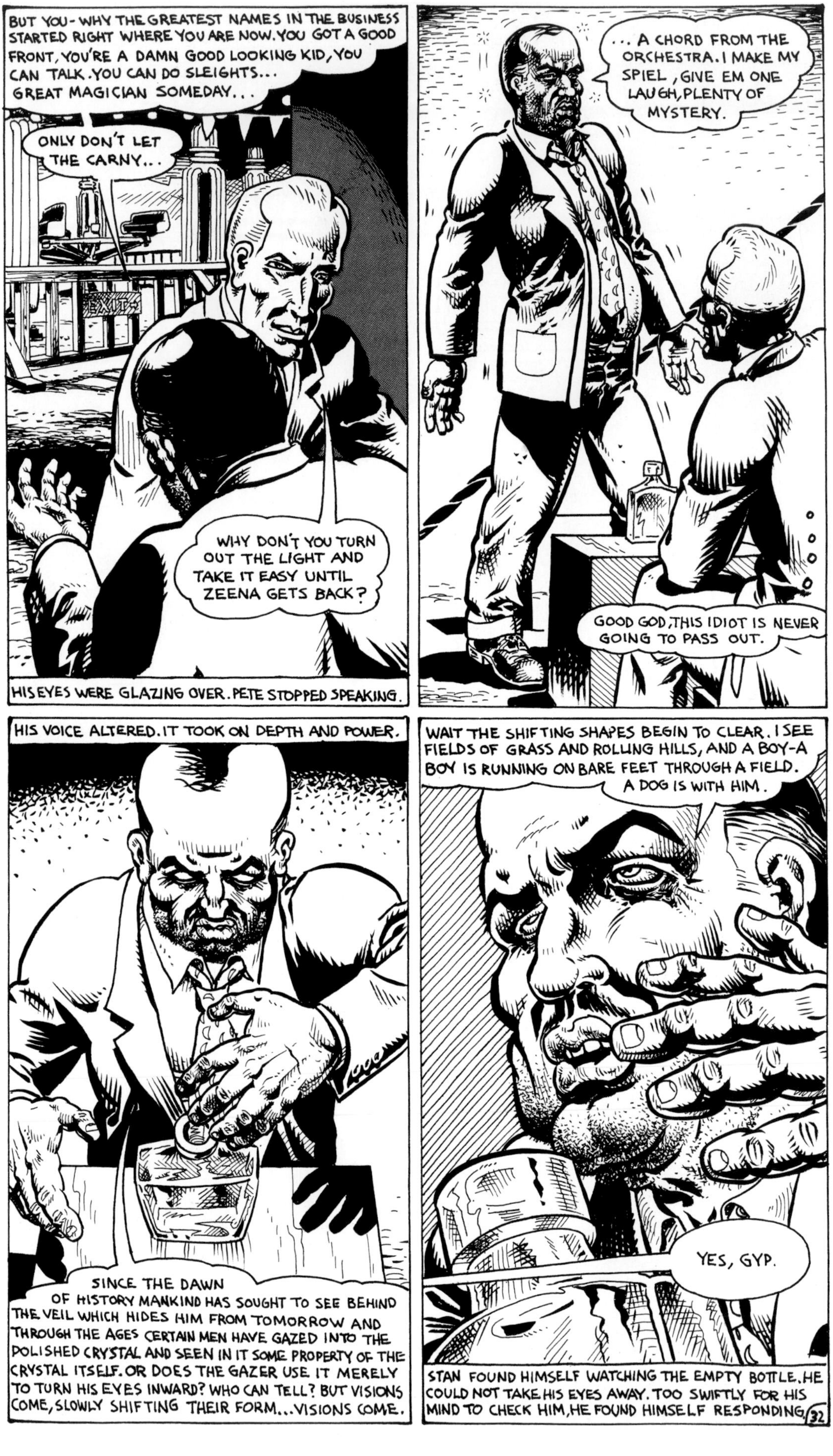
BUT YOU- WHY THE GREATEST NAMES IN THE BUSINESS STARTED RIGHT WHERE YOU ARE NOW. YOU GOT A GOOD FRONT, YOU'RE A DAMN GOOD LOOKING KID, YOU CAN TALK. YOU CAN DO SLEIGHTS... GREAT MAGICIAN SOMEDAY...
ONLY DON'T LET THE CARNY...
EXIT
WHY DON'T YOU TURN OUT THE LIGHT AND TAKE IT EASY UNTIL ZEENA GETS BACK?
HIS EYES WERE GLAZING OVER. PETE STOPPED SPEAKING.
... A CHORD FROM THE ORCHESTRA. I MAKE MY SPIEL, GIVE EM ONE LAUGH, PLENTY OF MYSTERY.
GOOD GOD, THIS IDIOT IS NEVER GOING TO PASS OUT.
HIS VOICE ALTERED. IT TOOK ON DEPTH AND POWER.
SINCE THE DAWN OF HISTORY MANKIND HAS SOUGHT TO SEE BEHIND THE VEIL WHICH HIDES HIM FROM TOMORROW AND THROUGH THE AGES CERTAIN MEN HAVE GAZED INTO THE POLISHED CRYSTAL AND SEEN IN IT SOME PROPERTY OF THE CRYSTAL ITSELF. OR DOES THE GAZER USE IT MERELY TO TURN HIS EYES INWARD? WHO CAN TELL? BUT VISIONS COME, SLOWLY SHIFTING THEIR FORM... VISIONS COME.
WAIT THE SHIFTING SHAPES BEGIN TO CLEAR. I SEE FIELDS OF GRASS AND ROLLING HILLS, AND A BOY-A BOY IS RUNNING ON BARE FEET THROUGH A FIELD. A DOG IS WITH HIM.
YES, GYP.
STAN FOUND HIMSELF WATCHING THE EMPTY BOTTLE. HE COULD NOT TAKE HIS EYES AWAY. TOO SWIFTLY FOR HIS MIND TO CHECK HIM, HE FOUND HIMSELF RESPONDING.

HAPPINESS THEN... BUT FOR A LITTLE WHILE. NOW DARK MISTS... SORROW. I SEE PEOPLE MOVING... ONE MAN STANDS OUT... EVIL... THE BOY HATES HIM, DEATH, AND THE WISH OF DEATH...

BTONK

I DIDN'T MEAN NOTHING, BOY. YOU AIN'T MAD AT ME, ARE YA? STOCK READING - FITS EVERYBODY, ONLY YOU GOT TO DRESS IT UP... EVERYBODY HAD SOME TROUBLE. SOMEBODY THEY WANTED TO KILL. USUALLY FOR A BOY IT'S THE OLD MAN. WHAT'S CHILDHOOD? HAPPY ONE MINUTE, HEARTBROKE THE NEXT. EVERY BOY HAD A DOG OR A NEIGHBOR'S DOG.

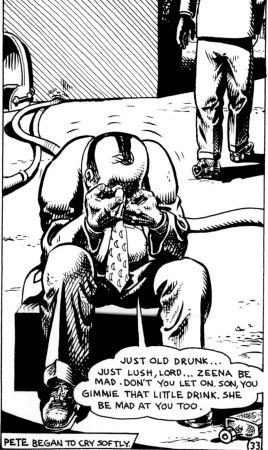

JUST OLD DRUNK... JUST LUSH, LORD... ZEENA BE MAD. DON'T YOU LET ON, SON, YOU GIMMIE THAT LITTLE DRINK. SHE BE MAD AT YOU TOO.

PETE BEGAN TO CRY SOFTLY.

33

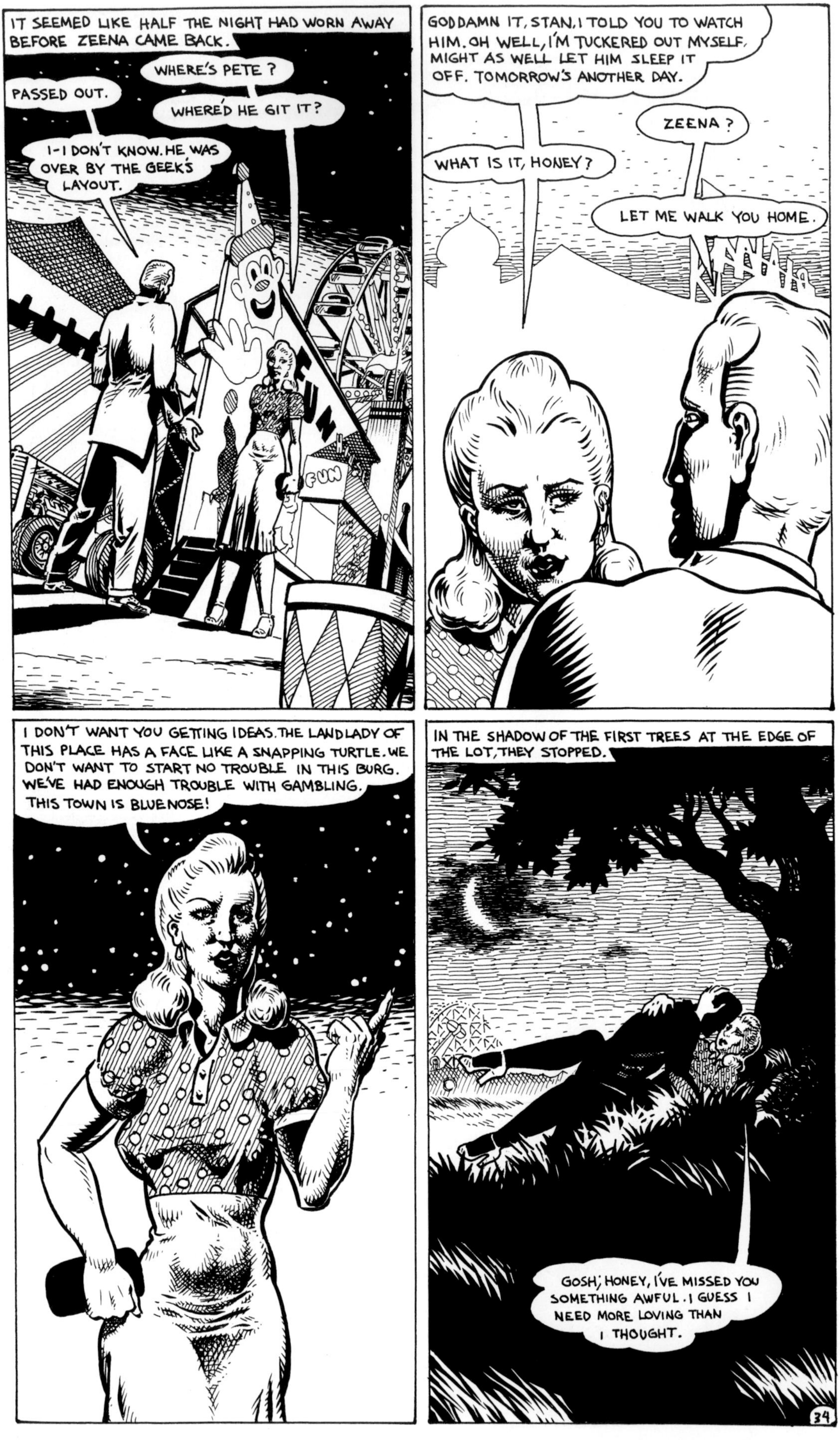
IT SEEMED LIKE HALF THE NIGHT HAD WORN AWAY BEFORE ZEENA CAME BACK.
WHERE'S PETE ?
PASSED OUT.
WHERE'D HE GIT IT?
I-I DON'T KNOW. HE WAS OVER BY THE GEEK'S LAYOUT.
FUN
FUN
GODDAMN IT, STAN, I TOLD YOU TO WATCH HIM. OH WELL, I'M TUCKERED OUT MYSELF. MIGHT AS WELL LET HIM SLEEP IT OFF. TOMORROW'S ANOTHER DAY.
ZEENA ?
WHAT IS IT, HONEY ?
LET ME WALK YOU HOME.
I DON'T WANT YOU GETTING IDEAS. THE LANDLADY OF THIS PLACE HAS A FACE LIKE A SNAPPING TURTLE. WE DON'T WANT TO START NO TROUBLE IN THIS BURG. WE'VE HAD ENOUGH TROUBLE WITH GAMBLING. THIS TOWN IS BLUENOSE!
IN THE SHADOW OF THE FIRST TREES AT THE EDGE OF THE LOT, THEY STOPPED.
GOSH, HONEY, I'VE MISSED YOU SOMETHING AWFUL. I GUESS I NEED MORE LOVING THAN I THOUGHT.

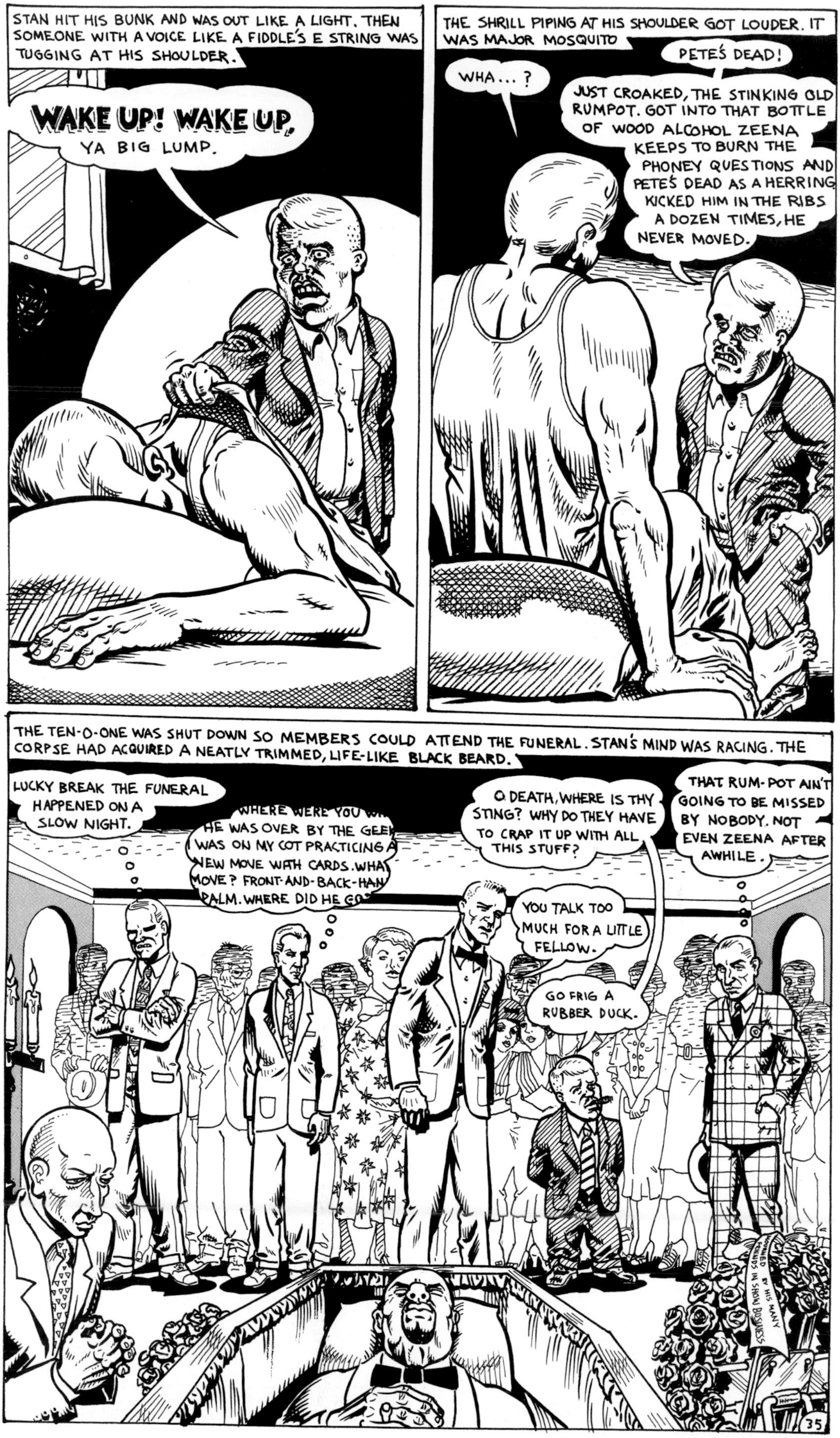

STAN HIT HIS BUNK AND WAS OUT LIKE A LIGHT. THEN SOMEONE WITH A VOICE LIKE A FIDDLE'S E STRING WAS TUGGING AT HIS SHOULDER.
WAKE UP! WAKE UP, YA BIG LUMP.
THE SHRILL PIPING AT HIS SHOULDER GOT LOUDER. IT WAS MAJOR MOSQUITO
WHA... ?
PETE'S DEAD!
JUST CROAKED, THE STINKING OLD RUMPOT. GOT INTO THAT BOTTLE OF WOOD ALCOHOL ZEENA KEEPS TO BURN THE PHONEY QUESTIONS AND PETE'S DEAD AS A HERRING. KICKED HIM IN THE RIBS A DOZEN TIMES, HE NEVER MOVED.
THE TEN-O-ONE WAS SHUT DOWN SO MEMBERS COULD ATTEND THE FUNERAL. STAN'S MIND WAS RACING. THE CORPSE HAD ACQUIRED A NEATLY TRIMMED, LIFE-LIKE BLACK BEARD.
LUCKY BREAK THE FUNERAL HAPPENED ON A SLOW NIGHT.
WHERE WERE YOU W HE WAS OVER BY THE GEEK WAS ON MY COT PRACTICING A NEW MOVE WITH CARDS. WHA MOVE? FRONT-AND-BACK-HAN PALM. WHERE DID HE GO
O DEATH, WHERE IS THY STING? WHY DO THEY HAVE TO CRAP IT UP WITH ALL THIS STUFF?
THAT RUM-POT AIN'T GOING TO BE MISSED BY NOBODY. NOT EVEN ZEENA AFTER AWHILE.
YOU TALK TOO MUCH FOR A LITTLE FELLOW.
GO FRIG A RUBBER DUCK.
MOURNED BY HIS MANY FRIENDS IN SHOW BUSINESS

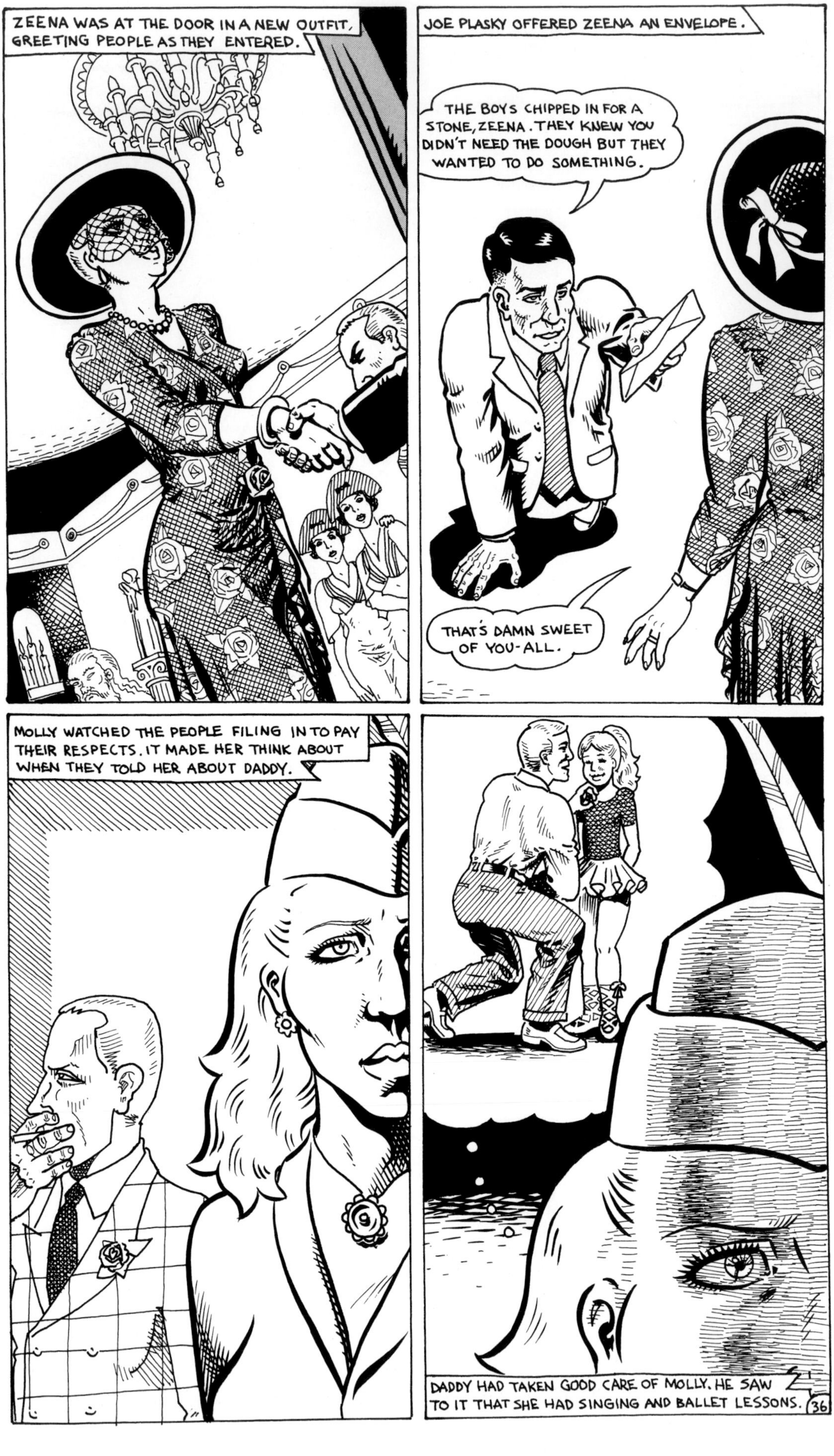

ZEENA WAS AT THE DOOR IN A NEW OUTFIT, GREETING PEOPLE AS THEY ENTERED.
JOE PLASKY OFFERED ZEENA AN ENVELOPE.
THE BOYS CHIPPED IN FOR A STONE, ZEENA. THEY KNEW YOU DIDN'T NEED THE DOUGH BUT THEY WANTED TO DO SOMETHING.
THAT'S DAMN SWEET OF YOU-ALL.
MOLLY WATCHED THE PEOPLE FILING IN TO PAY THEIR RESPECTS. IT MADE HER THINK ABOUT WHEN THEY TOLD HER ABOUT DADDY.
DADDY HAD TAKEN GOOD CARE OF MOLLY. HE SAW TO IT THAT SHE HAD SINGING AND BALLET LESSONS.

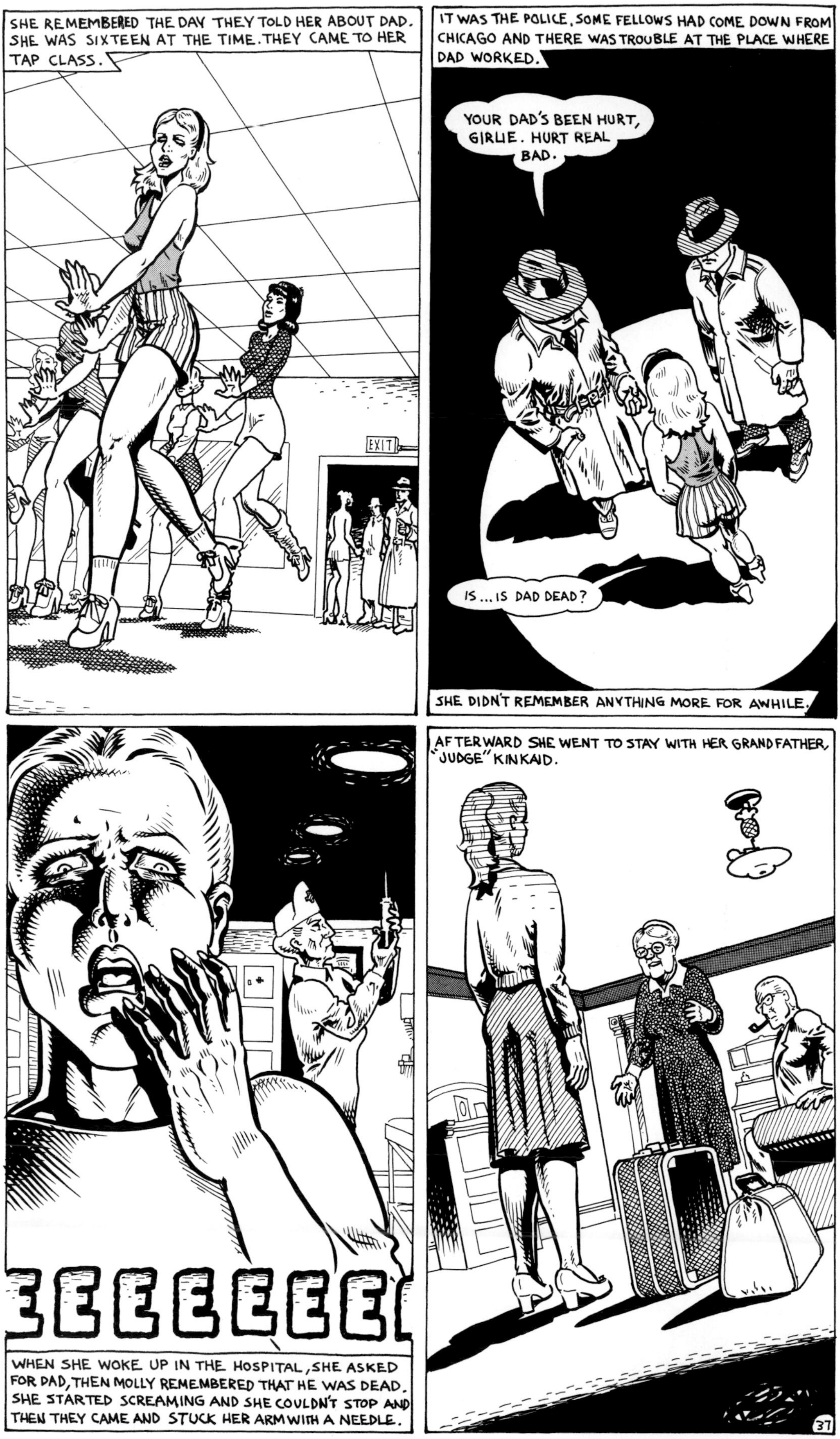
SHE REMEMBERED THE DAY THEY TOLD HER ABOUT DAD. SHE WAS SIXTEEN AT THE TIME. THEY CAME TO HER TAP CLASS.
EXIT
IT WAS THE POLICE. SOME FELLOWS HAD COME DOWN FROM CHICAGO AND THERE WAS TROUBLE AT THE PLACE WHERE DAD WORKED.
YOUR DAD'S BEEN HURT, GIRLIE. HURT REAL BAD.
IS ... IS DAD DEAD?
SHE DIDN'T REMEMBER ANYTHING MORE FOR AWHILE.
EEEEEEE
WHEN SHE WOKE UP IN THE HOSPITAL, SHE ASKED FOR DAD, THEN MOLLY REMEMBERED THAT HE WAS DEAD. SHE STARTED SCREAMING AND SHE COULDN'T STOP AND THEN THEY CAME AND STUCK HER ARM WITH A NEEDLE.
AFTERWARD SHE WENT TO STAY WITH HER GRANDFATHER, "JUDGE" KINKAID.

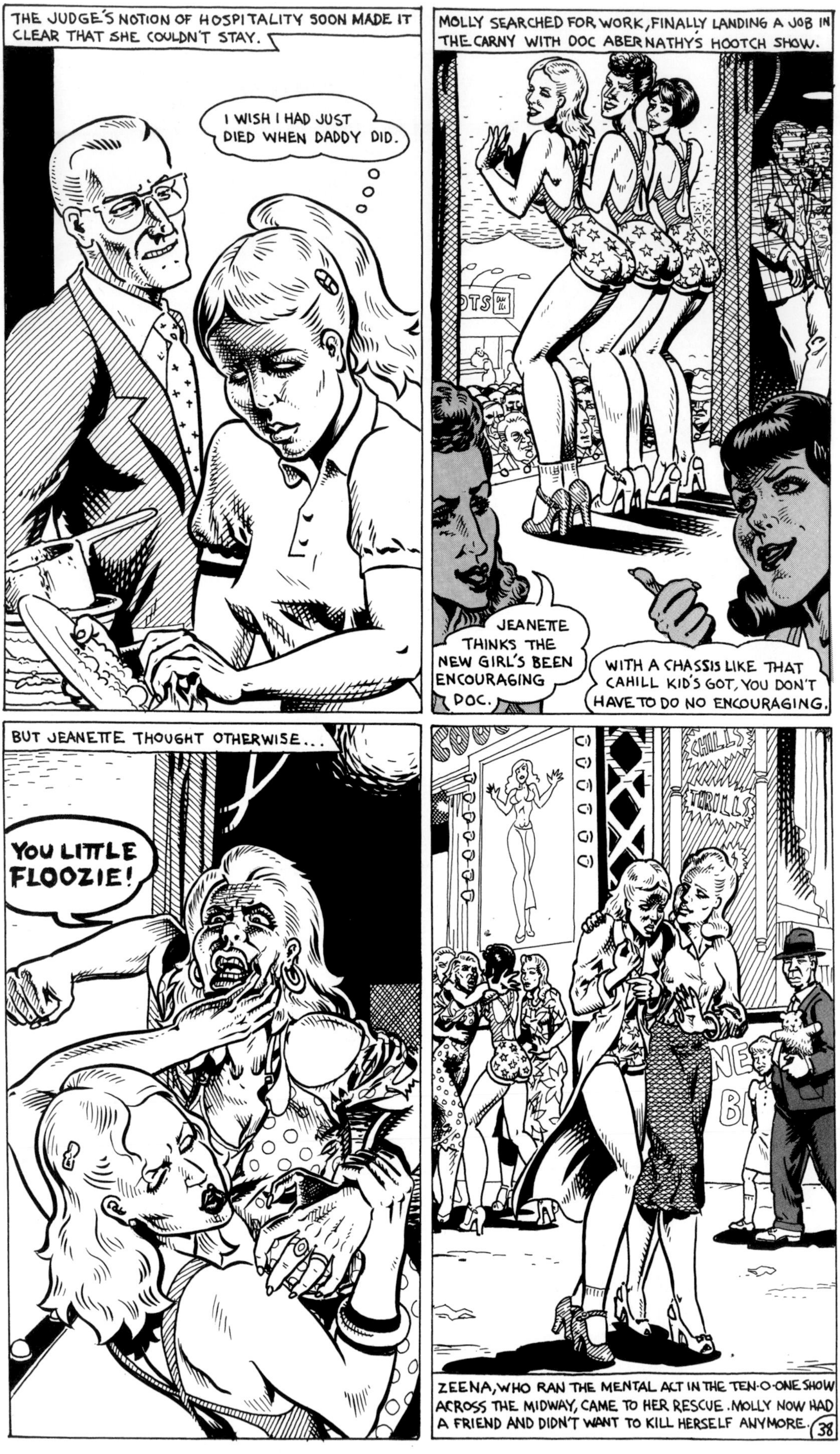
THE JUDGE'S NOTION OF HOSPITALITY SOON MADE IT CLEAR THAT SHE COULDN'T STAY.
I WISH I HAD JUST DIED WHEN DADDY DID.
MOLLY SEARCHED FOR WORK, FINALLY LANDING A JOB IN THE CARNY WITH DOC ABERNATHY'S HOOTCH SHOW.
JEANETTE THINKS THE NEW GIRL'S BEEN ENCOURAGING DOC.
WITH A CHASSIS LIKE THAT CAHILL KID'S GOT, YOU DON'T HAVE TO DO NO ENCOURAGING.
BUT JEANETTE THOUGHT OTHERWISE...
YOU LITTLE FLOOZIE!
CHILLS
THRILLS
ZEENA, WHO RAN THE MENTAL ACT IN THE TEN-O-ONE SHOW ACROSS THE MIDWAY, CAME TO HER RESCUE. MOLLY NOW HAD A FRIEND AND DIDN'T WANT TO KILL HERSELF ANYMORE.

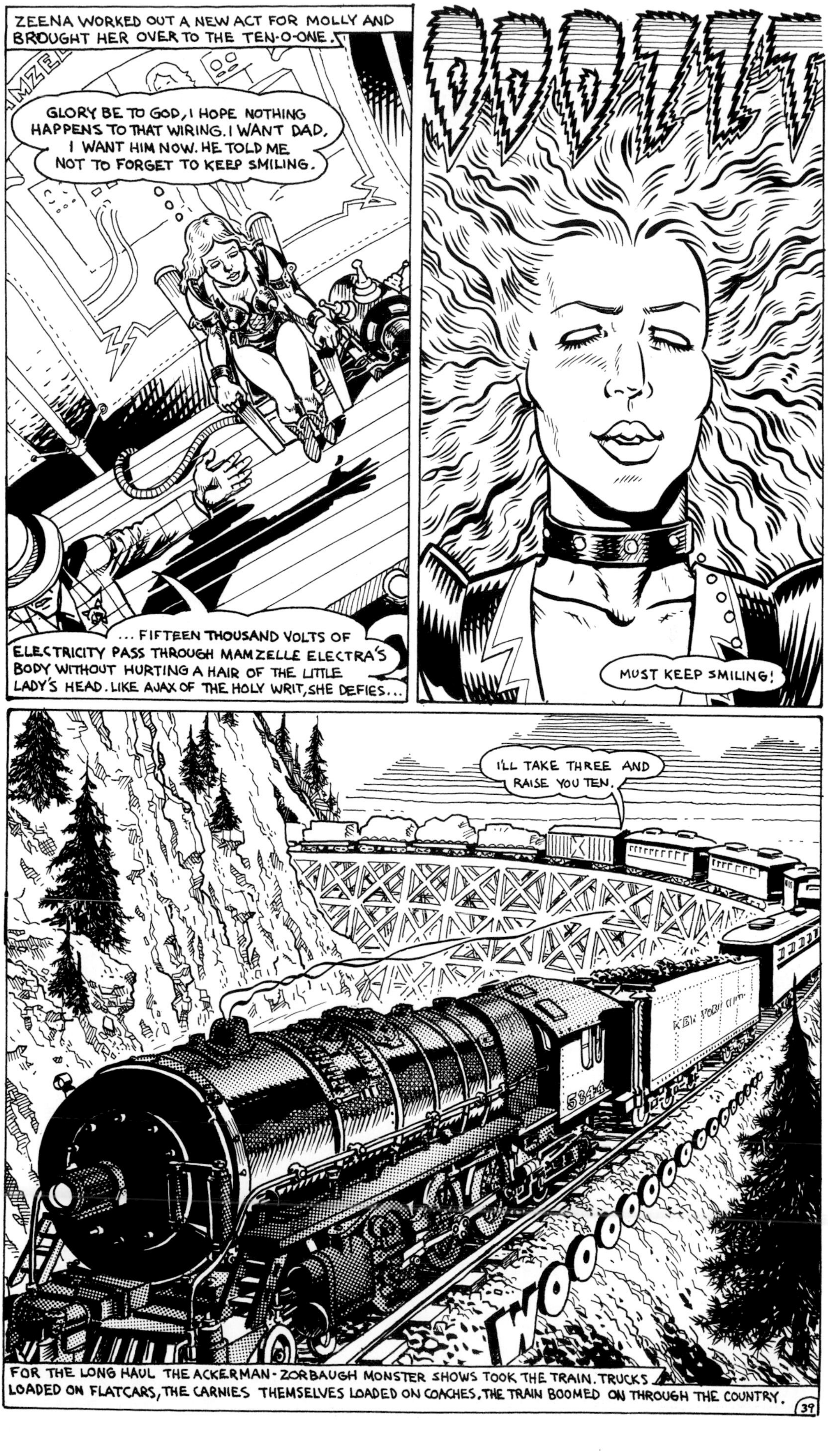
ZEENA WORKED OUT A NEW ACT FOR MOLLY AND BROUGHT HER OVER TO THE TEN-O-ONE.
GLORY BE TO GOD, I HOPE NOTHING HAPPENS TO THAT WIRING. I WANT DAD, I WANT HIM NOW. HE TOLD ME NOT TO FORGET TO KEEP SMILING.
... FIFTEEN THOUSAND VOLTS OF ELECTRICITY PASS THROUGH MAMZELLE ELECTRA'S BODY WITHOUT HURTING A HAIR OF THE LITTLE LADY'S HEAD. LIKE AJAX OF THE HOLY WRIT, SHE DEFIES...
MUST KEEP SMILING!
I'LL TAKE THREE AND RAISE YOU TEN.
FOR THE LONG HAUL THE ACKERMAN-ZORBAUGH MONSTER SHOWS TOOK THE TRAIN. TRUCKS LOADED ON FLATCARS, THE CARNIES THEMSELVES LOADED ON COACHES, THE TRAIN BOOMED ON THROUGH THE COUNTRY.

I'M STAYING.

I'M IN TOO.

IN A BAGGAGE CAR, AMONG PILES OF CANVASS AND GEAR, THE MAJOR'S VOICE HAD THE INSISTENCE OF A CRICKET'S.

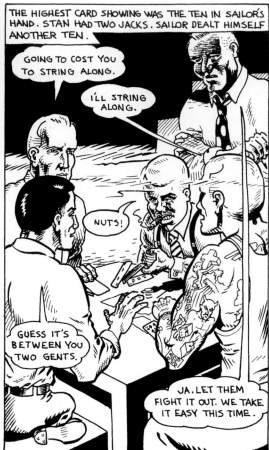

THE HIGHEST CARD SHOWING WAS THE TEN IN SAILOR'S HAND. STAN HAD TWO JACKS. SAILOR DEALT HIMSELF ANOTHER TEN.

GOING TO COST YOU TO STRING ALONG.

I'LL STRING ALONG.

NUTS!

GUESS IT'S BETWEEN YOU TWO GENTS.

JA. LET THEM FIGHT IT OUT. WE TAKE IT EASY THIS TIME.

THE SAILOR THREW OVER HIS HOLE CARD, A TEN. HE REACHED FOR THE POT. AT A SOUND LIKE A LONG DRAWN FIDDLE SCRAPE, THEY ALL JUMPED.

HEY

WHAT'S EATING YOU, BIG NOISE?

WAIT A MINUTE! THESE CARDS ARE MARKED WITH DAUB. THEY'RE SMEARED TO ACT LIKE READERS. YOU CAN SEE IT IF YOU KNOW HOW TO LOOK.

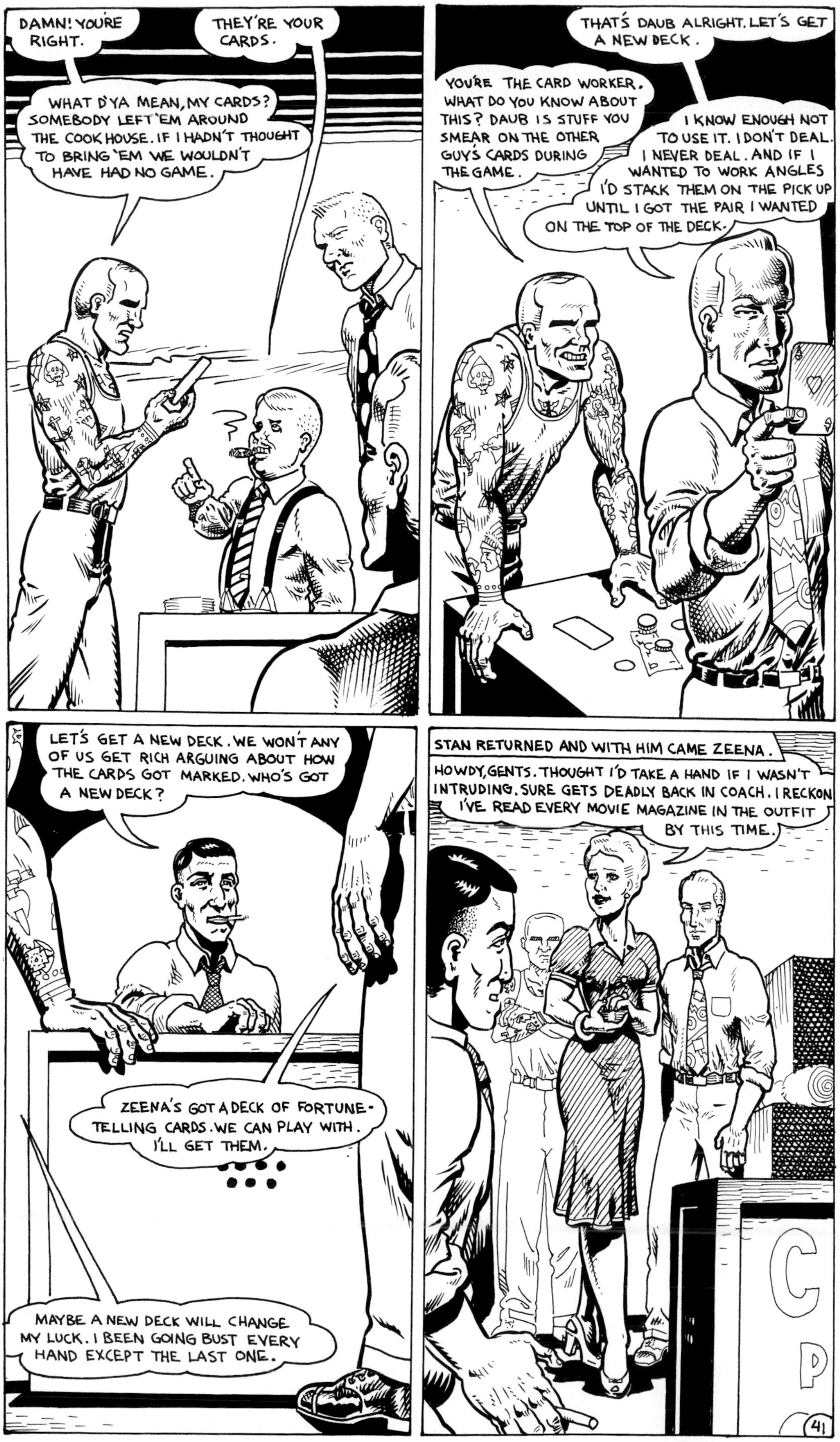
DAMN! YOU'RE RIGHT.
THEY'RE YOUR CARDS.
WHAT D'YA MEAN, MY CARDS? SOMEBODY LEFT 'EM AROUND THE COOK HOUSE. IF I HADN'T THOUGHT TO BRING 'EM WE WOULDN'T HAVE HAD NO GAME.
THAT'S DAUB ALRIGHT. LET'S GET A NEW DECK.
YOU'RE THE CARD WORKER. WHAT DO YOU KNOW ABOUT THIS? DAUB IS STUFF YOU SMEAR ON THE OTHER GUY'S CARDS DURING THE GAME.
I KNOW ENOUGH NOT TO USE IT. I DON'T DEAL. I NEVER DEAL. AND IF I WANTED TO WORK ANGLES I'D STACK THEM ON THE PICK UP UNTIL I GOT THE PAIR I WANTED ON THE TOP OF THE DECK.
LET'S GET A NEW DECK. WE WON'T ANY OF US GET RICH ARGUING ABOUT HOW THE CARDS GOT MARKED. WHO'S GOT A NEW DECK?
ZEENA'S GOT A DECK OF FORTUNE-TELLING CARDS. WE CAN PLAY WITH. I'LL GET THEM.
MAYBE A NEW DECK WILL CHANGE MY LUCK. I BEEN GOING BUST EVERY HAND EXCEPT THE LAST ONE.
STAN RETURNED AND WITH HIM CAME ZEENA.
HOWDY, GENTS. THOUGHT I'D TAKE A HAND IF I WASN'T INTRUDING. SURE GETS DEADLY BACK IN COACH. I RECKON I'VE READ EVERY MOVIE MAGAZINE IN THE OUTFIT BY THIS TIME.
C
P

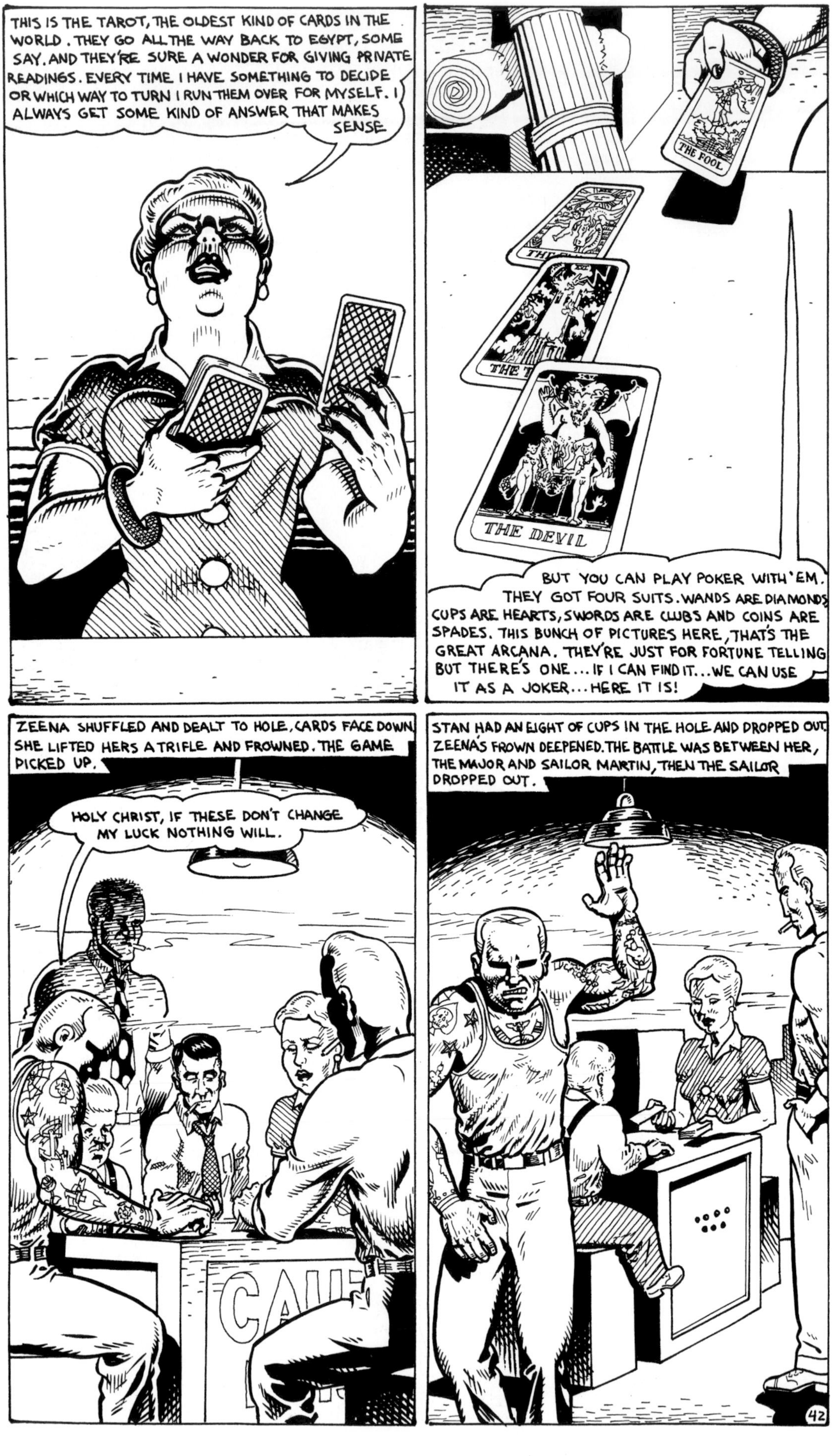
THIS IS THE TAROT, THE OLDEST KIND OF CARDS IN THE WORLD. THEY GO ALL THE WAY BACK TO EGYPT, SOME SAY. AND THEY'RE SURE A WONDER FOR GIVING PRIVATE READINGS. EVERY TIME I HAVE SOMETHING TO DECIDE OR WHICH WAY TO TURN I RUN THEM OVER FOR MYSELF. I ALWAYS GET SOME KIND OF ANSWER THAT MAKES SENSE
THE FOOL
THE DEVIL
BUT YOU CAN PLAY POKER WITH 'EM. THEY GOT FOUR SUITS. WANDS ARE DIAMONDS CUPS ARE HEARTS, SWORDS ARE CLUBS AND COINS ARE SPADES. THIS BUNCH OF PICTURES HERE, THAT'S THE GREAT ARCANA. THEY'RE JUST FOR FORTUNE TELLING BUT THERE'S ONE... IF I CAN FIND IT... WE CAN USE IT AS A JOKER... HERE IT IS!
ZEENA SHUFFLED AND DEALT TO HOLE, CARDS FACE DOWN. SHE LIFTED HERS A TRIFLE AND FROWNED. THE GAME PICKED UP.
HOLY CHRIST, IF THESE DON'T CHANGE MY LUCK NOTHING WILL.
STAN HAD AN EIGHT OF CUPS IN THE HOLE AND DROPPED OUT. ZEENA'S FROWN DEEPENED. THE BATTLE WAS BETWEEN HER, THE MAJOR AND SAILOR MARTIN, THEN THE SAILOR DROPPED OUT.

THE MAJOR'S HAND SHOWED THREE KNIGHTS. HE CALLED. ZEENA HAD A FLUSH IN COINS.

AIN'T YOU THE BLUFFER. FROWNING LIKE YOU HAD NOTHING AND YOU SITTING ON TOP OF A FLUSH.

I WASN'T MEANING TO BLUFF. IT WAS THE HOLE CARD I WAS FROWNING AT. THE ACE OF COINS. I ALWAYS READ THAT AS AN INJURY BY A TRUSTED FRIEND.

MAYBE THE SNAKES HAVE SOMETHING TO DO WITH IT. THEY'RE SCRAPPING AROUND LIKE THEY'RE UNCOMFORTABLE.

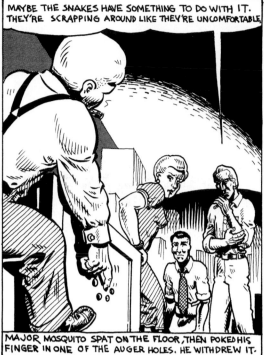

MAJOR MOSQUITO SPAT ON THE FLOOR, THEN POKED HIS FINGER IN ONE OF THE AUGER HOLES. HE WITHDREW IT.

FROM THE HOLE FLICKED A FORKED THREAD OF PINK. THE MAJOR QUICKLY TOUCHED THE LIGHTED EMBER OF HIS CIGAR TO THE TONGUE OF THE VIPER.

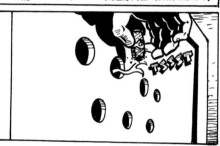

TSSST

IT FLASHED BACK INTO THE BOX AND THERE WAS A FRENZIED SCRAPING OF COILS AND WHIPPING INSIDE.

JESUS, YOU SHOULDN'T OF DONE THAT, YOU LITTLE STINKER, THEM DAMN THINGS GET MAD.

HO-HO-HO. NEXT TIME I'LL DO IT TO YOU!

CAUTION POISONOUS SNAKE

THRUMP THRUMP

STAN LEFT THE GAME AND PUSHED THROUGH TO THE BACK OF THE TRAIN. HIS RIGHT HAND SLID UNDER THE EDGE OF HIS COAT AND UNPINNED A TINY METAL BOX

WHY DO I HAVE TO FRIG AROUND WITH ALL THIS CHICKEN-SHIT STUFF? I DIDN'T WANT THEIR DIMES. I WANTED TO SEE IF I COULD TAKE THEM.

FLIP

DAUB

3257

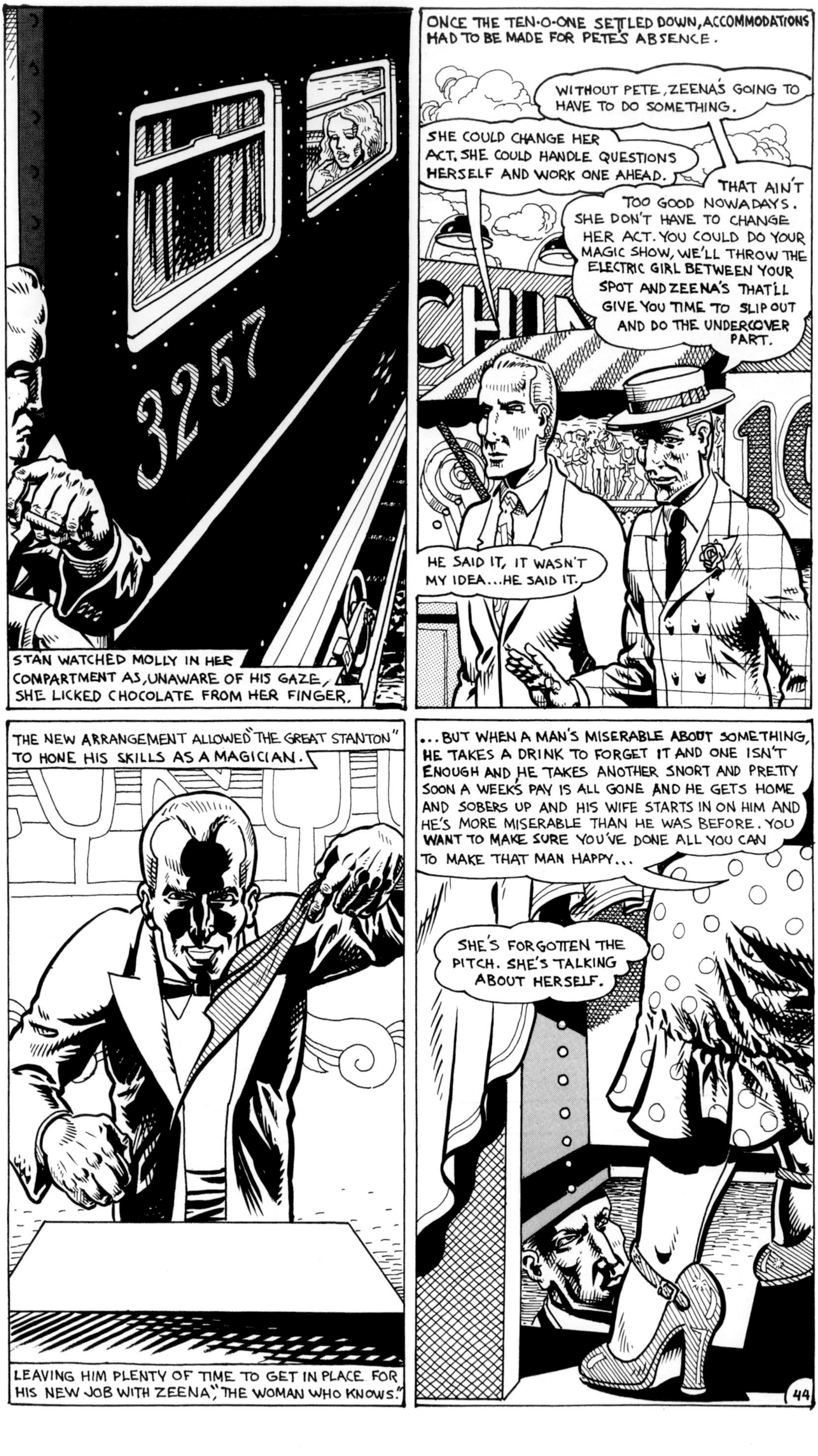
3257
STAN WATCHED MOLLY IN HER COMPARTMENT AS, UNAWARE OF HIS GAZE, SHE LICKED CHOCOLATE FROM HER FINGER.
ONCE THE TEN-O-ONE SETTLED DOWN, ACCOMMODATIONS HAD TO BE MADE FOR PETE'S ABSENCE.
WITHOUT PETE, ZEENA'S GOING TO HAVE TO DO SOMETHING.
SHE COULD CHANGE HER ACT. SHE COULD HANDLE QUESTIONS HERSELF AND WORK ONE AHEAD.
THAT AIN'T TOO GOOD NOWADAYS. SHE DON'T HAVE TO CHANGE HER ACT. YOU COULD DO YOUR MAGIC SHOW, WE'LL THROW THE ELECTRIC GIRL BETWEEN YOUR SPOT AND ZEENA'S THAT'LL GIVE YOU TIME TO SLIP OUT AND DO THE UNDERCOVER PART.
HE SAID IT, IT WASN'T MY IDEA...HE SAID IT.
THE NEW ARRANGEMENT ALLOWED "THE GREAT STANTON" TO HONE HIS SKILLS AS A MAGICIAN.
LEAVING HIM PLENTY OF TIME TO GET IN PLACE FOR HIS NEW JOB WITH ZEENA, "THE WOMAN WHO KNOWS."
...BUT WHEN A MAN'S MISERABLE ABOUT SOMETHING, HE TAKES A DRINK TO FORGET IT AND ONE ISN'T ENOUGH AND HE TAKES ANOTHER SNORT AND PRETTY SOON A WEEK'S PAY IS ALL GONE AND HE GETS HOME AND SOBERS UP AND HIS WIFE STARTS IN ON HIM AND HE'S MORE MISERABLE THAN HE WAS BEFORE. YOU WANT TO MAKE SURE YOU'VE DONE ALL YOU CAN TO MAKE THAT MAN HAPPY...
SHE'S FORGOTTEN THE PITCH. SHE'S TALKING ABOUT HERSELF.
44

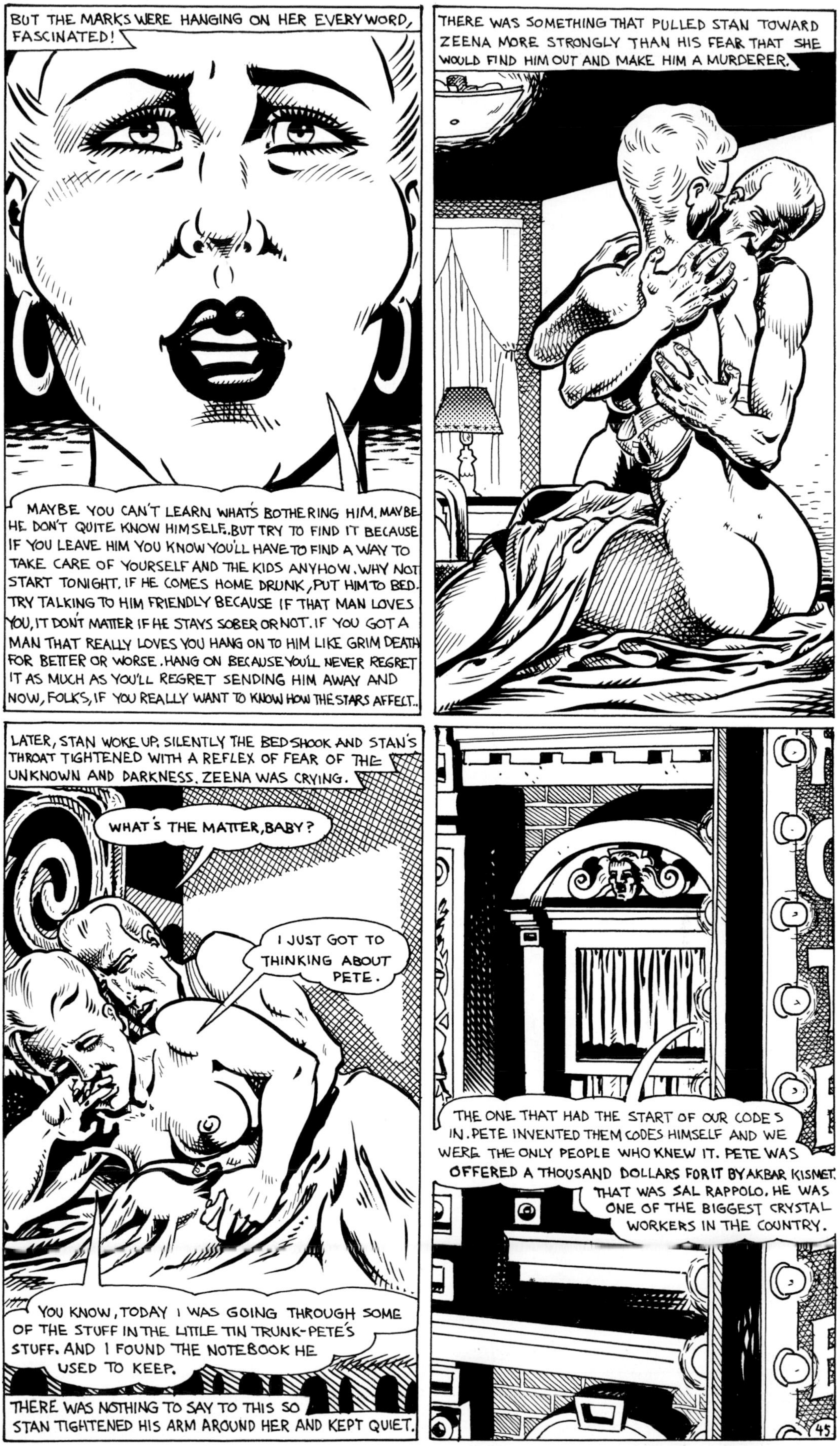

BUT THE MARKS WERE HANGING ON HER EVERY WORD, FASCINATED!
MAYBE YOU CAN'T LEARN WHAT'S BOTHERING HIM. MAYBE HE DON'T QUITE KNOW HIMSELF. BUT TRY TO FIND IT BECAUSE IF YOU LEAVE HIM YOU KNOW YOU'LL HAVE TO FIND A WAY TO TAKE CARE OF YOURSELF AND THE KIDS ANYHOW. WHY NOT START TONIGHT. IF HE COMES HOME DRUNK, PUT HIM TO BED. TRY TALKING TO HIM FRIENDLY BECAUSE IF THAT MAN LOVES YOU, IT DON'T MATTER IF HE STAYS SOBER OR NOT. IF YOU GOT A MAN THAT REALLY LOVES YOU HANG ON TO HIM LIKE GRIM DEATH FOR BETTER OR WORSE. HANG ON BECAUSE YOU'LL NEVER REGRET IT AS MUCH AS YOU'LL REGRET SENDING HIM AWAY AND NOW, FOLKS, IF YOU REALLY WANT TO KNOW HOW THE STARS AFFECT..
THERE WAS SOMETHING THAT PULLED STAN TOWARD ZEENA MORE STRONGLY THAN HIS FEAR THAT SHE WOULD FIND HIM OUT AND MAKE HIM A MURDERER.
LATER, STAN WOKE UP. SILENTLY THE BED SHOOK AND STAN'S THROAT TIGHTENED WITH A REFLEX OF FEAR OF THE UNKNOWN AND DARKNESS. ZEENA WAS CRYING.
WHAT'S THE MATTER, BABY?
I JUST GOT TO THINKING ABOUT PETE.
YOU KNOW, TODAY I WAS GOING THROUGH SOME OF THE STUFF IN THE LITTLE TIN TRUNK-PETE'S STUFF. AND I FOUND THE NOTEBOOK HE USED TO KEEP.
THERE WAS NOTHING TO SAY TO THIS SO STAN TIGHTENED HIS ARM AROUND HER AND KEPT QUIET.
THE ONE THAT HAD THE START OF OUR CODES IN. PETE INVENTED THEM CODES HIMSELF AND WE WERE THE ONLY PEOPLE WHO KNEW IT. PETE WAS OFFERED A THOUSAND DOLLARS FOR IT BY AKBAR KISMET.
THAT WAS SAL RAPPOLO. HE WAS ONE OF THE BIGGEST CRYSTAL WORKERS IN THE COUNTRY.

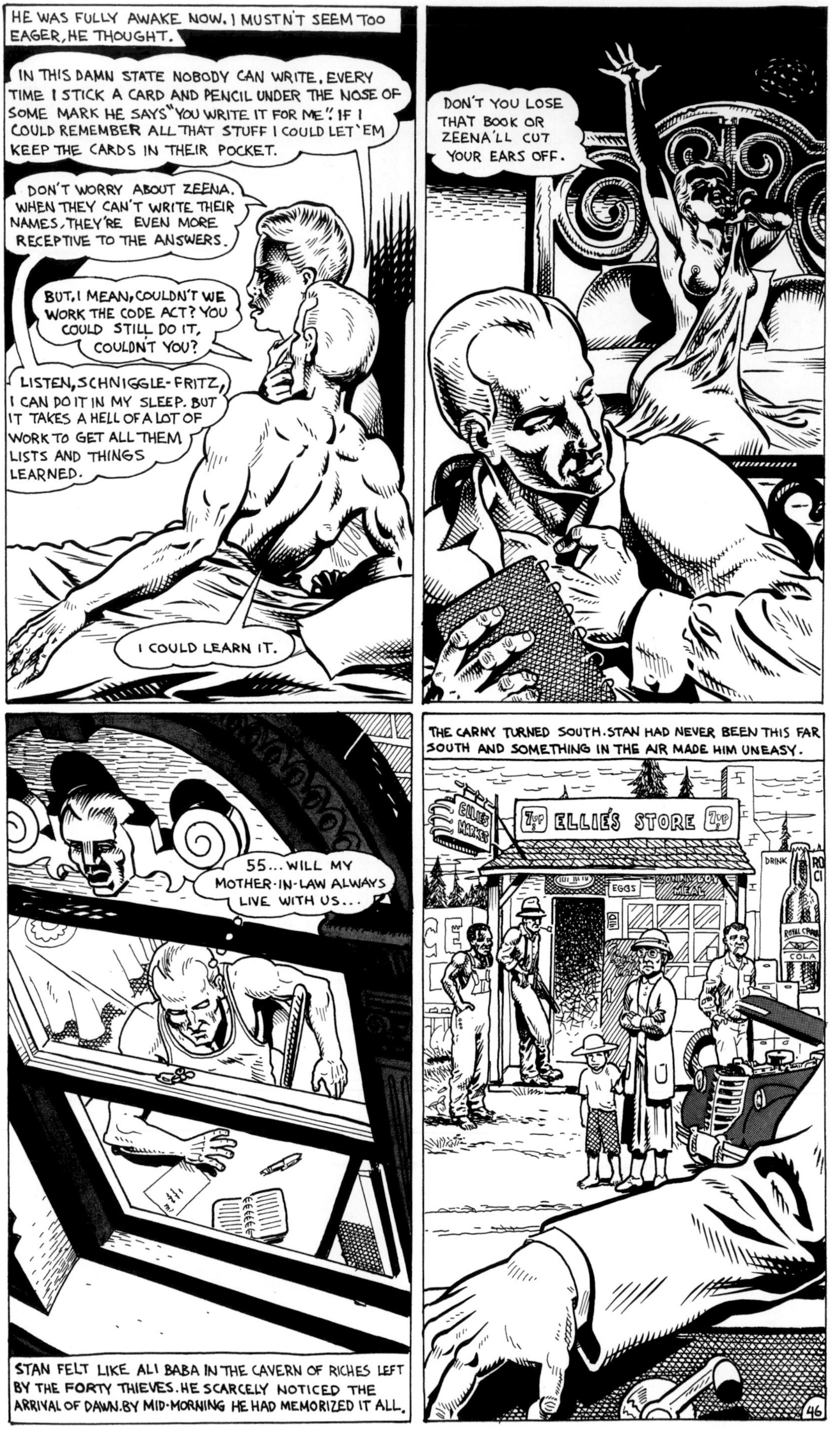
HE WAS FULLY AWAKE NOW. I MUSTN'T SEEM TOO EAGER, HE THOUGHT.
IN THIS DAMN STATE NOBODY CAN WRITE. EVERY TIME I STICK A CARD AND PENCIL UNDER THE NOSE OF SOME MARK HE SAYS "YOU WRITE IT FOR ME". IF I COULD REMEMBER ALL THAT STUFF I COULD LET 'EM KEEP THE CARDS IN THEIR POCKET.
DON'T WORRY ABOUT ZEENA. WHEN THEY CAN'T WRITE THEIR NAMES, THEY'RE EVEN MORE RECEPTIVE TO THE ANSWERS.
BUT, I MEAN, COULDN'T WE WORK THE CODE ACT? YOU COULD STILL DO IT, COULDN'T YOU?
LISTEN, SCHNIGGLE-FRITZ, I CAN DO IT IN MY SLEEP. BUT IT TAKES A HELL OF A LOT OF WORK TO GET ALL THEM LISTS AND THINGS LEARNED.
I COULD LEARN IT.
DON'T YOU LOSE THAT BOOK OR ZEENA'LL CUT YOUR EARS OFF.
55... WILL MY MOTHER-IN-LAW ALWAYS LIVE WITH US...
STAN FELT LIKE ALI BABA IN THE CAVERN OF RICHES LEFT BY THE FORTY THIEVES. HE SCARCELY NOTICED THE ARRIVAL OF DAWN. BY MID-MORNING HE HAD MEMORIZED IT ALL.
THE CARNY TURNED SOUTH. STAN HAD NEVER BEEN THIS FAR SOUTH AND SOMETHING IN THE AIR MADE HIM UNEASY.
ELLIE'S MARKET
7up ELLIE'S STORE 7up
EGGS
DRINK
ROYAL CROWN
COLA

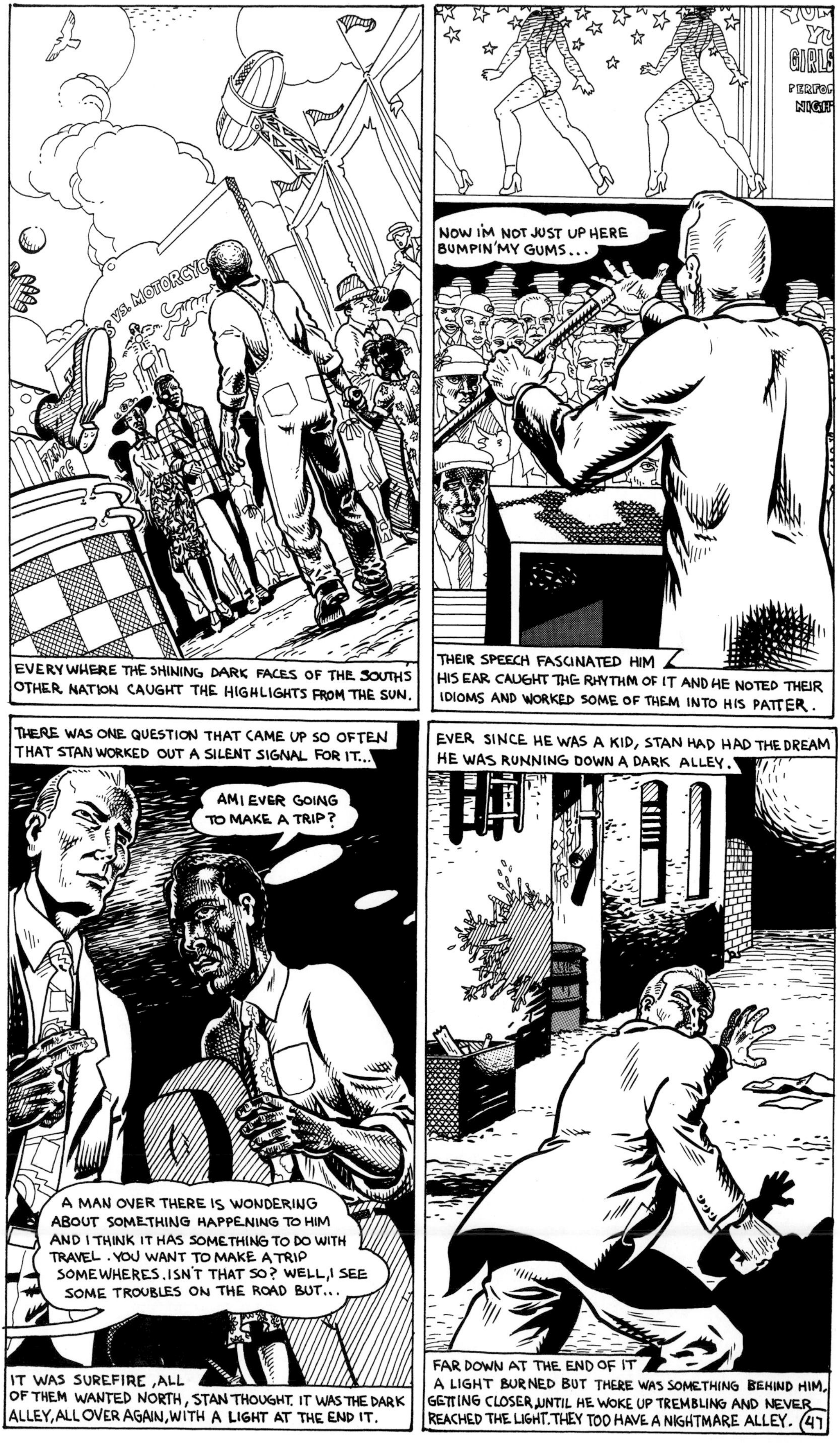

EVERYWHERE THE SHINING DARK FACES OF THE SOUTH'S OTHER NATION CAUGHT THE HIGHLIGHTS FROM THE SUN.
GIRLS
NOW I'M NOT JUST UP HERE BUMPIN' MY GUMS...
THEIR SPEECH FASCINATED HIM
HIS EAR CAUGHT THE RHYTHM OF IT AND HE NOTED THEIR IDIOMS AND WORKED SOME OF THEM INTO HIS PATTER.
THERE WAS ONE QUESTION THAT CAME UP SO OFTEN THAT STAN WORKED OUT A SILENT SIGNAL FOR IT...
AM I EVER GOING TO MAKE A TRIP?
A MAN OVER THERE IS WONDERING ABOUT SOMETHING HAPPENING TO HIM AND I THINK IT HAS SOMETHING TO DO WITH TRAVEL. YOU WANT TO MAKE A TRIP SOMEWHERES. ISN'T THAT SO? WELL, I SEE SOME TROUBLES ON THE ROAD BUT...
IT WAS SUREFIRE, ALL
OF THEM WANTED NORTH, STAN THOUGHT. IT WAS THE DARK ALLEY, ALL OVER AGAIN, WITH A LIGHT AT THE END IT.
EVER SINCE HE WAS A KID, STAN HAD HAD THE DREAM HE WAS RUNNING DOWN A DARK ALLEY.
FAR DOWN AT THE END OF IT
A LIGHT BURNED BUT THERE WAS SOMETHING BEHIND HIM, GETTING CLOSER, UNTIL HE WOKE UP TREMBLING AND NEVER REACHED THE LIGHT. THEY TOO HAVE A NIGHTMARE ALLEY.

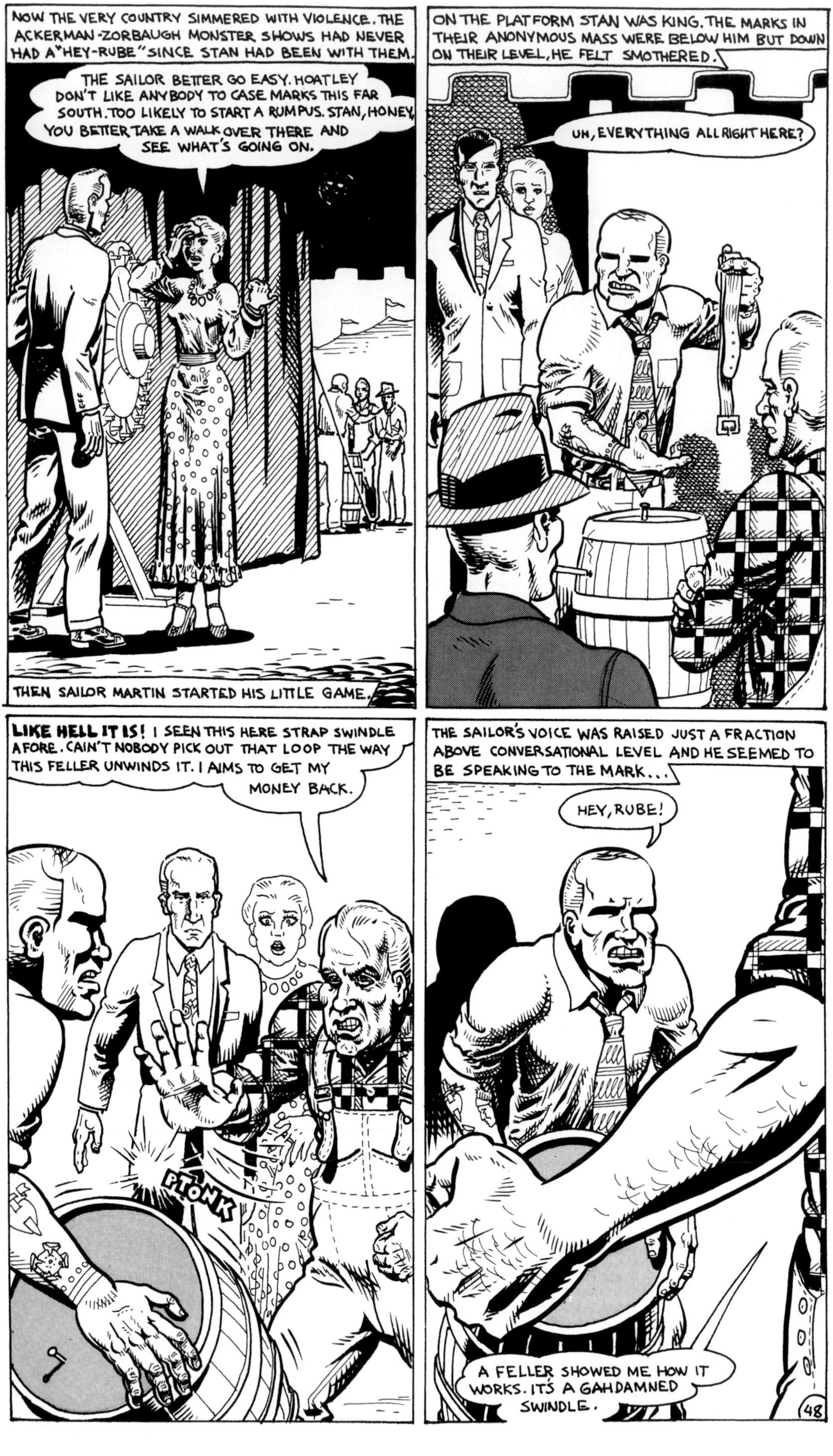

NOW THE VERY COUNTRY SIMMERED WITH VIOLENCE. THE ACKERMAN-ZORBAUGH MONSTER SHOWS HAD NEVER HAD A "HEY-RUBE" SINCE STAN HAD BEEN WITH THEM.
THE SAILOR BETTER GO EASY. HOATLEY DON'T LIKE ANYBODY TO CASE MARKS THIS FAR SOUTH. TOO LIKELY TO START A RUMPUS. STAN, HONEY, YOU BETTER TAKE A WALK OVER THERE AND SEE WHAT'S GOING ON.
THEN SAILOR MARTIN STARTED HIS LITTLE GAME.
ON THE PLATFORM STAN WAS KING. THE MARKS IN THEIR ANONYMOUS MASS WERE BELOW HIM BUT DOWN ON THEIR LEVEL, HE FELT SMOTHERED.
UH, EVERYTHING ALL RIGHT HERE?
LIKE HELL IT IS! I SEEN THIS HERE STRAP SWINDLE AFORE. CAIN'T NOBODY PICK OUT THAT LOOP THE WAY THIS FELLER UNWINDS IT. I AIMS TO GET MY MONEY BACK.
PTONK
THE SAILOR'S VOICE WAS RAISED JUST A FRACTION ABOVE CONVERSATIONAL LEVEL AND HE SEEMED TO BE SPEAKING TO THE MARK...
HEY, RUBE!
A FELLER SHOWED ME HOW IT WORKS. IT'S A GAHDAMNED SWINDLE.

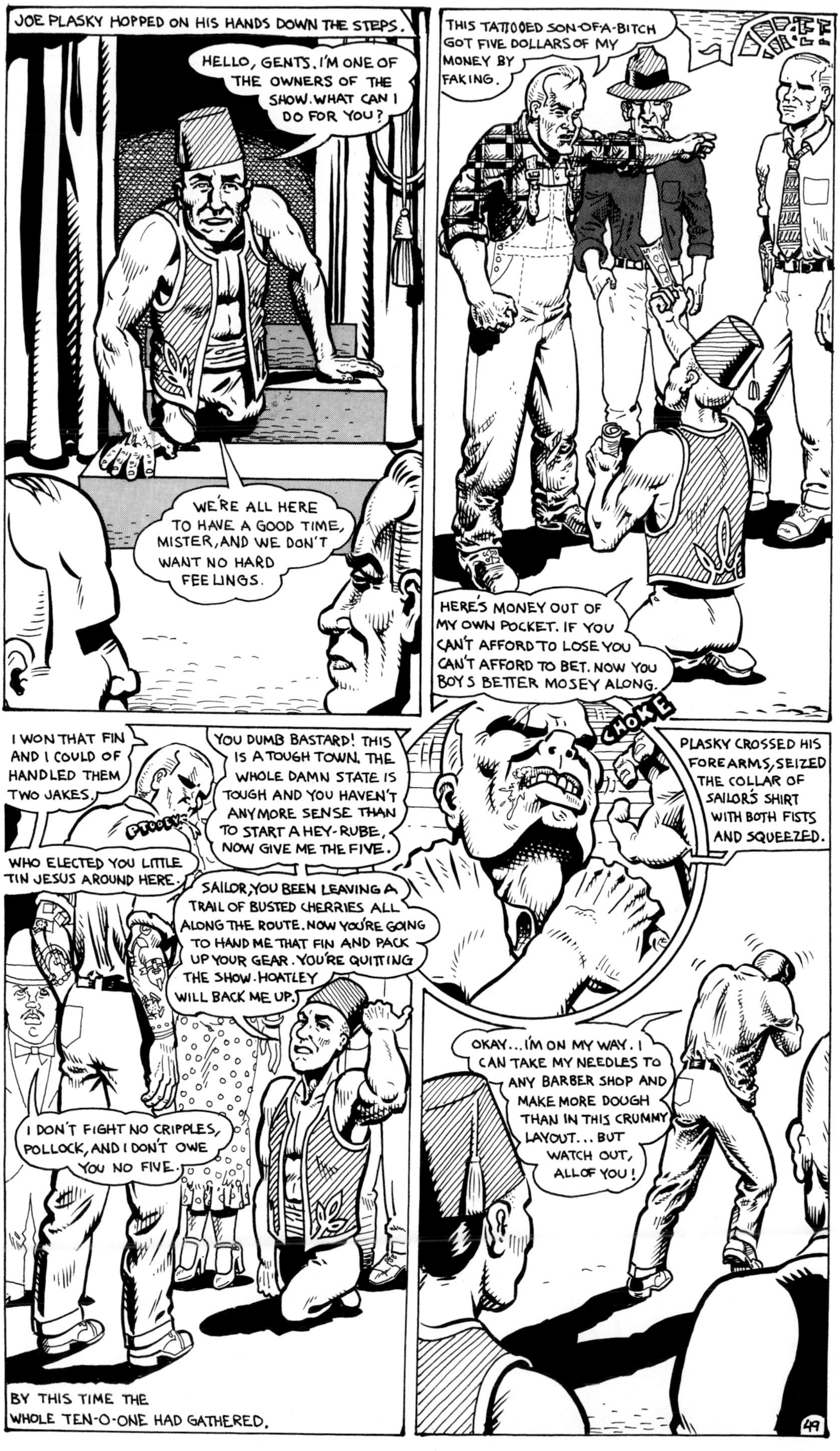
JOE PLASKY HOPPED ON HIS HANDS DOWN THE STEPS.
HELLO, GENTS. I'M ONE OF THE OWNERS OF THE SHOW. WHAT CAN I DO FOR YOU?
WE'RE ALL HERE TO HAVE A GOOD TIME, MISTER, AND WE DON'T WANT NO HARD FEELINGS.
THIS TATTOOED SON-OF-A-BITCH GOT FIVE DOLLARS OF MY MONEY BY FAKING.
HERE'S MONEY OUT OF MY OWN POCKET. IF YOU CAN'T AFFORD TO LOSE YOU CAN'T AFFORD TO BET. NOW YOU BOYS BETTER MOSEY ALONG.
I WON THAT FIN AND I COULD OF HANDLED THEM TWO JAKES.
PTOOEY
YOU DUMB BASTARD! THIS IS A TOUGH TOWN. THE WHOLE DAMN STATE IS TOUGH AND YOU HAVEN'T ANYMORE SENSE THAN TO START A HEY-RUBE. NOW GIVE ME THE FIVE.
WHO ELECTED YOU LITTLE TIN JESUS AROUND HERE.
SAILOR, YOU BEEN LEAVING A TRAIL OF BUSTED CHERRIES ALL ALONG THE ROUTE. NOW YOU'RE GOING TO HAND ME THAT FIN AND PACK UP YOUR GEAR. YOU'RE QUITTING THE SHOW. HOATLEY WILL BACK ME UP.
I DON'T FIGHT NO CRIPPLES, POLLOCK, AND I DON'T OWE YOU NO FIVE.
BY THIS TIME THE WHOLE TEN-O-ONE HAD GATHERED.
CHOKE
PLASKY CROSSED HIS FOREARMS, SEIZED THE COLLAR OF SAILOR'S SHIRT WITH BOTH FISTS AND SQUEEZED.
OKAY... I'M ON MY WAY. I CAN TAKE MY NEEDLES TO ANY BARBER SHOP AND MAKE MORE DOUGH THAN IN THIS CRUMMY LAYOUT... BUT WATCH OUT, ALL OF YOU!

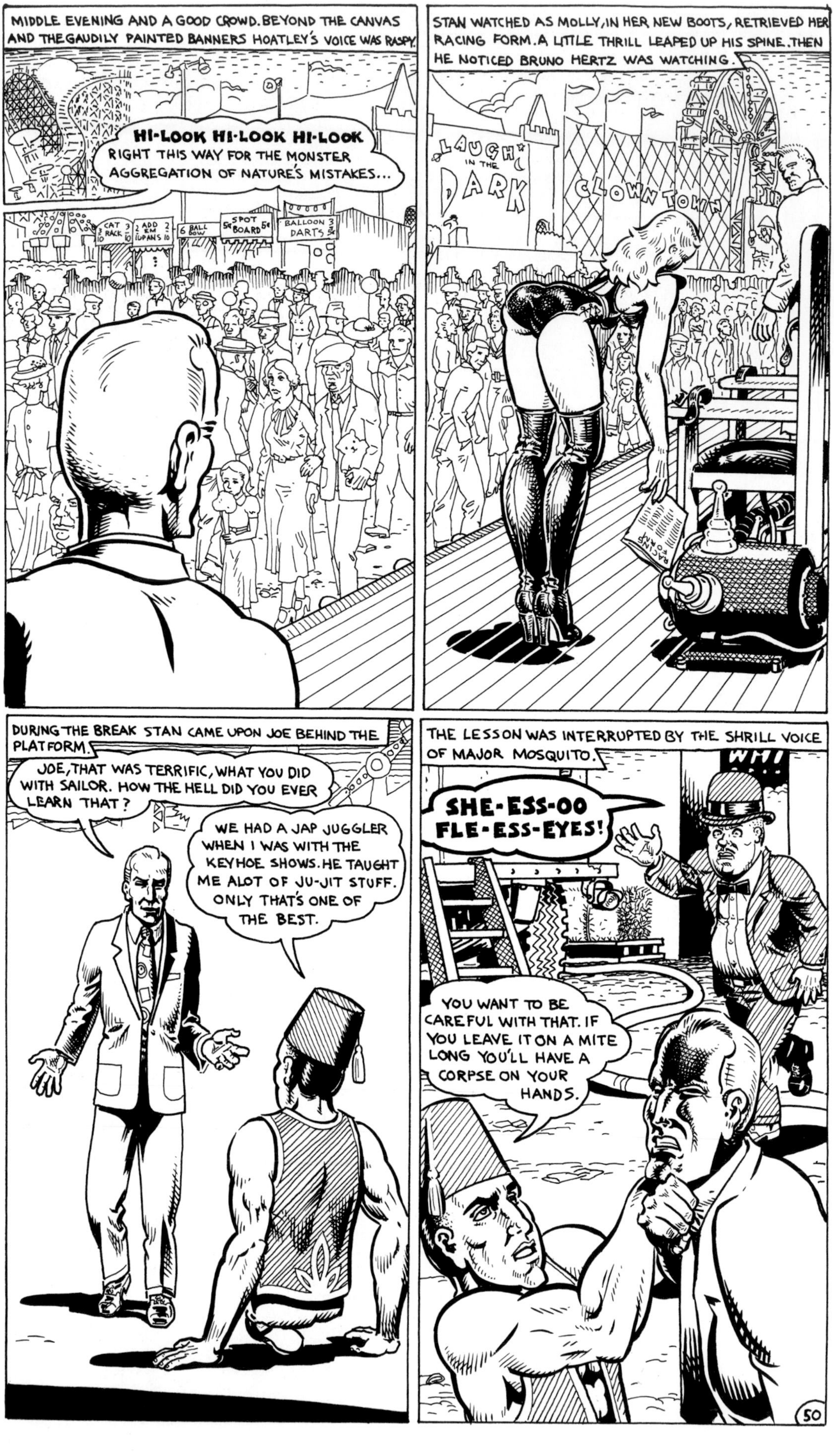
MIDDLE EVENING AND A GOOD CROWD. BEYOND THE CANVAS AND THE GAUDILY PAINTED BANNERS HOATLEY'S VOICE WAS RASPY.
HI-LOOK HI-LOOK HI-LOOK RIGHT THIS WAY FOR THE MONSTER AGGREGATION OF NATURE'S MISTAKES...
CAT RACK
ADD EM UP
BALL
SPOT BOARD
BALLOON DARTS
STAN WATCHED AS MOLLY, IN HER NEW BOOTS, RETRIEVED HER RACING FORM. A LITTLE THRILL LEAPED UP HIS SPINE. THEN HE NOTICED BRUNO HERTZ WAS WATCHING.
LAUGH IN THE DARK
CLOWN TOWN
RACING FORM
DURING THE BREAK STAN CAME UPON JOE BEHIND THE PLATFORM.
JOE, THAT WAS TERRIFIC, WHAT YOU DID WITH SAILOR. HOW THE HELL DID YOU EVER LEARN THAT?
WE HAD A JAP JUGGLER WHEN I WAS WITH THE KEYHOE SHOWS. HE TAUGHT ME ALOT OF JU-JIT STUFF. ONLY THAT'S ONE OF THE BEST.
THE LESSON WAS INTERRUPTED BY THE SHRILL VOICE OF MAJOR MOSQUITO.
SHE-ESS-OO FLE-ESS-EYES!
YOU WANT TO BE CAREFUL WITH THAT. IF YOU LEAVE IT ON A MITE LONG YOU'LL HAVE A CORPSE ON YOUR HANDS.

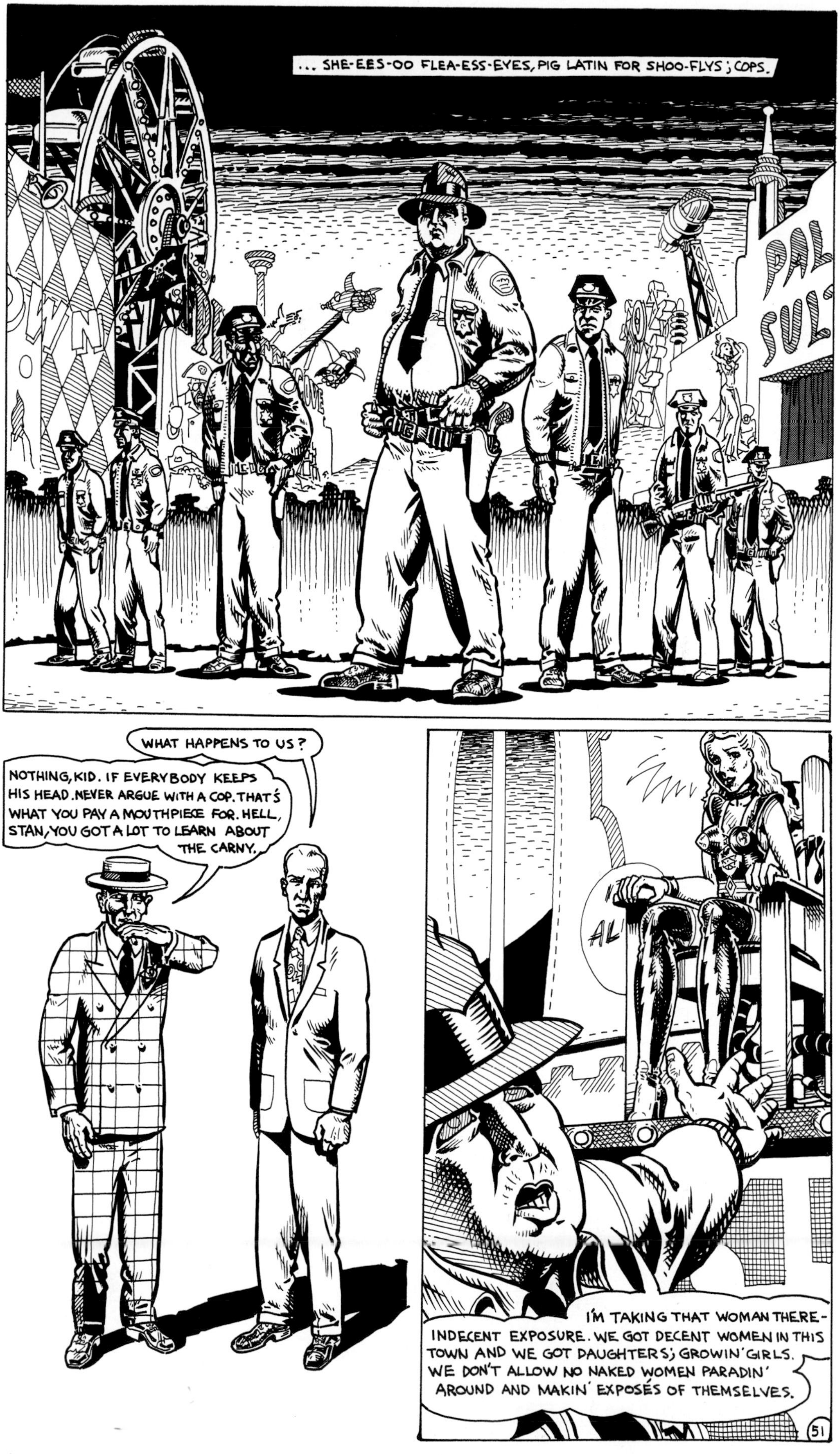
... SHE-EES-OO FLEA-ESS-EYES, PIG LATIN FOR SHOO-FLYS; COPS.
WHAT HAPPENS TO US?
NOTHING, KID. IF EVERYBODY KEEPS HIS HEAD. NEVER ARGUE WITH A COP. THAT'S WHAT YOU PAY A MOUTHPIECE FOR. HELL, STAN, YOU GOT A LOT TO LEARN ABOUT THE CARNY.
I'M TAKING THAT WOMAN THERE- INDECENT EXPOSURE. WE GOT DECENT WOMEN IN THIS TOWN AND WE GOT DAUGHTERS; GROWIN' GIRLS. WE DON'T ALLOW NO NAKED WOMEN PARADIN' AROUND AND MAKIN' EXPOSÉS OF THEMSELVES.

THE SHERIFF'S EYES WERE FASTENED ON MOLLY'S BARE THIGHS

LOOKY HERE, CHIEF, THAT GIRL'S NEVER HAD NO COMPLAINTS SHE'S GOT TO WEAR A COSTUME LIKE THAT ON ACCOUNT OF SHE HANDLES ELECTRIC WIRES AND ORDINARY CLOTH MIGHT CATCH FIRE. AND...

SHUT UP! I'LL ARREST ANYBODY I SEE FIT AND DON'T TRY OFFERING ME ANY BRIBES NEITHER, I AIN'T NONE O' YOUR THIEVIN' NORTHERN POLICE KISSIN' THE PRIEST'S TOE ON SUNDAY AND TAKING IN THE GRAFT, HELL-BENT FOR ELECTION SIX DAYS A WEEK.

FLIP FLIP FLIP

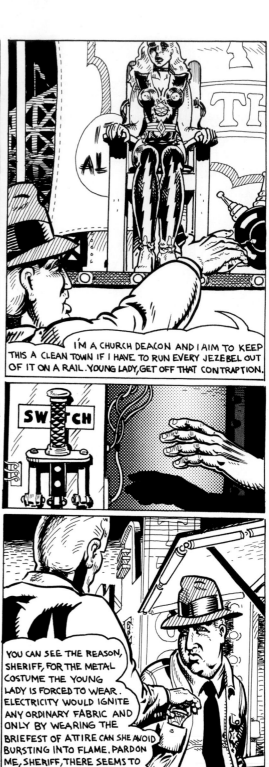

I'M A CHURCH DEACON AND I AIM TO KEEP THIS A CLEAN TOWN IF I HAVE TO RUN EVERY JEZEBEL OUT OF IT ON A RAIL. YOUNG LADY, GET OFF THAT CONTRAPTION.

SWITCH

YOU CAN SEE THE REASON, SHERIFF, FOR THE METAL COSTUME THE YOUNG LADY IS FORCED TO WEAR. ELECTRICITY WOULD IGNITE ANY ORDINARY FABRIC AND ONLY BY WEARING THE BRIEFEST OF ATTIRE CAN SHE AVOID BURSTING INTO FLAME. PARDON ME, SHERIFF, THERE SEEMS TO BE SEVERAL BILLS COMING OUT OF YOUR POCKET... ANOTHER MINUTE AND YOU WOULD HAVE LOST YOUR MONEY, SHERIFF.

MOLLY WAS ENVELOPED IN A BLUE FLAME.
...THE DEPUTY DREW BACK.

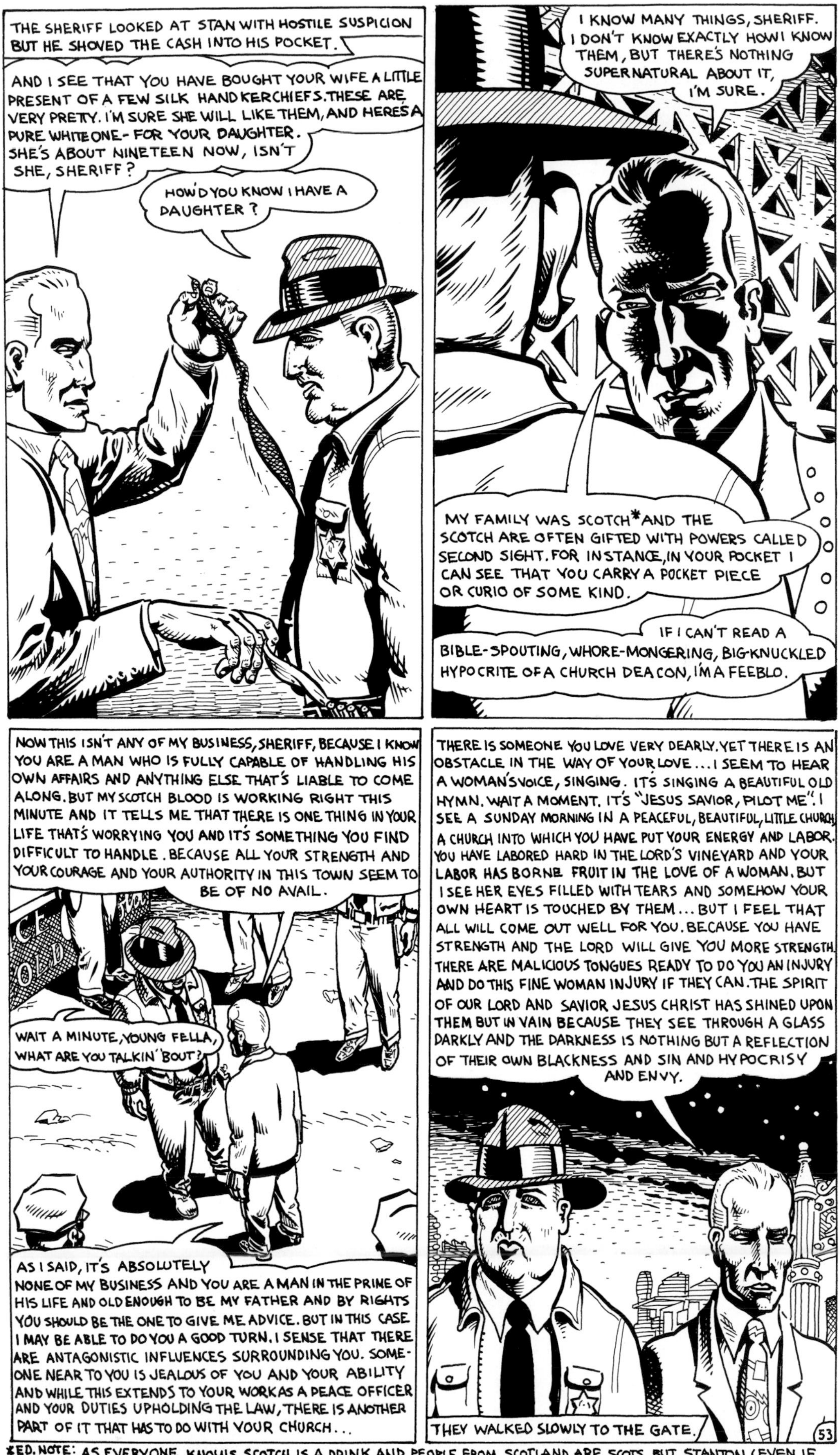
THE SHERIFF LOOKED AT STAN WITH HOSTILE SUSPICION BUT HE SHOVED THE CASH INTO HIS POCKET.
AND I SEE THAT YOU HAVE BOUGHT YOUR WIFE A LITTLE PRESENT OF A FEW SILK HANDKERCHIEFS. THESE ARE VERY PRETTY. I'M SURE SHE WILL LIKE THEM, AND HERE'S A PURE WHITE ONE- FOR YOUR DAUGHTER. SHE'S ABOUT NINETEEN NOW, ISN'T SHE, SHERIFF?
HOW'D YOU KNOW I HAVE A DAUGHTER?
I KNOW MANY THINGS, SHERIFF. I DON'T KNOW EXACTLY HOW I KNOW THEM, BUT THERE'S NOTHING SUPERNATURAL ABOUT IT, I'M SURE.
MY FAMILY WAS SCOTCH* AND THE SCOTCH ARE OFTEN GIFTED WITH POWERS CALLED SECOND SIGHT. FOR INSTANCE, IN YOUR POCKET I CAN SEE THAT YOU CARRY A POCKET PIECE OR CURIO OF SOME KIND.
IF I CAN'T READ A BIBLE-SPOUTING, WHORE-MONGERING, BIG-KNUCKLED HYPOCRITE OF A CHURCH DEACON, I'M A FEEBLO.
NOW THIS ISN'T ANY OF MY BUSINESS, SHERIFF, BECAUSE I KNOW YOU ARE A MAN WHO IS FULLY CAPABLE OF HANDLING HIS OWN AFFAIRS AND ANYTHING ELSE THAT'S LIABLE TO COME ALONG. BUT MY SCOTCH BLOOD IS WORKING RIGHT THIS MINUTE AND IT TELLS ME THAT THERE IS ONE THING IN YOUR LIFE THAT'S WORRYING YOU AND IT'S SOMETHING YOU FIND DIFFICULT TO HANDLE. BECAUSE ALL YOUR STRENGTH AND YOUR COURAGE AND YOUR AUTHORITY IN THIS TOWN SEEM TO BE OF NO AVAIL.
WAIT A MINUTE, YOUNG FELLA, WHAT ARE YOU TALKIN' 'BOUT?
AS I SAID, IT'S ABSOLUTELY NONE OF MY BUSINESS AND YOU ARE A MAN IN THE PRIME OF HIS LIFE AND OLD ENOUGH TO BE MY FATHER AND BY RIGHTS YOU SHOULD BE THE ONE TO GIVE ME ADVICE. BUT IN THIS CASE I MAY BE ABLE TO DO YOU A GOOD TURN. I SENSE THAT THERE ARE ANTAGONISTIC INFLUENCES SURROUNDING YOU. SOMEONE NEAR TO YOU IS JEALOUS OF YOU AND YOUR ABILITY AND WHILE THIS EXTENDS TO YOUR WORK AS A PEACE OFFICER AND YOUR DUTIES UPHOLDING THE LAW, THERE IS ANOTHER PART OF IT THAT HAS TO DO WITH YOUR CHURCH...
THERE IS SOMEONE YOU LOVE VERY DEARLY. YET THERE IS AN OBSTACLE IN THE WAY OF YOUR LOVE... I SEEM TO HEAR A WOMAN'S VOICE, SINGING. IT'S SINGING A BEAUTIFUL OLD HYMN. WAIT A MOMENT. IT'S "JESUS SAVIOR, PILOT ME". I SEE A SUNDAY MORNING IN A PEACEFUL, BEAUTIFUL, LITTLE CHURCH, A CHURCH INTO WHICH YOU HAVE PUT YOUR ENERGY AND LABOR. YOU HAVE LABORED HARD IN THE LORD'S VINEYARD AND YOUR LABOR HAS BORNE FRUIT IN THE LOVE OF A WOMAN. BUT I SEE HER EYES FILLED WITH TEARS AND SOMEHOW YOUR OWN HEART IS TOUCHED BY THEM... BUT I FEEL THAT ALL WILL COME OUT WELL FOR YOU. BECAUSE YOU HAVE STRENGTH AND THE LORD WILL GIVE YOU MORE STRENGTH. THERE ARE MALICIOUS TONGUES READY TO DO YOU AN INJURY AND DO THIS FINE WOMAN INJURY IF THEY CAN. THE SPIRIT OF OUR LORD AND SAVIOR JESUS CHRIST HAS SHINED UPON THEM BUT IN VAIN BECAUSE THEY SEE THROUGH A GLASS DARKLY AND THE DARKNESS IS NOTHING BUT A REFLECTION OF THEIR OWN BLACKNESS AND SIN AND HYPOCRISY AND ENVY.
THEY WALKED SLOWLY TO THE GATE.
53

*ED. NOTE: AS EVERYONE KNOWS, SCOTCH IS A DRINK AND PEOPLE FROM SCOTLAND ARE SCOTS. BUT STANTON (EVEN IF HE ACTUALLY DOES HAVE SCOTTISH BLOOD) IS APPARENTLY IGNORANT OF THIS FACT.

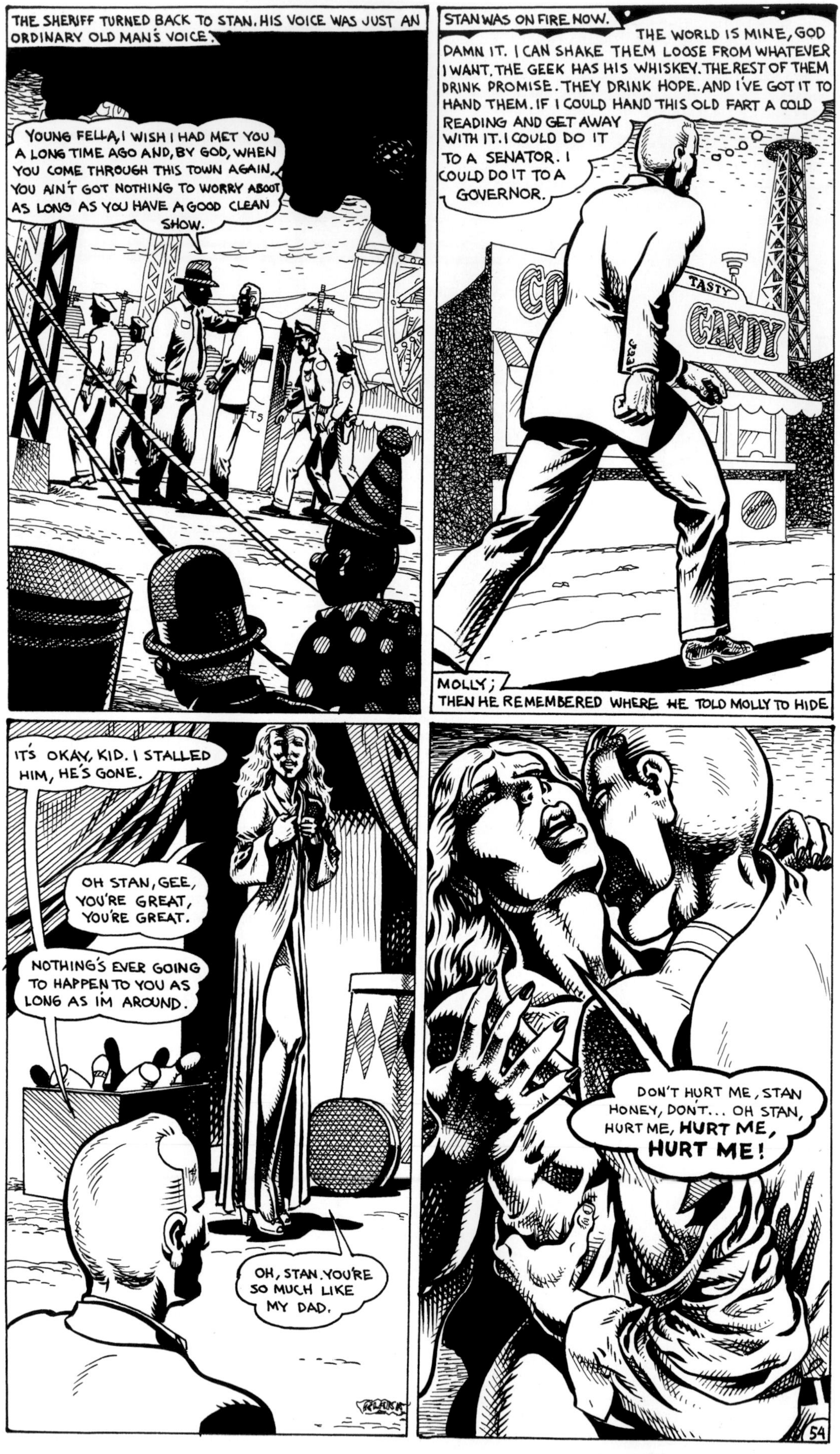

THE SHERIFF TURNED BACK TO STAN. HIS VOICE WAS JUST AN ORDINARY OLD MAN'S VOICE.
YOUNG FELLA, I WISH I HAD MET YOU A LONG TIME AGO AND, BY GOD, WHEN YOU COME THROUGH THIS TOWN AGAIN, YOU AIN'T GOT NOTHING TO WORRY ABOUT AS LONG AS YOU HAVE A GOOD CLEAN SHOW.
STAN WAS ON FIRE NOW.
THE WORLD IS MINE, GOD DAMN IT. I CAN SHAKE THEM LOOSE FROM WHATEVER I WANT. THE GEEK HAS HIS WHISKEY. THE REST OF THEM DRINK PROMISE. THEY DRINK HOPE. AND I'VE GOT IT TO HAND THEM. IF I COULD HAND THIS OLD FART A COLD READING AND GET AWAY WITH IT. I COULD DO IT TO A SENATOR. I COULD DO IT TO A GOVERNOR.
TASTY
CANDY
MOLLY;
THEN HE REMEMBERED WHERE HE TOLD MOLLY TO HIDE
IT'S OKAY, KID. I STALLED HIM, HE'S GONE.
OH STAN, GEE, YOU'RE GREAT, YOU'RE GREAT.
NOTHING'S EVER GOING TO HAPPEN TO YOU AS LONG AS IM AROUND.
OH, STAN. YOU'RE SO MUCH LIKE MY DAD.
DON'T HURT ME, STAN HONEY, DON'T... OH STAN, HURT ME, HURT ME, HURT ME!

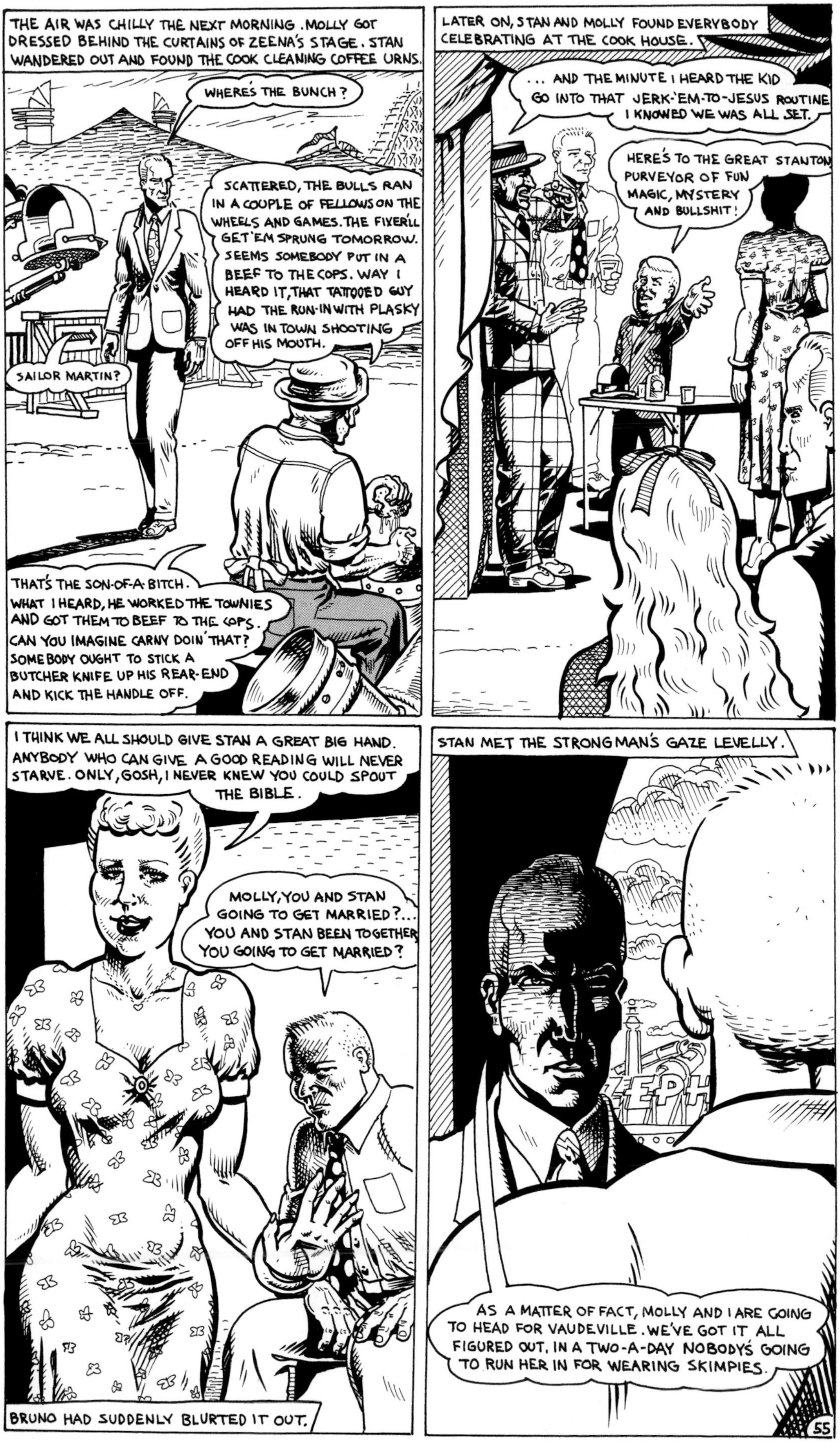
THE AIR WAS CHILLY THE NEXT MORNING. MOLLY GOT DRESSED BEHIND THE CURTAINS OF ZEENA'S STAGE. STAN WANDERED OUT AND FOUND THE COOK CLEANING COFFEE URNS.
WHERE'S THE BUNCH?
SCATTERED, THE BULLS RAN IN A COUPLE OF FELLOWS ON THE WHEELS AND GAMES. THE FIXER'LL GET 'EM SPRUNG TOMORROW. SEEMS SOMEBODY PUT IN A BEEF TO THE COPS. WAY I HEARD IT, THAT TATTOOED GUY HAD THE RUN-IN WITH PLASKY WAS IN TOWN SHOOTING OFF HIS MOUTH.
SAILOR MARTIN?
THAT'S THE SON-OF-A-BITCH. WHAT I HEARD, HE WORKED THE TOWNIES AND GOT THEM TO BEEF TO THE COPS. CAN YOU IMAGINE CARNY DOIN' THAT? SOMEBODY OUGHT TO STICK A BUTCHER KNIFE UP HIS REAR-END AND KICK THE HANDLE OFF.
LATER ON, STAN AND MOLLY FOUND EVERYBODY CELEBRATING AT THE COOK HOUSE.
... AND THE MINUTE I HEARD THE KID GO INTO THAT JERK-'EM-TO-JESUS ROUTINE I KNOWED WE WAS ALL SET.
HERE'S TO THE GREAT STANTON PURVEYOR OF FUN MAGIC, MYSTERY AND BULLSHIT!
I THINK WE ALL SHOULD GIVE STAN A GREAT BIG HAND. ANYBODY WHO CAN GIVE A GOOD READING WILL NEVER STARVE. ONLY, GOSH, I NEVER KNEW YOU COULD SPOUT THE BIBLE.
MOLLY, YOU AND STAN GOING TO GET MARRIED?... YOU AND STAN BEEN TOGETHER YOU GOING TO GET MARRIED?
BRUNO HAD SUDDENLY BLURTED IT OUT.
STAN MET THE STRONGMAN'S GAZE LEVELLY.
ZEPH
AS A MATTER OF FACT, MOLLY AND I ARE GOING TO HEAD FOR VAUDEVILLE. WE'VE GOT IT ALL FIGURED OUT, IN A TWO-A-DAY NOBODY'S GOING TO RUN HER IN FOR WEARING SKIMPIES.

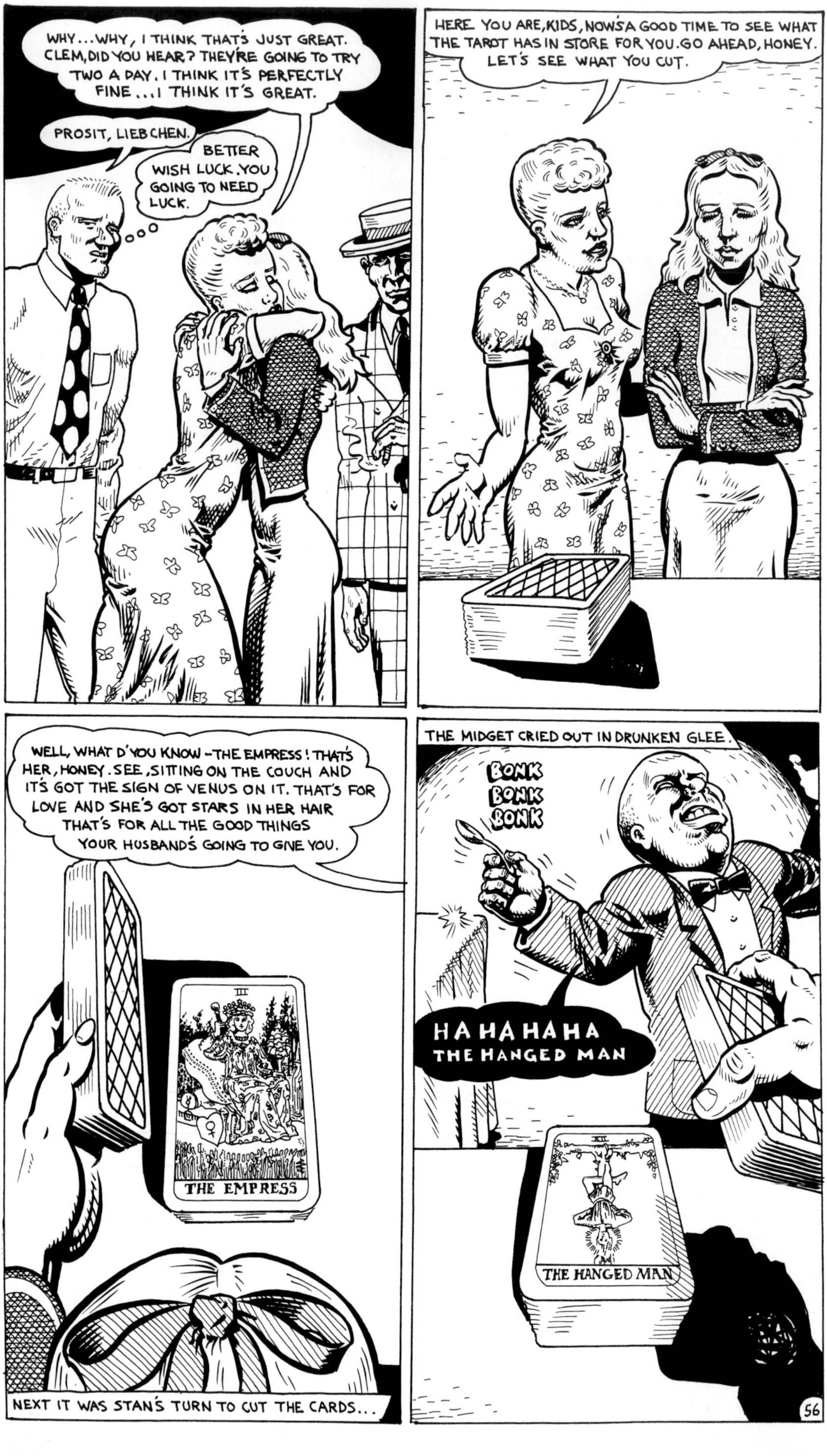

WHY...WHY, I THINK THAT'S JUST GREAT. CLEM, DID YOU HEAR? THEY'RE GOING TO TRY TWO A DAY. I THINK IT'S PERFECTLY FINE...I THINK IT'S GREAT.
PROSIT, LIEBCHEN.
BETTER WISH LUCK, YOU GOING TO NEED LUCK.
HERE YOU ARE, KIDS, NOW'S A GOOD TIME TO SEE WHAT THE TAROT HAS IN STORE FOR YOU. GO AHEAD, HONEY. LET'S SEE WHAT YOU CUT.
WELL, WHAT D'YOU KNOW - THE EMPRESS! THAT'S HER, HONEY. SEE, SITTING ON THE COUCH AND IT'S GOT THE SIGN OF VENUS ON IT. THAT'S FOR LOVE AND SHE'S GOT STARS IN HER HAIR THAT'S FOR ALL THE GOOD THINGS YOUR HUSBAND'S GOING TO GIVE YOU.
III
THE EMPRESS
NEXT IT WAS STAN'S TURN TO CUT THE CARDS...
THE MIDGET CRIED OUT IN DRUNKEN GLEE.
BONK
BONK
BONK
HAHAHAHA
THE HANGED MAN
XII
THE HANGED MAN

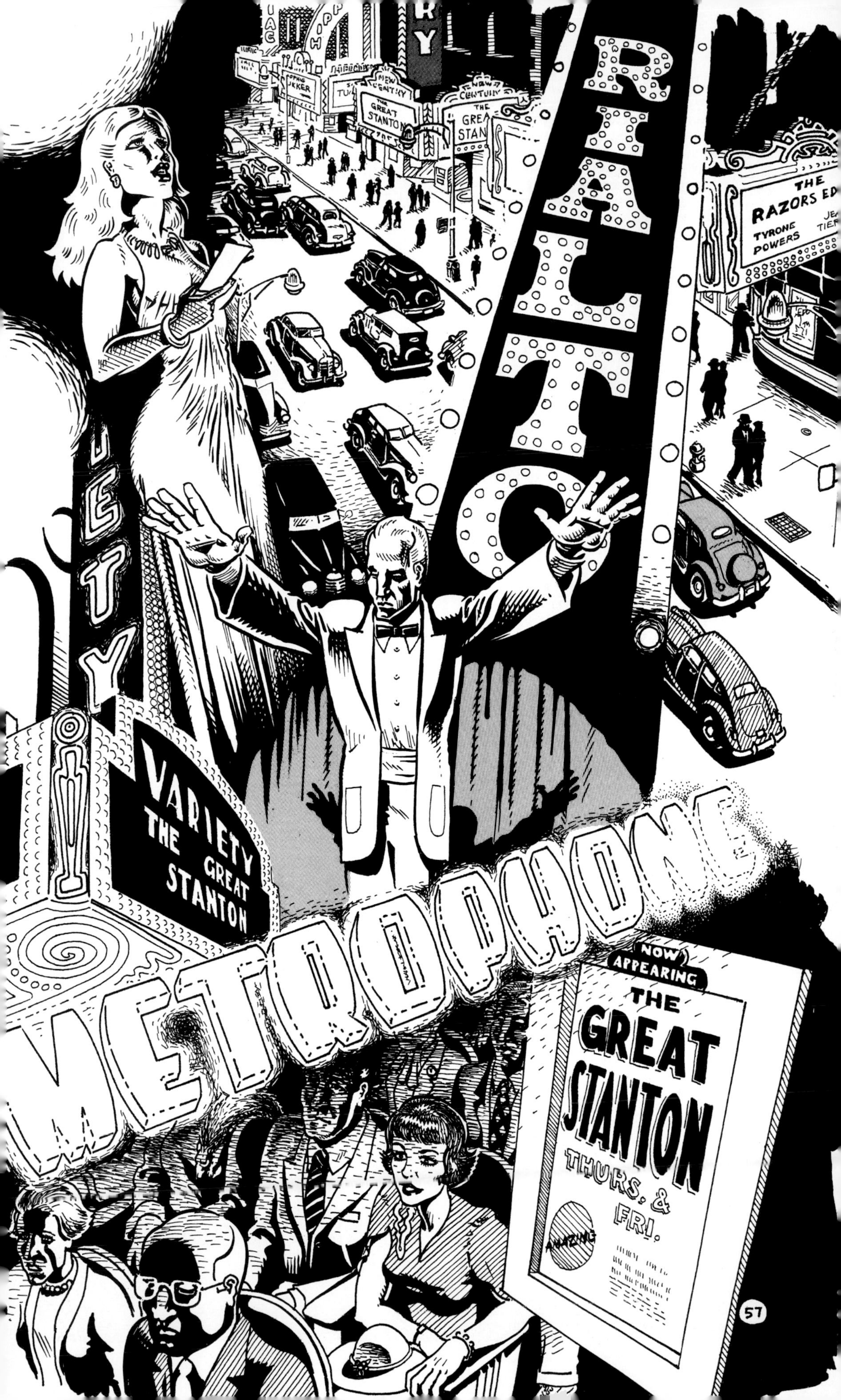

RIALTO
THE RAZORS ED
TYRONE POWERS
NEW CENTURY
THE GREAT STANTON
VARIETY
VARIETY THE GREAT STANTON
METROPHONE
NOW APPEARING
THE GREAT STANTON
THURS. & FRI.
AMAZING

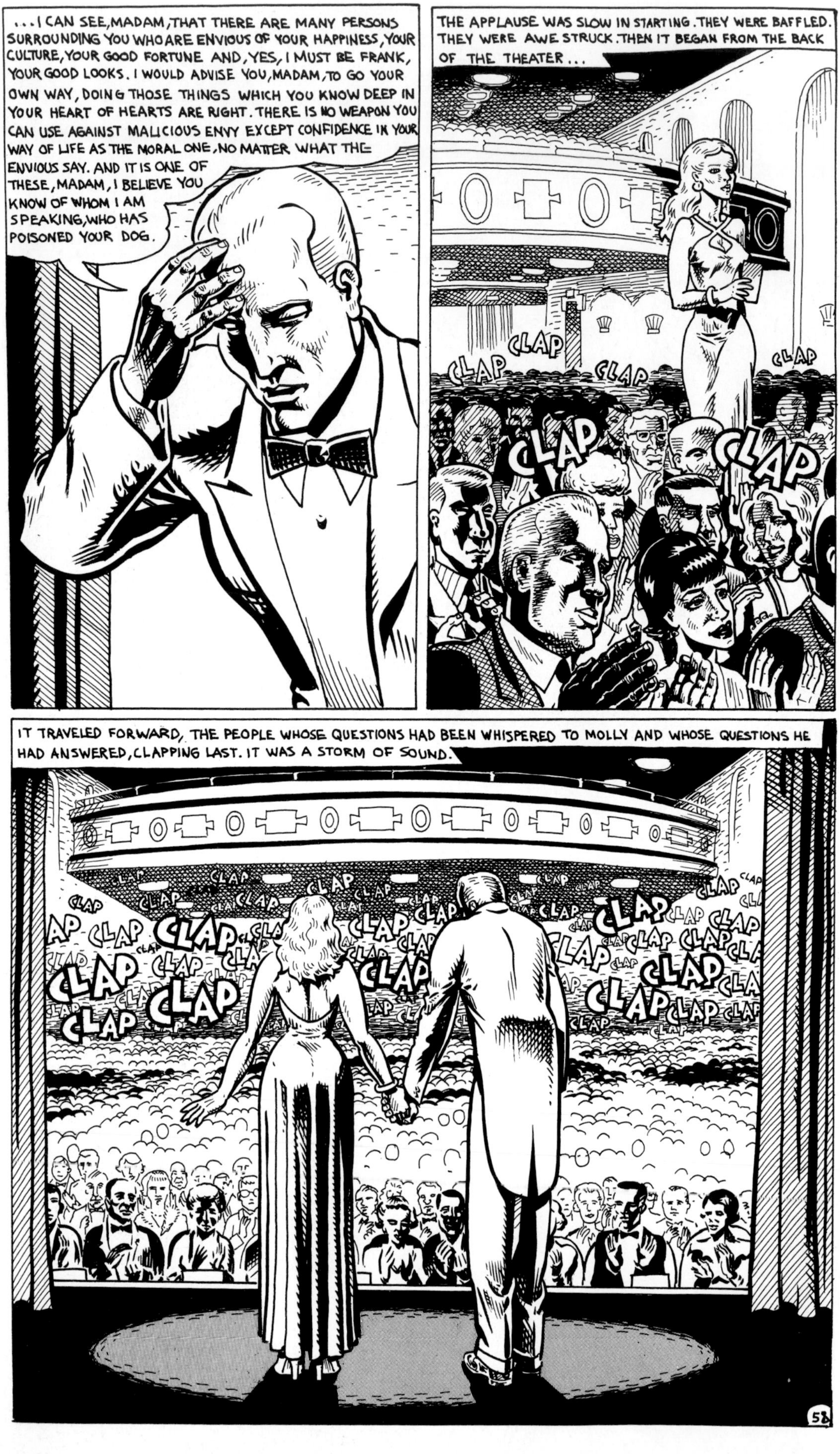

...I CAN SEE, MADAM, THAT THERE ARE MANY PERSONS SURROUNDING YOU WHO ARE ENVIOUS OF YOUR HAPPINESS, YOUR CULTURE, YOUR GOOD FORTUNE AND, YES, I MUST BE FRANK, YOUR GOOD LOOKS. I WOULD ADVISE YOU, MADAM, TO GO YOUR OWN WAY, DOING THOSE THINGS WHICH YOU KNOW DEEP IN YOUR HEART OF HEARTS ARE RIGHT. THERE IS NO WEAPON YOU CAN USE AGAINST MALICIOUS ENVY EXCEPT CONFIDENCE IN YOUR WAY OF LIFE AS THE MORAL ONE, NO MATTER WHAT THE ENVIOUS SAY. AND IT IS ONE OF THESE, MADAM, I BELIEVE YOU KNOW OF WHOM I AM SPEAKING, WHO HAS POISONED YOUR DOG.
THE APPLAUSE WAS SLOW IN STARTING. THEY WERE BAFFLED. THEY WERE AWE STRUCK. THEN IT BEGAN FROM THE BACK OF THE THEATER...
CLAP CLAP CLAP CLAP
CLAP CLAP
IT TRAVELED FORWARD, THE PEOPLE WHOSE QUESTIONS HAD BEEN WHISPERED TO MOLLY AND WHOSE QUESTIONS HE HAD ANSWERED, CLAPPING LAST. IT WAS A STORM OF SOUND.
CLAP CLAP CLAP CLAP CLAP CLAP CLAP CLAP

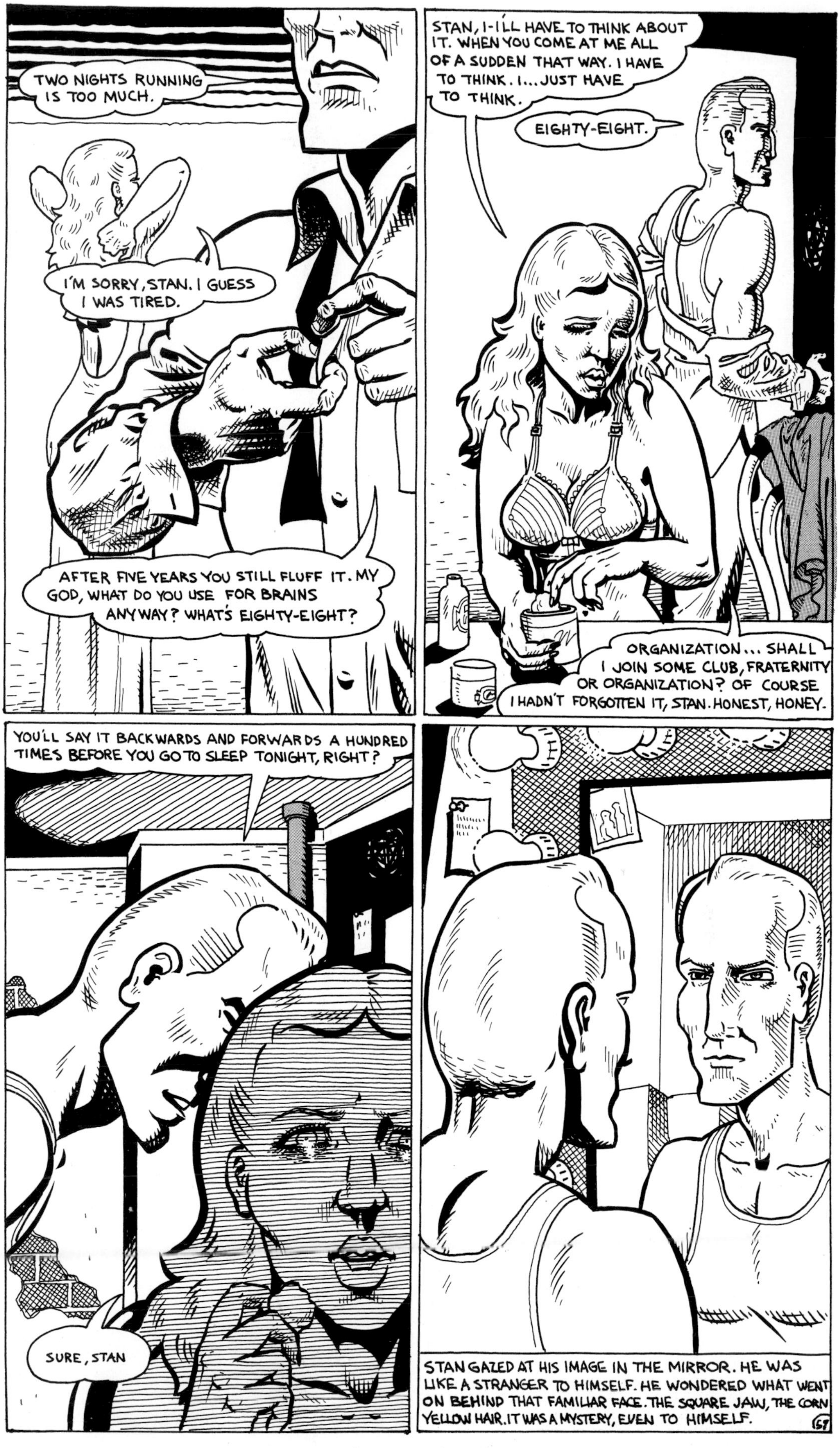
TWO NIGHTS RUNNING IS TOO MUCH.
I'M SORRY, STAN. I GUESS I WAS TIRED.
AFTER FIVE YEARS YOU STILL FLUFF IT. MY GOD, WHAT DO YOU USE FOR BRAINS ANYWAY? WHAT'S EIGHTY-EIGHT?
STAN, I-I'LL HAVE TO THINK ABOUT IT. WHEN YOU COME AT ME ALL OF A SUDDEN THAT WAY. I HAVE TO THINK. I... JUST HAVE TO THINK.
EIGHTY-EIGHT.
ORGANIZATION... SHALL I JOIN SOME CLUB, FRATERNITY OR ORGANIZATION? OF COURSE I HADN'T FORGOTTEN IT, STAN. HONEST, HONEY.
YOU'LL SAY IT BACKWARDS AND FORWARDS A HUNDRED TIMES BEFORE YOU GO TO SLEEP TONIGHT, RIGHT?
SURE, STAN
STAN GAZED AT HIS IMAGE IN THE MIRROR. HE WAS LIKE A STRANGER TO HIMSELF. HE WONDERED WHAT WENT ON BEHIND THAT FAMILIAR FACE. THE SQUARE JAW, THE CORN YELLOW HAIR. IT WAS A MYSTERY, EVEN TO HIMSELF.
58

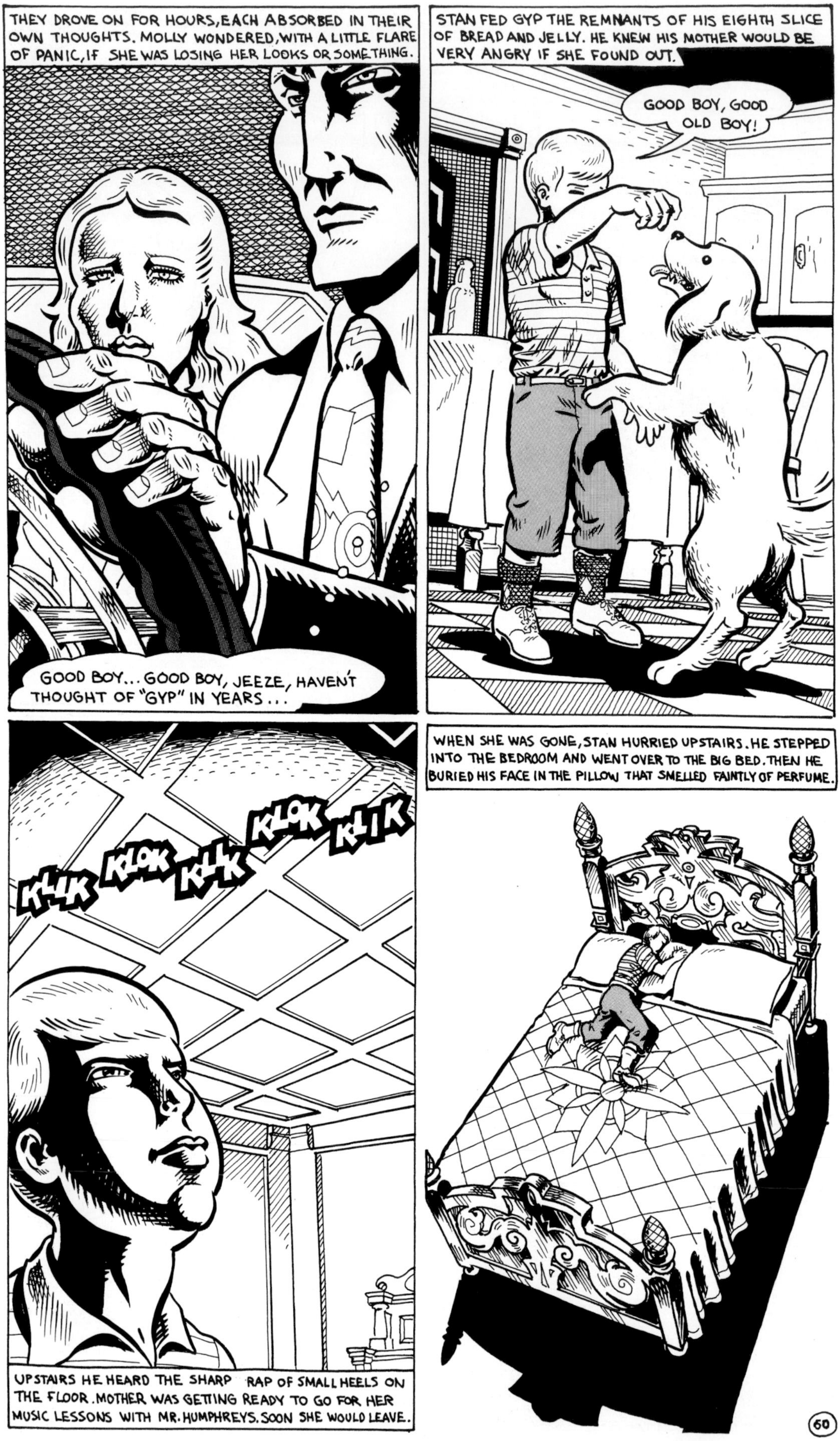
THEY DROVE ON FOR HOURS, EACH ABSORBED IN THEIR OWN THOUGHTS. MOLLY WONDERED, WITH A LITTLE FLARE OF PANIC, IF SHE WAS LOSING HER LOOKS OR SOMETHING.
GOOD BOY... GOOD BOY, JEEZE, HAVEN'T THOUGHT OF "GYP" IN YEARS...
STAN FED GYP THE REMNANTS OF HIS EIGHTH SLICE OF BREAD AND JELLY. HE KNEW HIS MOTHER WOULD BE VERY ANGRY IF SHE FOUND OUT.
GOOD BOY, GOOD OLD BOY!
KLIK KLOK KLIK KLOK KLIK
UPSTAIRS HE HEARD THE SHARP RAP OF SMALL HEELS ON THE FLOOR. MOTHER WAS GETTING READY TO GO FOR HER MUSIC LESSONS WITH MR. HUMPHREYS. SOON SHE WOULD LEAVE.
WHEN SHE WAS GONE, STAN HURRIED UPSTAIRS. HE STEPPED INTO THE BEDROOM AND WENT OVER TO THE BIG BED. THEN HE BURIED HIS FACE IN THE PILLOW THAT SMELLED FAINTLY OF PERFUME.

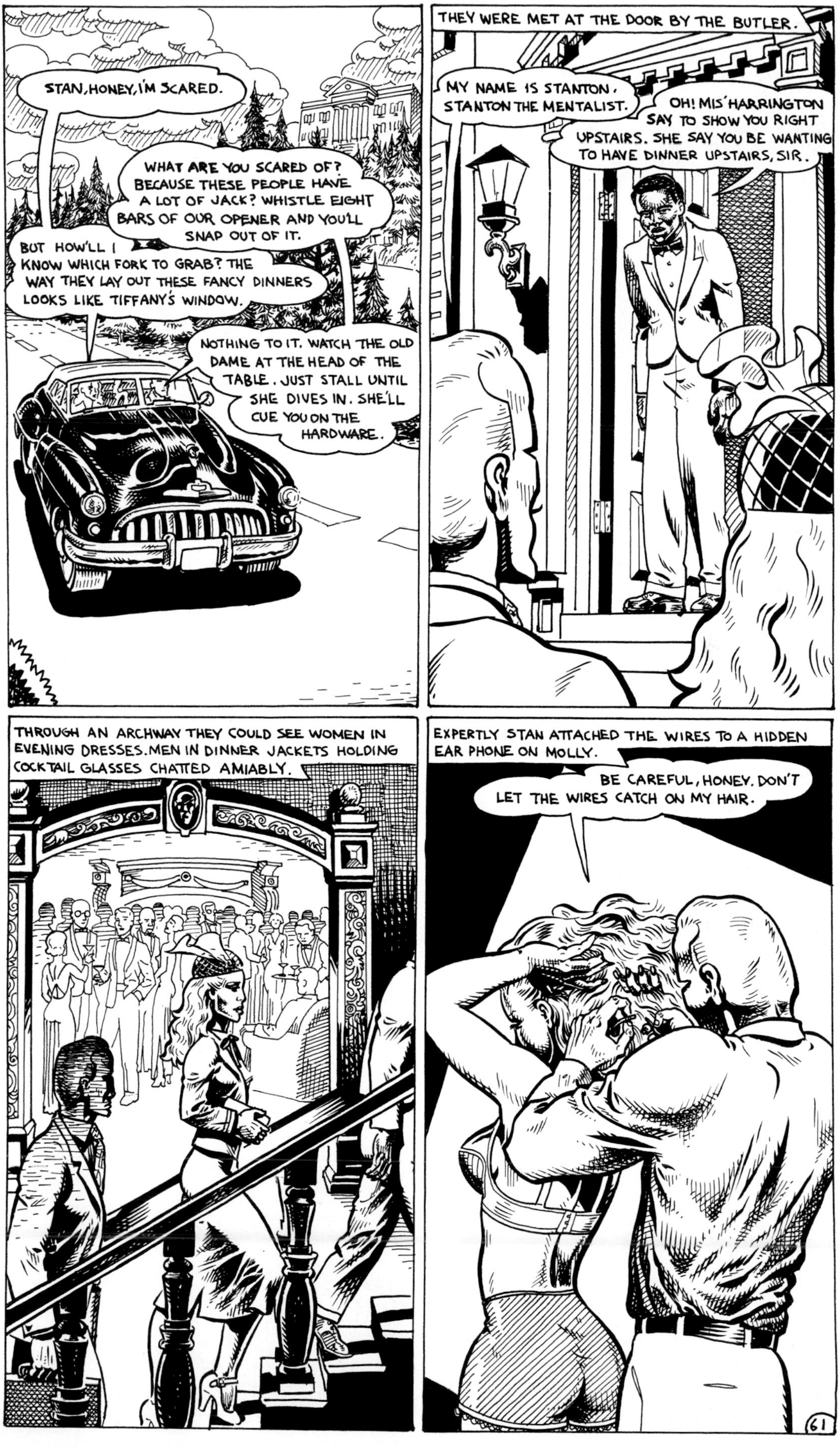
STAN, HONEY, I'M SCARED.
WHAT ARE YOU SCARED OF? BECAUSE THESE PEOPLE HAVE A LOT OF JACK? WHISTLE EIGHT BARS OF OUR OPENER AND YOU'LL SNAP OUT OF IT.
BUT HOW'LL I KNOW WHICH FORK TO GRAB? THE WAY THEY LAY OUT THESE FANCY DINNERS LOOKS LIKE TIFFANY'S WINDOW.
NOTHING TO IT. WATCH THE OLD DAME AT THE HEAD OF THE TABLE. JUST STALL UNTIL SHE DIVES IN. SHE'LL CUE YOU ON THE HARDWARE.
THEY WERE MET AT THE DOOR BY THE BUTLER.
MY NAME IS STANTON, STANTON THE MENTALIST.
OH! MIS' HARRINGTON SAY TO SHOW YOU RIGHT UPSTAIRS. SHE SAY YOU BE WANTING TO HAVE DINNER UPSTAIRS, SIR.
THROUGH AN ARCHWAY THEY COULD SEE WOMEN IN EVENING DRESSES. MEN IN DINNER JACKETS HOLDING COCKTAIL GLASSES CHATTED AMIABLY.
EXPERTLY STAN ATTACHED THE WIRES TO A HIDDEN EAR PHONE ON MOLLY.
BE CAREFUL, HONEY. DON'T LET THE WIRES CATCH ON MY HAIR.
61

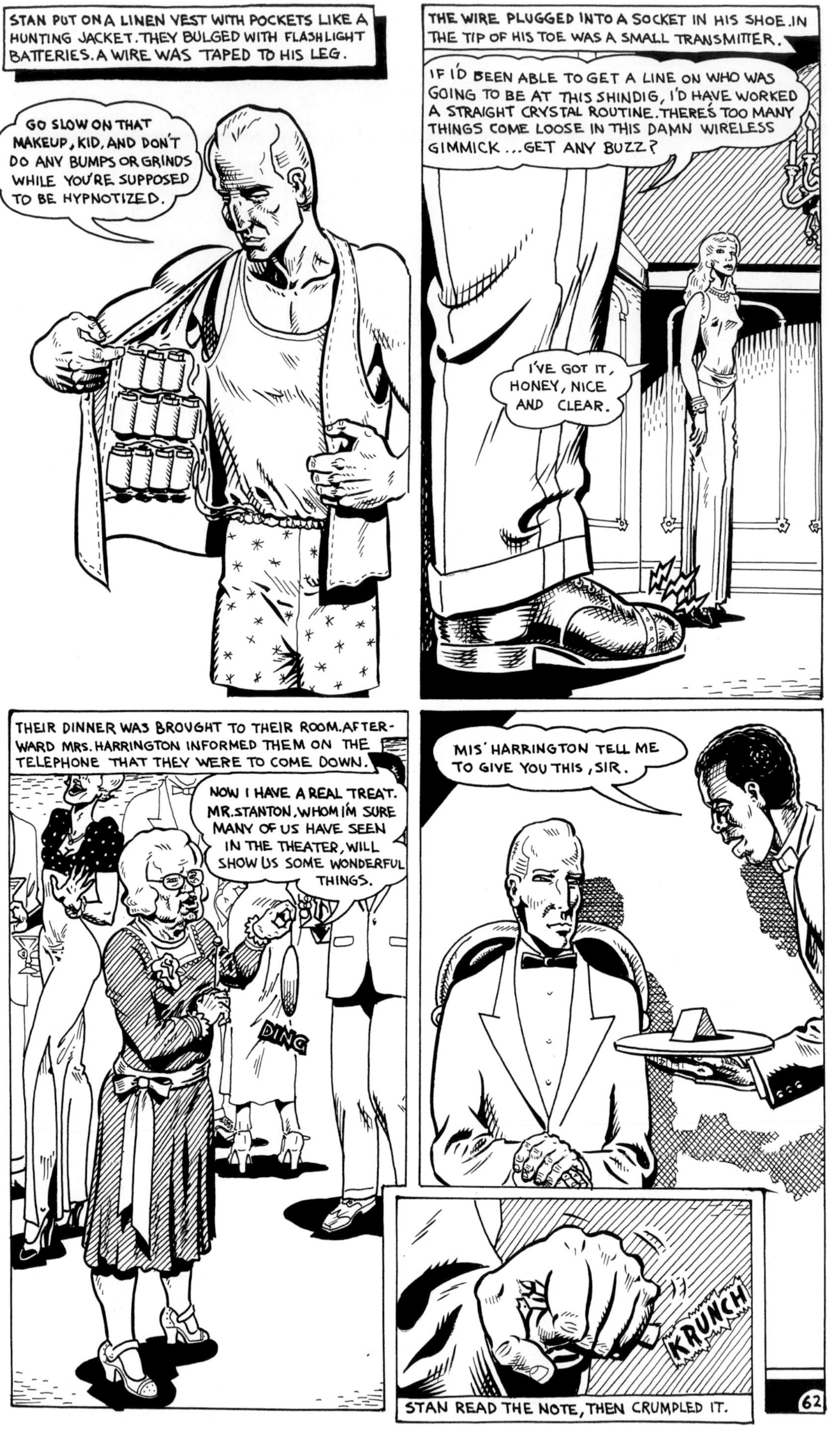

STAN PUT ON A LINEN VEST WITH POCKETS LIKE A HUNTING JACKET. THEY BULGED WITH FLASHLIGHT BATTERIES. A WIRE WAS TAPED TO HIS LEG.
GO SLOW ON THAT MAKEUP, KID, AND DON'T DO ANY BUMPS OR GRINDS WHILE YOU'RE SUPPOSED TO BE HYPNOTIZED.
THE WIRE PLUGGED INTO A SOCKET IN HIS SHOE. IN THE TIP OF HIS TOE WAS A SMALL TRANSMITTER.
IF I'D BEEN ABLE TO GET A LINE ON WHO WAS GOING TO BE AT THIS SHINDIG, I'D HAVE WORKED A STRAIGHT CRYSTAL ROUTINE. THERE'S TOO MANY THINGS COME LOOSE IN THIS DAMN WIRELESS GIMMICK ... GET ANY BUZZ?
I'VE GOT IT, HONEY, NICE AND CLEAR.
THEIR DINNER WAS BROUGHT TO THEIR ROOM. AFTERWARD MRS. HARRINGTON INFORMED THEM ON THE TELEPHONE THAT THEY WERE TO COME DOWN.
NOW I HAVE A REAL TREAT. MR. STANTON, WHOM I'M SURE MANY OF US HAVE SEEN IN THE THEATER, WILL SHOW US SOME WONDERFUL THINGS.
DING
MIS' HARRINGTON TELL ME TO GIVE YOU THIS, SIR.
KRUNCH
STAN READ THE NOTE, THEN CRUMPLED IT.

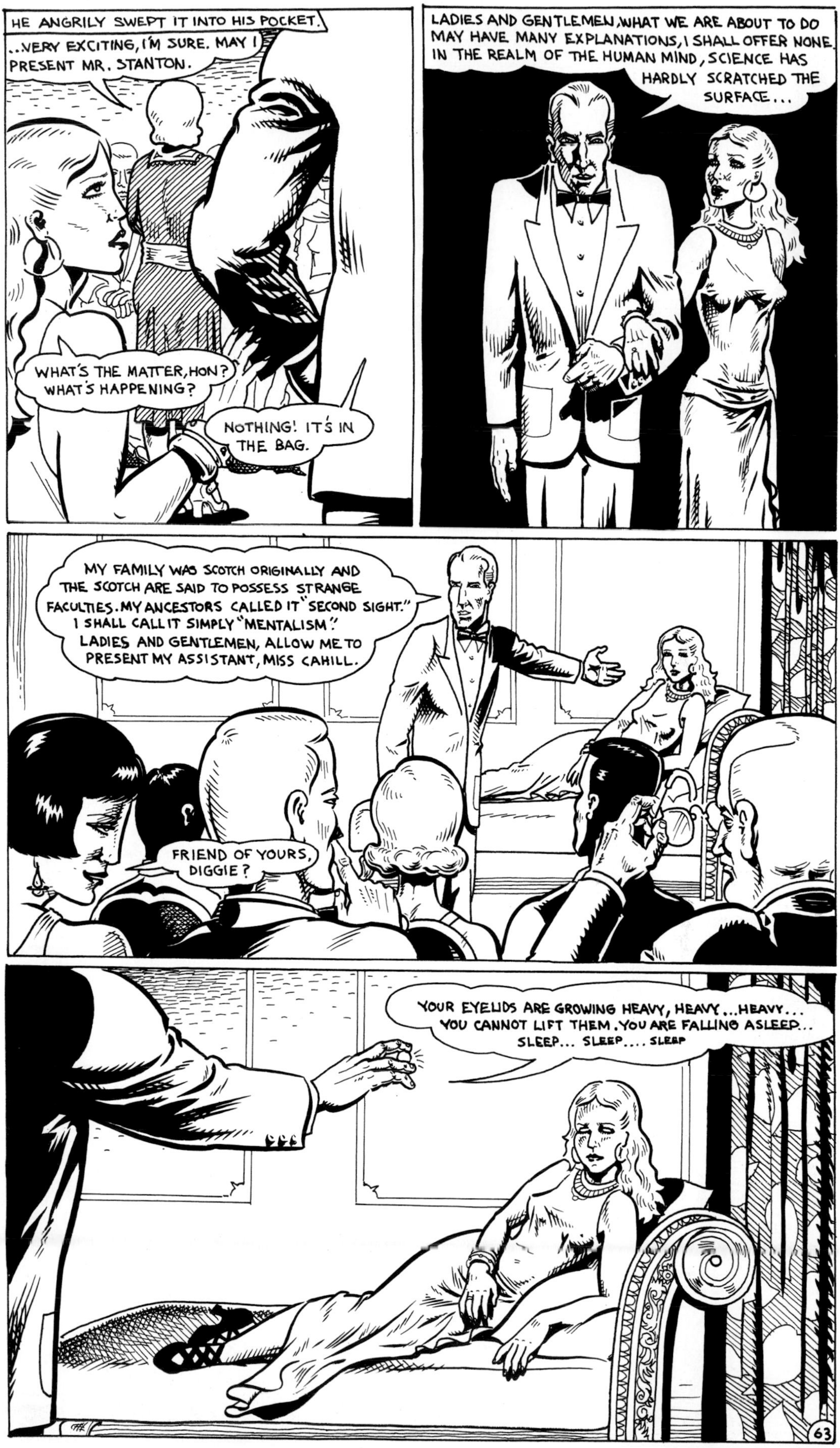
HE ANGRILY SWEPT IT INTO HIS POCKET.
...VERY EXCITING, I'M SURE. MAY I PRESENT MR. STANTON.
WHAT'S THE MATTER, HON? WHAT'S HAPPENING?
NOTHING! IT'S IN THE BAG.
LADIES AND GENTLEMEN, WHAT WE ARE ABOUT TO DO MAY HAVE MANY EXPLANATIONS, I SHALL OFFER NONE. IN THE REALM OF THE HUMAN MIND, SCIENCE HAS HARDLY SCRATCHED THE SURFACE...
MY FAMILY WAS SCOTCH ORIGINALLY AND THE SCOTCH ARE SAID TO POSSESS STRANGE FACULTIES. MY ANCESTORS CALLED IT "SECOND SIGHT." I SHALL CALL IT SIMPLY "MENTALISM." LADIES AND GENTLEMEN, ALLOW ME TO PRESENT MY ASSISTANT, MISS CAHILL.
FRIEND OF YOURS, DIGGIE?
YOUR EYELIDS ARE GROWING HEAVY, HEAVY...HEAVY... YOU CANNOT LIFT THEM. YOU ARE FALLING ASLEEP... SLEEP... SLEEP.... SLEEP

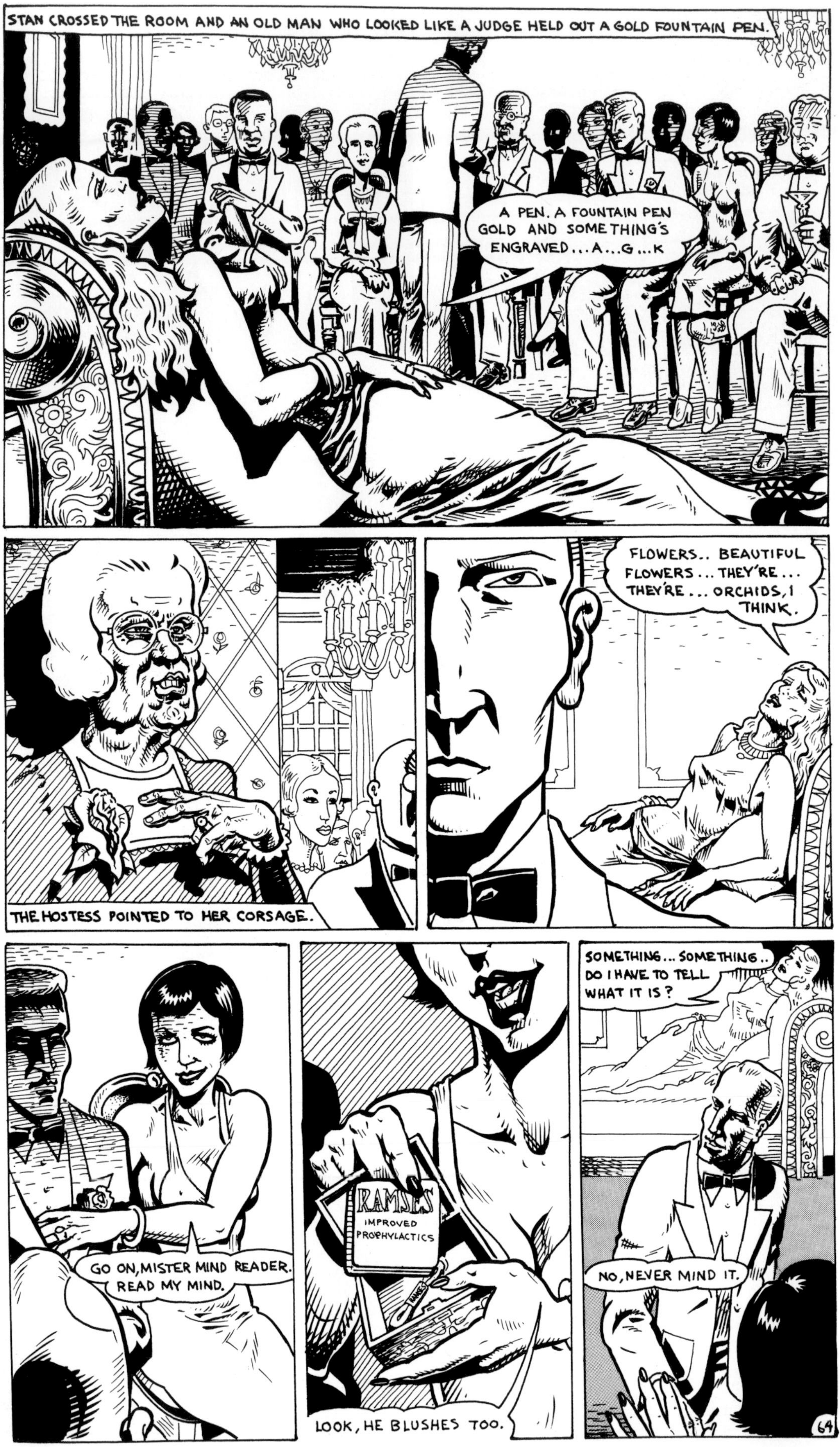
STAN CROSSED THE ROOM AND AN OLD MAN WHO LOOKED LIKE A JUDGE HELD OUT A GOLD FOUNTAIN PEN.
A PEN. A FOUNTAIN PEN GOLD AND SOMETHING'S ENGRAVED... A... G... K
THE HOSTESS POINTED TO HER CORSAGE.
FLOWERS.. BEAUTIFUL FLOWERS... THEY'RE... THEY'RE... ORCHIDS, I THINK.
GO ON, MISTER MIND READER. READ MY MIND.
RAMSES
IMPROVED PROPHYLACTICS
LOOK, HE BLUSHES TOO.
SOMETHING... SOMETHING.. DO I HAVE TO TELL WHAT IT IS?
NO, NEVER MIND IT.
64

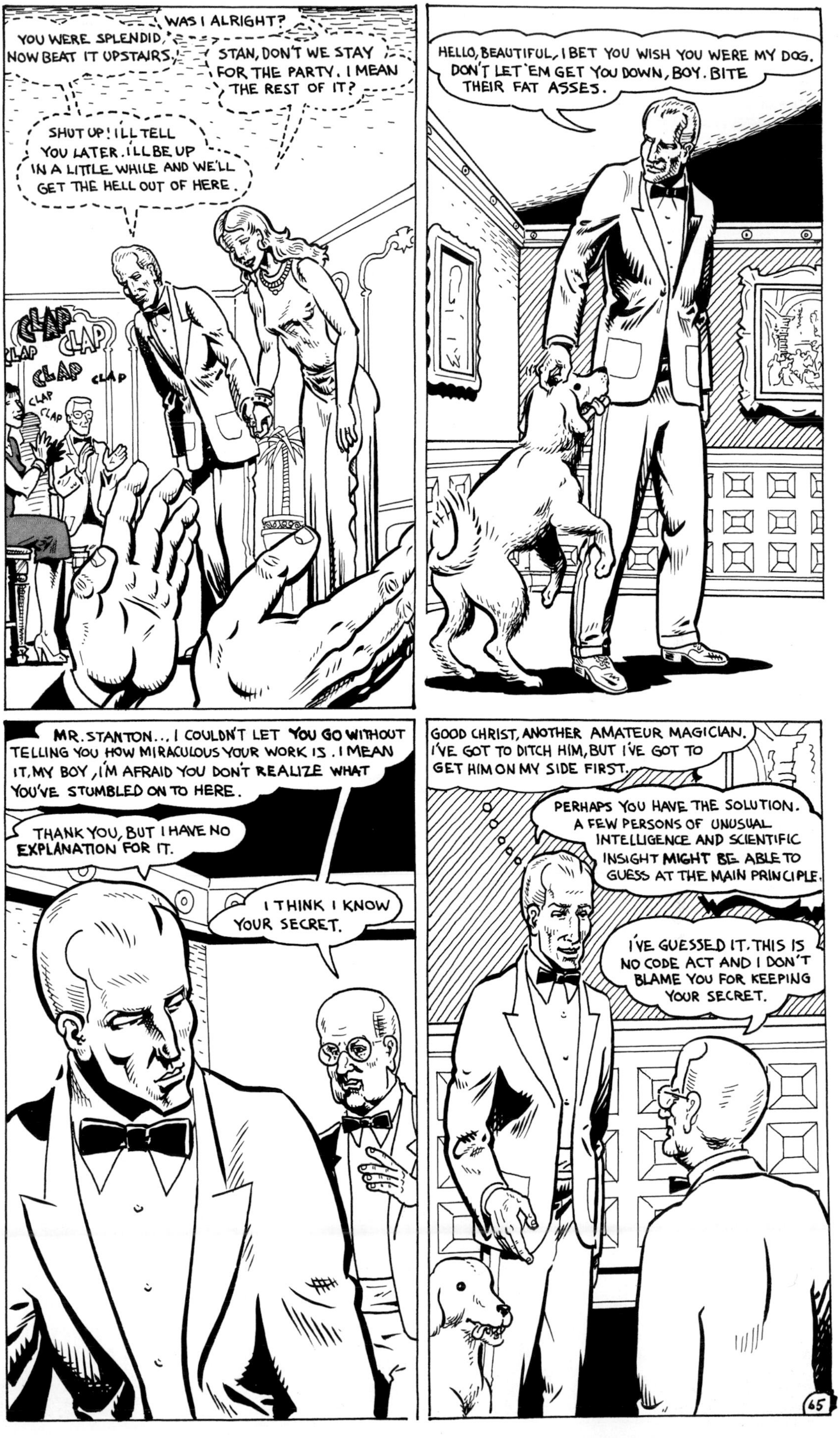
WAS I ALRIGHT?
YOU WERE SPLENDID, NOW BEAT IT UPSTAIRS.
STAN, DON'T WE STAY FOR THE PARTY. I MEAN THE REST OF IT?
SHUT UP! I'LL TELL YOU LATER. I'LL BE UP IN A LITTLE WHILE AND WE'LL GET THE HELL OUT OF HERE.
CLAP CLAP CLAP CLAP CLAP CLAP CLAP
HELLO, BEAUTIFUL, I BET YOU WISH YOU WERE MY DOG. DON'T LET 'EM GET YOU DOWN, BOY. BITE THEIR FAT ASSES.
MR. STANTON... I COULDN'T LET YOU GO WITHOUT TELLING YOU HOW MIRACULOUS YOUR WORK IS. I MEAN IT, MY BOY, I'M AFRAID YOU DON'T REALIZE WHAT YOU'VE STUMBLED ON TO HERE.
THANK YOU, BUT I HAVE NO EXPLANATION FOR IT.
I THINK I KNOW YOUR SECRET.
GOOD CHRIST, ANOTHER AMATEUR MAGICIAN. I'VE GOT TO DITCH HIM, BUT I'VE GOT TO GET HIM ON MY SIDE FIRST.
PERHAPS YOU HAVE THE SOLUTION. A FEW PERSONS OF UNUSUAL INTELLIGENCE AND SCIENTIFIC INSIGHT MIGHT BE ABLE TO GUESS AT THE MAIN PRINCIPLE.
I'VE GUESSED IT. THIS IS NO CODE ACT AND I DON'T BLAME YOU FOR KEEPING YOUR SECRET.
65

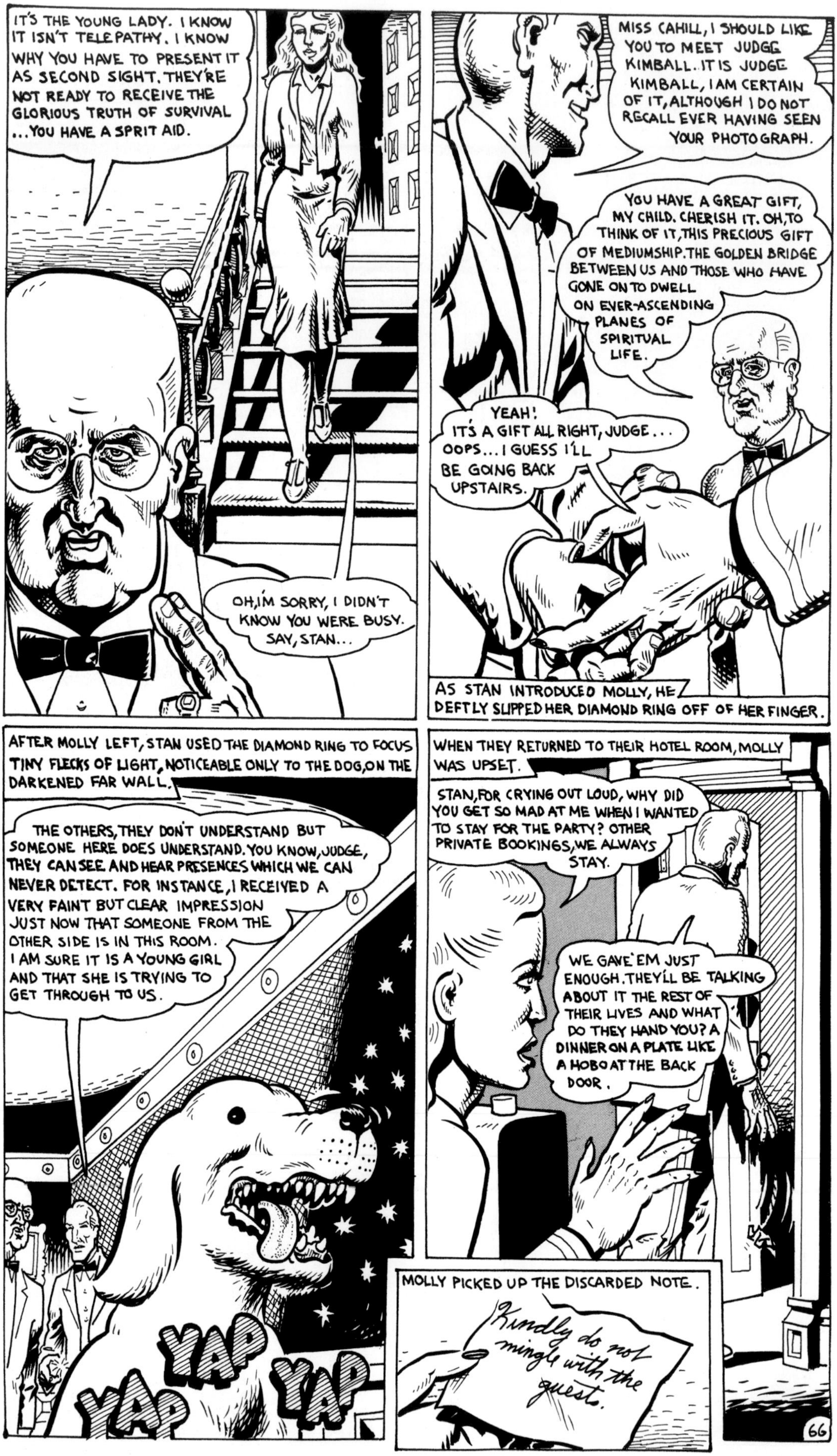
IT'S THE YOUNG LADY. I KNOW IT ISN'T TELEPATHY. I KNOW WHY YOU HAVE TO PRESENT IT AS SECOND SIGHT. THEY'RE NOT READY TO RECEIVE THE GLORIOUS TRUTH OF SURVIVAL ...YOU HAVE A SPRIT AID.
OH, I'M SORRY, I DIDN'T KNOW YOU WERE BUSY. SAY, STAN...
MISS CAHILL, I SHOULD LIKE YOU TO MEET JUDGE KIMBALL. IT IS JUDGE KIMBALL, I AM CERTAIN OF IT, ALTHOUGH I DO NOT RECALL EVER HAVING SEEN YOUR PHOTOGRAPH.
YOU HAVE A GREAT GIFT, MY CHILD. CHERISH IT. OH, TO THINK OF IT, THIS PRECIOUS GIFT OF MEDIUMSHIP. THE GOLDEN BRIDGE BETWEEN US AND THOSE WHO HAVE GONE ON TO DWELL ON EVER-ASCENDING PLANES OF SPIRITUAL LIFE.
YEAH! IT'S A GIFT ALL RIGHT, JUDGE... OOPS... I GUESS I'LL BE GOING BACK UPSTAIRS.
AS STAN INTRODUCED MOLLY, HE DEFTLY SLIPPED HER DIAMOND RING OFF OF HER FINGER.
AFTER MOLLY LEFT, STAN USED THE DIAMOND RING TO FOCUS TINY FLECKS OF LIGHT, NOTICEABLE ONLY TO THE DOG, ON THE DARKENED FAR WALL.
THE OTHERS, THEY DON'T UNDERSTAND BUT SOMEONE HERE DOES UNDERSTAND. YOU KNOW, JUDGE, THEY CAN SEE AND HEAR PRESENCES WHICH WE CAN NEVER DETECT. FOR INSTANCE, I RECEIVED A VERY FAINT BUT CLEAR IMPRESSION JUST NOW THAT SOMEONE FROM THE OTHER SIDE IS IN THIS ROOM. I AM SURE IT IS A YOUNG GIRL AND THAT SHE IS TRYING TO GET THROUGH TO US.
YAP YAP YAP
WHEN THEY RETURNED TO THEIR HOTEL ROOM, MOLLY WAS UPSET.
STAN, FOR CRYING OUT LOUD, WHY DID YOU GET SO MAD AT ME WHEN I WANTED TO STAY FOR THE PARTY? OTHER PRIVATE BOOKINGS, WE ALWAYS STAY.
WE GAVE 'EM JUST ENOUGH. THEY'LL BE TALKING ABOUT IT THE REST OF THEIR LIVES AND WHAT DO THEY HAND YOU? A DINNER ON A PLATE LIKE A HOBO AT THE BACK DOOR.
MOLLY PICKED UP THE DISCARDED NOTE.
Kindly do not mingle with the guest.

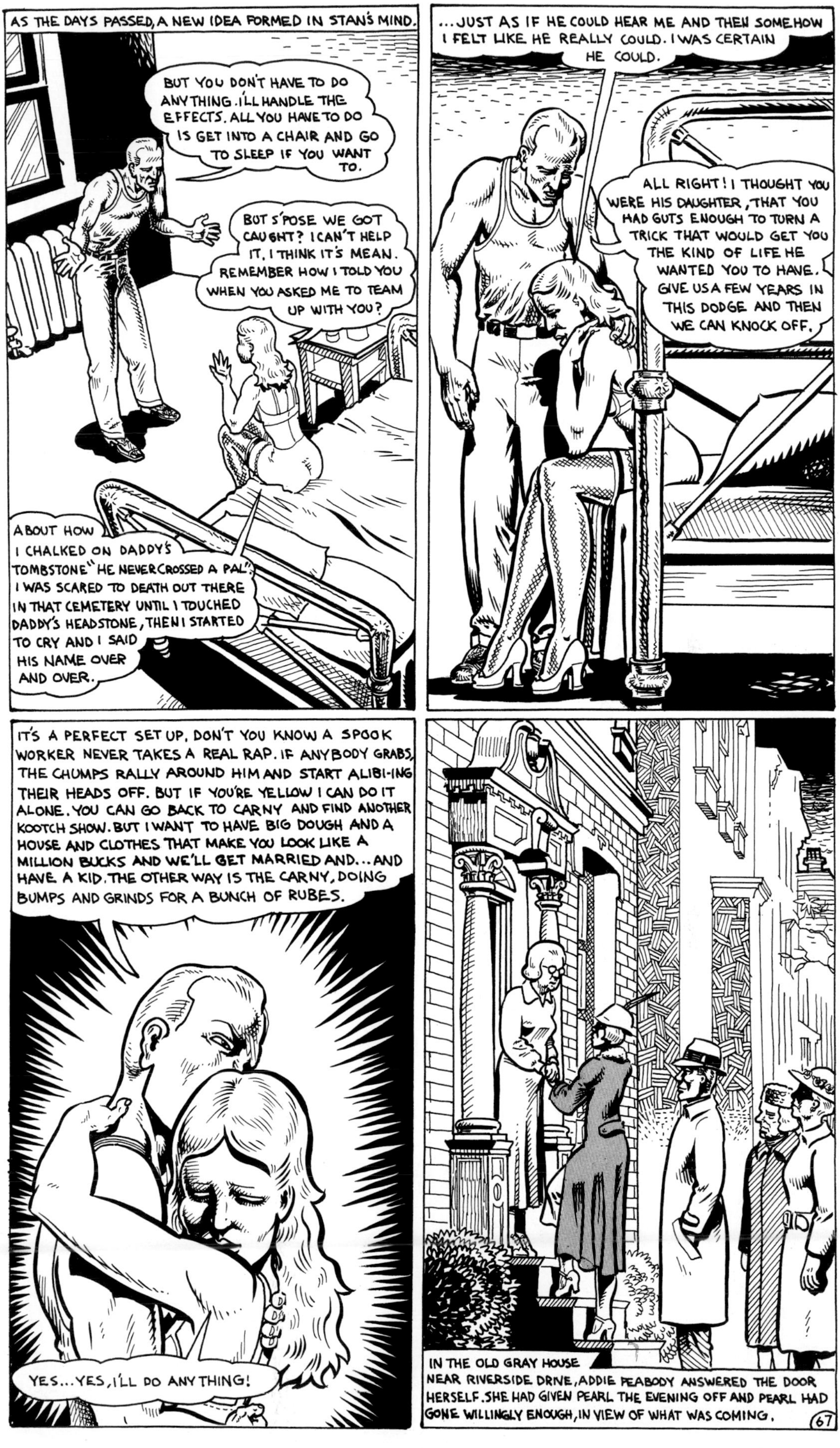

AS THE DAYS PASSED, A NEW IDEA FORMED IN STAN'S MIND.
BUT YOU DON'T HAVE TO DO ANYTHING. I'LL HANDLE THE EFFECTS. ALL YOU HAVE TO DO IS GET INTO A CHAIR AND GO TO SLEEP IF YOU WANT TO.
BUT S'POSE WE GOT CAUGHT? I CAN'T HELP IT, I THINK IT'S MEAN. REMEMBER HOW I TOLD YOU WHEN YOU ASKED ME TO TEAM UP WITH YOU?
ABOUT HOW I CHALKED ON DADDY'S TOMBSTONE "HE NEVER CROSSED A PAL". I WAS SCARED TO DEATH OUT THERE IN THAT CEMETERY UNTIL I TOUCHED DADDY'S HEADSTONE, THEN I STARTED TO CRY AND I SAID HIS NAME OVER AND OVER.
...JUST AS IF HE COULD HEAR ME AND THEN SOMEHOW I FELT LIKE HE REALLY COULD. I WAS CERTAIN HE COULD.
ALL RIGHT! I THOUGHT YOU WERE HIS DAUGHTER, THAT YOU HAD GUTS ENOUGH TO TURN A TRICK THAT WOULD GET YOU THE KIND OF LIFE HE WANTED YOU TO HAVE. GIVE US A FEW YEARS IN THIS DODGE AND THEN WE CAN KNOCK OFF.
IT'S A PERFECT SET UP, DON'T YOU KNOW A SPOOK WORKER NEVER TAKES A REAL RAP. IF ANYBODY GRABS, THE CHUMPS RALLY AROUND HIM AND START ALIBI-ING THEIR HEADS OFF. BUT IF YOU'RE YELLOW I CAN DO IT ALONE. YOU CAN GO BACK TO CARNY AND FIND ANOTHER KOOTCH SHOW. BUT I WANT TO HAVE BIG DOUGH AND A HOUSE AND CLOTHES THAT MAKE YOU LOOK LIKE A MILLION BUCKS AND WE'LL GET MARRIED AND... AND HAVE A KID. THE OTHER WAY IS THE CARNY, DOING BUMPS AND GRINDS FOR A BUNCH OF RUBES.
YES... YES, I'LL DO ANYTHING!
IN THE OLD GRAY HOUSE NEAR RIVERSIDE DRIVE, ADDIE PEABODY ANSWERED THE DOOR HERSELF. SHE HAD GIVEN PEARL THE EVENING OFF AND PEARL HAD GONE WILLINGLY ENOUGH, IN VIEW OF WHAT WAS COMING.

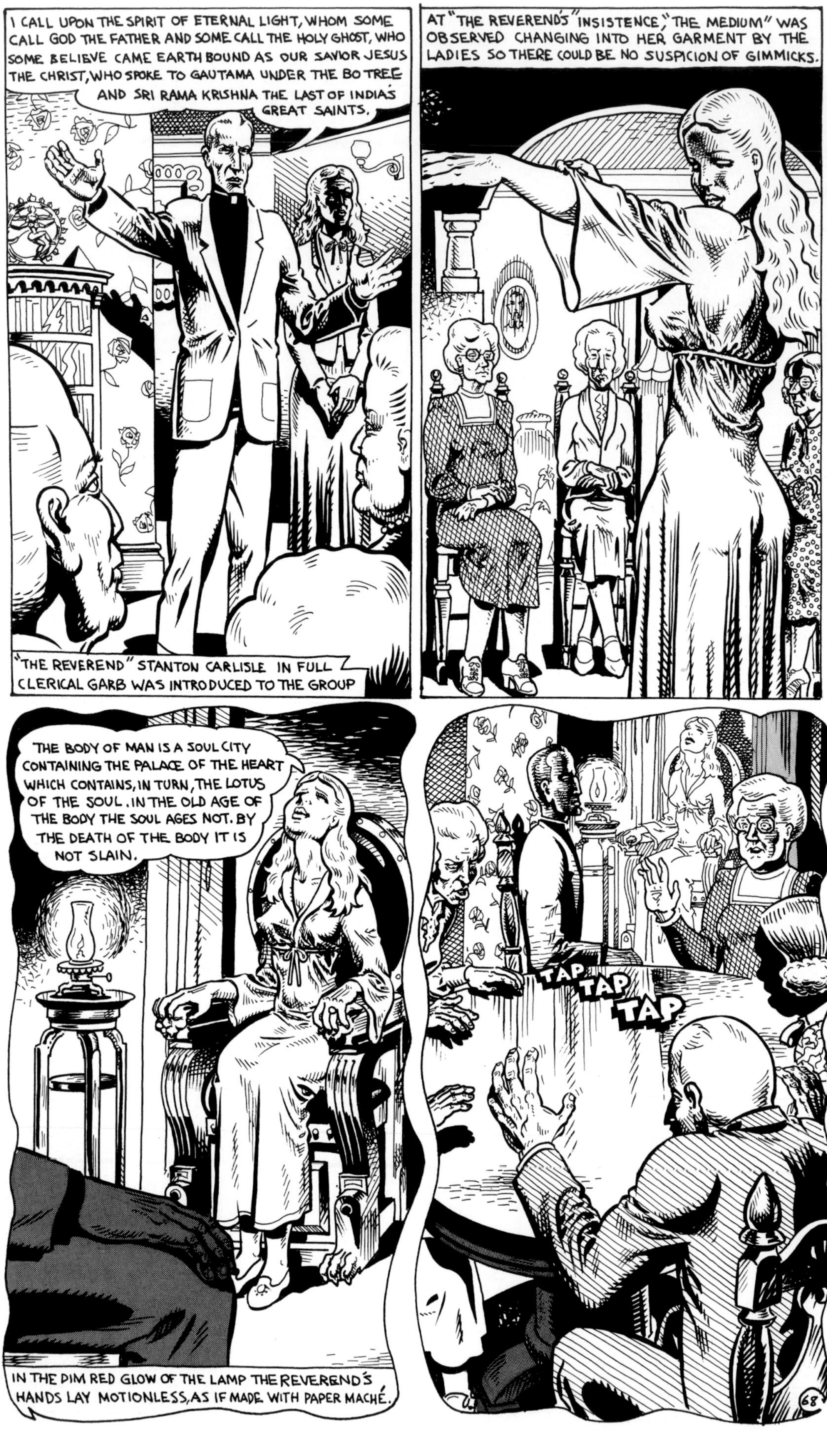
I CALL UPON THE SPIRIT OF ETERNAL LIGHT, WHOM SOME CALL GOD THE FATHER AND SOME CALL THE HOLY GHOST, WHO SOME BELIEVE CAME EARTH BOUND AS OUR SAVIOR JESUS THE CHRIST, WHO SPOKE TO GAUTAMA UNDER THE BO TREE
AND SRI RAMA KRISHNA THE LAST OF INDIA'S GREAT SAINTS.
"THE REVEREND" STANTON CARLISLE IN FULL CLERICAL GARB WAS INTRODUCED TO THE GROUP
AT "THE REVEREND'S" INSISTENCE, "THE MEDIUM" WAS OBSERVED CHANGING INTO HER GARMENT BY THE LADIES SO THERE COULD BE NO SUSPICION OF GIMMICKS.
THE BODY OF MAN IS A SOUL CITY CONTAINING THE PALACE OF THE HEART WHICH CONTAINS, IN TURN, THE LOTUS OF THE SOUL. IN THE OLD AGE OF THE BODY THE SOUL AGES NOT. BY THE DEATH OF THE BODY IT IS NOT SLAIN.
IN THE DIM RED GLOW OF THE LAMP THE REVEREND'S HANDS LAY MOTIONLESS, AS IF MADE WITH PAPER MACHÉ.
TAP TAP TAP

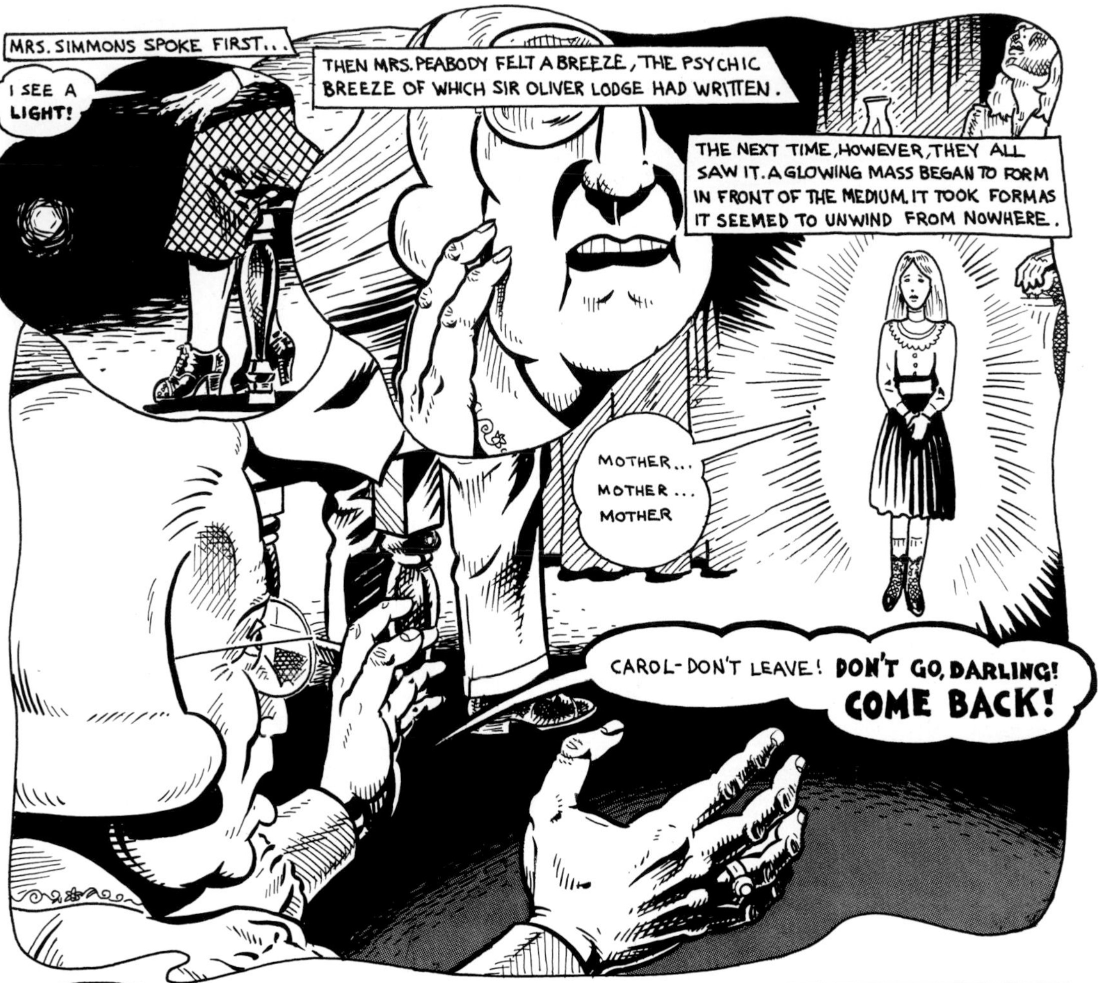
MRS. SIMMONS SPOKE FIRST...
I SEE A LIGHT!
THEN MRS. PEABODY FELT A BREEZE, THE PSYCHIC BREEZE OF WHICH SIR OLIVER LODGE HAD WRITTEN.
THE NEXT TIME, HOWEVER, THEY ALL SAW IT. A GLOWING MASS BEGAN TO FORM IN FRONT OF THE MEDIUM. IT TOOK FORM AS IT SEEMED TO UNWIND FROM NOWHERE.
MOTHER... MOTHER... MOTHER
CAROL- DON'T LEAVE! DON'T GO, DARLING! COME BACK!

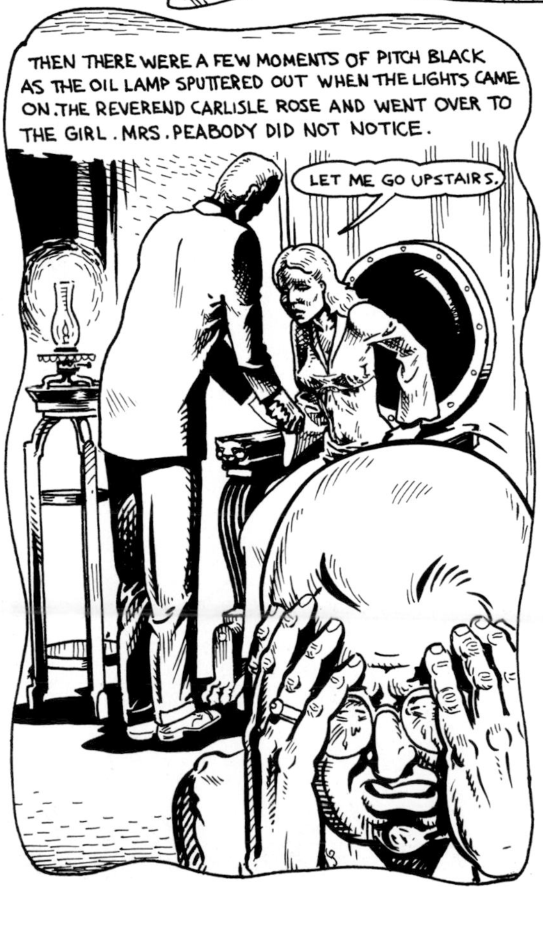
THEN THERE WERE A FEW MOMENTS OF PITCH BLACK AS THE OIL LAMP SPUTTERED OUT WHEN THE LIGHTS CAME ON. THE REVEREND CARLISLE ROSE AND WENT OVER TO THE GIRL. MRS. PEABODY DID NOT NOTICE.
LET ME GO UPSTAIRS.

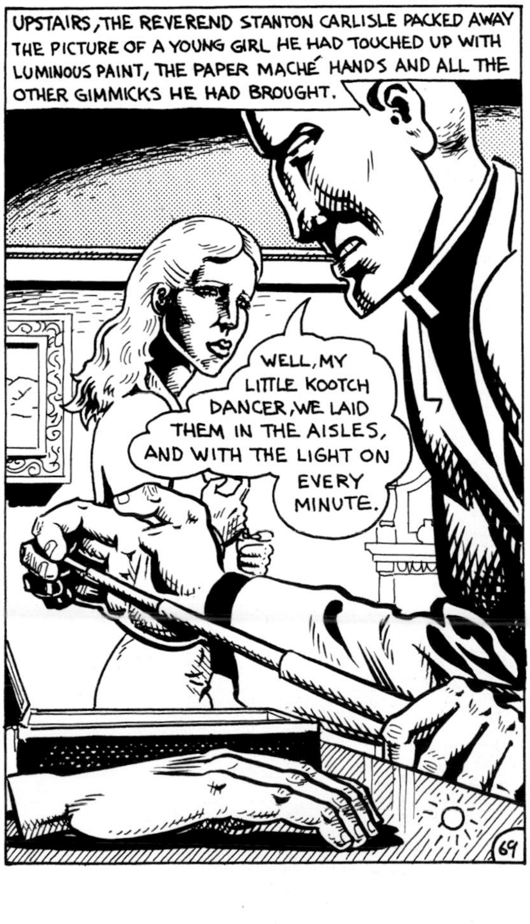
UPSTAIRS, THE REVEREND STANTON CARLISLE PACKED AWAY THE PICTURE OF A YOUNG GIRL HE HAD TOUCHED UP WITH LUMINOUS PAINT, THE PAPER MACHÉ HANDS AND ALL THE OTHER GIMMICKS HE HAD BROUGHT.
WELL, MY LITTLE KOOTCH DANCER, WE LAID THEM IN THE AISLES, AND WITH THE LIGHT ON EVERY MINUTE.

ALTHOUGH THE GUESTS HAD GONE, ADDIE PEABODY NO LONGER FELT SHE WAS QUITE ALONE IN THE HOUSE.

CAROLINE?

MOTHER... I LOVE YOU I WANT YOU TO KNOW...

I KNOW, DARLING, CAROLINE BABY.

MOTHER... I HAVE TO GO BACK. BE CAREFUL, THERE ARE BAD FORCES HERE TOO. ALL OF US ARE NOT GOOD. SOME ARE EVIL. I FEEL THEM ALL AROUND ME, MOTHER...

WITH THE REVEREND CARLISLE'S HELP, CAROLINE NOW BECAME A REGULAR VISITOR.

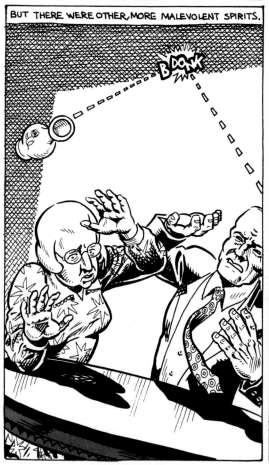

BUT THERE WERE OTHER, MORE MALEVOLENT SPIRITS.

BDONK

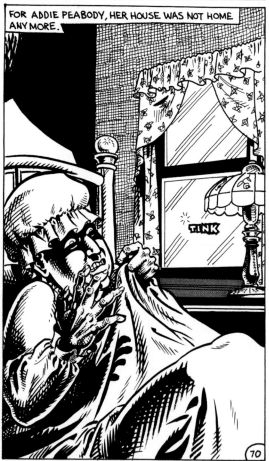

FOR ADDIE PEABODY, HER HOUSE WAS NOT HOME ANYMORE.

TINK

70

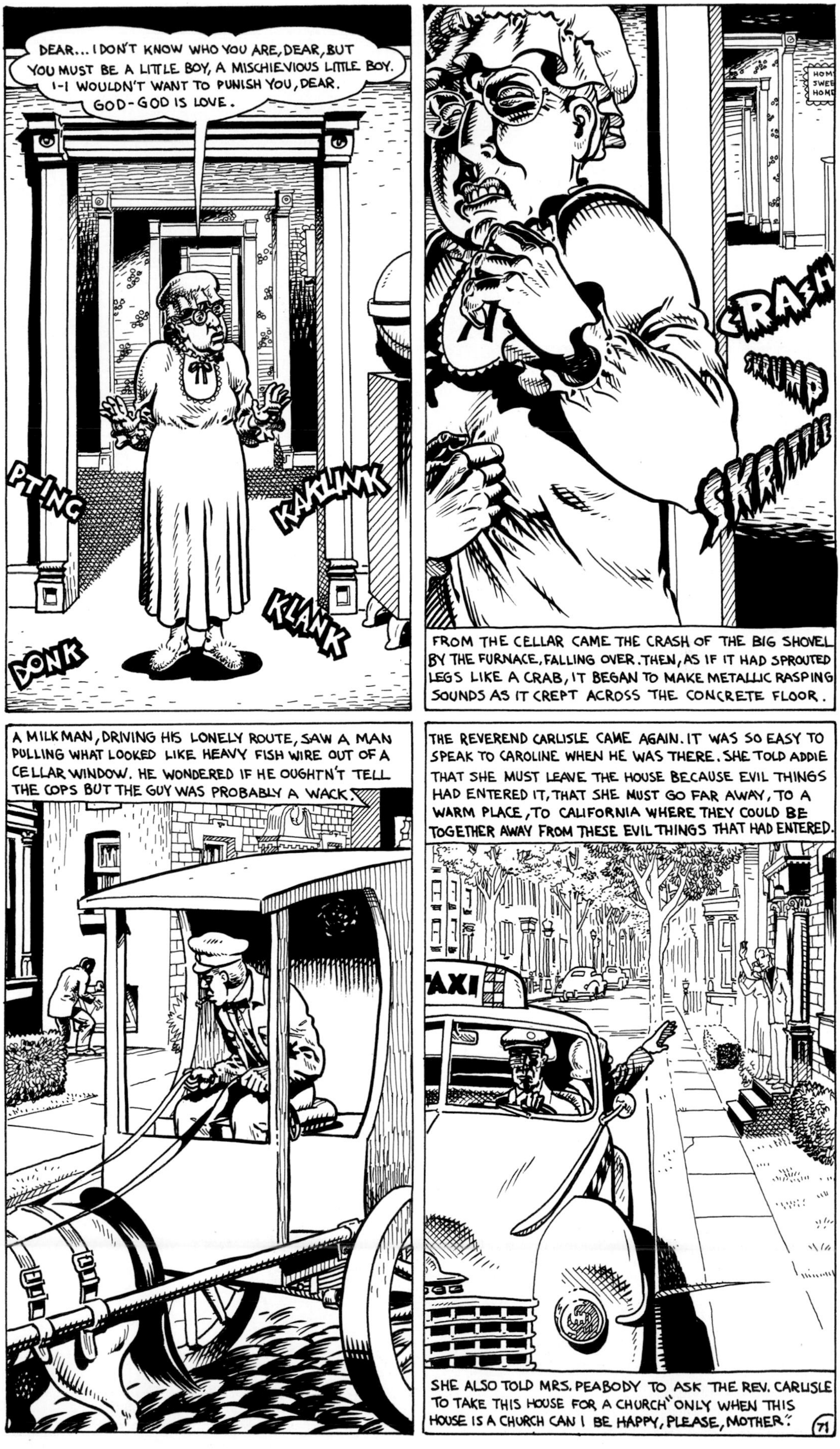
DEAR... I DON'T KNOW WHO YOU ARE, DEAR, BUT YOU MUST BE A LITTLE BOY, A MISCHIEVIOUS LITTLE BOY. I-I WOULDN'T WANT TO PUNISH YOU, DEAR. GOD-GOD IS LOVE.
PTING
KAKLINK
KLANK
DONK
CRASH
SKRUMP
SKRITTLE
FROM THE CELLAR CAME THE CRASH OF THE BIG SHOVEL BY THE FURNACE, FALLING OVER. THEN, AS IF IT HAD SPROUTED LEGS LIKE A CRAB, IT BEGAN TO MAKE METALLIC RASPING SOUNDS AS IT CREPT ACROSS THE CONCRETE FLOOR.
A MILKMAN, DRIVING HIS LONELY ROUTE, SAW A MAN PULLING WHAT LOOKED LIKE HEAVY FISH WIRE OUT OF A CELLAR WINDOW. HE WONDERED IF HE OUGHTN'T TELL THE COPS BUT THE GUY WAS PROBABLY A WACK.
THE REVEREND CARLISLE CAME AGAIN. IT WAS SO EASY TO SPEAK TO CAROLINE WHEN HE WAS THERE. SHE TOLD ADDIE THAT SHE MUST LEAVE THE HOUSE BECAUSE EVIL THINGS HAD ENTERED IT, THAT SHE MUST GO FAR AWAY, TO A WARM PLACE, TO CALIFORNIA WHERE THEY COULD BE TOGETHER AWAY FROM THESE EVIL THINGS THAT HAD ENTERED.
SHE ALSO TOLD MRS. PEABODY TO ASK THE REV. CARLISLE TO TAKE THIS HOUSE FOR A CHURCH "ONLY WHEN THIS HOUSE IS A CHURCH CAN I BE HAPPY, PLEASE, MOTHER."

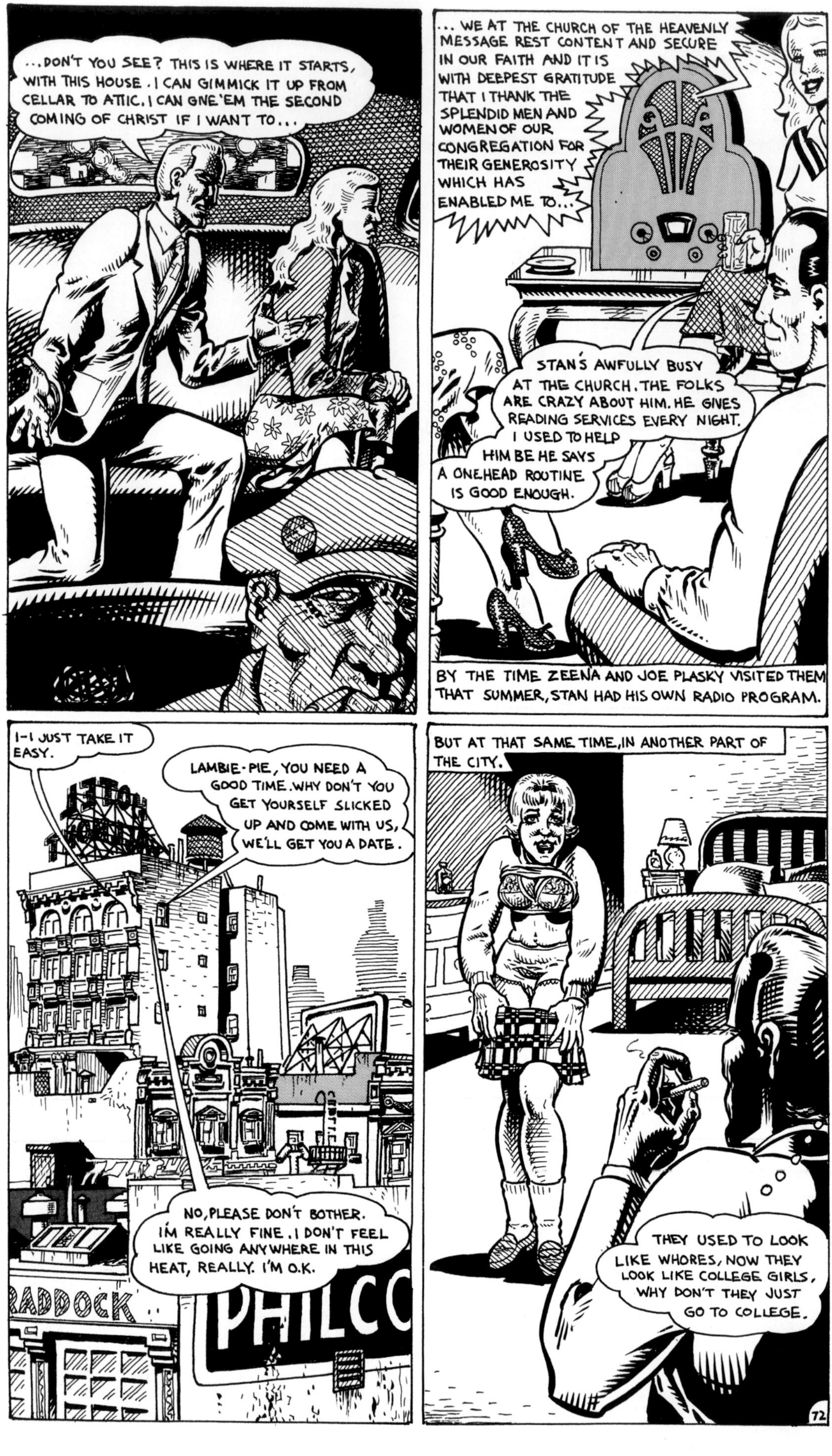
...DON'T YOU SEE? THIS IS WHERE IT STARTS, WITH THIS HOUSE. I CAN GIMMICK IT UP FROM CELLAR TO ATTIC. I CAN GIVE 'EM THE SECOND COMING OF CHRIST IF I WANT TO...
... WE AT THE CHURCH OF THE HEAVENLY MESSAGE REST CONTENT AND SECURE IN OUR FAITH AND IT IS WITH DEEPEST GRATITUDE THAT I THANK THE SPLENDID MEN AND WOMEN OF OUR CONGREGATION FOR THEIR GENEROSITY WHICH HAS ENABLED ME TO...
STAN'S AWFULLY BUSY AT THE CHURCH. THE FOLKS ARE CRAZY ABOUT HIM. HE GIVES READING SERVICES EVERY NIGHT. I USED TO HELP HIM BE HE SAYS A ONEHEAD ROUTINE IS GOOD ENOUGH.
BY THE TIME ZEENA AND JOE PLASKY VISITED THEM THAT SUMMER, STAN HAD HIS OWN RADIO PROGRAM.
I-I JUST TAKE IT EASY.
LAMBIE-PIE, YOU NEED A GOOD TIME. WHY DON'T YOU GET YOURSELF SLICKED UP AND COME WITH US, WE'LL GET YOU A DATE.
NO, PLEASE DON'T BOTHER. I'M REALLY FINE. I DON'T FEEL LIKE GOING ANYWHERE IN THIS HEAT, REALLY. I'M O.K.
RADDOCK
PHILCO
BUT AT THAT SAME TIME, IN ANOTHER PART OF THE CITY.
THEY USED TO LOOK LIKE WHORES, NOW THEY LOOK LIKE COLLEGE GIRLS, WHY DON'T THEY JUST GO TO COLLEGE.

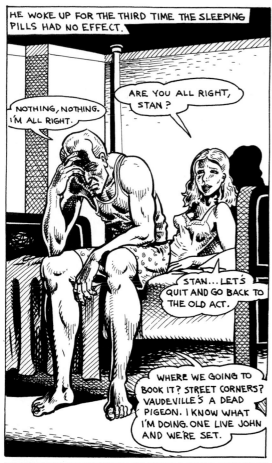

HE WOKE UP FOR THE THIRD TIME. THE SLEEPING PILLS HAD NO EFFECT.

NOTHING, NOTHING. I'M ALL RIGHT.

ARE YOU ALL RIGHT, STAN?

STAN...LET'S QUIT AND GO BACK TO THE OLD ACT.

WHERE WE GOING TO BOOK IT? STREET CORNERS? VAUDEVILLE'S A DEAD PIGEON. I KNOW WHAT I'M DOING. ONE LIVE JOHN AND WE'RE SET.

WHERE ARE YOU GOING?

OUT!

STAN MADE HIS WAY ALONG EMPTY STREETS TO THE OLD PEABODY HOUSE.

THE VAST ROOM, WHICH HAD BEEN A PARLOR AND DINING ROOM BEFORE HE KNOCKED THE PARTITION OUT, WAS CHILLY.

73

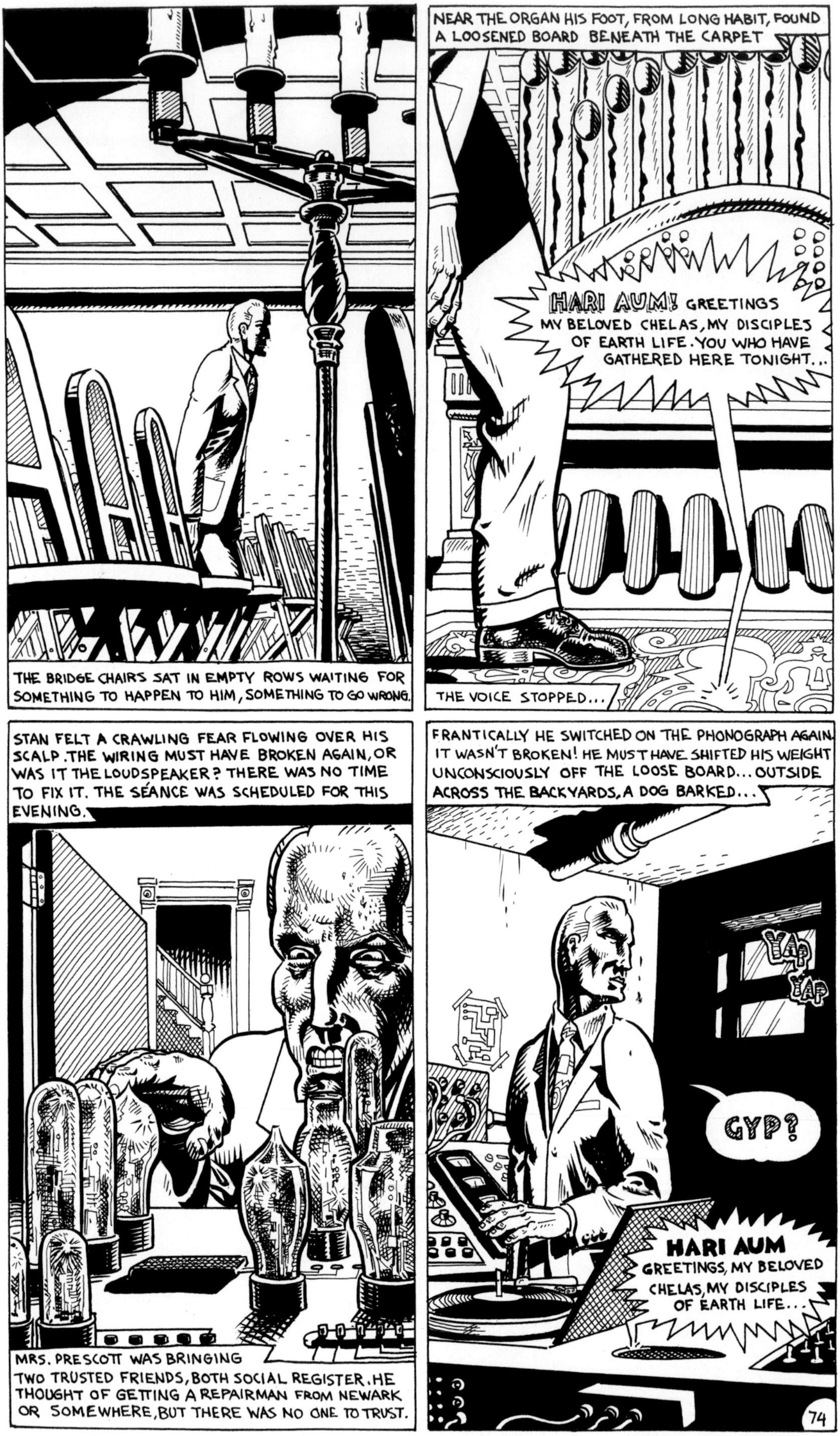
THE BRIDGE CHAIRS SAT IN EMPTY ROWS WAITING FOR SOMETHING TO HAPPEN TO HIM, SOMETHING TO GO WRONG.
NEAR THE ORGAN HIS FOOT, FROM LONG HABIT, FOUND A LOOSENED BOARD BENEATH THE CARPET
HARI AUM! GREETINGS MY BELOVED CHELAS, MY DISCIPLES OF EARTH LIFE. YOU WHO HAVE GATHERED HERE TONIGHT...
THE VOICE STOPPED...
STAN FELT A CRAWLING FEAR FLOWING OVER HIS SCALP. THE WIRING MUST HAVE BROKEN AGAIN, OR WAS IT THE LOUDSPEAKER? THERE WAS NO TIME TO FIX IT. THE SÉANCE WAS SCHEDULED FOR THIS EVENING.
MRS. PRESCOTT WAS BRINGING TWO TRUSTED FRIENDS, BOTH SOCIAL REGISTER. HE THOUGHT OF GETTING A REPAIRMAN FROM NEWARK OR SOMEWHERE, BUT THERE WAS NO ONE TO TRUST.
FRANTICALLY HE SWITCHED ON THE PHONOGRAPH AGAIN. IT WASN'T BROKEN! HE MUST HAVE SHIFTED HIS WEIGHT UNCONSCIOUSLY OFF THE LOOSE BOARD... OUTSIDE ACROSS THE BACKYARDS, A DOG BARKED...
YAP YAP
GYP?
HARI AUM GREETINGS, MY BELOVED CHELAS, MY DISCIPLES OF EARTH LIFE...
74

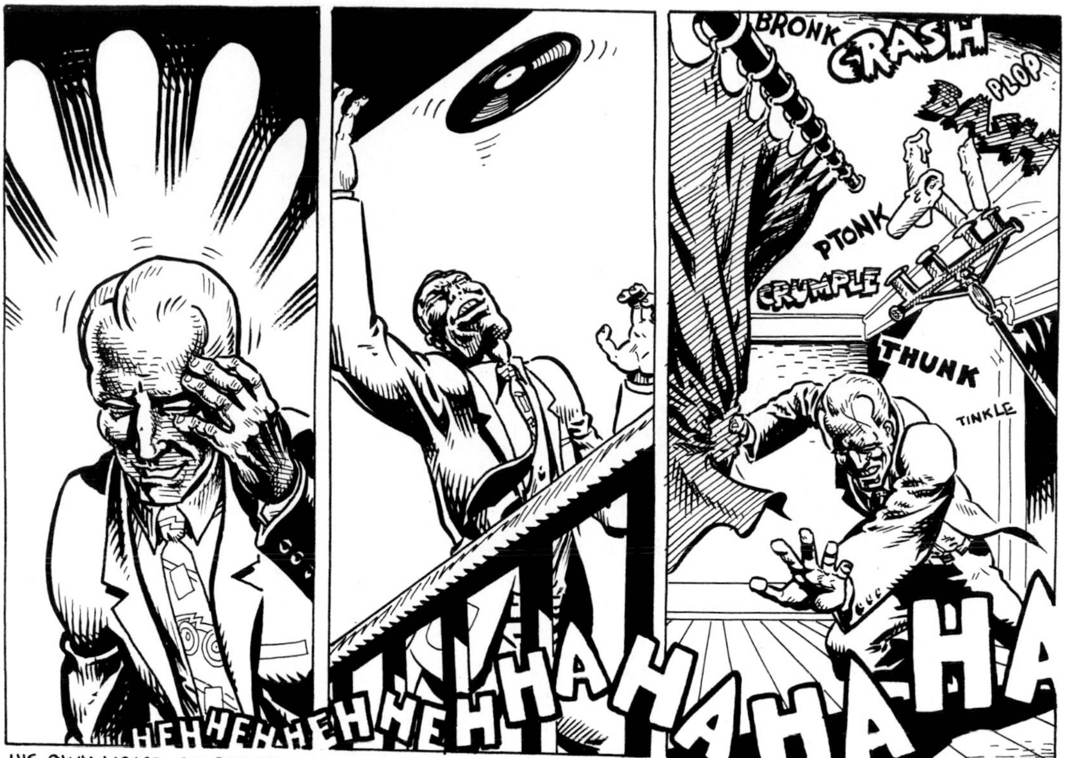
BRONK
CRASH
PLOP
PTONK
CRUMPLE
THUNK
TINKLE
HEH HEH HEH HEH HEH HAHAHAHA-HA

HIS OWN VOICE STARTLED HIM. THEN HE BEGAN TO LAUGH. LAUGHING UP THE STAIRS, IN AND OUT OF BEDROOMS, NOW CHASTELY BARE. IN THE SÉANCE ROOM HE SNAPPED ON THE LIGHT. STILL LAUGHING HE SNAPPED THE LIGHT OFF AND FELT FOR THE PANEL IN THE BASEBOARD WHERE HE KEPT THE PROJECTOR. HE BECAME ENTANGLED WITH THE CURTAINS. HE GRABBED THEM AND WRENCHED. THEN HE FOUND THE PROJECTOR AND TWISTED A KNOB. HE AIMED IT CRAZILY AND THE HAZY IMAGE OF A BABY FLOATED ON THE CEILING...

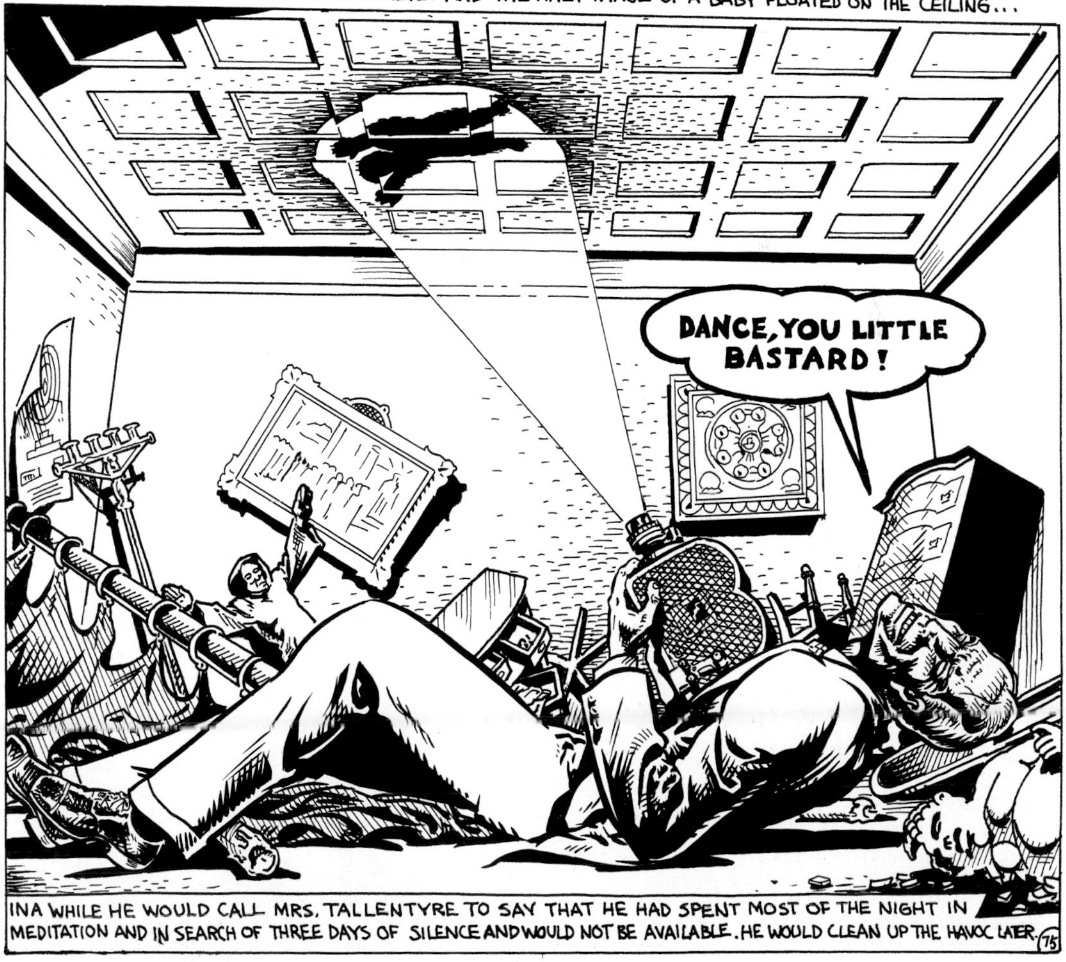
DANCE, YOU LITTLE BASTARD!

IN A WHILE HE WOULD CALL MRS. TALLENTYRE TO SAY THAT HE HAD SPENT MOST OF THE NIGHT IN MEDITATION AND IN SEARCH OF THREE DAYS OF SILENCE AND WOULD NOT BE AVAILABLE. HE WOULD CLEAN UP THE HAVOC LATER.

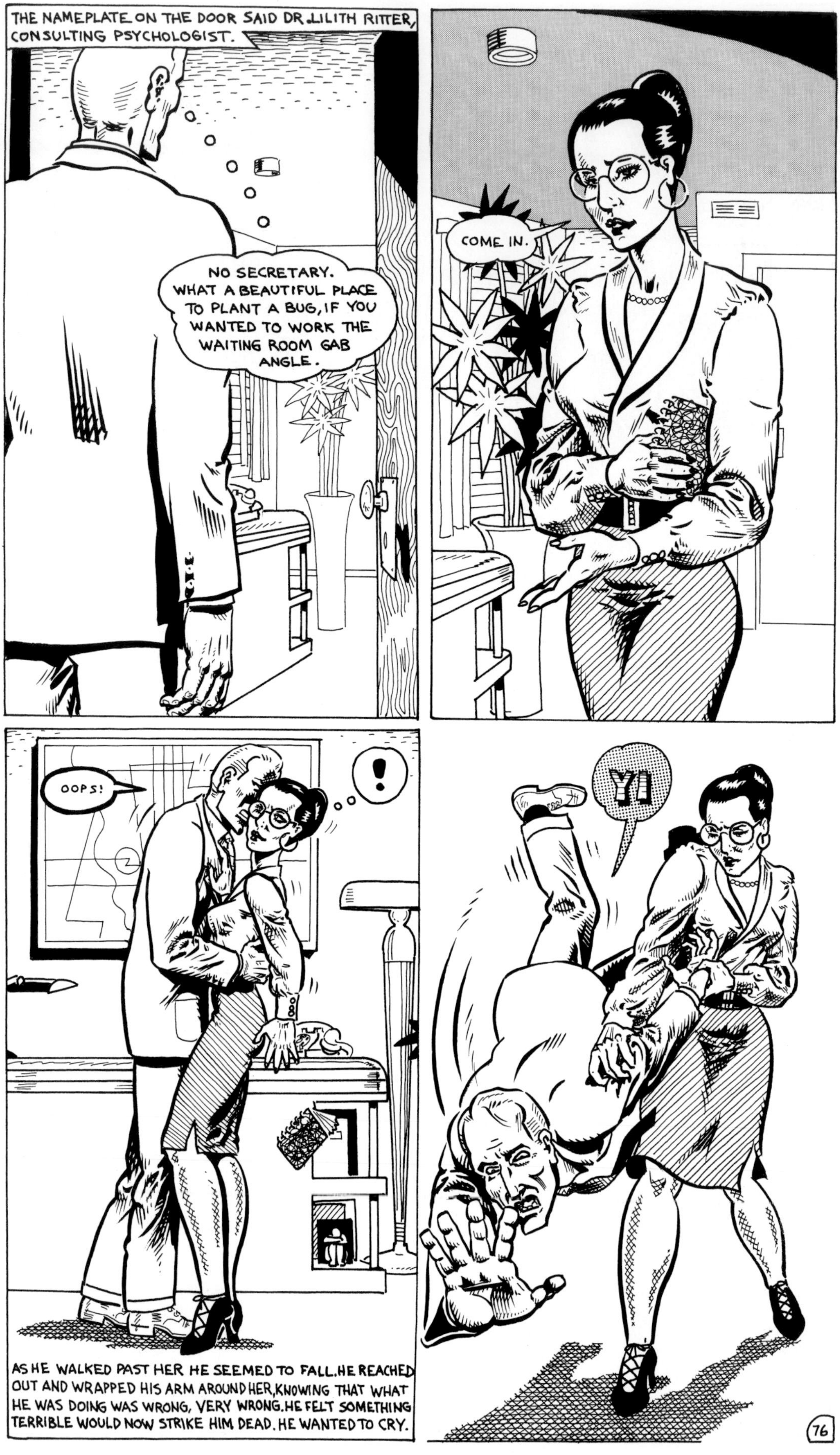
THE NAMEPLATE ON THE DOOR SAID DR. LILITH RITTER, CONSULTING PSYCHOLOGIST.
NO SECRETARY. WHAT A BEAUTIFUL PLACE TO PLANT A BUG, IF YOU WANTED TO WORK THE WAITING ROOM GAB ANGLE.
COME IN.
OOPS!
!
AS HE WALKED PAST HER HE SEEMED TO FALL. HE REACHED OUT AND WRAPPED HIS ARM AROUND HER, KNOWING THAT WHAT HE WAS DOING WAS WRONG, VERY WRONG. HE FELT SOMETHING TERRIBLE WOULD NOW STRIKE HIM DEAD. HE WANTED TO CRY.
YI

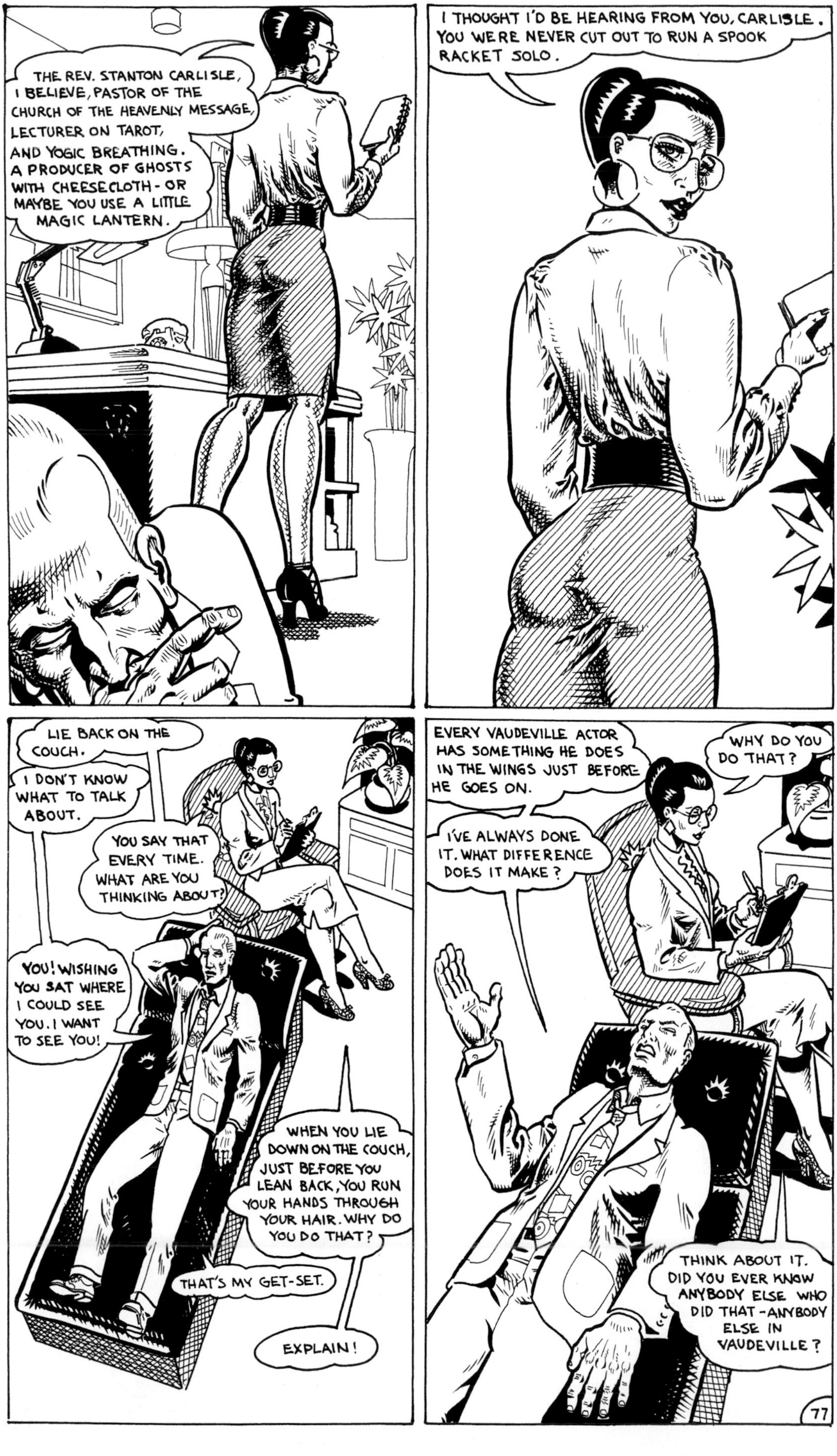
THE REV. STANTON CARLISLE, I BELIEVE, PASTOR OF THE CHURCH OF THE HEAVENLY MESSAGE, LECTURER ON TAROT, AND YOGIC BREATHING. A PRODUCER OF GHOSTS WITH CHEESECLOTH - OR MAYBE YOU USE A LITTLE MAGIC LANTERN.
I THOUGHT I'D BE HEARING FROM YOU, CARLISLE. YOU WERE NEVER CUT OUT TO RUN A SPOOK RACKET SOLO.
LIE BACK ON THE COUCH.
I DON'T KNOW WHAT TO TALK ABOUT.
YOU SAY THAT EVERY TIME. WHAT ARE YOU THINKING ABOUT?
YOU! WISHING YOU SAT WHERE I COULD SEE YOU. I WANT TO SEE YOU!
WHEN YOU LIE DOWN ON THE COUCH, JUST BEFORE YOU LEAN BACK, YOU RUN YOUR HANDS THROUGH YOUR HAIR. WHY DO YOU DO THAT?
THAT'S MY GET-SET.
EXPLAIN!
EVERY VAUDEVILLE ACTOR HAS SOMETHING HE DOES IN THE WINGS JUST BEFORE HE GOES ON.
WHY DO YOU DO THAT?
I'VE ALWAYS DONE IT. WHAT DIFFERENCE DOES IT MAKE?
THINK ABOUT IT. DID YOU EVER KNOW ANYBODY ELSE WHO DID THAT - ANYBODY ELSE IN VAUDEVILLE?
77

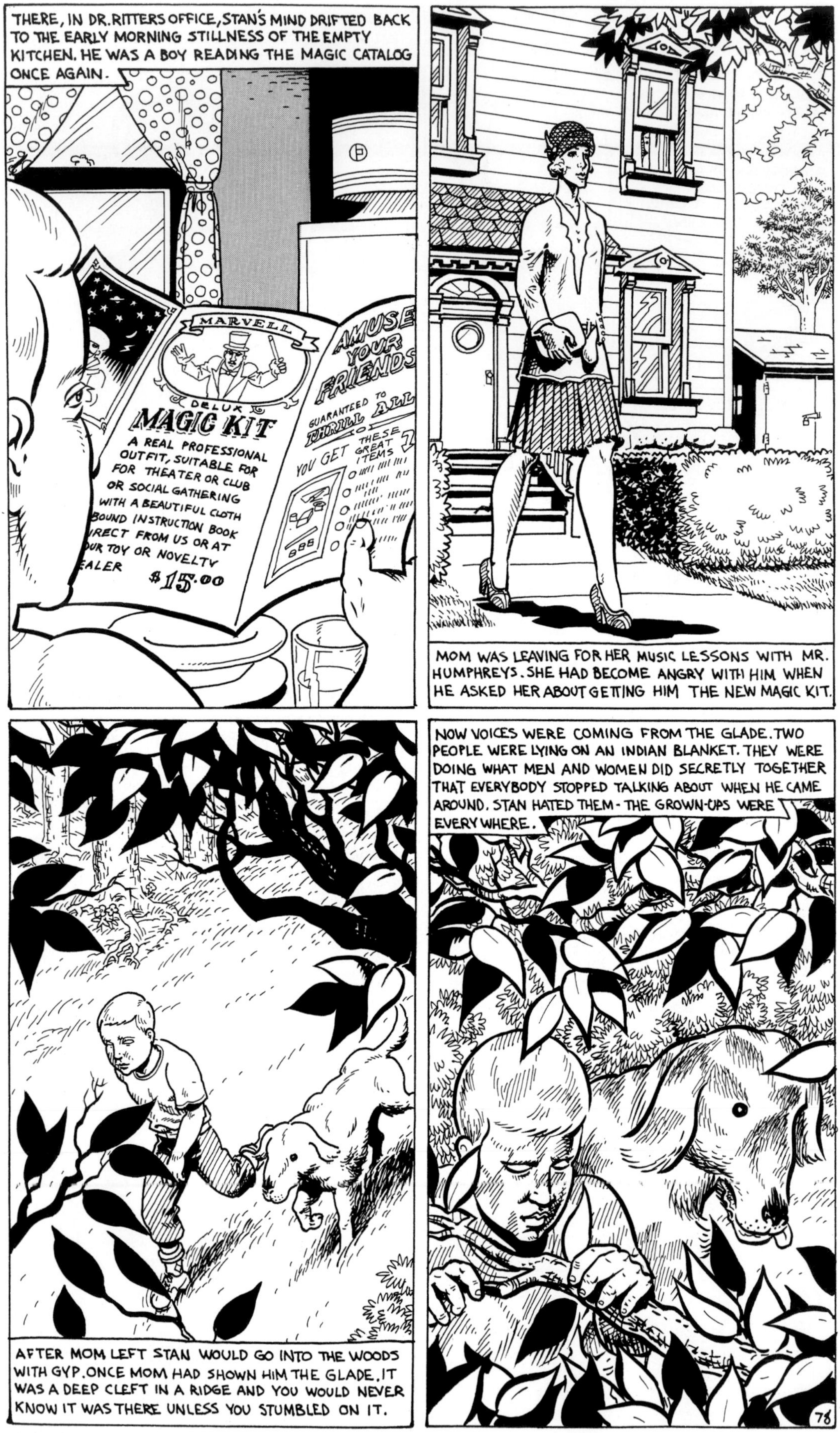
THERE, IN DR. RITTERS OFFICE, STAN'S MIND DRIFTED BACK TO THE EARLY MORNING STILLNESS OF THE EMPTY KITCHEN. HE WAS A BOY READING THE MAGIC CATALOG ONCE AGAIN.
MARVELL
DELUX
MAGIC KIT
A REAL PROFESSIONAL OUTFIT, SUITABLE FOR FOR THEATER OR CLUB OR SOCIAL GATHERING WITH A BEAUTIFUL CLOTH
$15.00
AMUSE YOUR FRIENDS
GUARANTEED TO THRILL ALL
YOU GET THESE GREAT ITEMS
MOM WAS LEAVING FOR HER MUSIC LESSONS WITH MR. HUMPHREYS. SHE HAD BECOME ANGRY WITH HIM WHEN HE ASKED HER ABOUT GETTING HIM THE NEW MAGIC KIT.
AFTER MOM LEFT STAN WOULD GO INTO THE WOODS WITH GYP. ONCE MOM HAD SHOWN HIM THE GLADE. IT WAS A DEEP CLEFT IN A RIDGE AND YOU WOULD NEVER KNOW IT WAS THERE UNLESS YOU STUMBLED ON IT.
NOW VOICES WERE COMING FROM THE GLADE. TWO PEOPLE WERE LYING ON AN INDIAN BLANKET. THEY WERE DOING WHAT MEN AND WOMEN DID SECRETLY TOGETHER THAT EVERYBODY STOPPED TALKING ABOUT WHEN HE CAME AROUND. STAN HATED THEM - THE GROWN-UPS WERE EVERY WHERE.

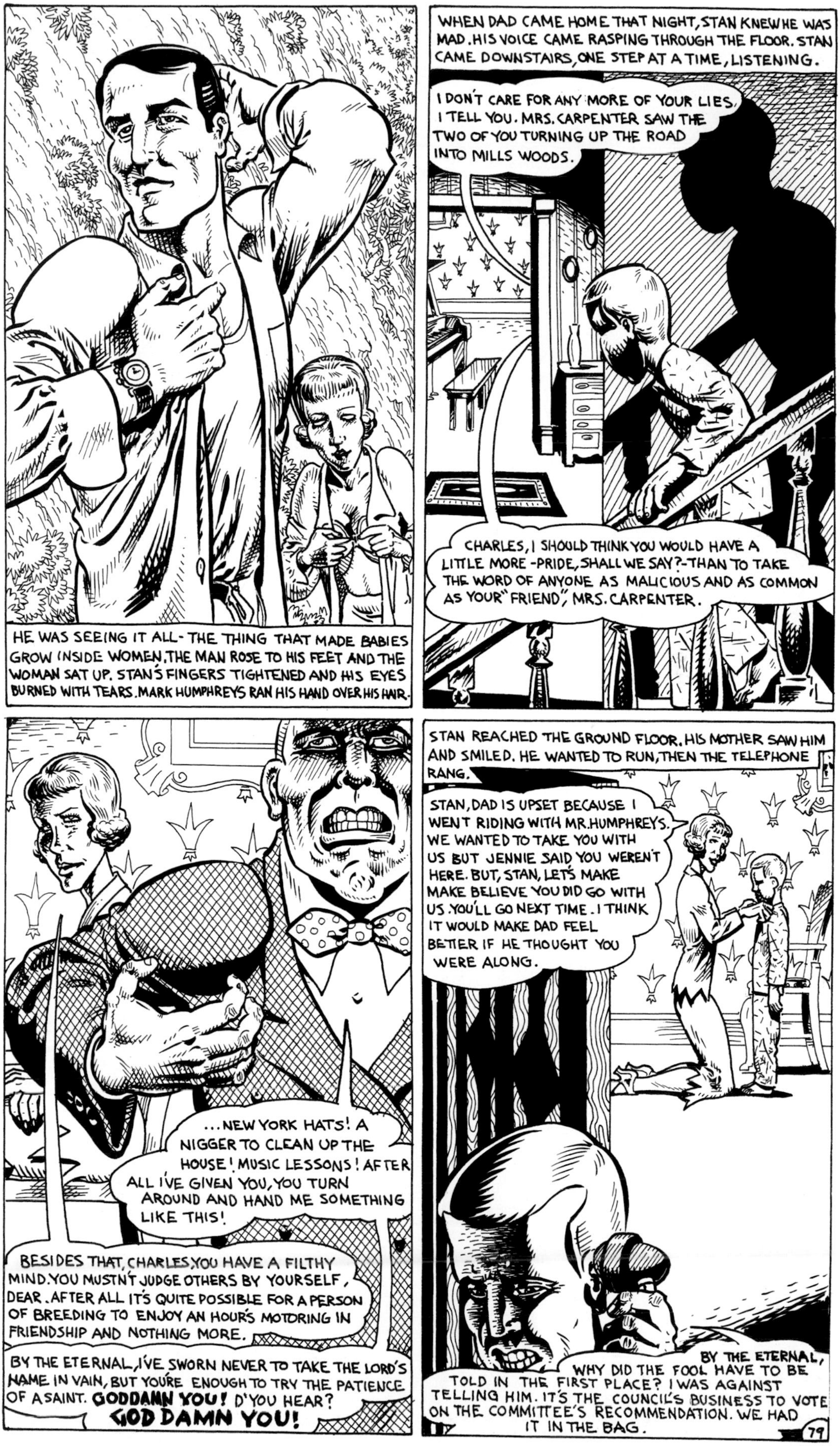
HE WAS SEEING IT ALL- THE THING THAT MADE BABIES GROW INSIDE WOMEN. THE MAN ROSE TO HIS FEET AND THE WOMAN SAT UP. STAN'S FINGERS TIGHTENED AND HIS EYES BURNED WITH TEARS. MARK HUMPHREYS RAN HIS HAND OVER HIS HAIR.
WHEN DAD CAME HOME THAT NIGHT, STAN KNEW HE WAS MAD. HIS VOICE CAME RASPING THROUGH THE FLOOR. STAN CAME DOWNSTAIRS, ONE STEP AT A TIME, LISTENING.
I DON'T CARE FOR ANY MORE OF YOUR LIES, I TELL YOU. MRS. CARPENTER SAW THE TWO OF YOU TURNING UP THE ROAD INTO MILLS WOODS.
CHARLES, I SHOULD THINK YOU WOULD HAVE A LITTLE MORE -PRIDE, SHALL WE SAY?- THAN TO TAKE THE WORD OF ANYONE AS MALICIOUS AND AS COMMON AS YOUR "FRIEND", MRS. CARPENTER.
...NEW YORK HATS! A NIGGER TO CLEAN UP THE HOUSE! MUSIC LESSONS! AFTER ALL I'VE GIVEN YOU, YOU TURN AROUND AND HAND ME SOMETHING LIKE THIS!
BESIDES THAT, CHARLES, YOU HAVE A FILTHY MIND. YOU MUSTN'T JUDGE OTHERS BY YOURSELF, DEAR. AFTER ALL IT'S QUITE POSSIBLE FOR A PERSON OF BREEDING TO ENJOY AN HOUR'S MOTORING IN FRIENDSHIP AND NOTHING MORE.
BY THE ETERNAL, I'VE SWORN NEVER TO TAKE THE LORD'S NAME IN VAIN, BUT YOU'RE ENOUGH TO TRY THE PATIENCE OF A SAINT. GODDAMN YOU! D'YOU HEAR? GOD DAMN YOU!
STAN REACHED THE GROUND FLOOR. HIS MOTHER SAW HIM AND SMILED. HE WANTED TO RUN, THEN THE TELEPHONE RANG.
STAN, DAD IS UPSET BECAUSE I WENT RIDING WITH MR. HUMPHREYS. WE WANTED TO TAKE YOU WITH US BUT JENNIE SAID YOU WEREN'T HERE. BUT, STAN, LET'S MAKE MAKE BELIEVE YOU DID GO WITH US. YOU'LL GO NEXT TIME. I THINK IT WOULD MAKE DAD FEEL BETTER IF HE THOUGHT YOU WERE ALONG.
BY THE ETERNAL, WHY DID THE FOOL HAVE TO BE TOLD IN THE FIRST PLACE? I WAS AGAINST TELLING HIM. IT'S THE COUNCIL'S BUSINESS TO VOTE ON THE COMMITTEE'S RECOMMENDATION. WE HAD IT IN THE BAG.

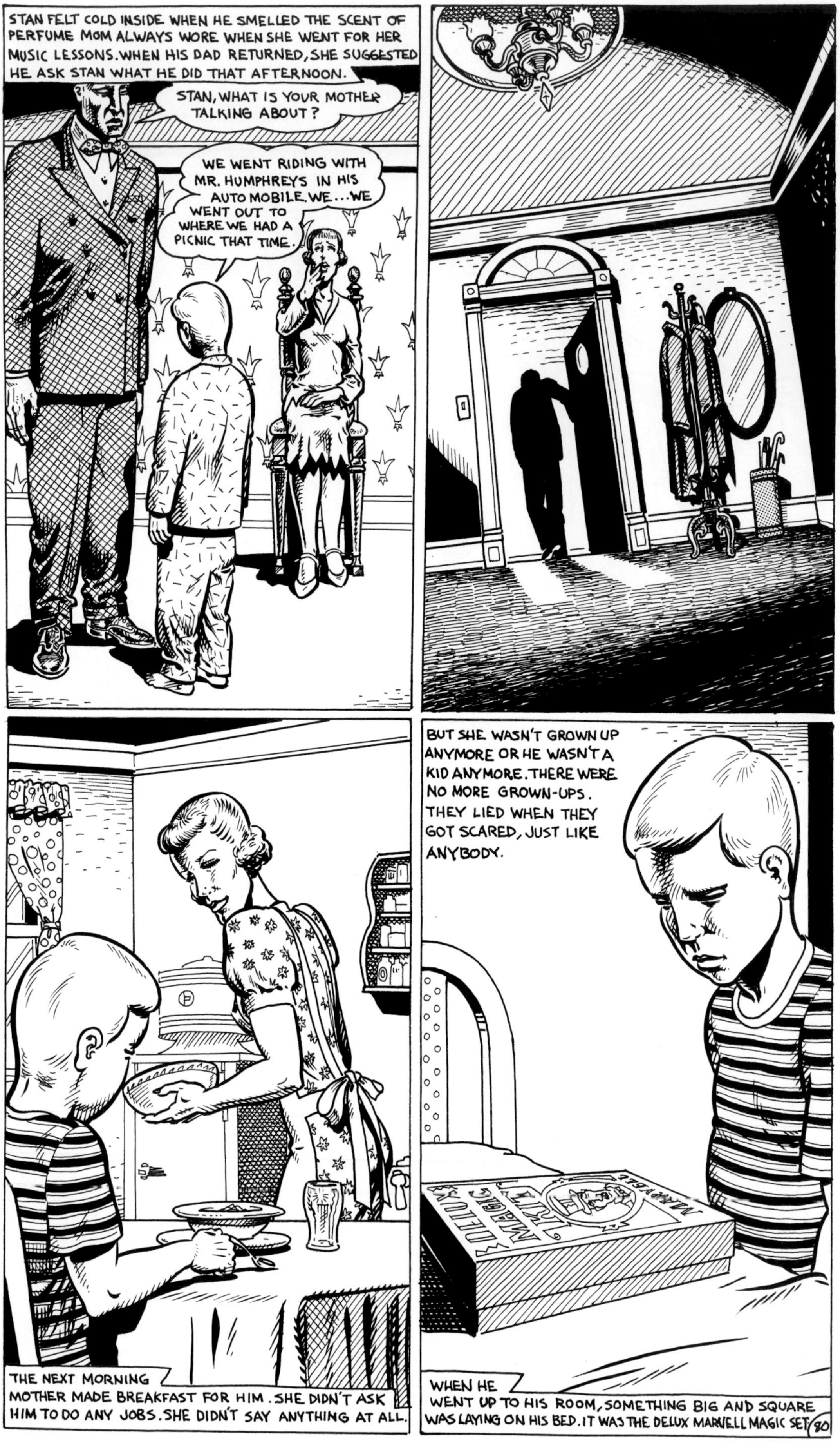
STAN FELT COLD INSIDE WHEN HE SMELLED THE SCENT OF PERFUME MOM ALWAYS WORE WHEN SHE WENT FOR HER MUSIC LESSONS. WHEN HIS DAD RETURNED, SHE SUGGESTED HE ASK STAN WHAT HE DID THAT AFTERNOON.
STAN, WHAT IS YOUR MOTHER TALKING ABOUT?
WE WENT RIDING WITH MR. HUMPHREYS IN HIS AUTO MOBILE. WE... WE WENT OUT TO WHERE WE HAD A PICNIC THAT TIME.
THE NEXT MORNING
MOTHER MADE BREAKFAST FOR HIM. SHE DIDN'T ASK HIM TO DO ANY JOBS. SHE DIDN'T SAY ANYTHING AT ALL.
BUT SHE WASN'T GROWN UP ANYMORE OR HE WASN'T A KID ANYMORE. THERE WERE NO MORE GROWN-UPS. THEY LIED WHEN THEY GOT SCARED, JUST LIKE ANYBODY.
WHEN HE
WENT UP TO HIS ROOM, SOMETHING BIG AND SQUARE WAS LAYING ON HIS BED. IT WAS THE DELUX MARVELL MAGIC SET

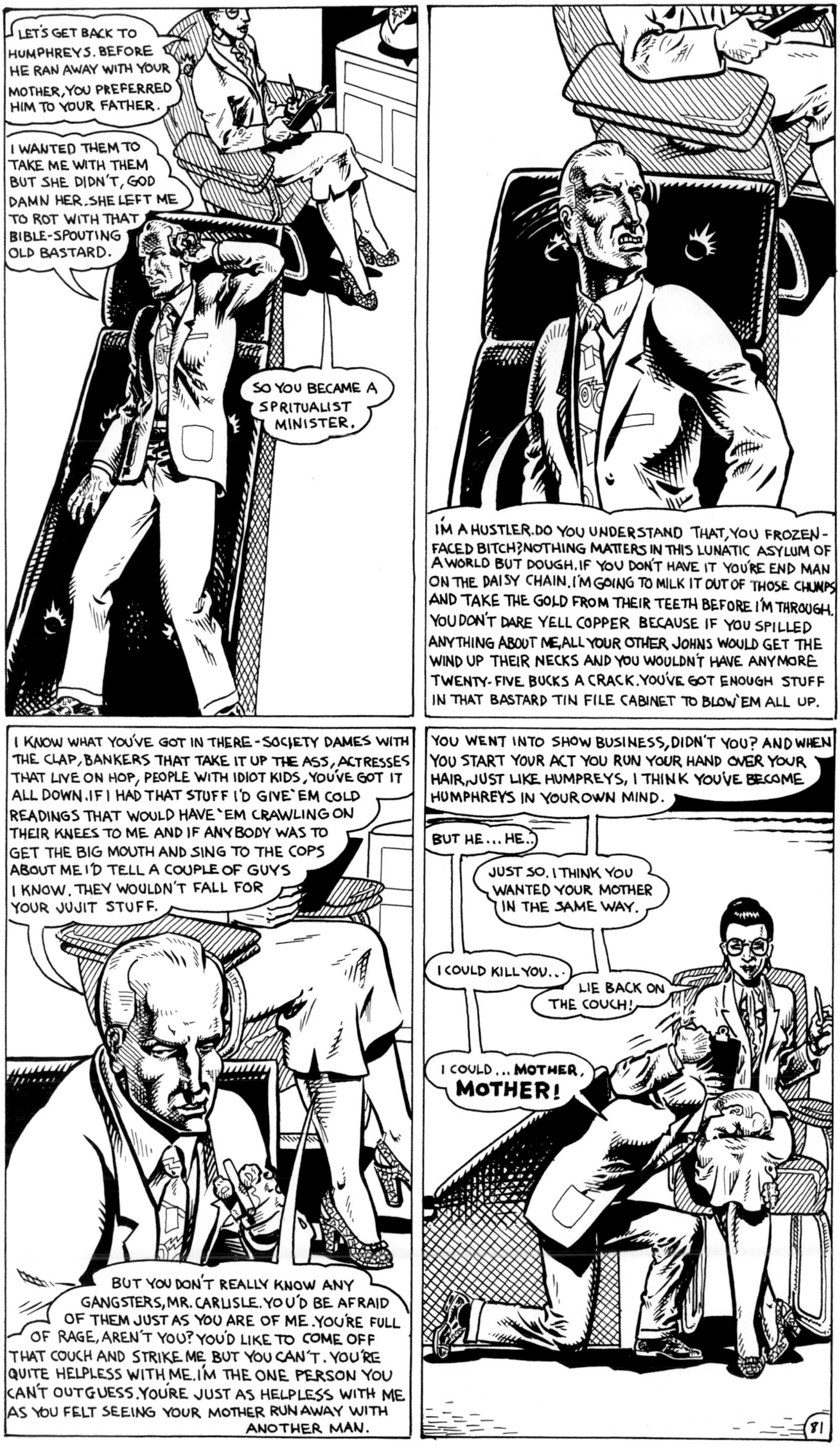
LET'S GET BACK TO HUMPHREYS. BEFORE HE RAN AWAY WITH YOUR MOTHER, YOU PREFERRED HIM TO YOUR FATHER.
I WANTED THEM TO TAKE ME WITH THEM BUT SHE DIDN'T, GOD DAMN HER. SHE LEFT ME TO ROT WITH THAT BIBLE-SPOUTING OLD BASTARD.
SO YOU BECAME A SPRITUALIST MINISTER.
I'M A HUSTLER. DO YOU UNDERSTAND THAT, YOU FROZEN-FACED BITCH? NOTHING MATTERS IN THIS LUNATIC ASYLUM OF A WORLD BUT DOUGH. IF YOU DON'T HAVE IT YOU'RE END MAN ON THE DAISY CHAIN. I'M GOING TO MILK IT OUT OF THOSE CHUMPS AND TAKE THE GOLD FROM THEIR TEETH BEFORE I'M THROUGH. YOU DON'T DARE YELL COPPER BECAUSE IF YOU SPILLED ANYTHING ABOUT ME, ALL YOUR OTHER JOHNS WOULD GET THE WIND UP THEIR NECKS AND YOU WOULDN'T HAVE ANYMORE TWENTY-FIVE BUCKS A CRACK. YOU'VE GOT ENOUGH STUFF IN THAT BASTARD TIN FILE CABINET TO BLOW 'EM ALL UP.
I KNOW WHAT YOU'VE GOT IN THERE - SOCIETY DAMES WITH THE CLAP, BANKERS THAT TAKE IT UP THE ASS, ACTRESSES THAT LIVE ON HOP, PEOPLE WITH IDIOT KIDS, YOU'VE GOT IT ALL DOWN. IF I HAD THAT STUFF I'D GIVE 'EM COLD READINGS THAT WOULD HAVE 'EM CRAWLING ON THEIR KNEES TO ME AND IF ANYBODY WAS TO GET THE BIG MOUTH AND SING TO THE COPS ABOUT ME I'D TELL A COUPLE OF GUYS I KNOW. THEY WOULDN'T FALL FOR YOUR JUJIT STUFF.
BUT YOU DON'T REALLY KNOW ANY GANGSTERS, MR. CARLISLE. YOU'D BE AFRAID OF THEM JUST AS YOU ARE OF ME. YOU'RE FULL OF RAGE, AREN'T YOU? YOU'D LIKE TO COME OFF THAT COUCH AND STRIKE ME BUT YOU CAN'T. YOU'RE QUITE HELPLESS WITH ME. I'M THE ONE PERSON YOU CAN'T OUTGUESS. YOU'RE JUST AS HELPLESS WITH ME AS YOU FELT SEEING YOUR MOTHER RUN AWAY WITH ANOTHER MAN.
YOU WENT INTO SHOW BUSINESS, DIDN'T YOU? AND WHEN YOU START YOUR ACT YOU RUN YOUR HAND OVER YOUR HAIR, JUST LIKE HUMPHREYS. I THINK YOU'VE BECOME HUMPHREYS IN YOUR OWN MIND.
BUT HE... HE..
JUST SO. I THINK YOU WANTED YOUR MOTHER IN THE SAME WAY.
I COULD KILL YOU...
LIE BACK ON THE COUCH!
I COULD... MOTHER, MOTHER!

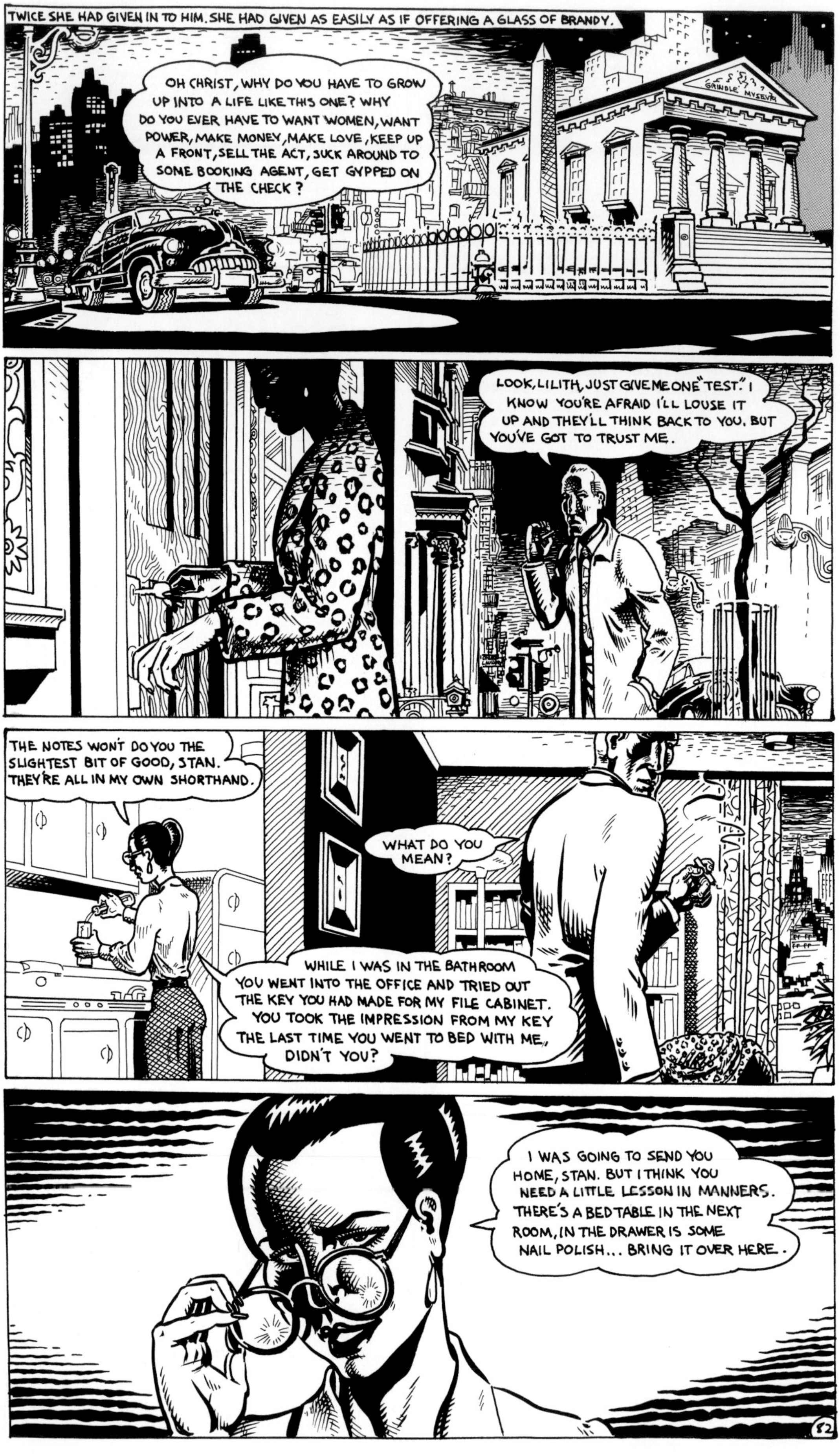
TWICE SHE HAD GIVEN IN TO HIM. SHE HAD GIVEN AS EASILY AS IF OFFERING A GLASS OF BRANDY.
OH CHRIST, WHY DO YOU HAVE TO GROW UP INTO A LIFE LIKE THIS ONE? WHY DO YOU EVER HAVE TO WANT WOMEN, WANT POWER, MAKE MONEY, MAKE LOVE, KEEP UP A FRONT, SELL THE ACT, SUCK AROUND TO SOME BOOKING AGENT, GET GYPPED ON THE CHECK?
GRINDLE MUSEUM
LOOK, LILITH, JUST GIVE ME ONE "TEST." I KNOW YOU'RE AFRAID I'LL LOUSE IT UP AND THEY'LL THINK BACK TO YOU. BUT YOU'VE GOT TO TRUST ME.
THE NOTES WON'T DO YOU THE SLIGHTEST BIT OF GOOD, STAN. THEY'RE ALL IN MY OWN SHORTHAND.
WHAT DO YOU MEAN?
WHILE I WAS IN THE BATHROOM YOU WENT INTO THE OFFICE AND TRIED OUT THE KEY YOU HAD MADE FOR MY FILE CABINET. YOU TOOK THE IMPRESSION FROM MY KEY THE LAST TIME YOU WENT TO BED WITH ME, DIDN'T YOU?
I WAS GOING TO SEND YOU HOME, STAN. BUT I THINK YOU NEED A LITTLE LESSON IN MANNERS. THERE'S A BED TABLE IN THE NEXT ROOM, IN THE DRAWER IS SOME NAIL POLISH... BRING IT OVER HERE.

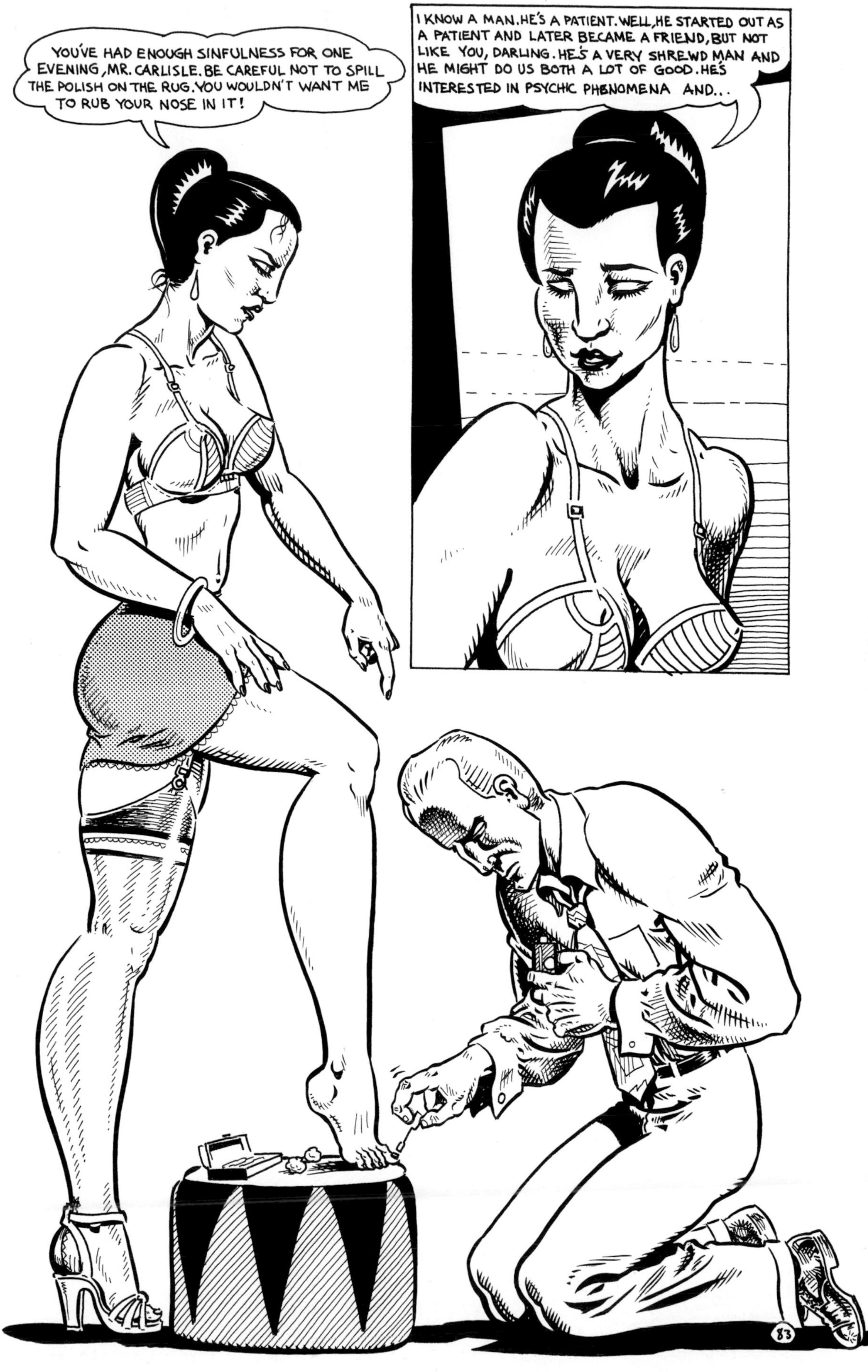
YOU'VE HAD ENOUGH SINFULNESS FOR ONE EVENING, MR. CARLISLE. BE CAREFUL NOT TO SPILL THE POLISH ON THE RUG. YOU WOULDN'T WANT ME TO RUB YOUR NOSE IN IT!
I KNOW A MAN. HE'S A PATIENT. WELL, HE STARTED OUT AS A PATIENT AND LATER BECAME A FRIEND, BUT NOT LIKE YOU, DARLING. HE'S A VERY SHREWD MAN AND HE MIGHT DO US BOTH A LOT OF GOOD. HE'S INTERESTED IN PSYCHIC PHENOMENA AND...

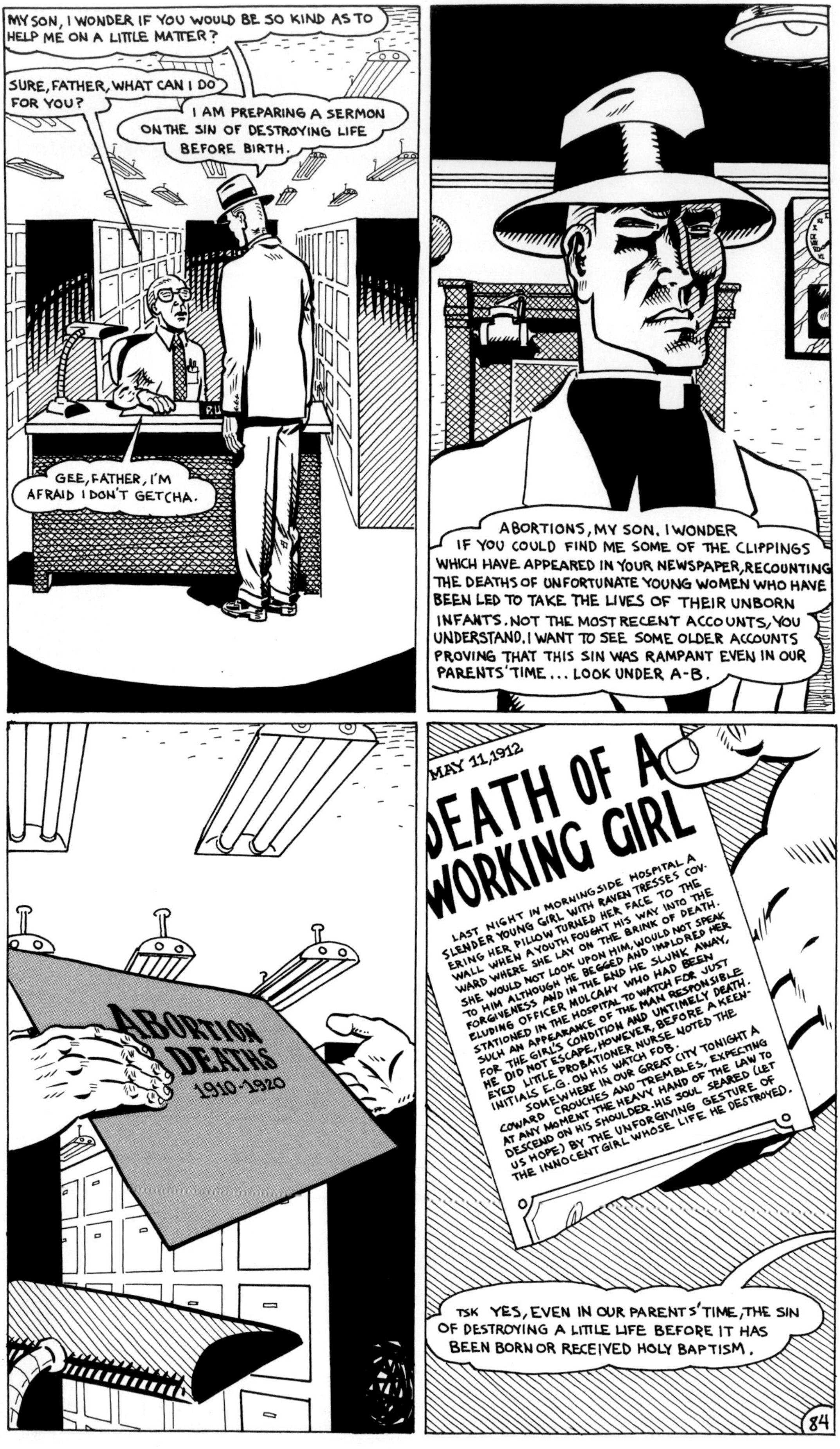
MY SON, I WONDER IF YOU WOULD BE SO KIND AS TO HELP ME ON A LITTLE MATTER?
SURE, FATHER, WHAT CAN I DO FOR YOU?
I AM PREPARING A SERMON ON THE SIN OF DESTROYING LIFE BEFORE BIRTH.
GEE, FATHER, I'M AFRAID I DON'T GETCHA.
ABORTIONS, MY SON. I WONDER IF YOU COULD FIND ME SOME OF THE CLIPPINGS WHICH HAVE APPEARED IN YOUR NEWSPAPER, RECOUNTING THE DEATHS OF UNFORTUNATE YOUNG WOMEN WHO HAVE BEEN LED TO TAKE THE LIVES OF THEIR UNBORN INFANTS. NOT THE MOST RECENT ACCOUNTS, YOU UNDERSTAND. I WANT TO SEE SOME OLDER ACCOUNTS PROVING THAT THIS SIN WAS RAMPANT EVEN IN OUR PARENTS' TIME... LOOK UNDER A-B.
ABORTION DEATHS 1910-1920
MAY 11, 1912
DEATH OF A WORKING GIRL
LAST NIGHT IN MORNINGSIDE HOSPITAL A SLENDER YOUNG GIRL WITH RAVEN TRESSES COVERING HER PILLOW TURNED HER FACE TO THE WALL WHEN A YOUTH FOUGHT HIS WAY INTO THE WARD WHERE SHE LAY ON THE BRINK OF DEATH. SHE WOULD NOT LOOK UPON HIM, WOULD NOT SPEAK TO HIM ALTHOUGH HE BEGGED AND IMPLORED HER FORGIVENESS AND IN THE END HE SLUNK AWAY, ELUDING OFFICER MULCAHY WHO HAD BEEN STATIONED IN THE HOSPITAL TO WATCH FOR JUST SUCH AN APPEARANCE OF THE MAN RESPONSIBLE FOR THE GIRL'S CONDITION AND UNTIMELY DEATH. HE DID NOT ESCAPE, HOWEVER, BEFORE A KEEN-EYED LITTLE PROBATIONER NURSE NOTED THE INITIALS E.G. ON HIS WATCH FOB.
SOMEWHERE IN OUR GREAT CITY TONIGHT A COWARD CROUCHES AND TREMBLES, EXPECTING AT ANY MOMENT THE HEAVY HAND OF THE LAW TO DESCEND ON HIS SHOULDER. HIS SOUL SEARED (LET US HOPE) BY THE UNFORGIVING GESTURE OF THE INNOCENT GIRL WHOSE LIFE HE DESTROYED.
TSK YES, EVEN IN OUR PARENTS' TIME, THE SIN OF DESTROYING A LITTLE LIFE BEFORE IT HAS BEEN BORN OR RECEIVED HOLY BAPTISM.

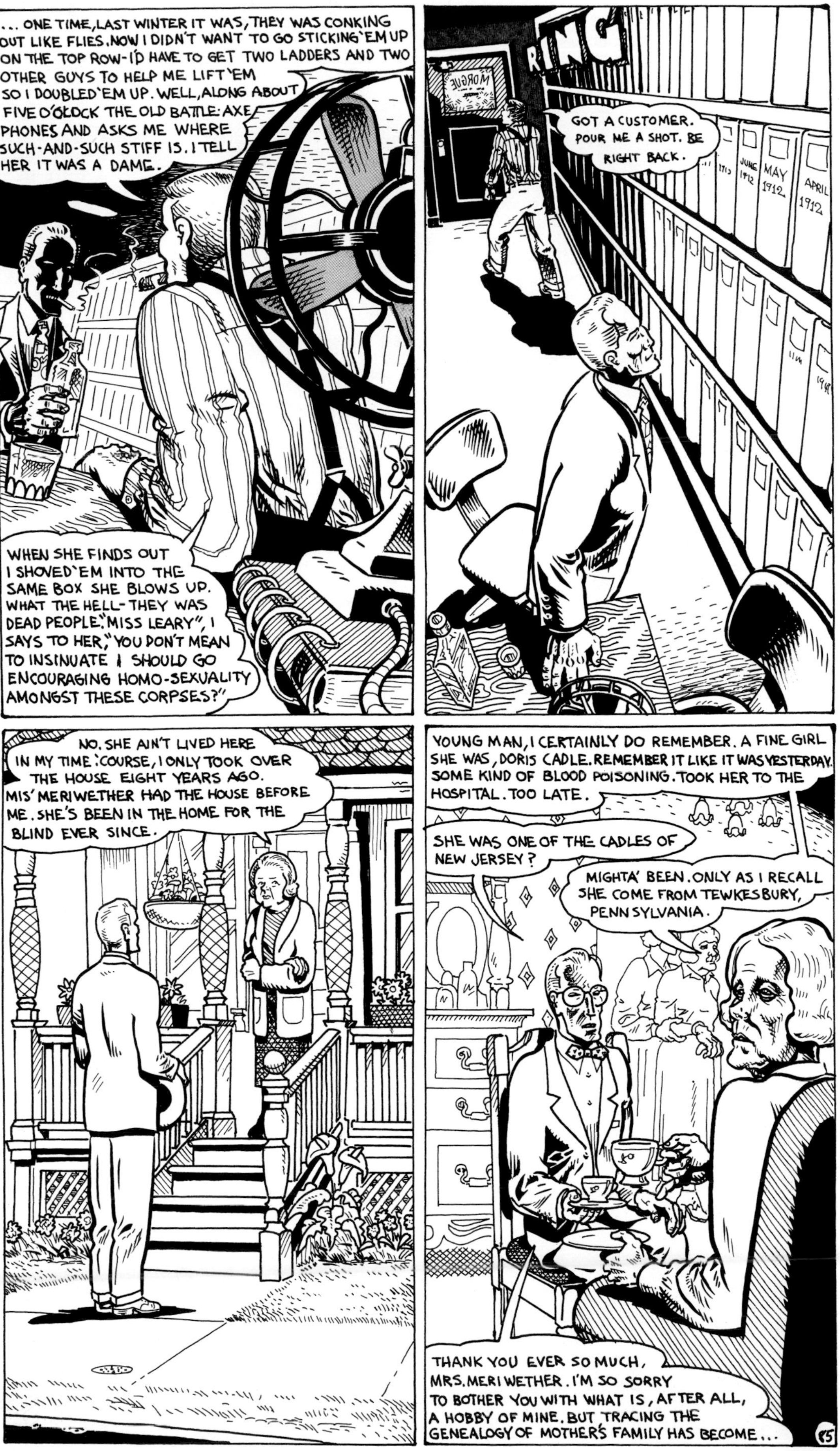
... ONE TIME, LAST WINTER IT WAS, THEY WAS CONKING OUT LIKE FLIES. NOW I DIDN'T WANT TO GO STICKING 'EM UP ON THE TOP ROW- I'D HAVE TO GET TWO LADDERS AND TWO OTHER GUYS TO HELP ME LIFT 'EM SO I DOUBLED 'EM UP. WELL, ALONG ABOUT FIVE O'CLOCK THE OLD BATTLE-AXE PHONES AND ASKS ME WHERE SUCH-AND-SUCH STIFF IS. I TELL HER IT WAS A DAME.
WHEN SHE FINDS OUT I SHOVED 'EM INTO THE SAME BOX SHE BLOWS UP. WHAT THE HELL- THEY WAS DEAD PEOPLE. "MISS LEARY", I SAYS TO HER, "YOU DON'T MEAN TO INSINUATE I SHOULD GO ENCOURAGING HOMO-SEXUALITY AMONGST THESE CORPSES?"
MORGUE
RING
GOT A CUSTOMER. POUR ME A SHOT. BE RIGHT BACK.
JUNE 1912
MAY 1912
APRIL 1912
NO, SHE AIN'T LIVED HERE IN MY TIME. 'COURSE, I ONLY TOOK OVER THE HOUSE EIGHT YEARS AGO. MIS' MERIWETHER HAD THE HOUSE BEFORE ME. SHE'S BEEN IN THE HOME FOR THE BLIND EVER SINCE.
YOUNG MAN, I CERTAINLY DO REMEMBER. A FINE GIRL SHE WAS, DORIS CADLE. REMEMBER IT LIKE IT WAS YESTERDAY. SOME KIND OF BLOOD POISONING. TOOK HER TO THE HOSPITAL. TOO LATE.
SHE WAS ONE OF THE CADLES OF NEW JERSEY?
MIGHTA' BEEN. ONLY AS I RECALL SHE COME FROM TEWKESBURY, PENNSYLVANIA.
THANK YOU EVER SO MUCH, MRS. MERIWETHER. I'M SO SORRY TO BOTHER YOU WITH WHAT IS, AFTER ALL, A HOBBY OF MINE. BUT TRACING THE GENEALOGY OF MOTHER'S FAMILY HAS BECOME...

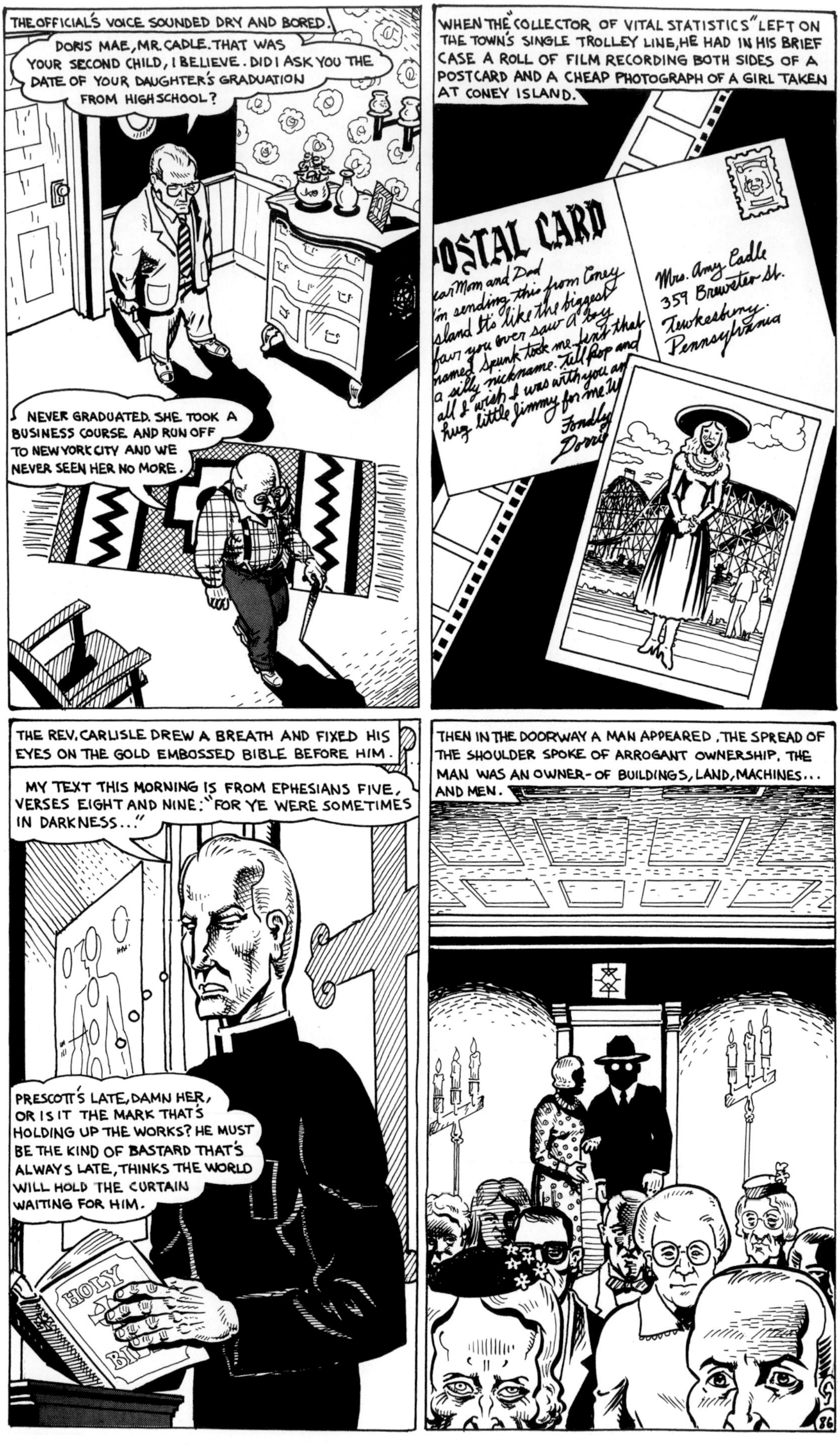
THE OFFICIAL'S VOICE SOUNDED DRY AND BORED.
DORIS MAE, MR. CADLE. THAT WAS YOUR SECOND CHILD, I BELIEVE. DID I ASK YOU THE DATE OF YOUR DAUGHTER'S GRADUATION FROM HIGH SCHOOL?
NEVER GRADUATED. SHE TOOK A BUSINESS COURSE AND RUN OFF TO NEW YORK CITY AND WE NEVER SEEN HER NO MORE.
WHEN THE "COLLECTOR OF VITAL STATISTICS" LEFT ON THE TOWN'S SINGLE TROLLEY LINE, HE HAD IN HIS BRIEF CASE A ROLL OF FILM RECORDING BOTH SIDES OF A POSTCARD AND A CHEAP PHOTOGRAPH OF A GIRL TAKEN AT CONEY ISLAND.
OSTAL CARD
ear Mom and Dad
'm sending this from Coney
sland It's like the biggest
fair you ever saw A boy
named Spunk took me. Isn't that
a silly nickname. Tell Pop and
all I wish I was with you an
hug little Jimmy for me.
Fondly
Dorri
Mrs. Amy Cadle
359 Brewster St.
Tewkesbury.
Pennsylvania
THE REV. CARLISLE DREW A BREATH AND FIXED HIS EYES ON THE GOLD EMBOSSED BIBLE BEFORE HIM.
MY TEXT THIS MORNING IS FROM EPHESIANS FIVE, VERSES EIGHT AND NINE: "FOR YE WERE SOMETIMES IN DARKNESS..."
PRESCOTT'S LATE, DAMN HER, OR IS IT THE MARK THAT'S HOLDING UP THE WORKS? HE MUST BE THE KIND OF BASTARD THAT'S ALWAYS LATE, THINKS THE WORLD WILL HOLD THE CURTAIN WAITING FOR HIM.
HOLY
BI
THEN IN THE DOORWAY A MAN APPEARED. THE SPREAD OF THE SHOULDER SPOKE OF ARROGANT OWNERSHIP. THE MAN WAS AN OWNER- OF BUILDINGS, LAND, MACHINES... AND MEN.

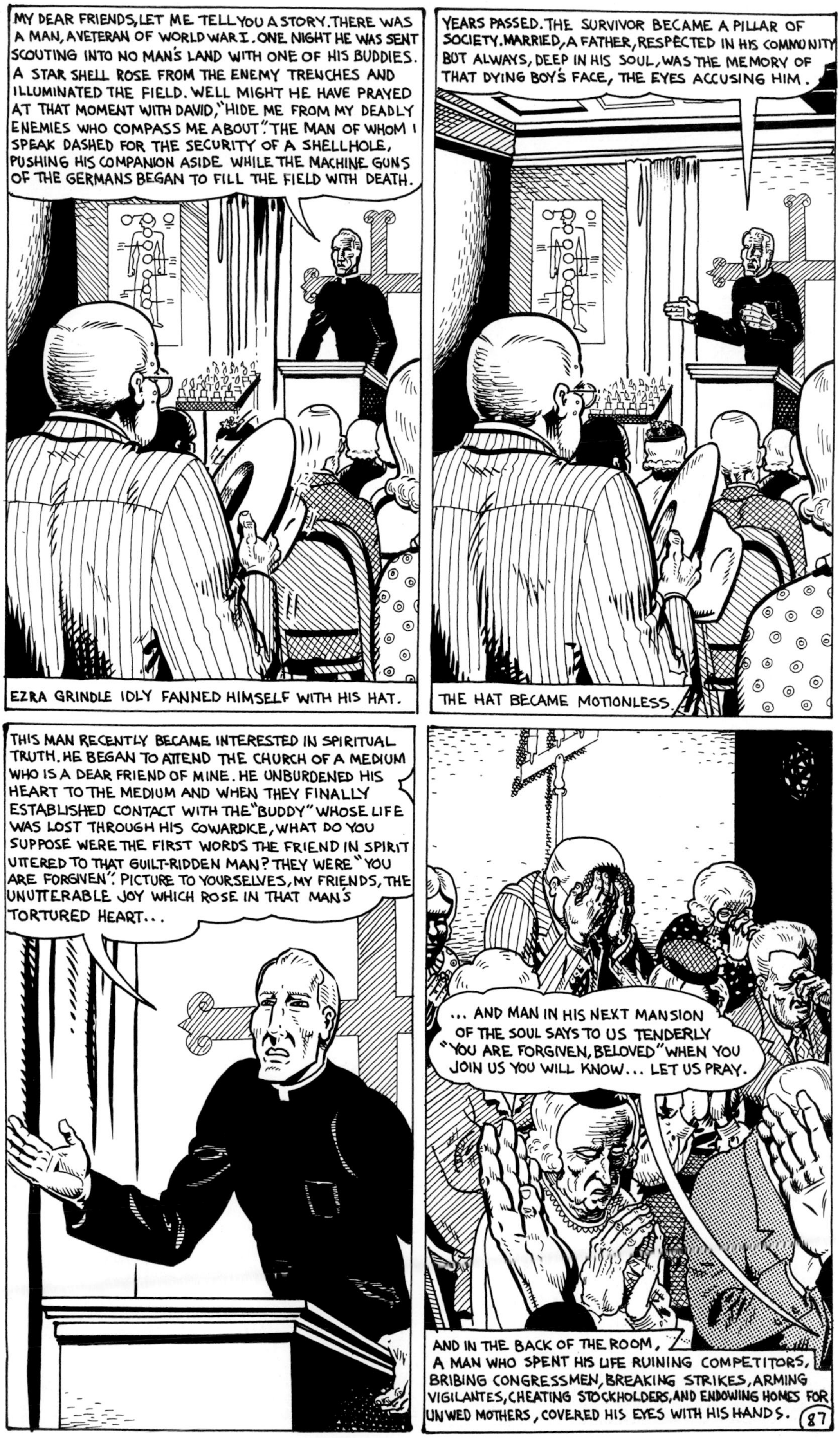
MY DEAR FRIENDS, LET ME TELL YOU A STORY. THERE WAS A MAN, A VETERAN OF WORLD WAR I. ONE NIGHT HE WAS SENT SCOUTING INTO NO MAN'S LAND WITH ONE OF HIS BUDDIES. A STAR SHELL ROSE FROM THE ENEMY TRENCHES AND ILLUMINATED THE FIELD. WELL MIGHT HE HAVE PRAYED AT THAT MOMENT WITH DAVID, "HIDE ME FROM MY DEADLY ENEMIES WHO COMPASS ME ABOUT". THE MAN OF WHOM I SPEAK DASHED FOR THE SECURITY OF A SHELLHOLE, PUSHING HIS COMPANION ASIDE WHILE THE MACHINE GUNS OF THE GERMANS BEGAN TO FILL THE FIELD WITH DEATH.
EZRA GRINDLE IDLY FANNED HIMSELF WITH HIS HAT.
YEARS PASSED. THE SURVIVOR BECAME A PILLAR OF SOCIETY. MARRIED, A FATHER, RESPECTED IN HIS COMMUNITY BUT ALWAYS, DEEP IN HIS SOUL, WAS THE MEMORY OF THAT DYING BOY'S FACE, THE EYES ACCUSING HIM.
THE HAT BECAME MOTIONLESS.
THIS MAN RECENTLY BECAME INTERESTED IN SPIRITUAL TRUTH. HE BEGAN TO ATTEND THE CHURCH OF A MEDIUM WHO IS A DEAR FRIEND OF MINE. HE UNBURDENED HIS HEART TO THE MEDIUM AND WHEN THEY FINALLY ESTABLISHED CONTACT WITH THE "BUDDY" WHOSE LIFE WAS LOST THROUGH HIS COWARDICE, WHAT DO YOU SUPPOSE WERE THE FIRST WORDS THE FRIEND IN SPIRIT UTTERED TO THAT GUILT-RIDDEN MAN? THEY WERE "YOU ARE FORGIVEN". PICTURE TO YOURSELVES, MY FRIENDS, THE UNUTTERABLE JOY WHICH ROSE IN THAT MAN'S TORTURED HEART...
... AND MAN IN HIS NEXT MANSION OF THE SOUL SAYS TO US TENDERLY "YOU ARE FORGIVEN, BELOVED" WHEN YOU JOIN US YOU WILL KNOW... LET US PRAY.
AND IN THE BACK OF THE ROOM, A MAN WHO SPENT HIS LIFE RUINING COMPETITORS, BRIBING CONGRESSMEN, BREAKING STRIKES, ARMING VIGILANTES, CHEATING STOCKHOLDERS, AND ENDOWING HOMES FOR UNWED MOTHERS, COVERED HIS EYES WITH HIS HANDS.

REVEREND, THEY TELL ME YOU BRING VOICES OUT OF TRUMPETS.

I HAVE HEARD VOICES FROM TRUMPETS, I DON'T BRING THEM. MEDIUMSHIP IS EITHER A NATURAL GIFT OR ACQUIRED BY DEVOTION AND STUDY.

I FOLLOW YOU THERE, CARLISLE. IN ONE OF YOUR SERMONS YOU SAID SOMETHING ABOUT SPIRITUALISM BEING THE ONLY FAITH THAT OFFERS PROOF OF SURVIVAL. I REMEMBER YOU SAID THAT "SHOW ME" IS THE WATCHWORD OF AMERICAN BUSINESS. WELL, YOU HIT THE NAIL ON THE HEAD THAT TIME. I'M JUST ASKING TO BE SHOWN, THAT'S ALL.

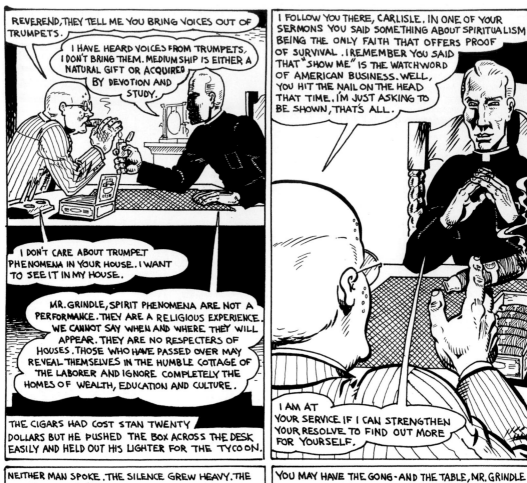

I DON'T CARE ABOUT TRUMPET PHENOMENA IN YOUR HOUSE. I WANT TO SEE IT IN MY HOUSE.

MR. GRINDLE, SPIRIT PHENOMENA ARE NOT A PERFORMANCE. THEY ARE A RELIGIOUS EXPERIENCE. WE CANNOT SAY WHEN AND WHERE THEY WILL APPEAR. THEY ARE NO RESPECTERS OF HOUSES. THOSE WHO HAVE PASSED OVER MAY REVEAL THEMSELVES IN THE HUMBLE COTTAGE OF THE LABORER AND IGNORE COMPLETELY THE HOMES OF WEALTH, EDUCATION AND CULTURE.

THE CIGARS HAD COST STAN TWENTY DOLLARS BUT HE PUSHED THE BOX ACROSS THE DESK EASILY AND HELD OUT HIS LIGHTER FOR THE TYCOON.

I AM AT YOUR SERVICE IF I CAN STRENGTHEN YOUR RESOLVE TO FIND OUT MORE FOR YOURSELF.

NEITHER MAN SPOKE. THE SILENCE GREW HEAVY. THE INDUSTRIALIST SEEMED TO BE TRYING TO FORCE THE OTHER TO BREAK IT FIRST.

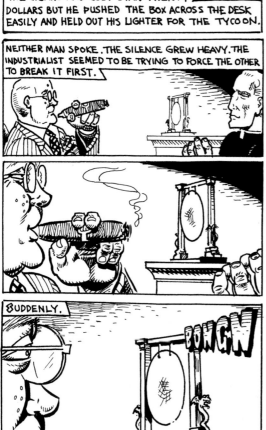

SUDDENLY.

BONGN

YOU MAY HAVE THE GONG - AND THE TABLE, MR. GRINDLE. IT NEVER BEFORE HAS RUNG BY WHAT WE CALL THE ODETIC FORCE. SOMEONE MUST BE TRYING TO GET THROUGH TO YOU, BUT IT IS DIFFICULT - YOUR INNATE SKEPTICISM IS THE BARRIER.

ON THE BIG MAN'S FACE, STAN COULD READ THE CONFLICT - THE FEAR OF BEING DECEIVED AGAINST THE DESIRE TO BE FORGIVEN BY DORIS CADLE.

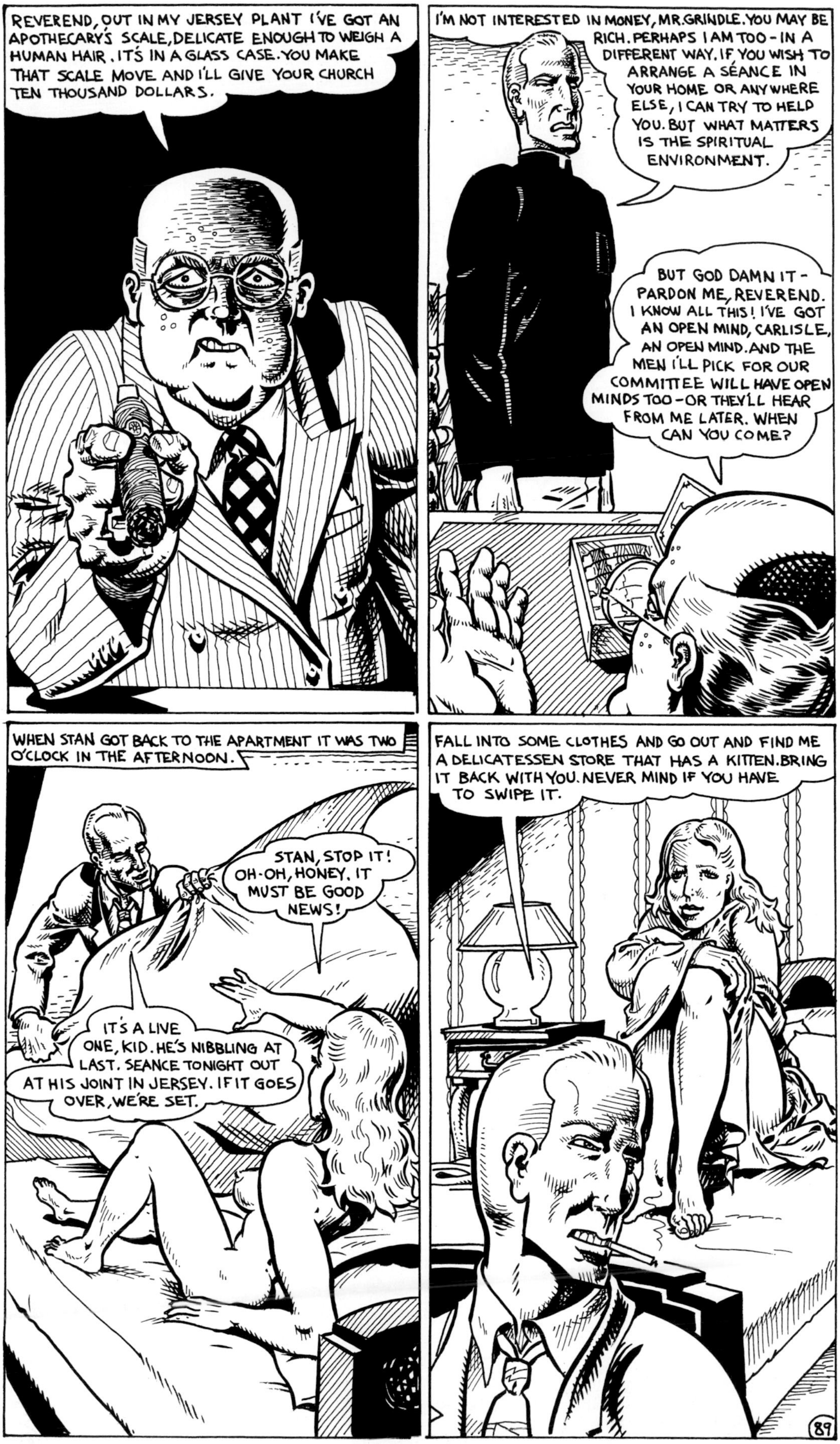
REVEREND, OUT IN MY JERSEY PLANT I'VE GOT AN APOTHECARY'S SCALE, DELICATE ENOUGH TO WEIGH A HUMAN HAIR. IT'S IN A GLASS CASE. YOU MAKE THAT SCALE MOVE AND I'LL GIVE YOUR CHURCH TEN THOUSAND DOLLARS.
I'M NOT INTERESTED IN MONEY, MR. GRINDLE. YOU MAY BE RICH. PERHAPS I AM TOO - IN A DIFFERENT WAY. IF YOU WISH TO ARRANGE A SÉANCE IN YOUR HOME OR ANYWHERE ELSE, I CAN TRY TO HELP YOU. BUT WHAT MATTERS IS THE SPIRITUAL ENVIRONMENT.
BUT GOD DAMN IT - PARDON ME, REVEREND. I KNOW ALL THIS! I'VE GOT AN OPEN MIND, CARLISLE, AN OPEN MIND. AND THE MEN I'LL PICK FOR OUR COMMITTEE WILL HAVE OPEN MINDS TOO - OR THEY'LL HEAR FROM ME LATER. WHEN CAN YOU COME?
WHEN STAN GOT BACK TO THE APARTMENT IT WAS TWO O'CLOCK IN THE AFTERNOON.
STAN, STOP IT! OH-OH, HONEY, IT MUST BE GOOD NEWS!
IT'S A LIVE ONE, KID. HE'S NIBBLING AT LAST. SEANCE TONIGHT OUT AT HIS JOINT IN JERSEY. IF IT GOES OVER, WE'RE SET.
FALL INTO SOME CLOTHES AND GO OUT AND FIND ME A DELICATESSEN STORE THAT HAS A KITTEN. BRING IT BACK WITH YOU. NEVER MIND IF YOU HAVE TO SWIPE IT.

WHEN SHE HAD GONE HE EASED THE ERASER FROM THE END OF A PENCIL AND BORED INTO THE SHAFT WITH A HAND DRILL.

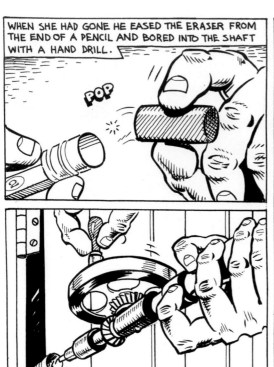

POP

THEN HE PUSHED THE ERASER BACK AND PUT THE PENCIL IN HIS POCKET.

THE LIMOUSINE ROLLED THROUGH MANHATTAN, UNDER THE RIVER WITH TUNNEL WALLS GLEAMING, PAST THE SMOKE OF NORTH JERSEY AND ACROSS A DESOLATION OF SALTMARSHES. THE CAR SLOWED DOWN AT A WIRE FENCE.

WHEN MOLLY CAME BACK WITH A KITTEN, STAN TOOK IT INSIDE THE BATHROOM AND SHUT HIMSELF IN.

GOLLY, STAN'S BEEN IN THERE A HALF AN HOUR.

INSIDE THE CONCRETE SHACK THE REVEREND STANTON CARLISLE WAS SEARCHED AND FINGERPRINTED.

DOES MR. GRINDLE KNOW ABOUT THIS?

SEARCH ME, REVEREND; YOU CAN ASK HIM. NOTHING PERSONAL. THE NEXT GUY MIGHT BE A SENATOR, ORDERS OF MR. ANDERSON, HEAD OF PLANT SECURITY.

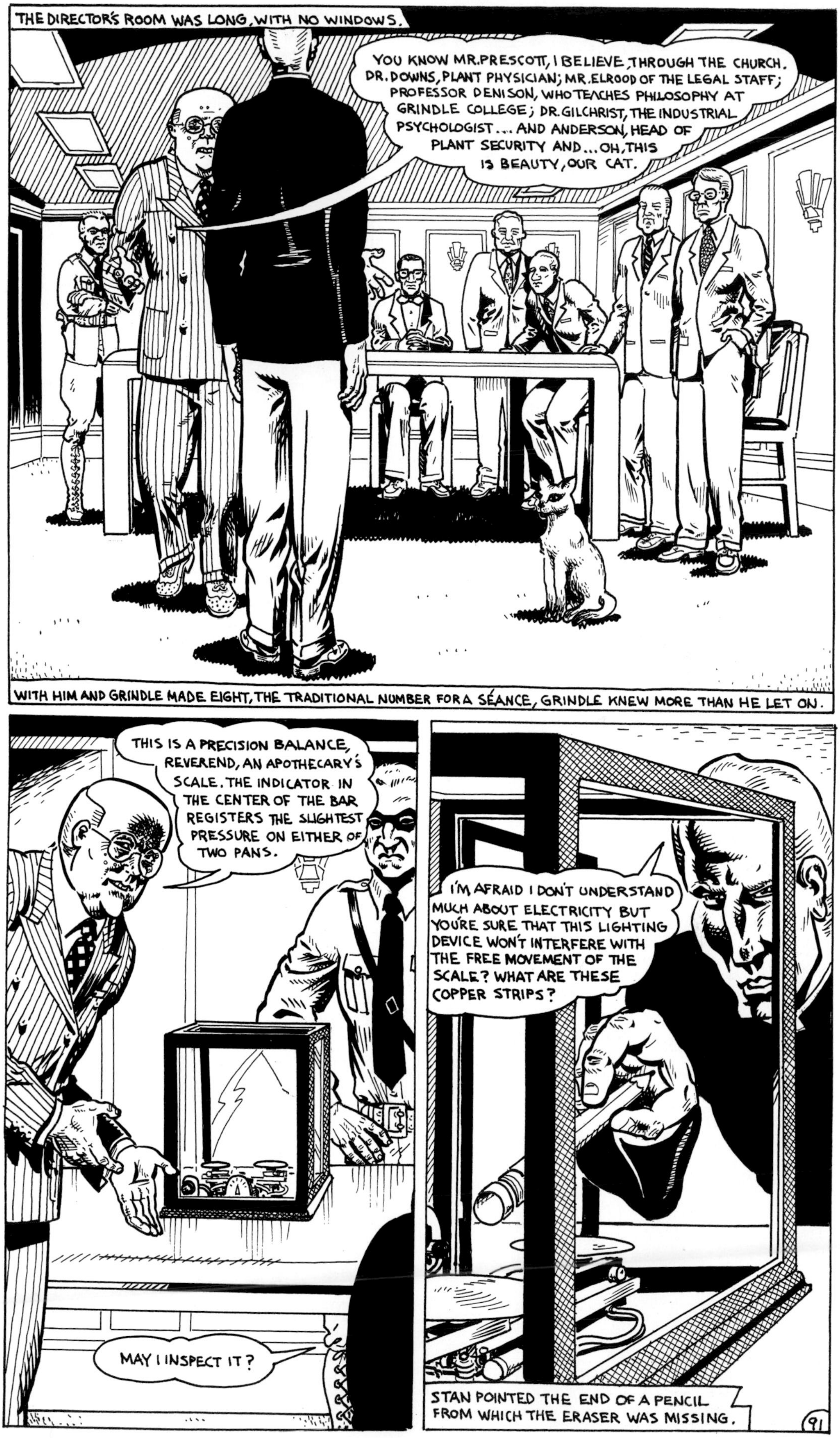
THE DIRECTOR'S ROOM WAS LONG, WITH NO WINDOWS.
YOU KNOW MR. PRESCOTT, I BELIEVE, THROUGH THE CHURCH. DR. DOWNS, PLANT PHYSICIAN; MR. ELROOD OF THE LEGAL STAFF; PROFESSOR DENISON, WHO TEACHES PHILOSOPHY AT GRINDLE COLLEGE; DR. GILCHRIST, THE INDUSTRIAL PSYCHOLOGIST... AND ANDERSON, HEAD OF PLANT SECURITY AND... OH, THIS IS BEAUTY, OUR CAT.
WITH HIM AND GRINDLE MADE EIGHT, THE TRADITIONAL NUMBER FOR A SÉANCE, GRINDLE KNEW MORE THAN HE LET ON.
THIS IS A PRECISION BALANCE, REVEREND, AN APOTHECARY'S SCALE. THE INDICATOR IN THE CENTER OF THE BAR REGISTERS THE SLIGHTEST PRESSURE ON EITHER OF TWO PANS.
MAY I INSPECT IT?
I'M AFRAID I DON'T UNDERSTAND MUCH ABOUT ELECTRICITY BUT YOU'RE SURE THAT THIS LIGHTING DEVICE WON'T INTERFERE WITH THE FREE MOVEMENT OF THE SCALE? WHAT ARE THESE COPPER STRIPS?
STAN POINTED THE END OF A PENCIL FROM WHICH THE ERASER WAS MISSING.

ANDERSON SWIFTLY SHUT THE GLASS DOOR.

DON'T TOUCH ANYTHING, REVEREND.

THE MEDIUM HAD BEEN SEARCHED AT THE GATE. THEIR EYES HAD BEEN ON HIM EVERY SECOND SINCE HE ARRIVED. HE HAD NEVER TOUCHED THE INSTRUMENT. THEY HAD ALL BEEN WARNED TO LOOK FOR THREADS...

..MNG...KGIFF,

HE FELT THE SALIVA IN HIS MOUTH THICKENING. HIS TONGUE WAS DRY. HE FORCED THE SALIVA OUT OVER HIS LOWER LIP. THIS WAS ONE TIME WHEN HE DIDN'T HAVE TO FAKE THE FOAM.

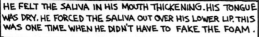

A GASP RAN AROUND THE WAITING CIRCLE.

THE HENLEY COLLEGE LIBRARY

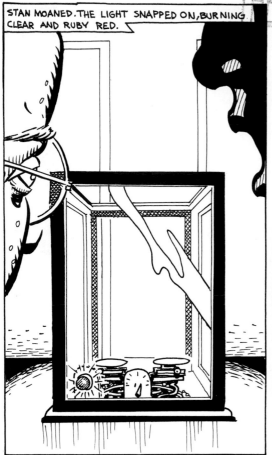

STAN MOANED. THE LIGHT SNAPPED ON, BURNING CLEAR AND RUBY RED.

I COULD GIVE YOU A GOOD SPECIMEN, RIGHT IN THE EYE.

STAN FELT SOMETHING TOUCH HIS LIPS; HE LET HIS EYELIDS FLICK OPEN. THE DOCTOR WAS STANDING OVER HIM COLLECTING SAMPLES FROM THE SIDE OF HIS MOUTH.

ALONE, WITH GRINDLE, STAN BEGAN TO RECOVER. LATER, ON THE STEPS OF THE PLANT, THE OWNER TOOK OUT TWO ENVELOPES.

HERE, MIGHT AS WELL GIVE THIS TO YOU NOW.

PLEASE, MR. GRINDLE, LET'S NOT TALK ABOUT MONEY. IF I HAVE GIVEN YOU PROOF...

YOU HAVE SHOWN ME SOMETHING THAT CANNOT BE EXPLAINED THROUGH TRICKERY OR FRAUD.

WELL, THE CHURCH CAN ALWAYS USE DONATIONS, MR. GRINDLE.

RRRUP

THIS OTHER WE WON'T NEED... IT WAS A WARRANT FOR YOUR ARREST FOR CONSPIRACY WITH INTENT TO DEFRAUD.

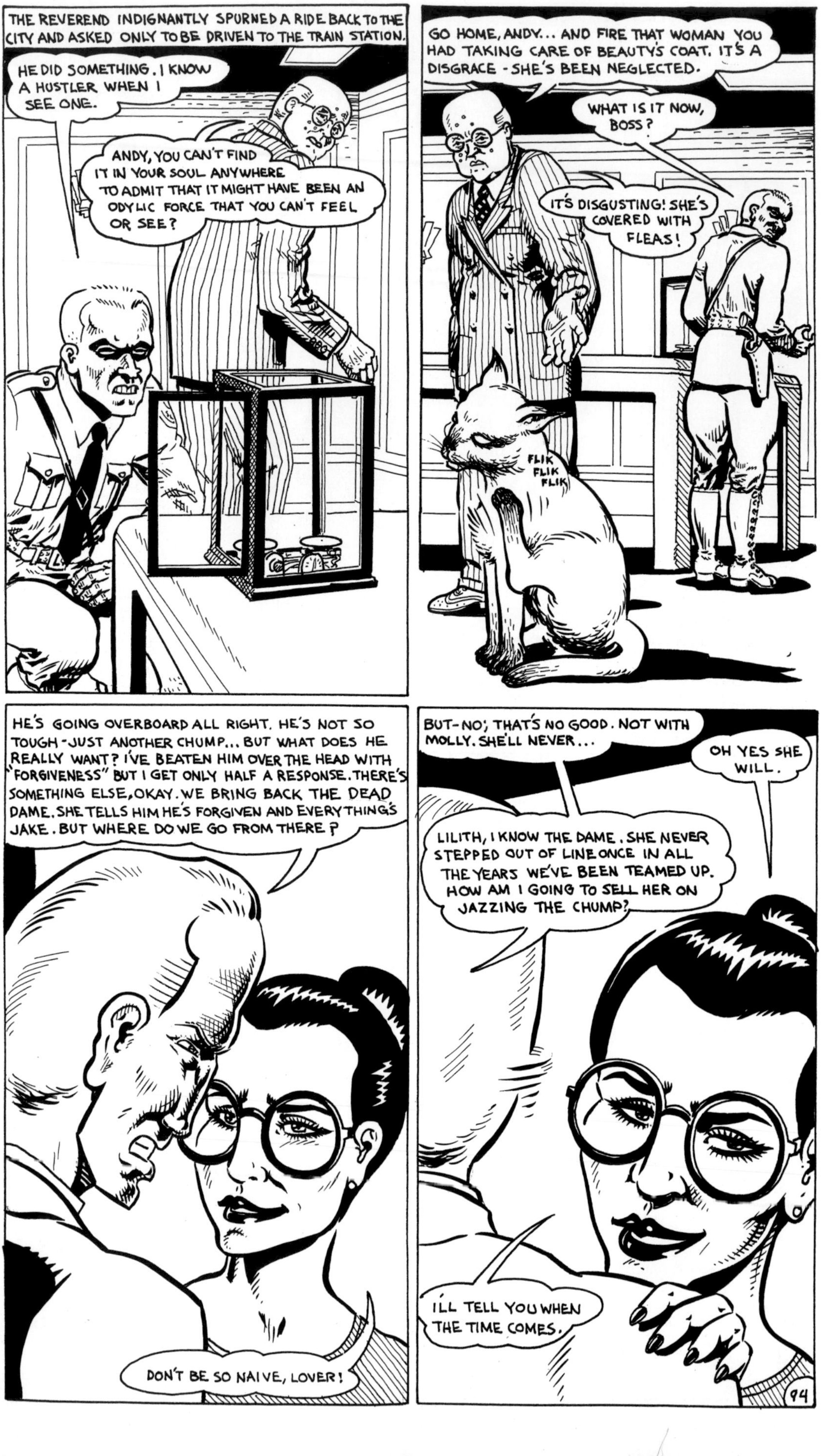
THE REVEREND INDIGNANTLY SPURNED A RIDE BACK TO THE CITY AND ASKED ONLY TO BE DRIVEN TO THE TRAIN STATION.
HE DID SOMETHING. I KNOW A HUSTLER WHEN I SEE ONE.
ANDY, YOU CAN'T FIND IT IN YOUR SOUL ANYWHERE TO ADMIT THAT IT MIGHT HAVE BEEN AN ODYLIC FORCE THAT YOU CAN'T FEEL OR SEE?
GO HOME, ANDY... AND FIRE THAT WOMAN YOU HAD TAKING CARE OF BEAUTY'S COAT. IT'S A DISGRACE - SHE'S BEEN NEGLECTED.
WHAT IS IT NOW, BOSS?
IT'S DISGUSTING! SHE'S COVERED WITH FLEAS!
FLIK FLIK FLIK
HE'S GOING OVERBOARD ALL RIGHT. HE'S NOT SO TOUGH - JUST ANOTHER CHUMP... BUT WHAT DOES HE REALLY WANT? I'VE BEATEN HIM OVER THE HEAD WITH "FORGIVENESS" BUT I GET ONLY HALF A RESPONSE. THERE'S SOMETHING ELSE, OKAY. WE BRING BACK THE DEAD DAME. SHE TELLS HIM HE'S FORGIVEN AND EVERYTHING'S JAKE. BUT WHERE DO WE GO FROM THERE?
DON'T BE SO NAIVE, LOVER!
BUT - NO; THAT'S NO GOOD. NOT WITH MOLLY. SHE'LL NEVER...
LILITH, I KNOW THE DAME. SHE NEVER STEPPED OUT OF LINE ONCE IN ALL THE YEARS WE'VE BEEN TEAMED UP. HOW AM I GOING TO SELL HER ON JAZZING THE CHUMP?
OH YES SHE WILL.
I'LL TELL YOU WHEN THE TIME COMES.

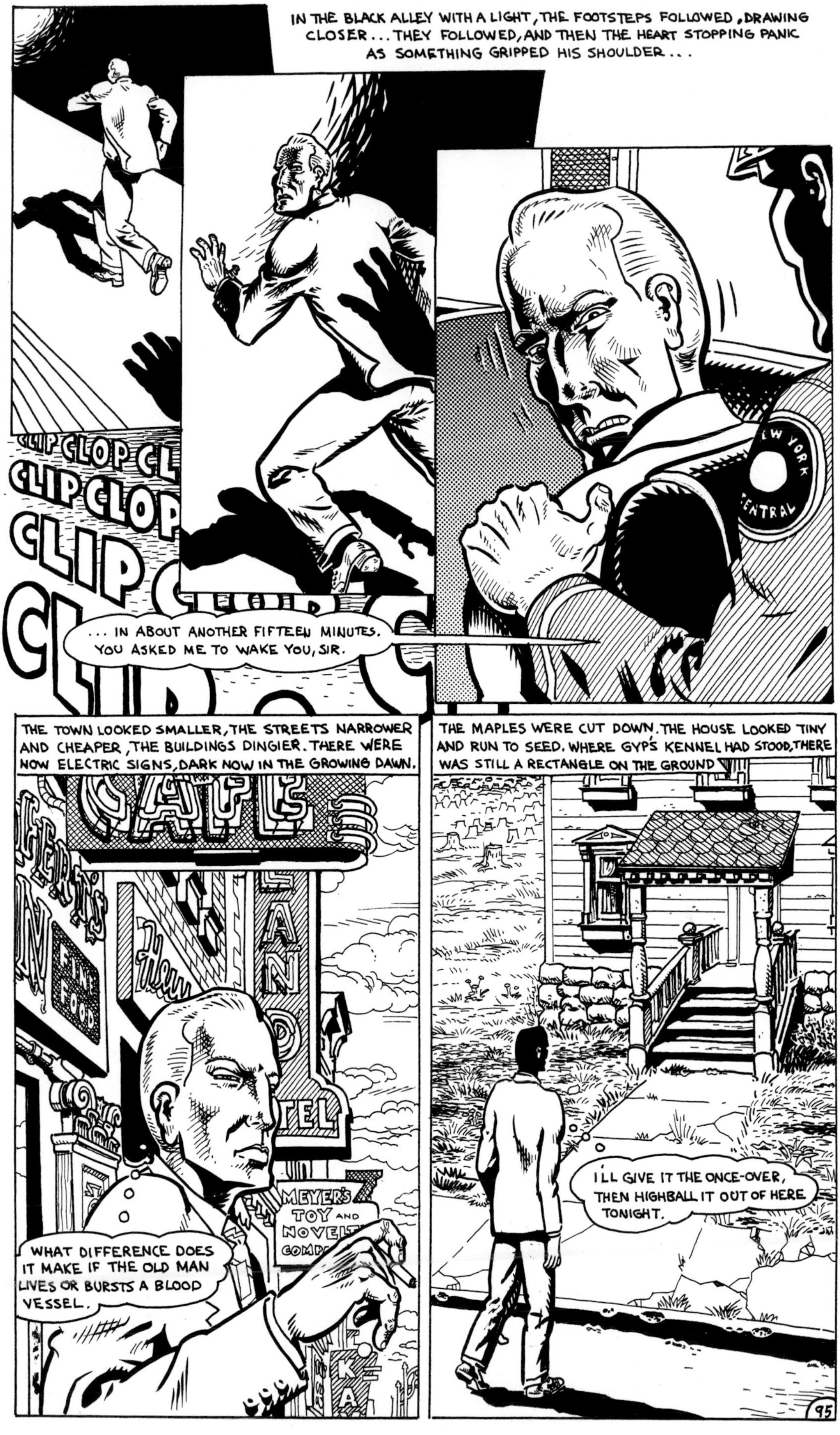

IN THE BLACK ALLEY WITH A LIGHT, THE FOOTSTEPS FOLLOWED, DRAWING CLOSER... THEY FOLLOWED, AND THEN THE HEART STOPPING PANIC AS SOMETHING GRIPPED HIS SHOULDER...
CLIP CLOP CL
CLIP CLOP
CLIP
NEW YORK CENTRAL
... IN ABOUT ANOTHER FIFTEEN MINUTES. YOU ASKED ME TO WAKE YOU, SIR.
THE TOWN LOOKED SMALLER, THE STREETS NARROWER AND CHEAPER, THE BUILDINGS DINGIER. THERE WERE NOW ELECTRIC SIGNS, DARK NOW IN THE GROWING DAWN.
CAFE
FINE FOOD
TEL
MEYER'S TOY AND NOVELT COMP
WHAT DIFFERENCE DOES IT MAKE IF THE OLD MAN LIVES OR BURSTS A BLOOD VESSEL.
THE MAPLES WERE CUT DOWN. THE HOUSE LOOKED TINY AND RUN TO SEED. WHERE GYP'S KENNEL HAD STOOD, THERE WAS STILL A RECTANGLE ON THE GROUND
I'LL GIVE IT THE ONCE-OVER, THEN HIGHBALL IT OUT OF HERE TONIGHT.

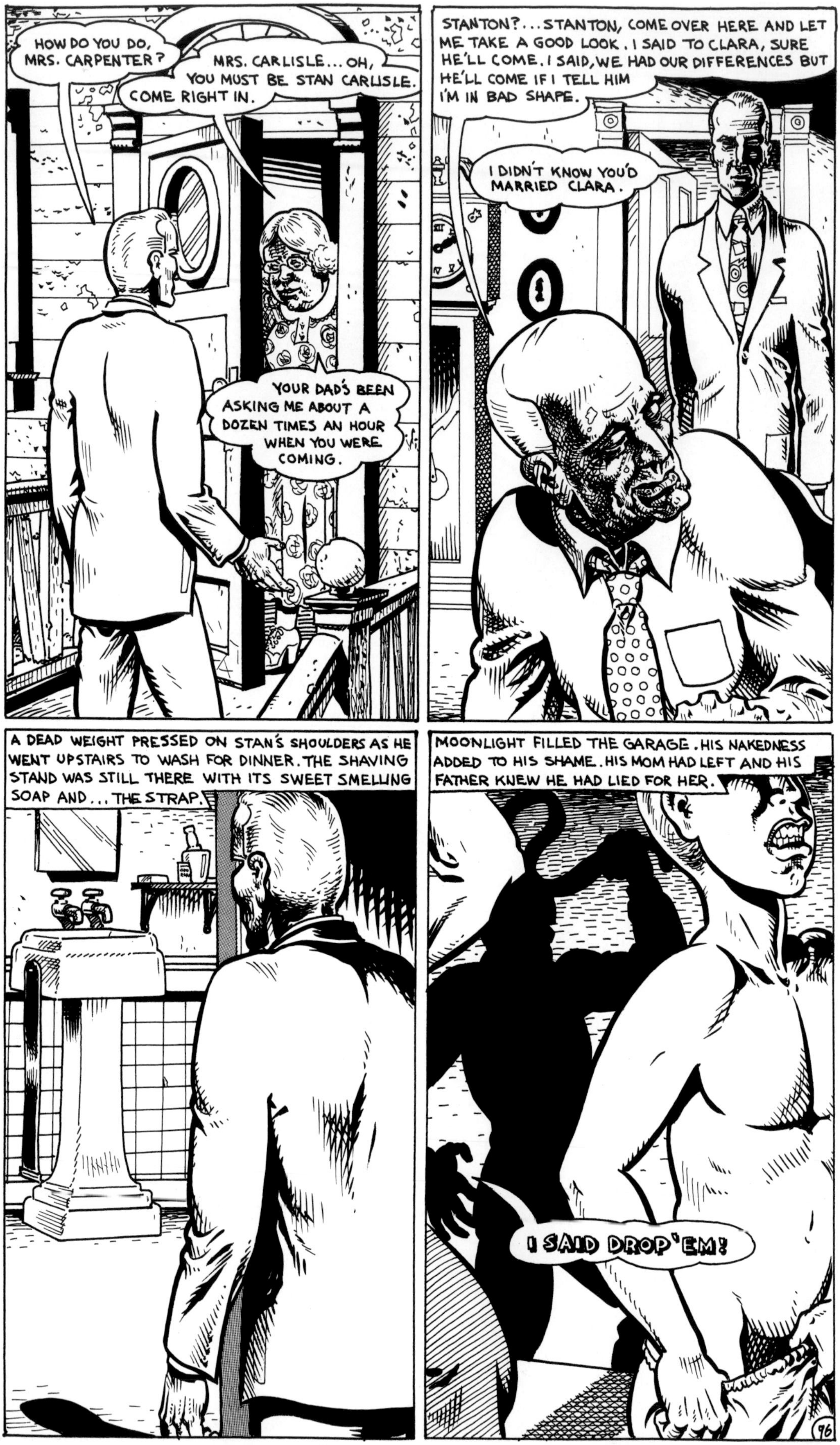
HOW DO YOU DO, MRS. CARPENTER?
MRS. CARLISLE... OH, YOU MUST BE STAN CARLISLE. COME RIGHT IN.
YOUR DAD'S BEEN ASKING ME ABOUT A DOZEN TIMES AN HOUR WHEN YOU WERE COMING.
STANTON?... STANTON, COME OVER HERE AND LET ME TAKE A GOOD LOOK. I SAID TO CLARA, SURE HE'LL COME. I SAID, WE HAD OUR DIFFERENCES BUT HE'LL COME IF I TELL HIM I'M IN BAD SHAPE.
I DIDN'T KNOW YOU'D MARRIED CLARA.
A DEAD WEIGHT PRESSED ON STAN'S SHOULDERS AS HE WENT UPSTAIRS TO WASH FOR DINNER. THE SHAVING STAND WAS STILL THERE WITH ITS SWEET SMELLING SOAP AND... THE STRAP.
MOONLIGHT FILLED THE GARAGE. HIS NAKEDNESS ADDED TO HIS SHAME. HIS MOM HAD LEFT AND HIS FATHER KNEW HE HAD LIED FOR HER.
I SAID DROP 'EM!
96

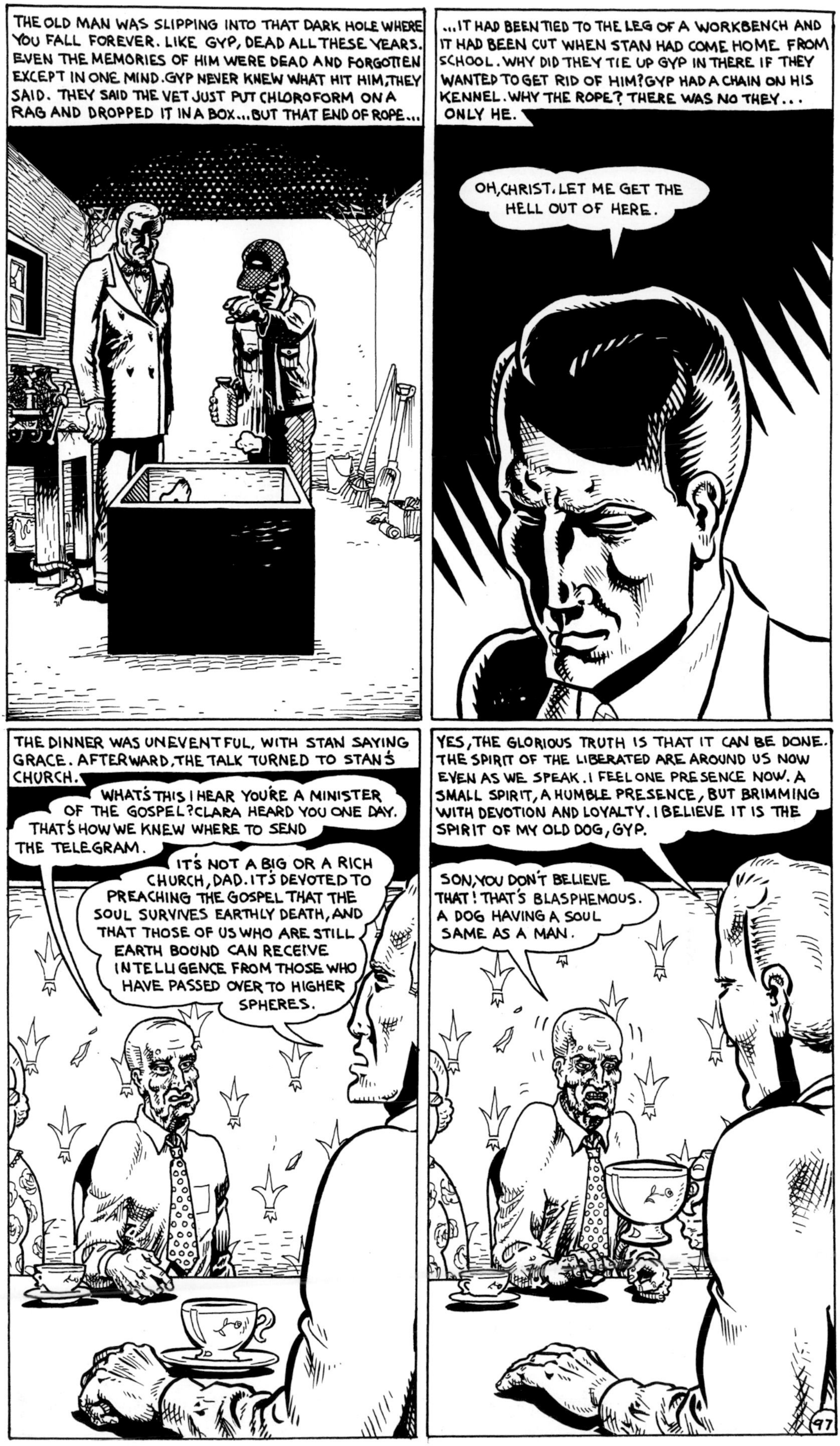
THE OLD MAN WAS SLIPPING INTO THAT DARK HOLE WHERE YOU FALL FOREVER. LIKE GYP, DEAD ALL THESE YEARS. EVEN THE MEMORIES OF HIM WERE DEAD AND FORGOTTEN EXCEPT IN ONE MIND. GYP NEVER KNEW WHAT HIT HIM, THEY SAID. THEY SAID THE VET JUST PUT CHLOROFORM ON A RAG AND DROPPED IT IN A BOX... BUT THAT END OF ROPE...
...IT HAD BEEN TIED TO THE LEG OF A WORKBENCH AND IT HAD BEEN CUT WHEN STAN HAD COME HOME FROM SCHOOL. WHY DID THEY TIE UP GYP IN THERE IF THEY WANTED TO GET RID OF HIM? GYP HAD A CHAIN ON HIS KENNEL. WHY THE ROPE? THERE WAS NO THEY... ONLY HE.
OH, CHRIST. LET ME GET THE HELL OUT OF HERE.
THE DINNER WAS UNEVENTFUL, WITH STAN SAYING GRACE. AFTERWARD, THE TALK TURNED TO STAN'S CHURCH.
WHAT'S THIS I HEAR YOU'RE A MINISTER OF THE GOSPEL? CLARA HEARD YOU ONE DAY. THAT'S HOW WE KNEW WHERE TO SEND THE TELEGRAM.
IT'S NOT A BIG OR A RICH CHURCH, DAD. IT'S DEVOTED TO PREACHING THE GOSPEL THAT THE SOUL SURVIVES EARTHLY DEATH, AND THAT THOSE OF US WHO ARE STILL EARTH BOUND CAN RECEIVE INTELLIGENCE FROM THOSE WHO HAVE PASSED OVER TO HIGHER SPHERES.
YES, THE GLORIOUS TRUTH IS THAT IT CAN BE DONE. THE SPIRIT OF THE LIBERATED ARE AROUND US NOW EVEN AS WE SPEAK. I FEEL ONE PRESENCE NOW. A SMALL SPIRIT, A HUMBLE PRESENCE, BUT BRIMMING WITH DEVOTION AND LOYALTY. I BELIEVE IT IS THE SPIRIT OF MY OLD DOG, GYP.
SON, YOU DON'T BELIEVE THAT! THAT'S BLASPHEMOUS. A DOG HAVING A SOUL SAME AS A MAN.
97

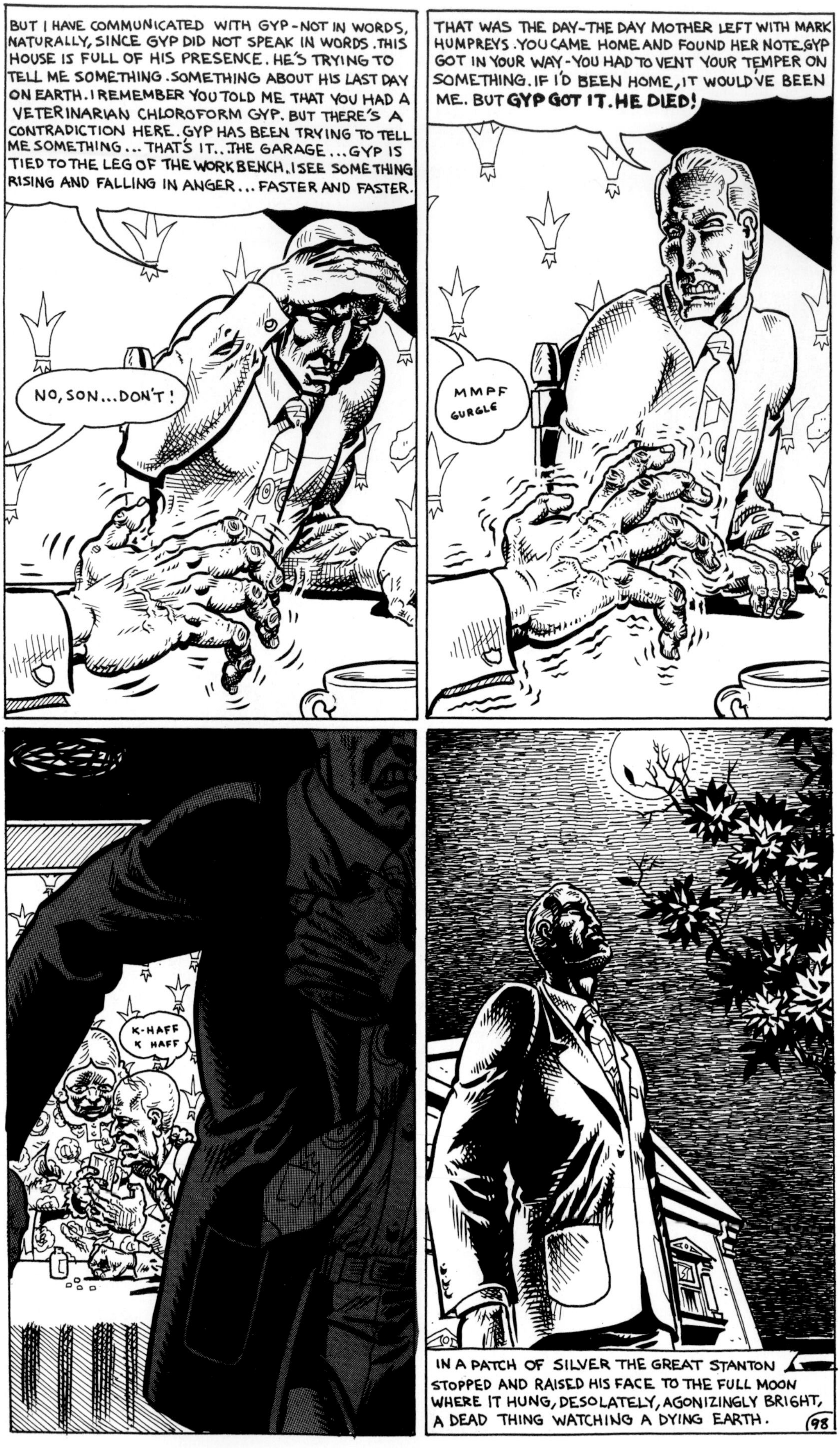
BUT I HAVE COMMUNICATED WITH GYP - NOT IN WORDS, NATURALLY, SINCE GYP DID NOT SPEAK IN WORDS. THIS HOUSE IS FULL OF HIS PRESENCE. HE'S TRYING TO TELL ME SOMETHING. SOMETHING ABOUT HIS LAST DAY ON EARTH. I REMEMBER YOU TOLD ME THAT YOU HAD A VETERINARIAN CHLOROFORM GYP. BUT THERE'S A CONTRADICTION HERE. GYP HAS BEEN TRYING TO TELL ME SOMETHING... THAT'S IT.. THE GARAGE... GYP IS TIED TO THE LEG OF THE WORKBENCH. I SEE SOMETHING RISING AND FALLING IN ANGER... FASTER AND FASTER.
NO, SON... DON'T!
THAT WAS THE DAY - THE DAY MOTHER LEFT WITH MARK HUMPREYS. YOU CAME HOME AND FOUND HER NOTE. GYP GOT IN YOUR WAY - YOU HAD TO VENT YOUR TEMPER ON SOMETHING. IF I'D BEEN HOME, IT WOULD'VE BEEN ME. BUT GYP GOT IT. HE DIED!
MMPF GURGLE
K-HAFF K HAFF
IN A PATCH OF SILVER THE GREAT STANTON STOPPED AND RAISED HIS FACE TO THE FULL MOON WHERE IT HUNG, DESOLATELY, AGONIZINGLY BRIGHT, A DEAD THING WATCHING A DYING EARTH.
98

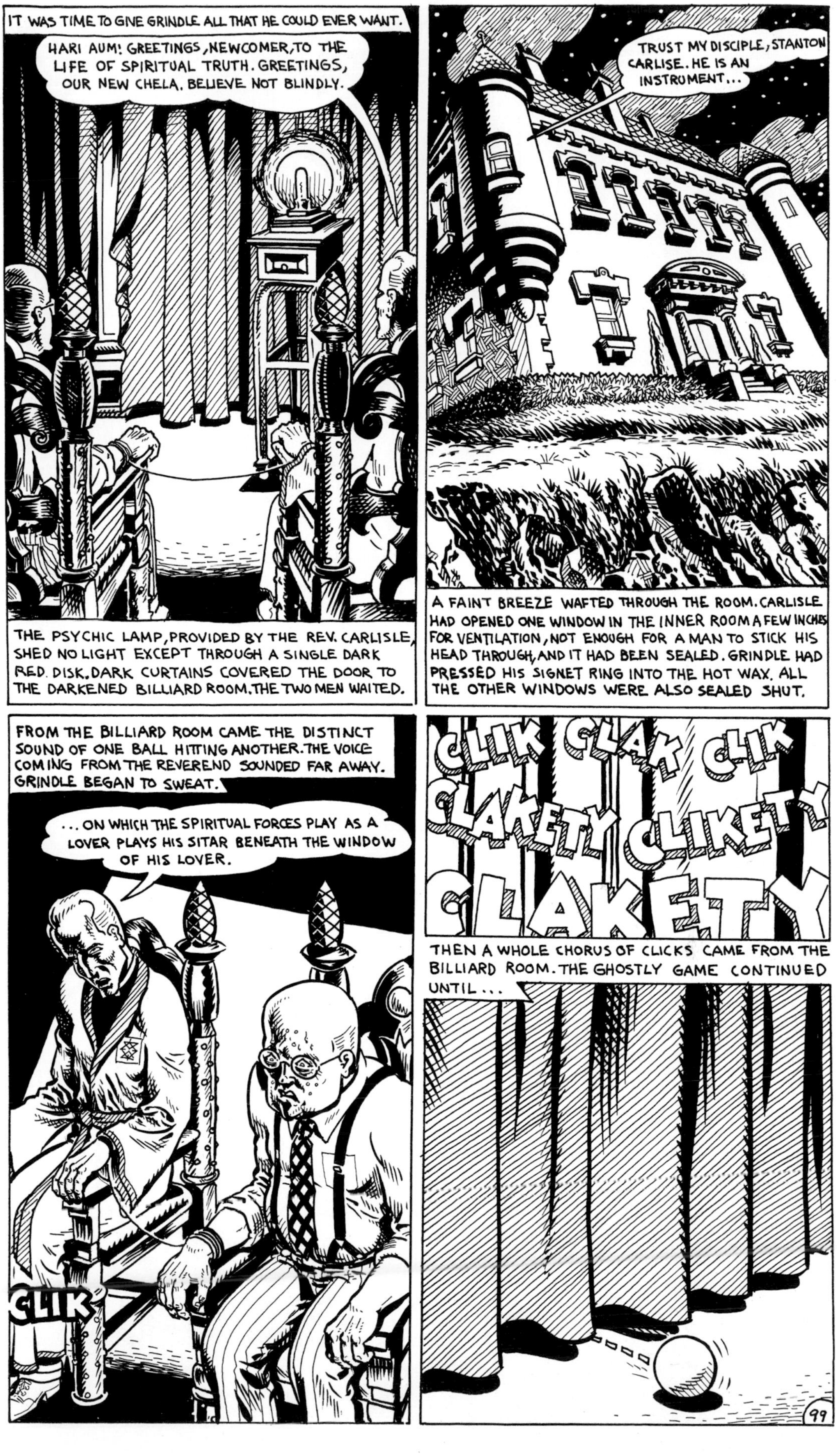
IT WAS TIME TO GIVE GRINDLE ALL THAT HE COULD EVER WANT.
HARI AUM! GREETINGS, NEWCOMER, TO THE LIFE OF SPIRITUAL TRUTH. GREETINGS, OUR NEW CHELA. BELIEVE NOT BLINDLY.
THE PSYCHIC LAMP, PROVIDED BY THE REV. CARLISLE, SHED NO LIGHT EXCEPT THROUGH A SINGLE DARK RED DISK. DARK CURTAINS COVERED THE DOOR TO THE DARKENED BILLIARD ROOM. THE TWO MEN WAITED.
TRUST MY DISCIPLE, STANTON CARLISLE. HE IS AN INSTRUMENT...
A FAINT BREEZE WAFTED THROUGH THE ROOM. CARLISLE HAD OPENED ONE WINDOW IN THE INNER ROOM A FEW INCHES FOR VENTILATION, NOT ENOUGH FOR A MAN TO STICK HIS HEAD THROUGH, AND IT HAD BEEN SEALED. GRINDLE HAD PRESSED HIS SIGNET RING INTO THE HOT WAX. ALL THE OTHER WINDOWS WERE ALSO SEALED SHUT.
FROM THE BILLIARD ROOM CAME THE DISTINCT SOUND OF ONE BALL HITTING ANOTHER. THE VOICE COMING FROM THE REVEREND SOUNDED FAR AWAY. GRINDLE BEGAN TO SWEAT.
...ON WHICH THE SPIRITUAL FORCES PLAY AS A LOVER PLAYS HIS SITAR BENEATH THE WINDOW OF HIS LOVER.
CLIK
CLIK CLAK CLIK
CLAKETY CLIKETY
CLAKETY
THEN A WHOLE CHORUS OF CLICKS CAME FROM THE BILLIARD ROOM. THE GHOSTLY GAME CONTINUED UNTIL...

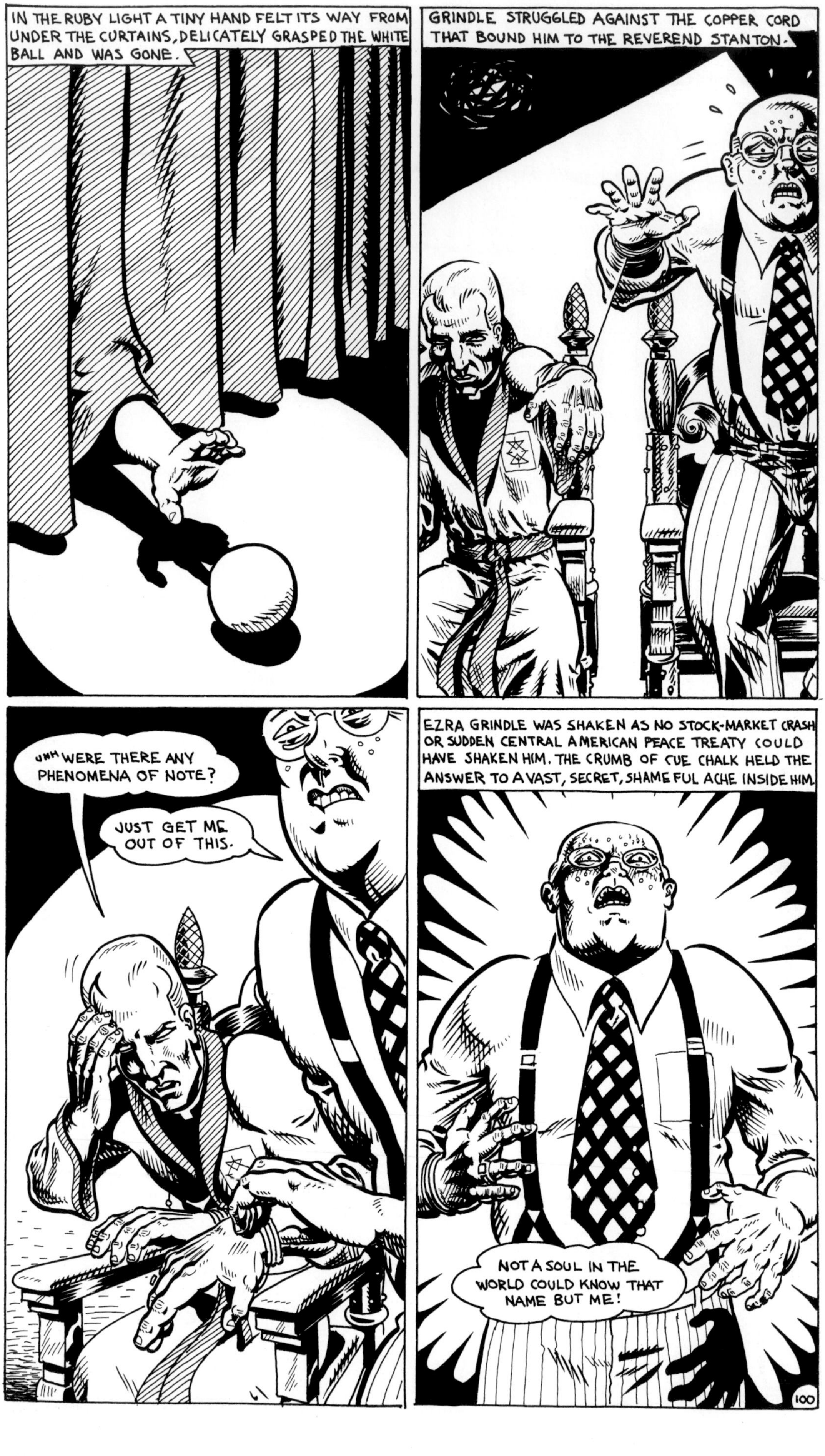
IN THE RUBY LIGHT A TINY HAND FELT ITS WAY FROM UNDER THE CURTAINS, DELICATELY GRASPED THE WHITE BALL AND WAS GONE.
GRINDLE STRUGGLED AGAINST THE COPPER CORD THAT BOUND HIM TO THE REVEREND STANTON.
UHM WERE THERE ANY PHENOMENA OF NOTE?
JUST GET ME OUT OF THIS.
EZRA GRINDLE WAS SHAKEN AS NO STOCK-MARKET CRASH OR SUDDEN CENTRAL AMERICAN PEACE TREATY COULD HAVE SHAKEN HIM. THE CRUMB OF CUE CHALK HELD THE ANSWER TO A VAST, SECRET, SHAMEFUL ACHE INSIDE HIM.
NOT A SOUL IN THE WORLD COULD KNOW THAT NAME BUT ME!

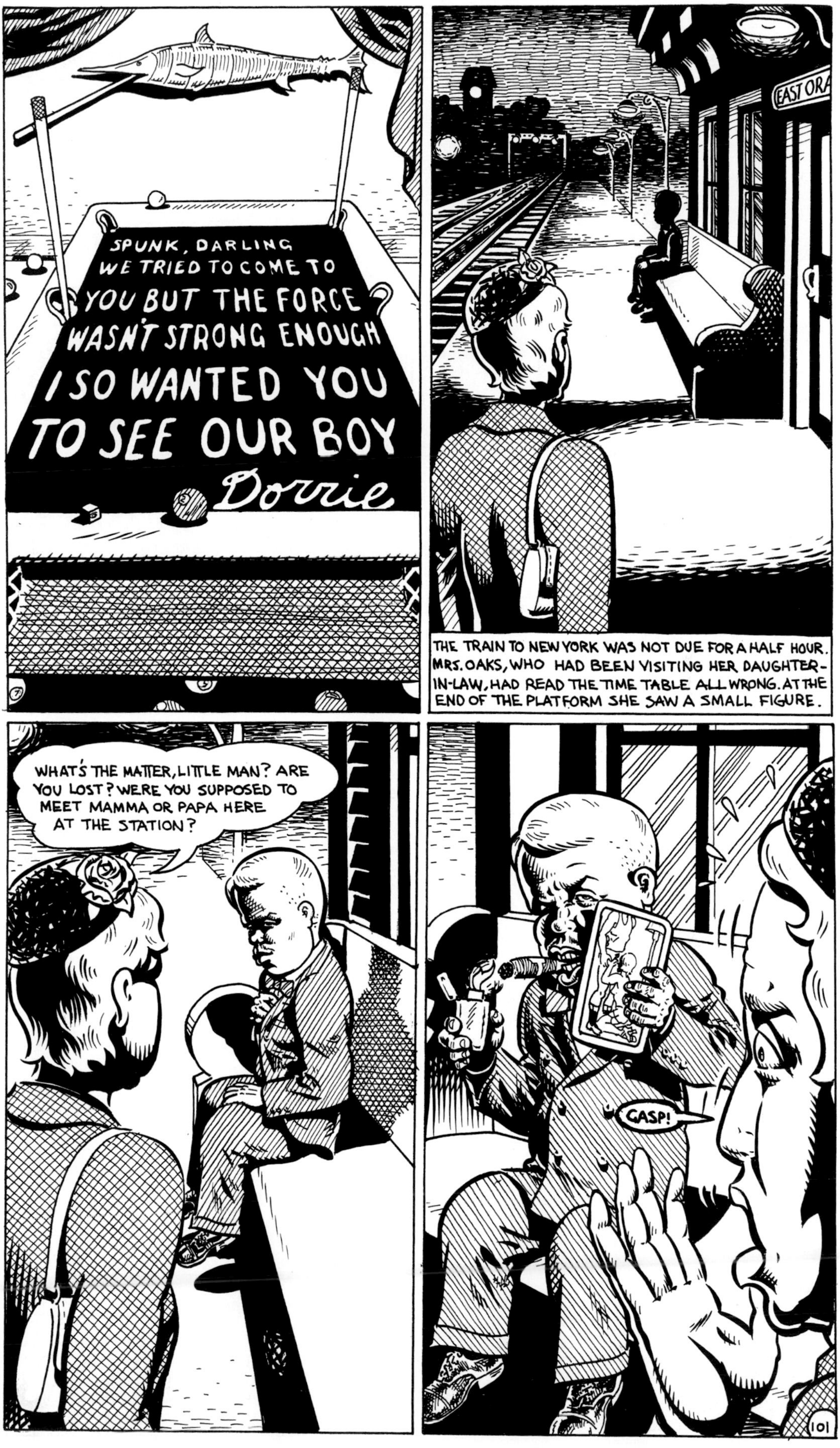
SPUNK, DARLING
WE TRIED TO COME TO YOU BUT THE FORCE WASN'T STRONG ENOUGH
I SO WANTED YOU TO SEE OUR BOY
Dorrie
EAST ORA
THE TRAIN TO NEW YORK WAS NOT DUE FOR A HALF HOUR. MRS. OAKS, WHO HAD BEEN VISITING HER DAUGHTER-IN-LAW, HAD READ THE TIME TABLE ALL WRONG. AT THE END OF THE PLATFORM SHE SAW A SMALL FIGURE.
WHAT'S THE MATTER, LITTLE MAN? ARE YOU LOST? WERE YOU SUPPOSED TO MEET MAMMA OR PAPA HERE AT THE STATION?
GASP!

IT'S GROWING CLEARER. IT'S A CITY, A GOLDEN CITY, TOWERS, DOMES. A BEAUTIFUL CITY... AND NOW IT'S GONE.

GRINDLE'S VOICE WAS FLACCID AND DREAMY. ALL THE BITE HAD GONE OUT OF IT.

YOU HAVE SEEN IT- THE CITY OF SPIRITUAL LIGHT. MY CONTROL SPIRIT, RAMA KRISHNA, HAS DIRECTED US TO BUILD IT. IT WILL BE PATTERNED AFTER A SIMILAR CITY - WHICH FEW OUTSIDERS HAVE EVER SEEN- IN THE MOUNTAINS OF NEPAL.

THE REV. CARLISLE SLIPPED BACK INTO HIS POCKET A "PATENT GHOST THROWER, COMPLETE WITH BATTERIES AND LENSES TO HOLD 16 MILLIMETER FILM $7.98" FROM A SPIRITUALIST'S SUPPLY HOUSE IN CHICAGO.

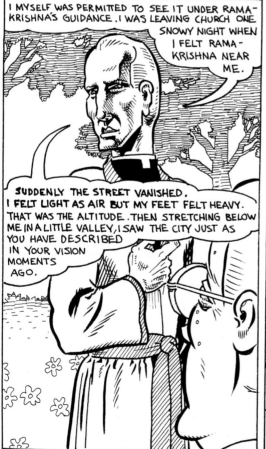

I MYSELF WAS PERMITTED TO SEE IT UNDER RAMA-KRISHNA'S GUIDANCE. I WAS LEAVING CHURCH ONE SNOWY NIGHT WHEN I FELT RAMA-KRISHNA NEAR ME.

SUDDENLY THE STREET VANISHED. I FELT LIGHT AS AIR BUT MY FEET FELT HEAVY. THAT WAS THE ALTITUDE. THEN STRETCHING BELOW ME IN A LITTLE VALLEY, I SAW THE CITY JUST AS YOU HAVE DESCRIBED IN YOUR VISION MOMENTS AGO.

AND I KNEW THAT IT HAD BEEN REVEALED TO ME FOR A PURPOSE. ONCE THIS REALIZATION HAD DAWNED ON ME, THE MOUNTAINS, THE RUGGED OUTLINE OF BARE PEAKS AND GLACIERS SOFTENED. THEY SEEMED TO CLOSE IN AND I WAS BACK ON THE DOORSTEP OF THE CHURCH OF THE HEAVENLY MESSAGE.

BUT THERE, STRETCHING AWAY UP THE SIDEWALK, WERE MY OWN TRACKS OF A FEW MINUTES BEFORE. A FEW YARDS FARTHER ON, THEY STOPPED, THEY HAD DEMATERIALIZED WHEN I REACHED THAT SPOT. (102)

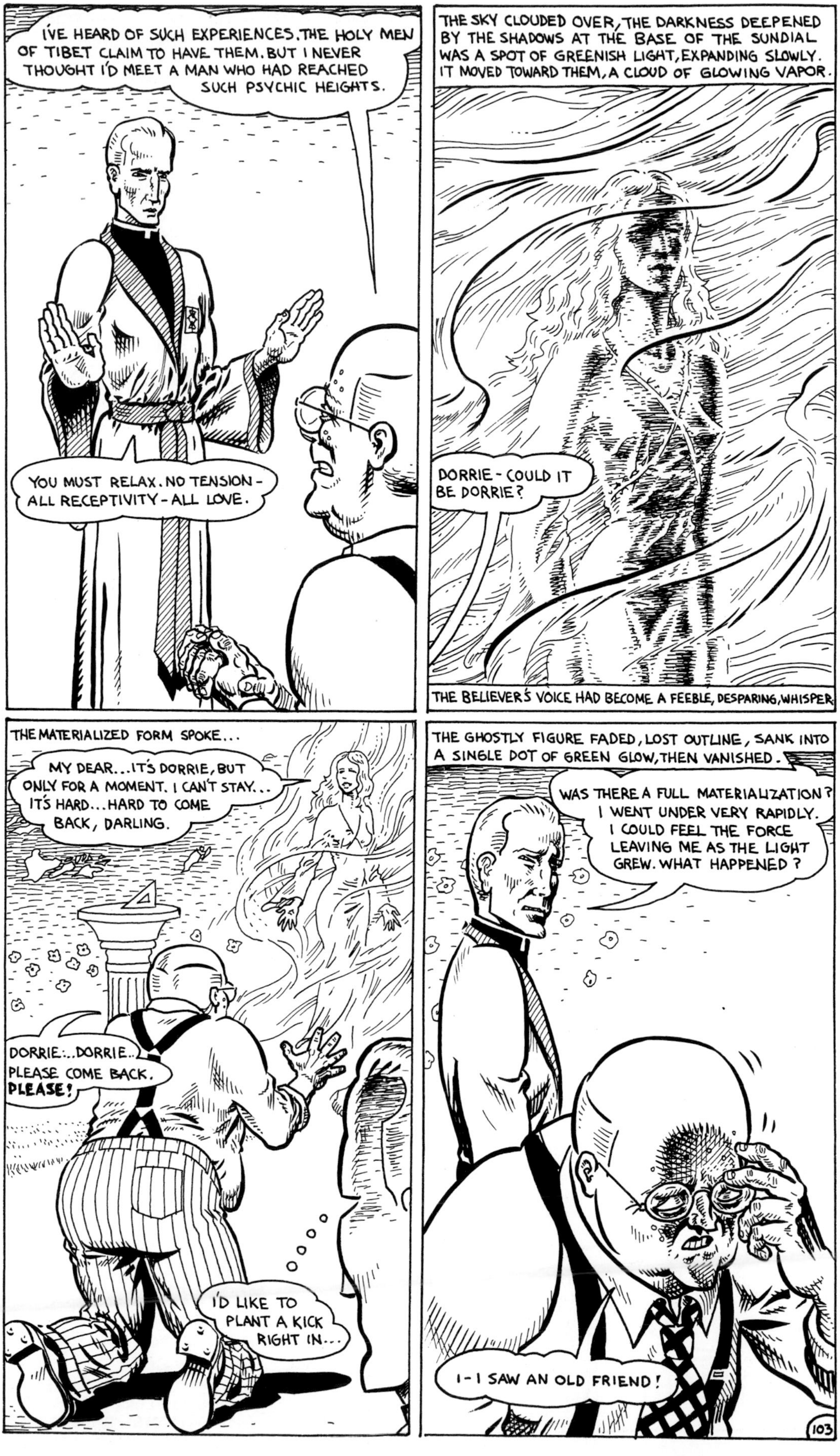
I'VE HEARD OF SUCH EXPERIENCES. THE HOLY MEN OF TIBET CLAIM TO HAVE THEM. BUT I NEVER THOUGHT I'D MEET A MAN WHO HAD REACHED SUCH PSYCHIC HEIGHTS.
YOU MUST RELAX. NO TENSION - ALL RECEPTIVITY - ALL LOVE.
THE SKY CLOUDED OVER, THE DARKNESS DEEPENED BY THE SHADOWS AT THE BASE OF THE SUNDIAL WAS A SPOT OF GREENISH LIGHT, EXPANDING SLOWLY. IT MOVED TOWARD THEM, A CLOUD OF GLOWING VAPOR.
DORRIE - COULD IT BE DORRIE?
THE BELIEVER'S VOICE HAD BECOME A FEEBLE, DESPARING, WHISPER.
THE MATERIALIZED FORM SPOKE...
MY DEAR... IT'S DORRIE, BUT ONLY FOR A MOMENT. I CAN'T STAY... IT'S HARD... HARD TO COME BACK, DARLING.
DORRIE... DORRIE.. PLEASE COME BACK. PLEASE!
I'D LIKE TO PLANT A KICK RIGHT IN...
THE GHOSTLY FIGURE FADED, LOST OUTLINE, SANK INTO A SINGLE DOT OF GREEN GLOW, THEN VANISHED.
WAS THERE A FULL MATERIALIZATION? I WENT UNDER VERY RAPIDLY. I COULD FEEL THE FORCE LEAVING ME AS THE LIGHT GREW. WHAT HAPPENED?
I- I SAW AN OLD FRIEND!

MOLLY WAS SO HAPPY, SHE COULD CRY. IT HAD BEEN A LONG TIME SINCE THEY'D HAD ANYTHING LIKE A HOLIDAY TOGETHER.

OH, STAN, LET'S STOP HERE.

SURE, BABY.

STAN HAD BEEN ACTING SO SCREWY, THEN ALL OF A SUDDEN THEY WERE JUST DRIVING ANYWHERE, STOPPING AT CHICKEN SHACKS, DANCING AND IN THE DAYTIME...

...TAKING A SWIM WHEREVER IT LOOKED GOOD. BUT STAN WAS STILL AWFULLY JUMPY. SOMETIMES, YOU'D TALK TO HIM AND YOU'D THINK HE'D BEEN LISTENING, THEN...

WHAT WAS THAT, KID?

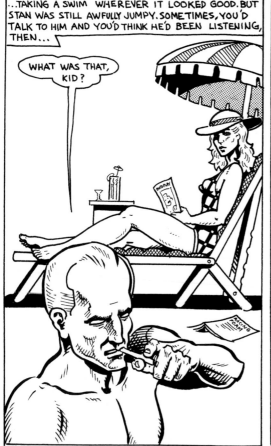

OH, STAN, DON'T EVER LET ANYTHING BUST US UP, HONEY! ALL I WANT IS YOU.

BABY, HOW'D YOU LIKE TO DO THIS EVERY DAY IN THE YEAR? HUH? WELL, IF THIS DEAL GOES OVER, WE'RE SET, AND EVERY DAY IS CHRISTMAS.

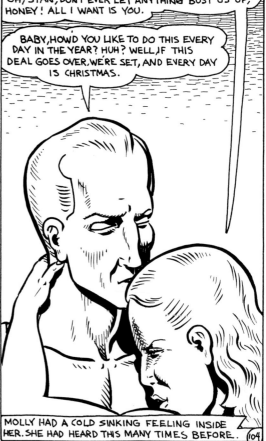

MOLLY HAD A COLD SINKING FEELING INSIDE HER. SHE HAD HEARD THIS MANY TIMES BEFORE. 104

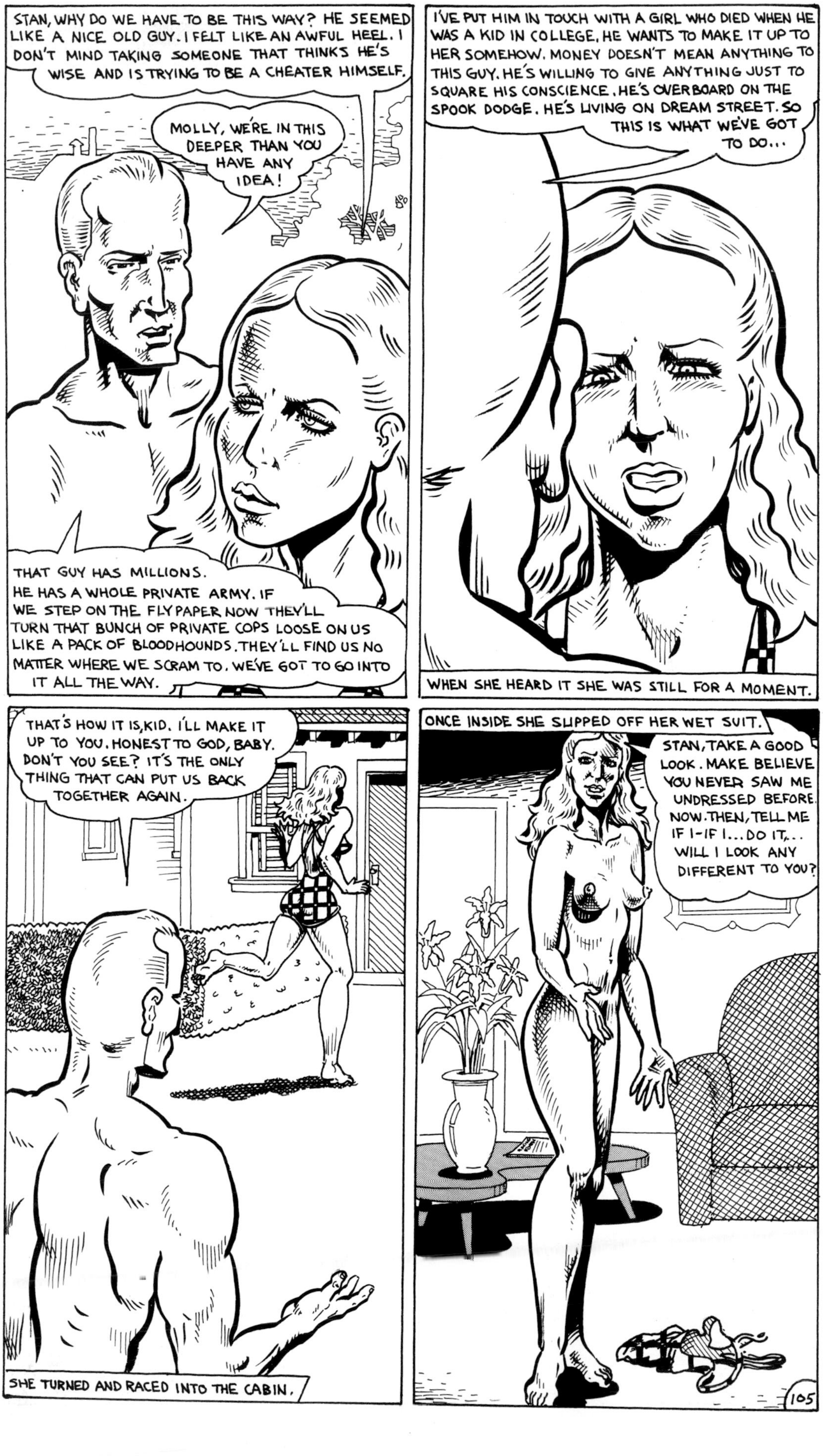
STAN, WHY DO WE HAVE TO BE THIS WAY? HE SEEMED LIKE A NICE OLD GUY. I FELT LIKE AN AWFUL HEEL. I DON'T MIND TAKING SOMEONE THAT THINKS HE'S WISE AND IS TRYING TO BE A CHEATER HIMSELF.
MOLLY, WE'RE IN THIS DEEPER THAN YOU HAVE ANY IDEA!
THAT GUY HAS MILLIONS. HE HAS A WHOLE PRIVATE ARMY. IF WE STEP ON THE FLYPAPER NOW THEY'LL TURN THAT BUNCH OF PRIVATE COPS LOOSE ON US LIKE A PACK OF BLOODHOUNDS. THEY'LL FIND US NO MATTER WHERE WE SCRAM TO. WE'VE GOT TO GO INTO IT ALL THE WAY.
I'VE PUT HIM IN TOUCH WITH A GIRL WHO DIED WHEN HE WAS A KID IN COLLEGE. HE WANTS TO MAKE IT UP TO HER SOMEHOW. MONEY DOESN'T MEAN ANYTHING TO THIS GUY. HE'S WILLING TO GIVE ANYTHING JUST TO SQUARE HIS CONSCIENCE. HE'S OVERBOARD ON THE SPOOK DODGE. HE'S LIVING ON DREAM STREET. SO THIS IS WHAT WE'VE GOT TO DO...
WHEN SHE HEARD IT SHE WAS STILL FOR A MOMENT.
THAT'S HOW IT IS, KID. I'LL MAKE IT UP TO YOU. HONEST TO GOD, BABY. DON'T YOU SEE? IT'S THE ONLY THING THAT CAN PUT US BACK TOGETHER AGAIN.
SHE TURNED AND RACED INTO THE CABIN.
ONCE INSIDE SHE SLIPPED OFF HER WET SUIT.
STAN, TAKE A GOOD LOOK. MAKE BELIEVE YOU NEVER SAW ME UNDRESSED BEFORE. NOW. THEN, TELL ME IF I-IF I... DO IT... WILL I LOOK ANY DIFFERENT TO YOU?

SHE'S HOOKED!

THE VIRTUOUS MOLLY?

SURE, IT TOOK SOME SELLING, BUT SHE'LL PLAY BALL. NOW LET'S LAY OUT THE MOVES FROM HERE ON IN. I PLANTED THE "CITY OF SPIRITUAL LIGHT" WITH HIM JUST BEFORE THE FIRST FULL-FORM JOB IN THE GARDEN UP AT HIS PLACE.

NEXT SÉANCE, WE'LL START WARMING HIM UP TO THE IDEA OF KICKING IN SOME DOUGH.

VERY PRETTY, REVEREND.

THERE'S MORE!

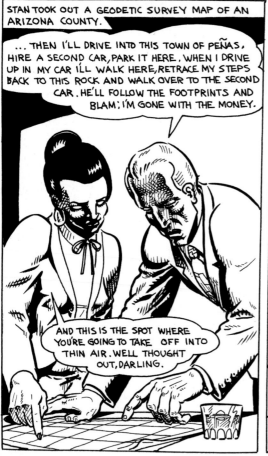

STAN TOOK OUT A GEODETIC SURVEY MAP OF AN ARIZONA COUNTY.

... THEN I'LL DRIVE INTO THIS TOWN OF PEÑAS, HIRE A SECOND CAR, PARK IT HERE. WHEN I DRIVE UP IN MY CAR I'LL WALK HERE, RETRACE MY STEPS BACK TO THIS ROCK AND WALK OVER TO THE SECOND CAR. HE'LL FOLLOW THE FOOTPRINTS AND BLAM: I'M GONE WITH THE MONEY.

AND THIS IS THE SPOT WHERE YOU'RE GOING TO TAKE OFF INTO THIN AIR. WELL THOUGHT OUT, DARLING.

HOW ARE YOU GOING TO BRUSH OFF THE FAITHFUL PENELOPE?

MOLLY? I'LL GIVE HER A COUPLE OF GRAND AND TELL HER TO MEET ME SOMEPLACE IN FLORIDA...

ALL SHE NEEDS IS A FEW BUCKS AND A RACE TRACK TO KEEP HER HAPPY. IF SHE WINS, SHE'LL FORGET THE DAY AND THE MONTH AND EVERYTHING ELSE. WHEN SHE'S BROKE, SHE CAN GO BACK TO THE TEN-O-ONE. SHE WON'T STARVE.

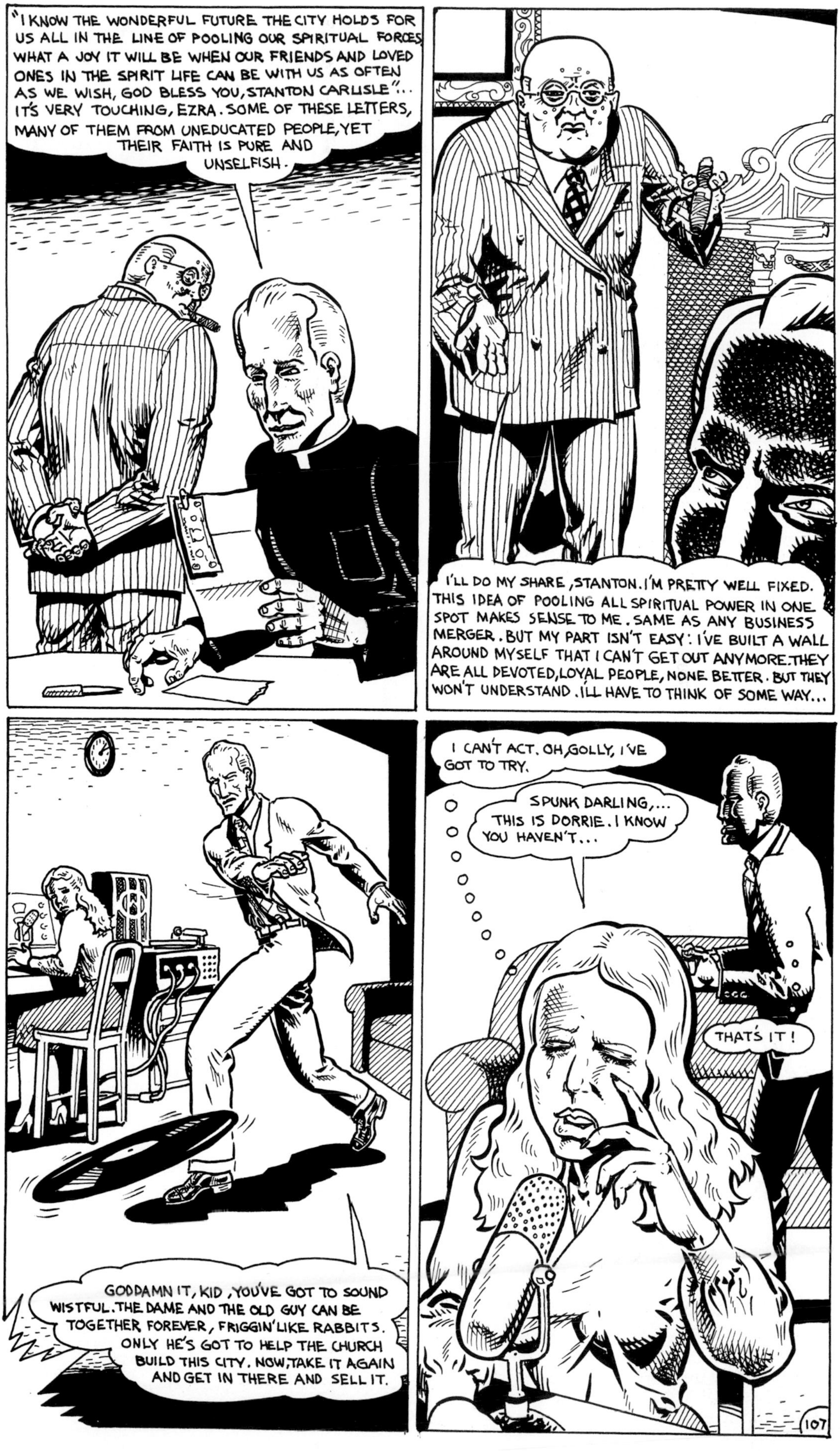
"I KNOW THE WONDERFUL FUTURE THE CITY HOLDS FOR US ALL IN THE LINE OF POOLING OUR SPIRITUAL FORCES. WHAT A JOY IT WILL BE WHEN OUR FRIENDS AND LOVED ONES IN THE SPIRIT LIFE CAN BE WITH US AS OFTEN AS WE WISH, GOD BLESS YOU, STANTON CARLISLE"... IT'S VERY TOUCHING, EZRA. SOME OF THESE LETTERS, MANY OF THEM FROM UNEDUCATED PEOPLE, YET THEIR FAITH IS PURE AND UNSELFISH.
I'LL DO MY SHARE, STANTON. I'M PRETTY WELL FIXED. THIS IDEA OF POOLING ALL SPIRITUAL POWER IN ONE SPOT MAKES SENSE TO ME. SAME AS ANY BUSINESS MERGER. BUT MY PART ISN'T EASY: I'VE BUILT A WALL AROUND MYSELF THAT I CAN'T GET OUT ANYMORE. THEY ARE ALL DEVOTED, LOYAL PEOPLE, NONE BETTER. BUT THEY WON'T UNDERSTAND. I'LL HAVE TO THINK OF SOME WAY...
GODDAMN IT, KID, YOU'VE GOT TO SOUND WISTFUL. THE DAME AND THE OLD GUY CAN BE TOGETHER FOREVER, FRIGGIN' LIKE RABBITS. ONLY HE'S GOT TO HELP THE CHURCH BUILD THIS CITY. NOW, TAKE IT AGAIN AND GET IN THERE AND SELL IT.
I CAN'T ACT. OH, GOLLY, I'VE GOT TO TRY.
SPUNK DARLING,... THIS IS DORRIE. I KNOW YOU HAVEN'T...
THAT'S IT!

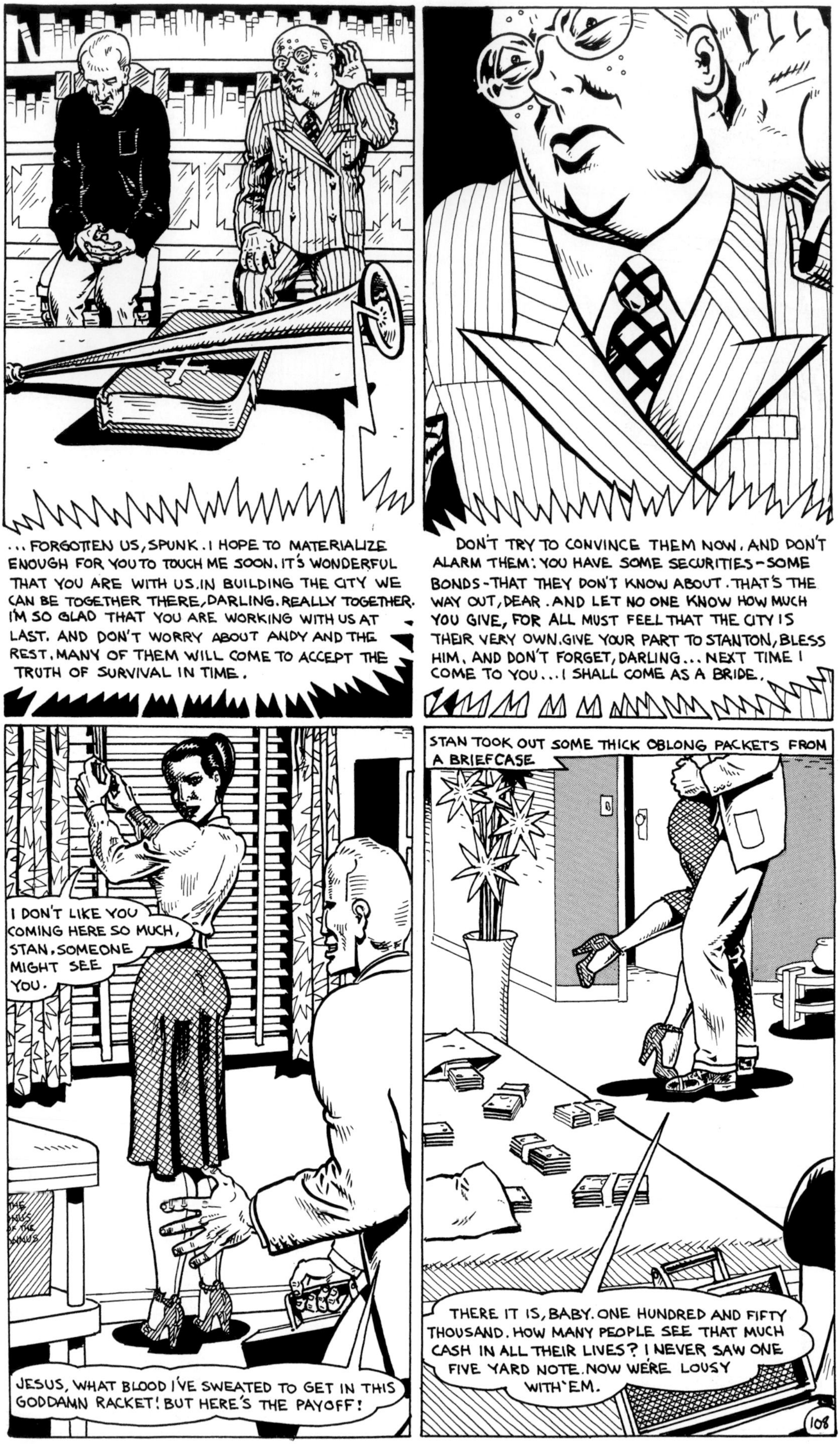

...FORGOTTEN US, SPUNK. I HOPE TO MATERIALIZE ENOUGH FOR YOU TO TOUCH ME SOON. IT'S WONDERFUL THAT YOU ARE WITH US. IN BUILDING THE CITY WE CAN BE TOGETHER THERE, DARLING. REALLY TOGETHER. I'M SO GLAD THAT YOU ARE WORKING WITH US AT LAST. AND DON'T WORRY ABOUT ANDY AND THE REST. MANY OF THEM WILL COME TO ACCEPT THE TRUTH OF SURVIVAL IN TIME.
DON'T TRY TO CONVINCE THEM NOW. AND DON'T ALARM THEM: YOU HAVE SOME SECURITIES - SOME BONDS - THAT THEY DON'T KNOW ABOUT. THAT'S THE WAY OUT, DEAR. AND LET NO ONE KNOW HOW MUCH YOU GIVE, FOR ALL MUST FEEL THAT THE CITY IS THEIR VERY OWN. GIVE YOUR PART TO STANTON, BLESS HIM. AND DON'T FORGET, DARLING... NEXT TIME I COME TO YOU... I SHALL COME AS A BRIDE.
I DON'T LIKE YOU COMING HERE SO MUCH, STAN. SOMEONE MIGHT SEE YOU.
JESUS, WHAT BLOOD I'VE SWEATED TO GET IN THIS GODDAMN RACKET! BUT HERE'S THE PAYOFF!
STAN TOOK OUT SOME THICK OBLONG PACKETS FROM A BRIEFCASE
THERE IT IS, BABY. ONE HUNDRED AND FIFTY THOUSAND. HOW MANY PEOPLE SEE THAT MUCH CASH IN ALL THEIR LIVES? I NEVER SAW ONE FIVE YARD NOTE. NOW WE'RE LOUSY WITH 'EM.

SHE HANDED HIM A DOUBLE BRANDY AND POURED ONE FOR HERSELF. THEN SHE OPENED A DUMMY DRAWER IN HER DESK.

WE'D BETTER PUT IT AWAY, DARLING. THAT'S A LOT OF MONEY FOR ONE PERSON TO CARRY IN HIS POCKET. YOU MIGHT SPEND IT FOOLISHLY.

GOD, THIS HIGH CLASS LAYOUT HAD ME DIZZY BUT I GET IT GOOD AND CLEAR NOW. WE'RE A COUPLE OF HUSTLERS, A PAIR OF BIG TIME THIEVES.

DR. LILITH RITTER DID NOT GO TO BED RIGHT AWAY. AFTER CARLISLE HAD LEFT, SHE TOOK OUT A FOLDER IDENTIFIED ONLY BY A NUMBER. ON GRAPH PAPER WAS A CHART SHOWING A JAGGED RISE AND FALL. IT WAS AN EMOTIONAL DIAGRAM OF STANTON CARLISLE.

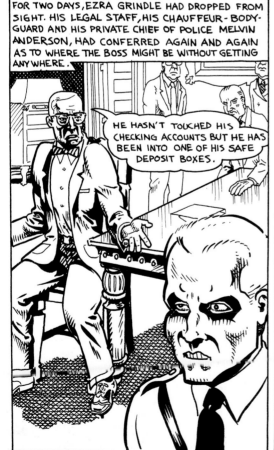

FOR TWO DAYS, EZRA GRINDLE HAD DROPPED FROM SIGHT. HIS LEGAL STAFF, HIS CHAUFFEUR-BODYGUARD AND HIS PRIVATE CHIEF OF POLICE MELVIN ANDERSON, HAD CONFERRED AGAIN AND AGAIN AS TO WHERE THE BOSS MIGHT BE WITHOUT GETTING ANYWHERE.

HE HASN'T TOUCHED HIS CHECKING ACCOUNTS BUT HE HAS BEEN INTO ONE OF HIS SAFE DEPOSIT BOXES.

IN A TINY BEDROOM, LIT ONLY BY A SKYLIGHT ON THE TOP FLOOR OF THE CHURCH OF THE HEAVENLY MESSAGE, THE GREAT MAN SAT IN THE ROBE OF A TIBETAN LAMA.

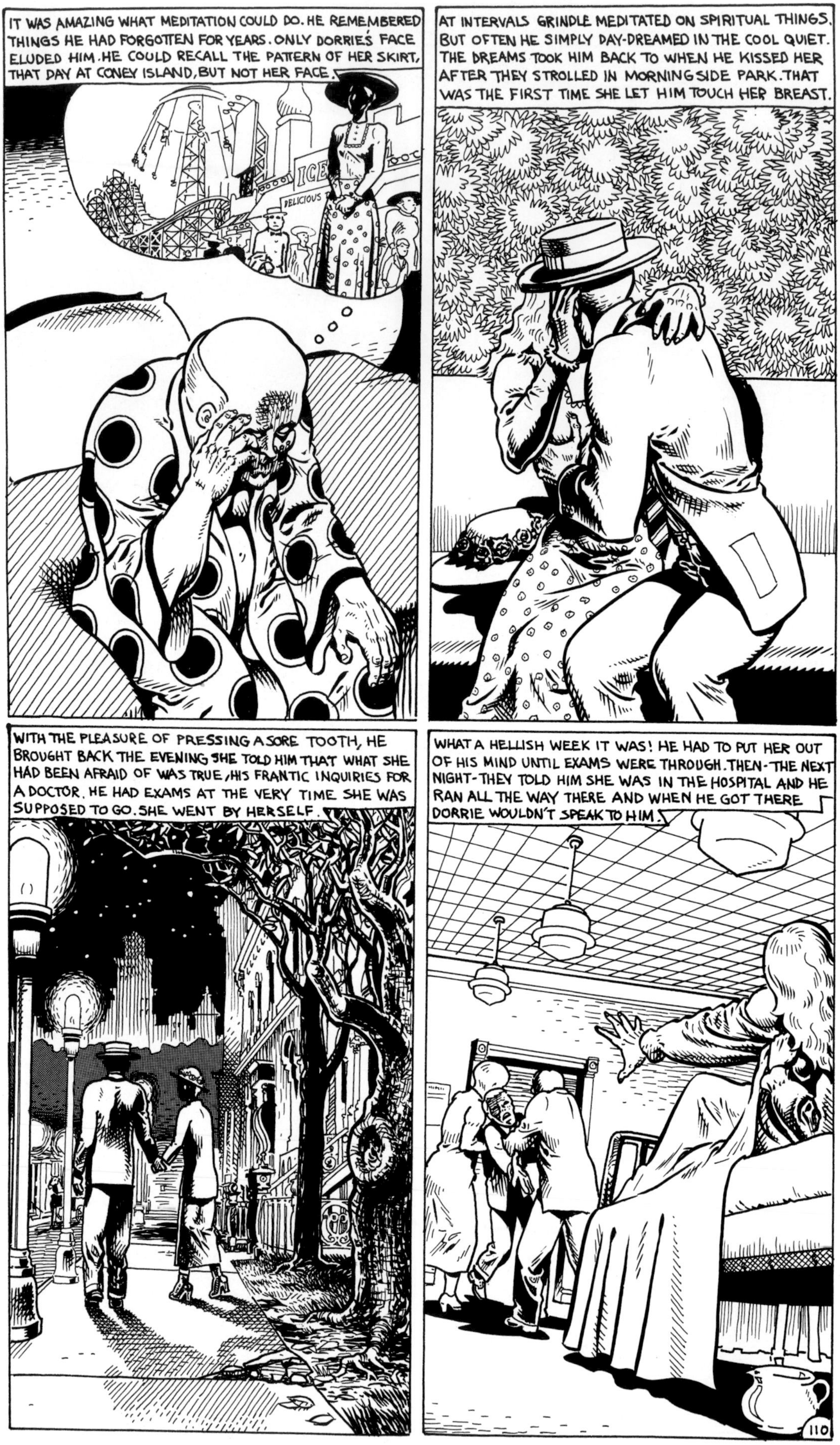
IT WAS AMAZING WHAT MEDITATION COULD DO. HE REMEMBERED THINGS HE HAD FORGOTTEN FOR YEARS. ONLY DORRIE'S FACE ELUDED HIM. HE COULD RECALL THE PATTERN OF HER SKIRT, THAT DAY AT CONEY ISLAND, BUT NOT HER FACE.
ICE
DELICIOUS
AT INTERVALS GRINDLE MEDITATED ON SPIRITUAL THINGS. BUT OFTEN HE SIMPLY DAY-DREAMED IN THE COOL QUIET. THE DREAMS TOOK HIM BACK TO WHEN HE KISSED HER AFTER THEY STROLLED IN MORNINGSIDE PARK. THAT WAS THE FIRST TIME SHE LET HIM TOUCH HER BREAST.
WITH THE PLEASURE OF PRESSING A SORE TOOTH, HE BROUGHT BACK THE EVENING SHE TOLD HIM THAT WHAT SHE HAD BEEN AFRAID OF WAS TRUE, HIS FRANTIC INQUIRIES FOR A DOCTOR. HE HAD EXAMS AT THE VERY TIME SHE WAS SUPPOSED TO GO. SHE WENT BY HERSELF.
WHAT A HELLISH WEEK IT WAS! HE HAD TO PUT HER OUT OF HIS MIND UNTIL EXAMS WERE THROUGH. THEN- THE NEXT NIGHT- THEY TOLD HIM SHE WAS IN THE HOSPITAL AND HE RAN ALL THE WAY THERE AND WHEN HE GOT THERE DORRIE WOULDN'T SPEAK TO HIM.

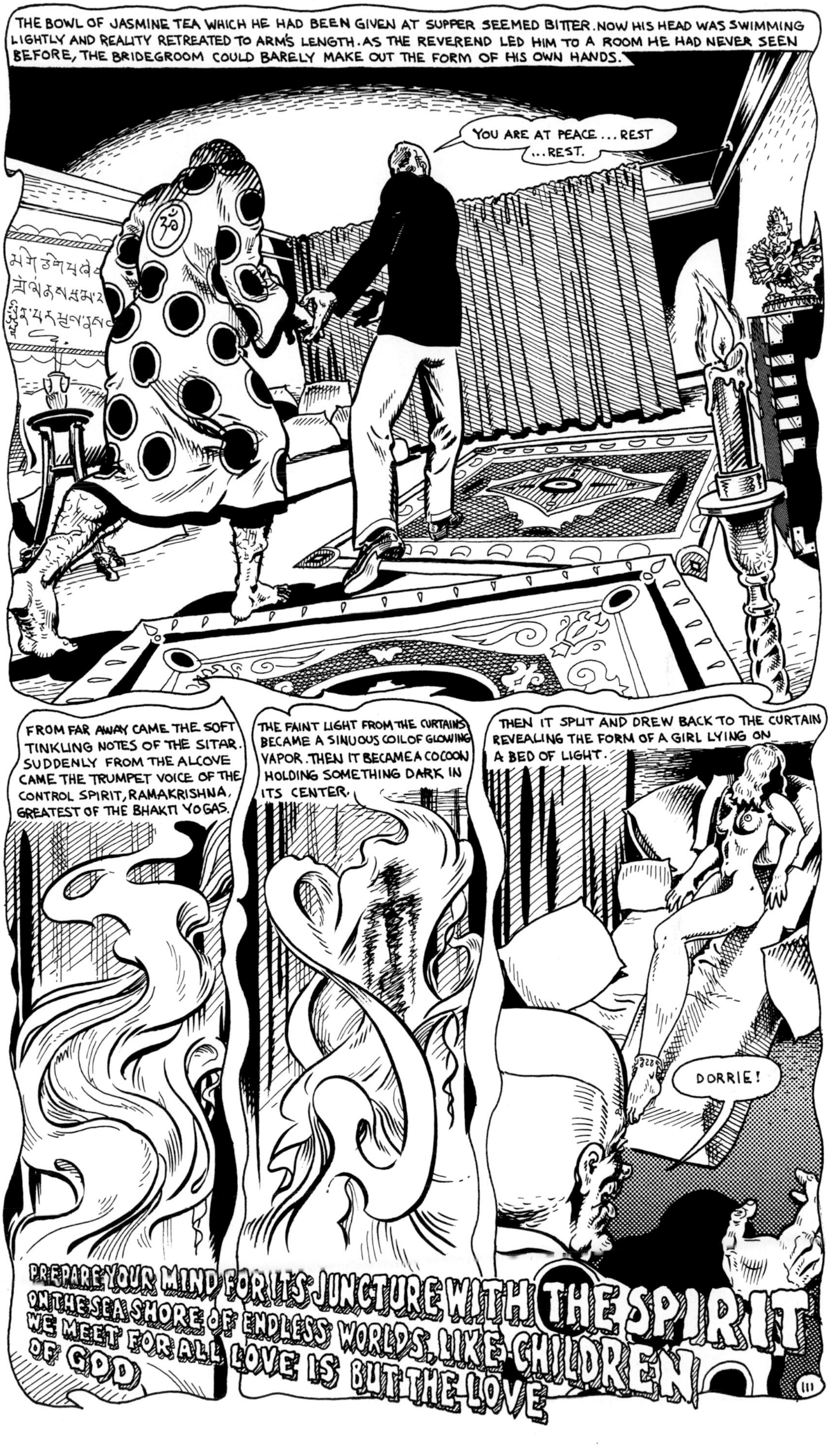
THE BOWL OF JASMINE TEA WHICH HE HAD BEEN GIVEN AT SUPPER SEEMED BITTER. NOW HIS HEAD WAS SWIMMING LIGHTLY AND REALITY RETREATED TO ARM'S LENGTH. AS THE REVEREND LED HIM TO A ROOM HE HAD NEVER SEEN BEFORE, THE BRIDEGROOM COULD BARELY MAKE OUT THE FORM OF HIS OWN HANDS.
YOU ARE AT PEACE ... REST ... REST.
FROM FAR AWAY CAME THE SOFT TINKLING NOTES OF THE SITAR. SUDDENLY FROM THE ALCOVE CAME THE TRUMPET VOICE OF THE CONTROL SPIRIT, RAMAKRISHNA, GREATEST OF THE BHAKTI YOGAS.
THE FAINT LIGHT FROM THE CURTAINS BECAME A SINUOUS COIL OF GLOWING VAPOR. THEN IT BECAME A COCOON HOLDING SOMETHING DARK IN ITS CENTER.
THEN IT SPLIT AND DREW BACK TO THE CURTAIN REVEALING THE FORM OF A GIRL LYING ON A BED OF LIGHT.
DORRIE!
PREPARE YOUR MIND FOR ITS JUNCTURE WITH THE SPIRIT
ON THE SEA SHORE OF ENDLESS WORLDS, LIKE CHILDREN
WE MEET FOR ALL LOVE IS BUT THE LOVE
OF GOD

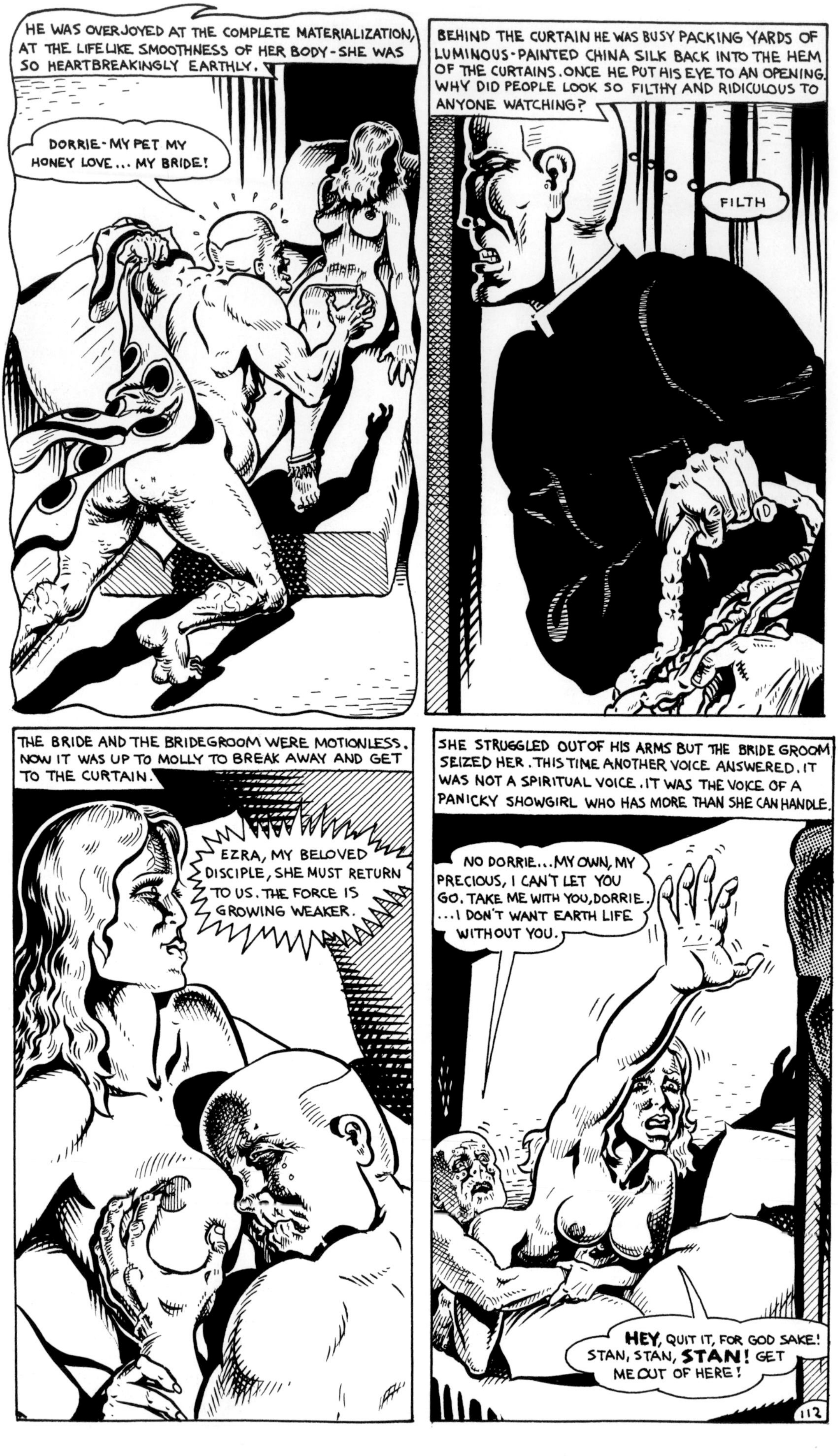
HE WAS OVERJOYED AT THE COMPLETE MATERIALIZATION, AT THE LIFELIKE SMOOTHNESS OF HER BODY - SHE WAS SO HEARTBREAKINGLY EARTHLY.
DORRIE - MY PET MY HONEY LOVE... MY BRIDE!
BEHIND THE CURTAIN HE WAS BUSY PACKING YARDS OF LUMINOUS - PAINTED CHINA SILK BACK INTO THE HEM OF THE CURTAINS. ONCE HE PUT HIS EYE TO AN OPENING. WHY DID PEOPLE LOOK SO FILTHY AND RIDICULOUS TO ANYONE WATCHING?
FILTH
THE BRIDE AND THE BRIDEGROOM WERE MOTIONLESS. NOW IT WAS UP TO MOLLY TO BREAK AWAY AND GET TO THE CURTAIN.
EZRA, MY BELOVED DISCIPLE, SHE MUST RETURN TO US. THE FORCE IS GROWING WEAKER.
SHE STRUGGLED OUT OF HIS ARMS BUT THE BRIDEGROOM SEIZED HER. THIS TIME ANOTHER VOICE ANSWERED. IT WAS NOT A SPIRITUAL VOICE. IT WAS THE VOICE OF A PANICKY SHOWGIRL WHO HAS MORE THAN SHE CAN HANDLE.
NO DORRIE... MY OWN, MY PRECIOUS, I CAN'T LET YOU GO. TAKE ME WITH YOU, DORRIE. ...I DON'T WANT EARTH LIFE WITHOUT YOU.
HEY, QUIT IT, FOR GOD SAKE! STAN, STAN, STAN! GET ME OUT OF HERE!
112

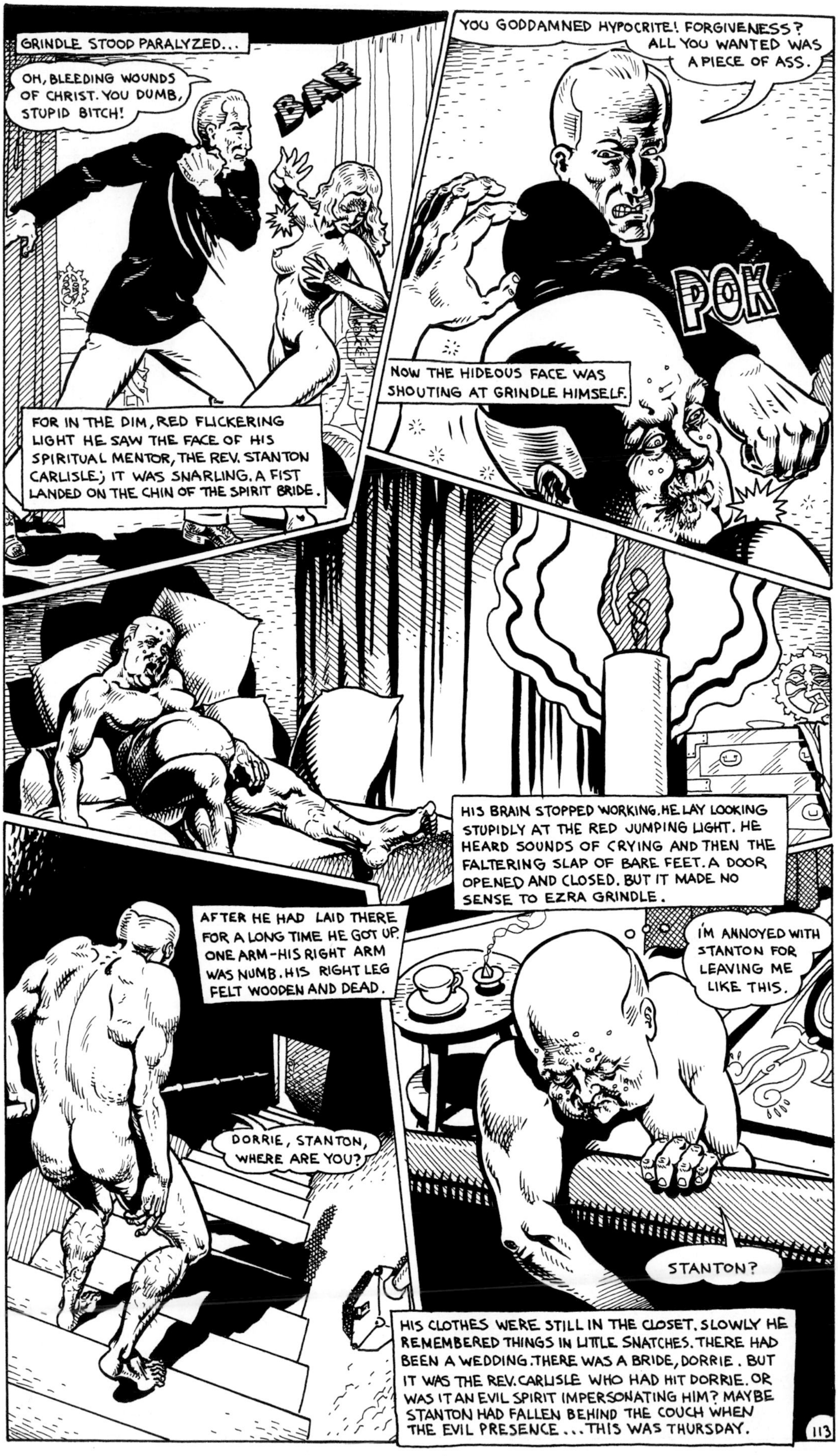
GRINDLE STOOD PARALYZED...
OH, BLEEDING WOUNDS OF CHRIST. YOU DUMB, STUPID BITCH!
BAF
FOR IN THE DIM, RED FLICKERING LIGHT HE SAW THE FACE OF HIS SPIRITUAL MENTOR, THE REV. STANTON CARLISLE; IT WAS SNARLING. A FIST LANDED ON THE CHIN OF THE SPIRIT BRIDE.
YOU GODDAMNED HYPOCRITE! FORGIVENESS? ALL YOU WANTED WAS A PIECE OF ASS.
POK
NOW THE HIDEOUS FACE WAS SHOUTING AT GRINDLE HIMSELF.
HIS BRAIN STOPPED WORKING. HE LAY LOOKING STUPIDLY AT THE RED JUMPING LIGHT. HE HEARD SOUNDS OF CRYING AND THEN THE FALTERING SLAP OF BARE FEET. A DOOR OPENED AND CLOSED. BUT IT MADE NO SENSE TO EZRA GRINDLE.
AFTER HE HAD LAID THERE FOR A LONG TIME HE GOT UP. ONE ARM-HIS RIGHT ARM WAS NUMB. HIS RIGHT LEG FELT WOODEN AND DEAD.
DORRIE, STANTON, WHERE ARE YOU?
I'M ANNOYED WITH STANTON FOR LEAVING ME LIKE THIS.
STANTON?
HIS CLOTHES WERE STILL IN THE CLOSET. SLOWLY HE REMEMBERED THINGS IN LITTLE SNATCHES. THERE HAD BEEN A WEDDING. THERE WAS A BRIDE, DORRIE. BUT IT WAS THE REV. CARLISLE WHO HAD HIT DORRIE. OR WAS IT AN EVIL SPIRIT IMPERSONATING HIM? MAYBE STANTON HAD FALLEN BEHIND THE COUCH WHEN THE EVIL PRESENCE... THIS WAS THURSDAY.

HE CAME TO A ROOM WITH SWITCHES AND DIALS. THE FIRST PRODUCED THE GHOSTLY MUSIC OF A SITAR. HE PRESSED A SECOND.

...EVERYBODY'S GONE, DEMATERIALIZED. I'VE MISSED AN IMPORTANT BOARD MEETING. I SHOULD HAVE BEEN THERE TO ACT AS AN ANCHOR FOR GRANGERFORD, A DEPENDABLE MAN... BUT COULD HE CONVINCE THEM BY HIMSELF OF THE SOUNDNESS OF THE COLORED LABOR POLICY?... MOB RULE GROWS EVER MORE MENACING EVEN AS WE SPEAK...

HARI AUM MY CHELAS

THE SOUND OF RAMAKRISHNA'S VOICE SEEMED TO TURN ON HIS OWN REASON. IN ONE JAGGED, SEARING FLASH HE SAW EVERYTHING. THE LONG BUILD-UP, THE BARRAGE OF SUGGESTION, THE MANUFACTURED MIRACLES

SOMEHOW HE GOT ON HIS CLOTHES AND STUMBLED OUTSIDE TO A PHONE BOOTH.

...NEVER MIND, ANDY, I'VE JUST BEEN... AWAY. I'M PEFECTLY ALL RIGHT, JUST CAN'T TALK VERY PLAIN. SOMETHING THE MATTER WITH THE SIDE OF MY FACE.

ONE QUESTION, CHIEF, ARE YOU WITH THAT SPIRIT PREACHER?

ANDY, I FORBID YOU EVER TO MENTION THAT MAN'S NAME TO ME AGAIN: THAT'S AN ORDER. YOU AND EVERYONE IN THE ORGANIZATION, IS THAT CLEAR? AND I FORBID ANYONE TO ASK ME WHERE I'VE BEEN.

THERE WAS ONE CHAMBER IN HIS MIND THAT HE DARE NOT OPEN UNTIL HE WAS SAFELY IN DR. RITTER'S OFFICE.

LILITH OPENED THE DOOR, SHE SAID NOTHING UNTIL THEY WERE IN THE OFFICE.

DID SHE?

SHE WENT ALL THE WAY THEN SHE BLEW UP, I KNOCKED OUT THE PAIR OF THEM AND LEFT THEM THERE.

WAS THAT NECESSARY?

THE OLD BASTARD WAS LIKE A STALLION, KICKING DOWN A STALL TO GET TO A MARE. IF MOLLY HAD ANY BRAINS SHE COULD PUT THE CON ON FOR HUSH MONEY.

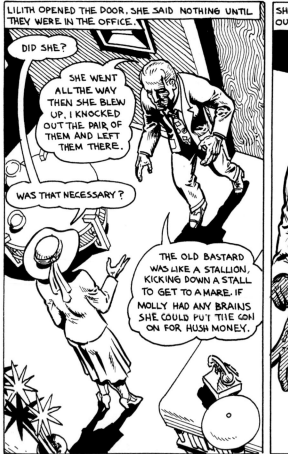

SHE TOOK THE BROWN ENVELOPES WITH THE MONEY OUT OF THE SAFE AND PLACED THEM ON THE TABLE.

I DON'T WANT TO KEEP THIS ANY LONGER, STAN. IT MAY BE SOME TIME BEFORE I CAN MEET YOU AGAIN.

I'VE GOT A KIESTER PARKED UPTOWN IN A CHECKROOM. PHONEY CREDENTIALS AND EVERYTHING.

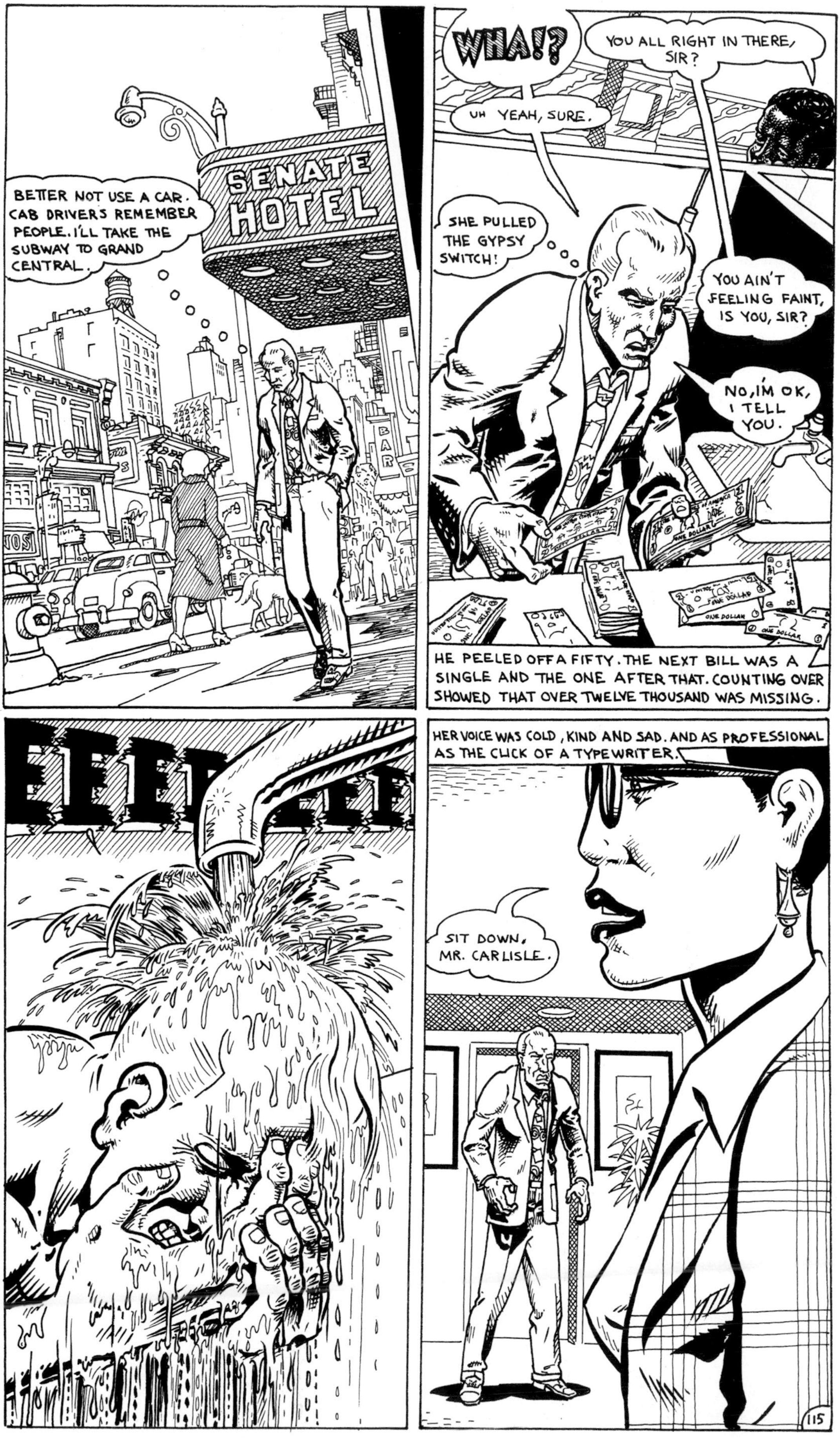
BETTER NOT USE A CAR. CAB DRIVERS REMEMBER PEOPLE. I'LL TAKE THE SUBWAY TO GRAND CENTRAL.
SENATE HOTEL
BAR
WHA!?
YOU ALL RIGHT IN THERE, SIR?
UH YEAH, SURE.
SHE PULLED THE GYPSY SWITCH!
YOU AIN'T FEELING FAINT, IS YOU, SIR?
NO, I'M OK, I TELL YOU.
HE PEELED OFF A FIFTY. THE NEXT BILL WAS A SINGLE AND THE ONE AFTER THAT. COUNTING OVER SHOWED THAT OVER TWELVE THOUSAND WAS MISSING.
HER VOICE WAS COLD, KIND AND SAD. AND AS PROFESSIONAL AS THE CLICK OF A TYPEWRITER.
SIT DOWN, MR. CARLISLE.

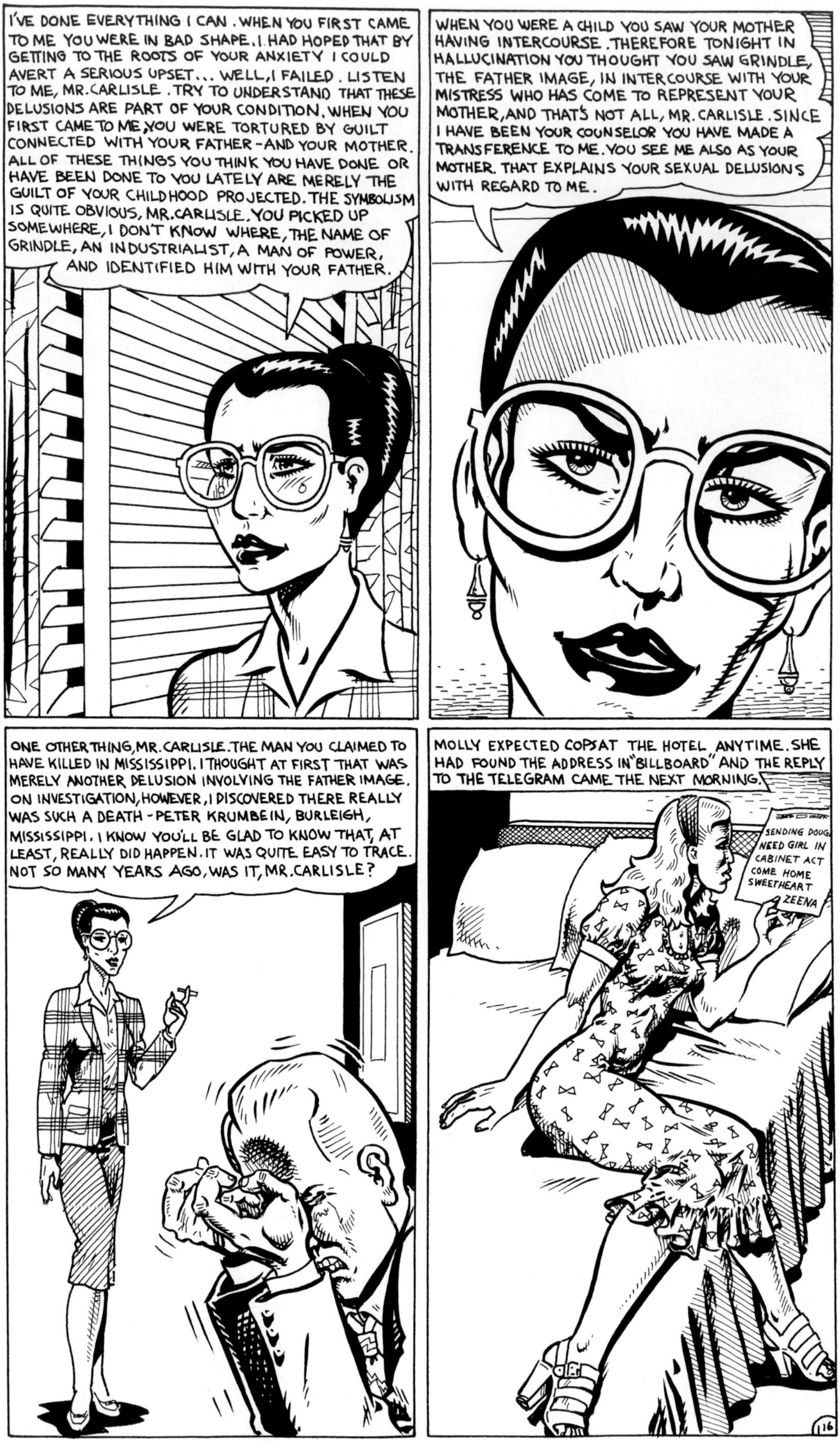
I'VE DONE EVERYTHING I CAN. WHEN YOU FIRST CAME TO ME YOU WERE IN BAD SHAPE. I HAD HOPED THAT BY GETTING TO THE ROOTS OF YOUR ANXIETY I COULD AVERT A SERIOUS UPSET... WELL, I FAILED. LISTEN TO ME, MR. CARLISLE. TRY TO UNDERSTAND THAT THESE DELUSIONS ARE PART OF YOUR CONDITION. WHEN YOU FIRST CAME TO ME, YOU WERE TORTURED BY GUILT CONNECTED WITH YOUR FATHER - AND YOUR MOTHER. ALL OF THESE THINGS YOU THINK YOU HAVE DONE OR HAVE BEEN DONE TO YOU LATELY ARE MERELY THE GUILT OF YOUR CHILDHOOD PROJECTED. THE SYMBOLISM IS QUITE OBVIOUS, MR. CARLISLE. YOU PICKED UP SOMEWHERE, I DON'T KNOW WHERE, THE NAME OF GRINDLE, AN INDUSTRIALIST, A MAN OF POWER, AND IDENTIFIED HIM WITH YOUR FATHER.
WHEN YOU WERE A CHILD YOU SAW YOUR MOTHER HAVING INTERCOURSE. THEREFORE TONIGHT IN HALLUCINATION YOU THOUGHT YOU SAW GRINDLE, THE FATHER IMAGE, IN INTERCOURSE WITH YOUR MISTRESS WHO HAS COME TO REPRESENT YOUR MOTHER, AND THAT'S NOT ALL, MR. CARLISLE. SINCE I HAVE BEEN YOUR COUNSELOR YOU HAVE MADE A TRANSFERENCE TO ME. YOU SEE ME ALSO AS YOUR MOTHER. THAT EXPLAINS YOUR SEXUAL DELUSIONS WITH REGARD TO ME.
ONE OTHER THING, MR. CARLISLE. THE MAN YOU CLAIMED TO HAVE KILLED IN MISSISSIPPI. I THOUGHT AT FIRST THAT WAS MERELY ANOTHER DELUSION INVOLVING THE FATHER IMAGE. ON INVESTIGATION, HOWEVER, I DISCOVERED THERE REALLY WAS SUCH A DEATH - PETER KRUMBEIN, BURLEIGH, MISSISSIPPI. I KNOW YOU'LL BE GLAD TO KNOW THAT, AT LEAST, REALLY DID HAPPEN. IT WAS QUITE EASY TO TRACE. NOT SO MANY YEARS AGO, WAS IT, MR. CARLISLE?
MOLLY EXPECTED COPS AT THE HOTEL ANYTIME. SHE HAD FOUND THE ADDRESS IN "BILLBOARD" AND THE REPLY TO THE TELEGRAM CAME THE NEXT MORNING.
SENDING DOUG NEED GIRL IN CABINET ACT COME HOME SWEETHEART ZEENA

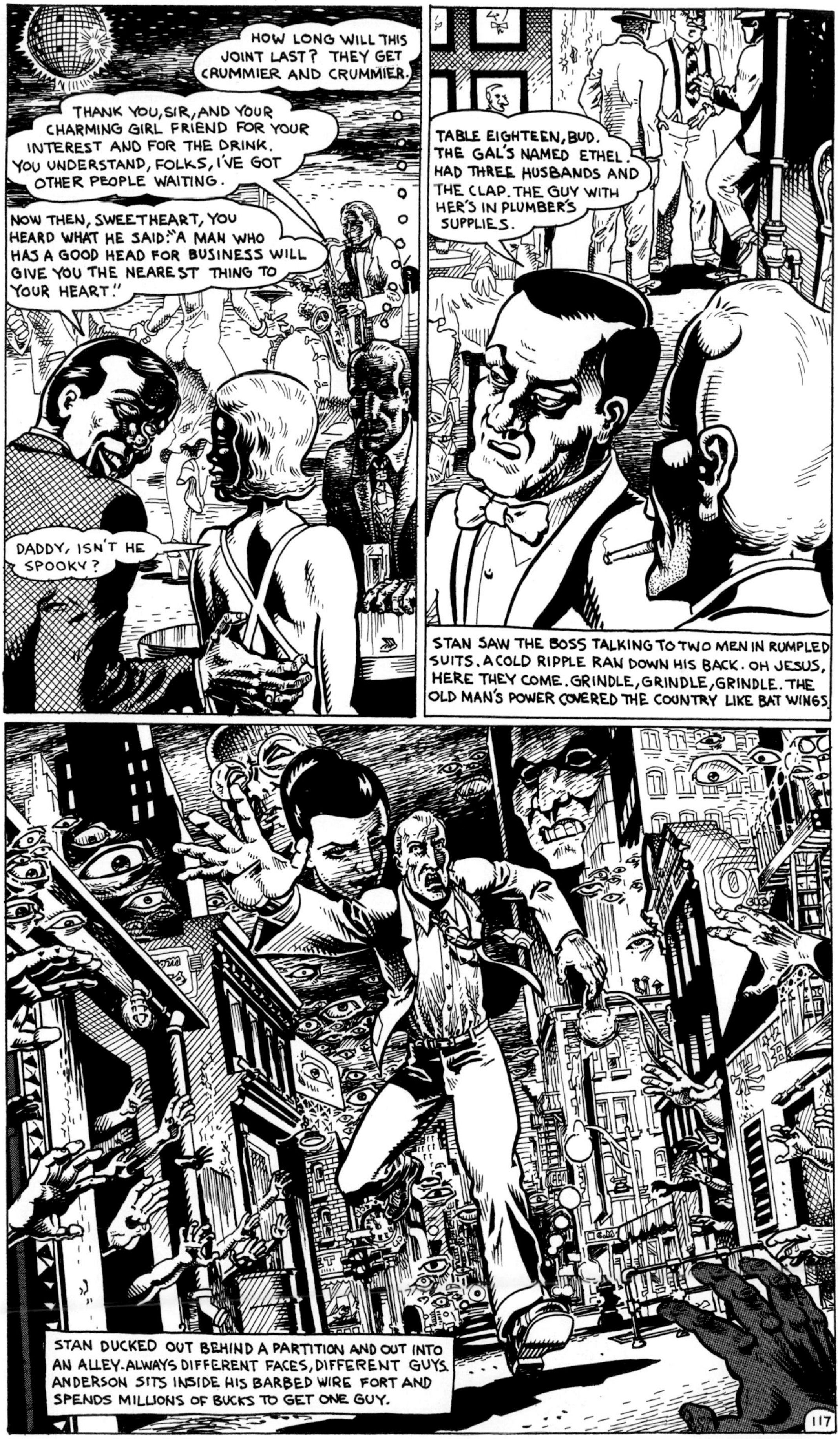
HOW LONG WILL THIS JOINT LAST? THEY GET CRUMMIER AND CRUMMIER.
THANK YOU, SIR, AND YOUR CHARMING GIRL FRIEND FOR YOUR INTEREST AND FOR THE DRINK. YOU UNDERSTAND, FOLKS, I'VE GOT OTHER PEOPLE WAITING.
NOW THEN, SWEETHEART, YOU HEARD WHAT HE SAID: "A MAN WHO HAS A GOOD HEAD FOR BUSINESS WILL GIVE YOU THE NEAREST THING TO YOUR HEART."
DADDY, ISN'T HE SPOOKY?
TABLE EIGHTEEN, BUD. THE GAL'S NAMED ETHEL. HAD THREE HUSBANDS AND THE CLAP. THE GUY WITH HER'S IN PLUMBER'S SUPPLIES.
STAN SAW THE BOSS TALKING TO TWO MEN IN RUMPLED SUITS. A COLD RIPPLE RAN DOWN HIS BACK. OH JESUS, HERE THEY COME. GRINDLE, GRINDLE, GRINDLE. THE OLD MAN'S POWER COVERED THE COUNTRY LIKE BAT WINGS.
STAN DUCKED OUT BEHIND A PARTITION AND OUT INTO AN ALLEY. ALWAYS DIFFERENT FACES, DIFFERENT GUYS. ANDERSON SITS INSIDE HIS BARBED WIRE FORT AND SPENDS MILLIONS OF BUCKS TO GET ONE GUY.

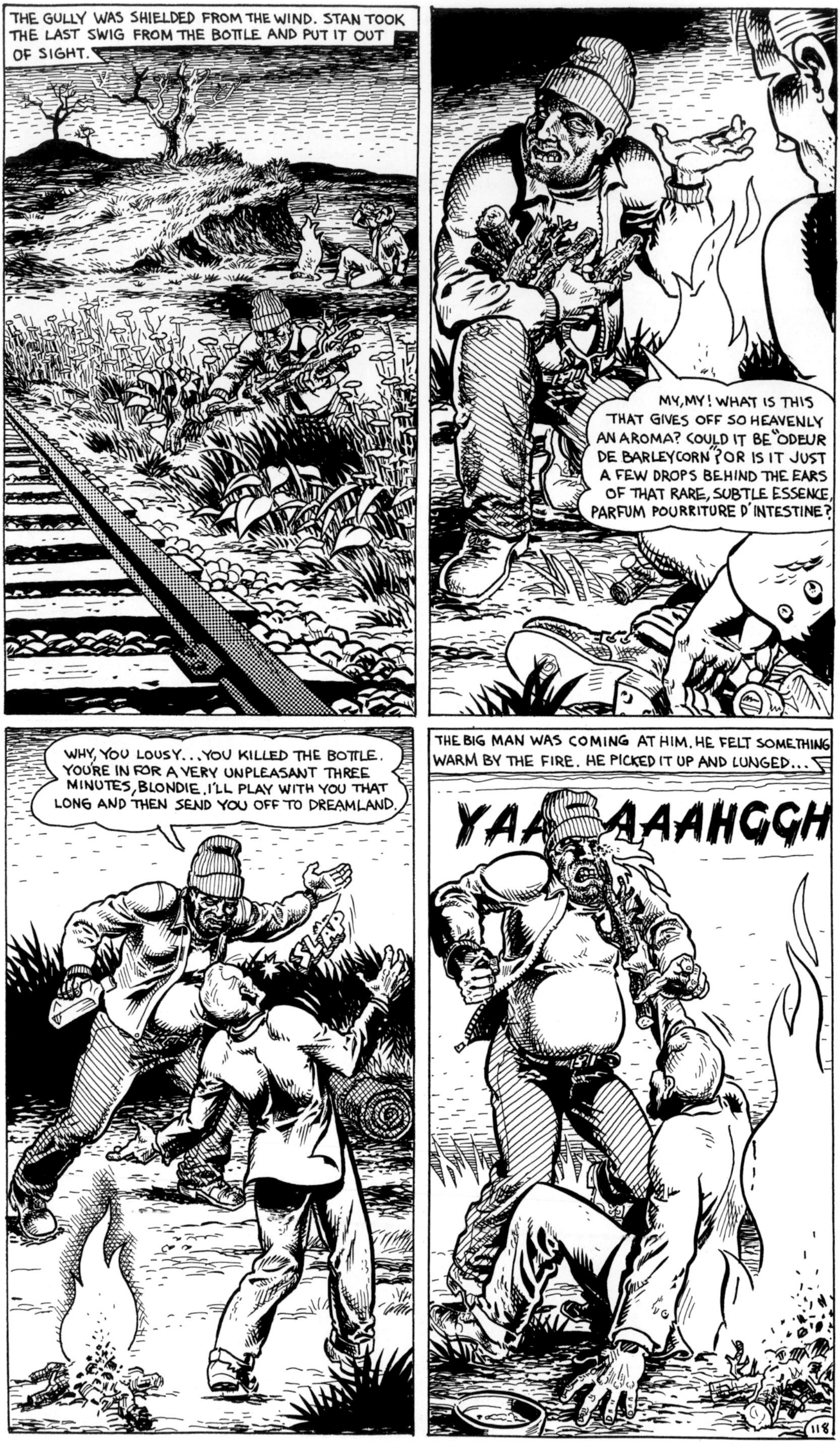
THE GULLY WAS SHIELDED FROM THE WIND. STAN TOOK THE LAST SWIG FROM THE BOTTLE AND PUT IT OUT OF SIGHT.
MY, MY! WHAT IS THIS THAT GIVES OFF SO HEAVENLY AN AROMA? COULD IT BE "ODEUR DE BARLEYCORN"? OR IS IT JUST A FEW DROPS BEHIND THE EARS OF THAT RARE, SUBTLE ESSENCE, PARFUM POURRITURE D'INTESTINE?
WHY, YOU LOUSY... YOU KILLED THE BOTTLE. YOU'RE IN FOR A VERY UNPLEASANT THREE MINUTES, BLONDIE. I'LL PLAY WITH YOU THAT LONG AND THEN SEND YOU OFF TO DREAMLAND.
SLAP
THE BIG MAN WAS COMING AT HIM. HE FELT SOMETHING WARM BY THE FIRE. HE PICKED IT UP AND LUNGED...
YAA AAAHGGH

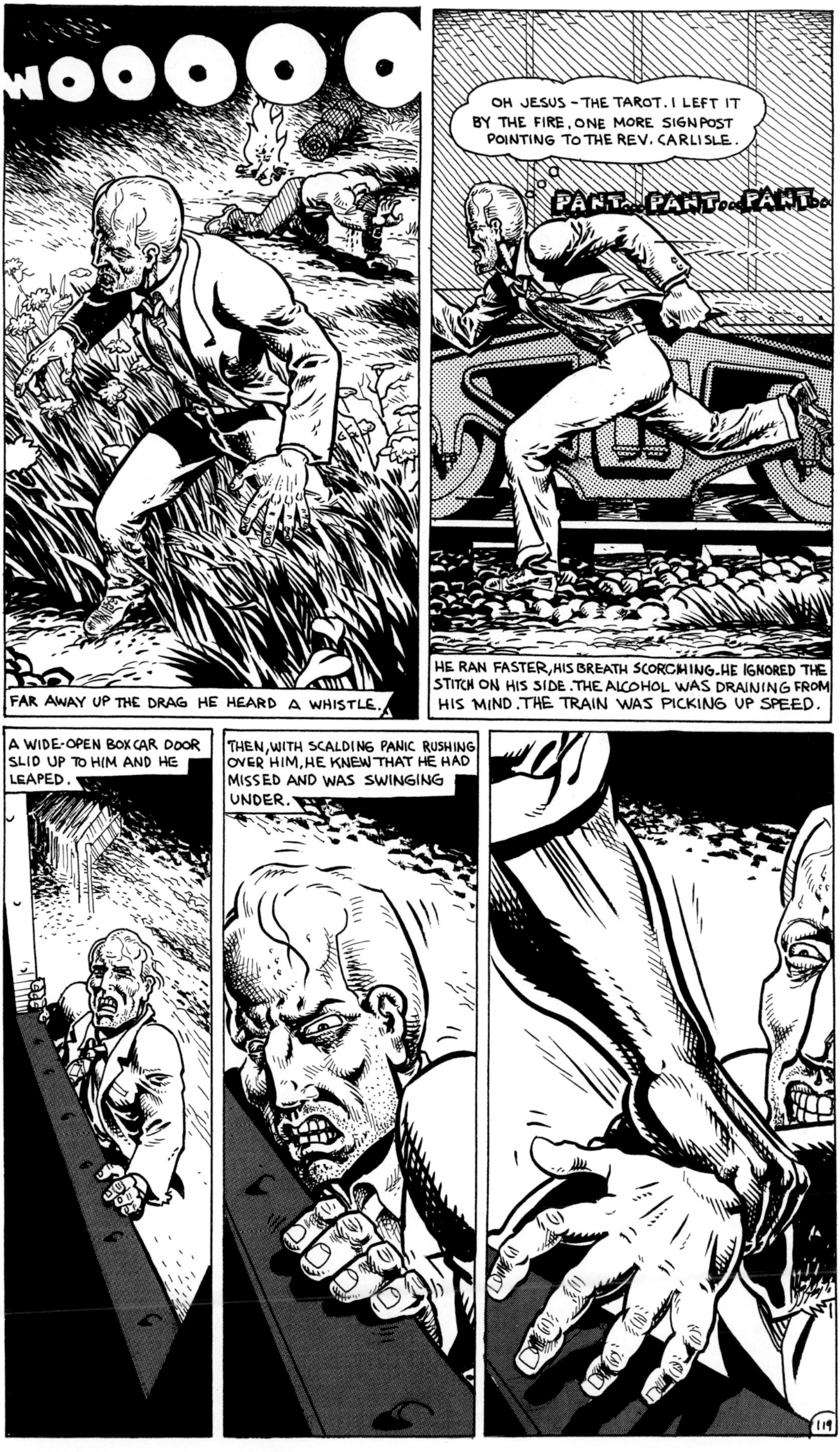
WOOOOO
FAR AWAY UP THE DRAG HE HEARD A WHISTLE.
OH JESUS - THE TAROT. I LEFT IT BY THE FIRE, ONE MORE SIGNPOST POINTING TO THE REV. CARLISLE.
PANT... PANT... PANT...
HE RAN FASTER, HIS BREATH SCORCHING. HE IGNORED THE STITCH ON HIS SIDE. THE ALCOHOL WAS DRAINING FROM HIS MIND. THE TRAIN WAS PICKING UP SPEED.
A WIDE-OPEN BOXCAR DOOR SLID UP TO HIM AND HE LEAPED.
THEN, WITH SCALDING PANIC RUSHING OVER HIM, HE KNEW THAT HE HAD MISSED AND WAS SWINGING UNDER.
119

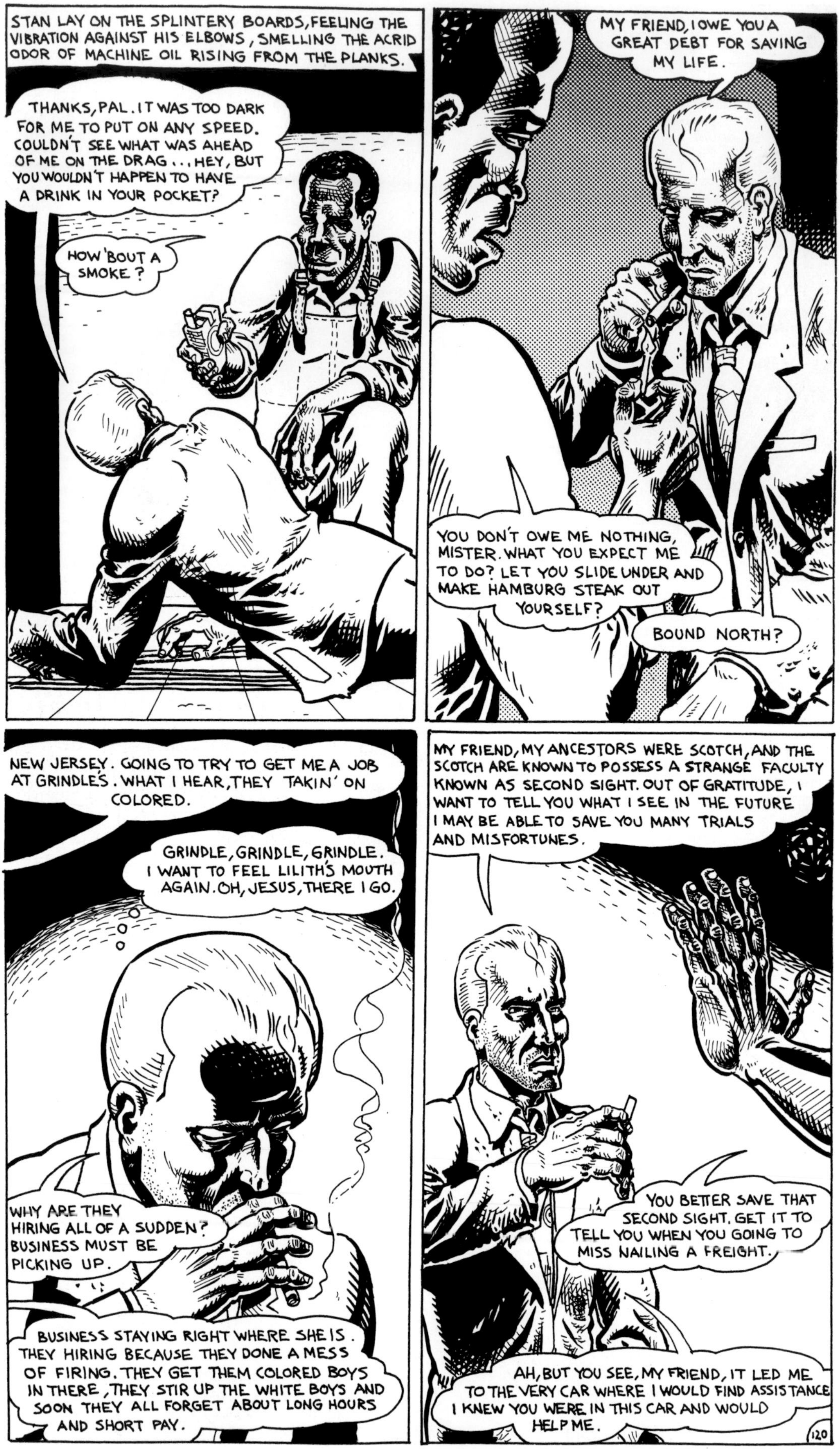
STAN LAY ON THE SPLINTERY BOARDS, FEELING THE VIBRATION AGAINST HIS ELBOWS, SMELLING THE ACRID ODOR OF MACHINE OIL RISING FROM THE PLANKS.
THANKS, PAL. IT WAS TOO DARK FOR ME TO PUT ON ANY SPEED. COULDN'T SEE WHAT WAS AHEAD OF ME ON THE DRAG... HEY, BUT YOU WOULDN'T HAPPEN TO HAVE A DRINK IN YOUR POCKET?
HOW 'BOUT A SMOKE?
MY FRIEND, I OWE YOU A GREAT DEBT FOR SAVING MY LIFE.
YOU DON'T OWE ME NOTHING, MISTER. WHAT YOU EXPECT ME TO DO? LET YOU SLIDE UNDER AND MAKE HAMBURG STEAK OUT YOURSELF?
BOUND NORTH?
NEW JERSEY. GOING TO TRY TO GET ME A JOB AT GRINDLE'S. WHAT I HEAR, THEY TAKIN' ON COLORED.
GRINDLE, GRINDLE, GRINDLE. I WANT TO FEEL LILITH'S MOUTH AGAIN. OH, JESUS, THERE I GO.
WHY ARE THEY HIRING ALL OF A SUDDEN? BUSINESS MUST BE PICKING UP.
BUSINESS STAYING RIGHT WHERE SHE IS. THEY HIRING BECAUSE THEY DONE A MESS OF FIRING. THEY GET THEM COLORED BOYS IN THERE, THEY STIR UP THE WHITE BOYS AND SOON THEY ALL FORGET ABOUT LONG HOURS AND SHORT PAY.
MY FRIEND, MY ANCESTORS WERE SCOTCH, AND THE SCOTCH ARE KNOWN TO POSSESS A STRANGE FACULTY KNOWN AS SECOND SIGHT. OUT OF GRATITUDE, I WANT TO TELL YOU WHAT I SEE IN THE FUTURE I MAY BE ABLE TO SAVE YOU MANY TRIALS AND MISFORTUNES.
YOU BETTER SAVE THAT SECOND SIGHT. GET IT TO TELL YOU WHEN YOU GOING TO MISS NAILING A FREIGHT.
AH, BUT YOU SEE, MY FRIEND, IT LED ME TO THE VERY CAR WHERE I WOULD FIND ASSISTANCE I KNEW YOU WERE IN THIS CAR AND WOULD HELP ME.
120

MISTER, YOU OUGHT TO PLAY THE RACES AND GET RICH.

TELL ME THIS—I GET THE DECIDED IMPRESSION THAT YOU HAVE A SCAR ON ONE KNEE. ISN'T THAT SO?

SURE, I GOT SCARS ON BOTH MY KNEES. I GOT SCARS ON MY ASS TOO.

YOU GOT EVERYTHING FIGURED OUT SO CLOSE, WHAT SENSE DOES IT ALL MAKE? WHAT SORT OF GOD WOULD PUT US HERE IN THIS GODDAMNED STINKING SLAUGHTERHOUSE OF A WORLD? SOME GUY THAT LIKES TO TEAR THE WINGS OFF FLIES. WHAT USE IS THERE LIVING AND STARVING AND FIGHTING THE NEXT GUY FOR A FULL BELLY. AND THE BIGGEST LOONIES ARE AT THE TOP. JUST WHAT'S THE PURPOSE—WHY ARE WE PUT HERE?

NOW YOU TALKING, BROTHER. YOU LET THAT CRAP ALONE AND TALK TO ME. WE GOT A LONG RIDE AHEAD. THE WAY I LOOK AT IT, WE AIN'T PUT, WE JUST GROWED. DIDN'T HAVE NO START. IT'S ALWAYS BEEN DOING BUSINESS. PEOPLE ASK ME: HOW THIS WORLD GET MADE WITHOUT GOD MAKE IT? I ASK 'EM RIGHT BACK: WHO MAKE GOD? THEY SAY HE DON'T NEED NO MAKING, HE ALWAYS BEEN THERE. I SAY: WELL, THEN WHY YOU GOT TO GO BRINGING HIM IN AT ALL? THE OLD WORLD'S ALWAYS BEEN THERE TOO. THEY ASK ME: HOW ABOUT SIN? WHO PUT ALL THAT SIN AND WICKEDNESS AND CUSSEDNESS IN THE WORLD? I SAY: WHO PUT THE BOLL WEEVIL? HE GROWED!

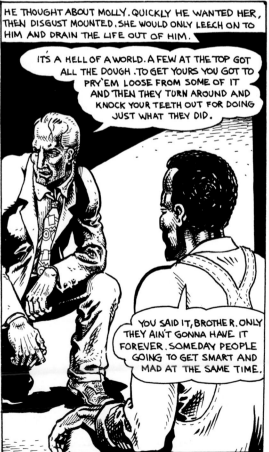

HE THOUGHT ABOUT MOLLY. QUICKLY HE WANTED HER, THEN DISGUST MOUNTED. SHE WOULD ONLY LEECH ON TO HIM AND DRAIN THE LIFE OUT OF HIM.

IT'S A HELL OF A WORLD. A FEW AT THE TOP GOT ALL THE DOUGH. TO GET YOURS YOU GOT TO PRY 'EM LOOSE FROM SOME OF IT AND THEN THEY TURN AROUND AND KNOCK YOUR TEETH OUT FOR DOING JUST WHAT THEY DID.

YOU SAID IT, BROTHER R. ONLY THEY AIN'T GONNA HAVE IT FOREVER. SOMEDAY PEOPLE GOING TO GET SMART AND MAD AT THE SAME TIME.

YOU SOUND LIKE A LABOR AGITATOR.

THIS AIN'T GOOD. GOT NO BUSINESS STOPPING HERE. OH-OH. IT'S A FRISK. SOMETHING FUNNY. THIS DIVISION NEVER BEEN HOSTILE BEFORE.

OH, JESUS. THIS IS IT. GRINDLE, EVERY SECOND MOVING CLOSER.

121

COME ON, YOU BASTARD, GET YOUR HANDS UP... I GOT ONE BUT HE AIN'T NO COON.

WE GOT IT FROM ANDERSON, HE'S ON THIS TRAIN.

THIS IS IT, THIS IS IT, THIS IS IT!

WHAT'S IN YOUR POCKET, BUD?... IT'S JUST A BIBLE.

MAYBE IT'S A PINEAPPLE MADE TO LOOK LIKE A BIBLE.

BROTHER, YOU HAVE IN YOUR HAND THE MOST POWERFUL WEAPON IN THE WORLD.

WE'RE LOOKING FOR A COLORED LAD. WE KNOW HE BOARDED THIS TRAIN. IF YOU CAN GIVE US INFORMATION LEADING TO HIS ARREST, YOU WOULD BE SERVING THE FORCES OF JUSTICE. AND THERE MIGHT BE SOMETHING IN IT FOR YOU.

JUSTICE..."SOMETHING IN IT" COULD BE FOLDING MONEY JUSTICE... A BUCK-TEN CANS OF ALKY... A BUCK-TWENTY SHOTS!

BROTHER, I MET A COLORED BROTHER-IN-GOD WHEN I WAS WAITING TO NAIL THIS JOB. I TRIED TO BRING HIM TO JESUS, BUT HE WOULDN'T LISTEN TO THE WORD. I GAVE HIM MY LAST TRACT...

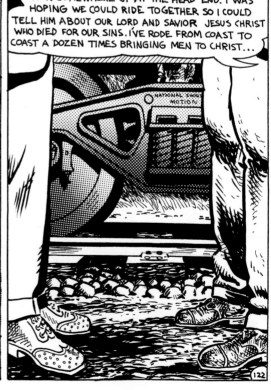

OK, PARSON, GIVE JESUS A REST. WE'RE LOOKING FOR A GODDAMNED NIGGER RED. WE KNOW HE WAS RIDING HERE IN THE CAR WITH YOU.

BROTHER, THIS COLORED BROTHER-IN-GOD NAILED HER SOMEWHERE UP AT THE HEAD-END. I WAS HOPING WE COULD RIDE TOGETHER SO I COULD TELL HIM ABOUT OUR LORD AND SAVIOR JESUS CHRIST WHO DIED FOR OUR SINS. I'VE RODE FROM COAST TO COAST A DOZEN TIMES BRINGING MEN TO CHRIST...

122

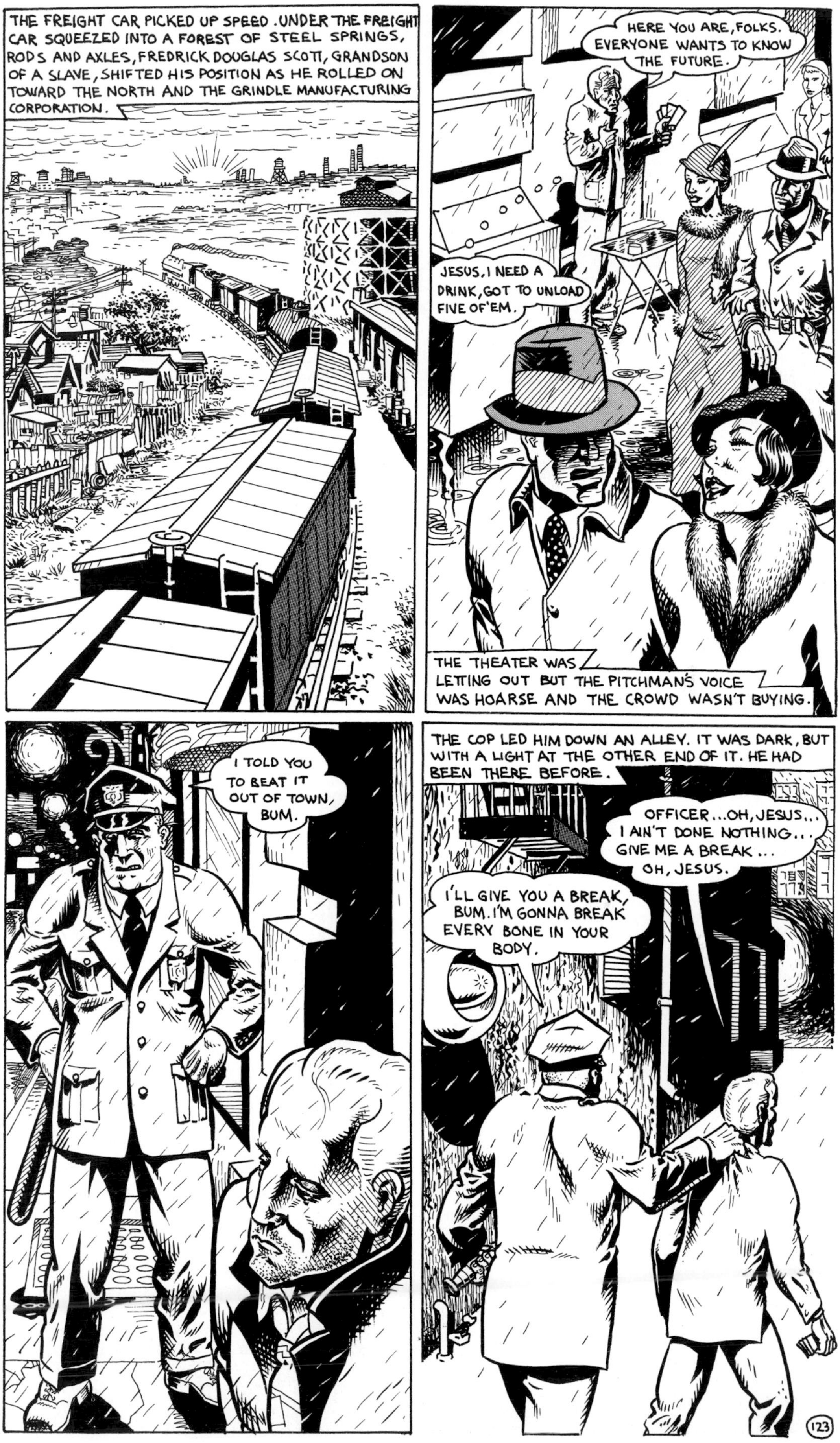
THE FREIGHT CAR PICKED UP SPEED. UNDER THE FREIGHT CAR SQUEEZED INTO A FOREST OF STEEL SPRINGS, RODS AND AXLES, FREDRICK DOUGLAS SCOTT, GRANDSON OF A SLAVE, SHIFTED HIS POSITION AS HE ROLLED ON TOWARD THE NORTH AND THE GRINDLE MANUFACTURING CORPORATION.
HERE YOU ARE, FOLKS. EVERYONE WANTS TO KNOW THE FUTURE.
JESUS, I NEED A DRINK, GOT TO UNLOAD FIVE OF 'EM.
THE THEATER WAS LETTING OUT BUT THE PITCHMAN'S VOICE WAS HOARSE AND THE CROWD WASN'T BUYING.
I TOLD YOU TO BEAT IT OUT OF TOWN, BUM.
THE COP LED HIM DOWN AN ALLEY. IT WAS DARK, BUT WITH A LIGHT AT THE OTHER END OF IT. HE HAD BEEN THERE BEFORE.
OFFICER... OH, JESUS... I AIN'T DONE NOTHING... GIVE ME A BREAK... OH, JESUS.
I'LL GIVE YOU A BREAK, BUM. I'M GONNA BREAK EVERY BONE IN YOUR BODY.

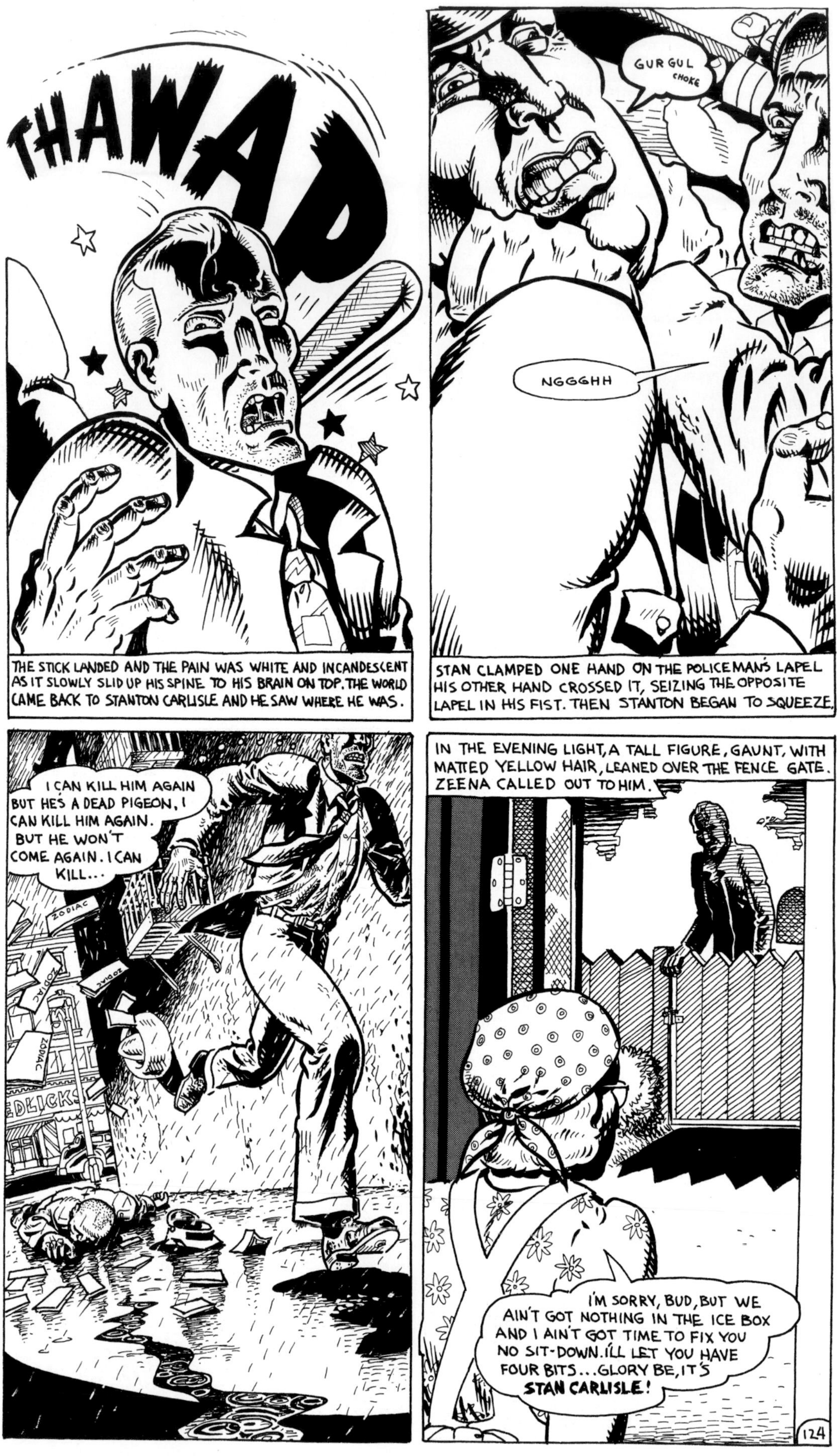
THAWAP
THE STICK LANDED AND THE PAIN WAS WHITE AND INCANDESCENT AS IT SLOWLY SLID UP HIS SPINE TO HIS BRAIN ON TOP. THE WORLD CAME BACK TO STANTON CARLISLE AND HE SAW WHERE HE WAS.
GURGUL CHOKE
NGGGHH
STAN CLAMPED ONE HAND ON THE POLICEMAN'S LAPEL HIS OTHER HAND CROSSED IT, SEIZING THE OPPOSITE LAPEL IN HIS FIST. THEN STANTON BEGAN TO SQUEEZE.
I CAN KILL HIM AGAIN BUT HE'S A DEAD PIGEON, I CAN KILL HIM AGAIN. BUT HE WON'T COME AGAIN. I CAN KILL...
ZODIAC
ZODIAC
ZODIAC
ZODIAC
EDLICKS
IN THE EVENING LIGHT, A TALL FIGURE, GAUNT, WITH MATTED YELLOW HAIR, LEANED OVER THE FENCE GATE. ZEENA CALLED OUT TO HIM.
I'M SORRY, BUD, BUT WE AIN'T GOT NOTHING IN THE ICE BOX AND I AIN'T GOT TIME TO FIX YOU NO SIT-DOWN. I'LL LET YOU HAVE FOUR BITS... GLORY BE, IT'S **STAN CARLISLE!**

HI, ZEENA. SAW YOUR AD IN THE PAPER...

STANTON CARLISLE, I SWORE IF I EVER SET MY EYES ON YOU AGAIN I'D SURE GIVE YOU A PIECE OF MY MIND. WHY, THAT CHILD WAS PRETTY NEAR OUT OF HER HEAD BY THE TIME SHE GOT TO THE CARNY. OH, YOU WAS GOING TO GET MIGHTY BIGGETY AND WHAT DO YOU DO BUT END UP PUTTING THAT SWEET KID ON THE TURF — SAME AS ANY TWO-BIT PIMP!

JOE, C'MON OVER HERE, STAN'S PASSED OUT. WE GOT TO GET HIM IN THE HOUSE.

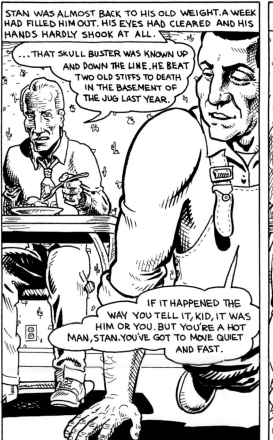

STAN WAS ALMOST BACK TO HIS OLD WEIGHT. A WEEK HAD FILLED HIM OUT. HIS EYES HAD CLEARED AND HIS HANDS HARDLY SHOOK AT ALL.

...THAT SKULL BUSTER WAS KNOWN UP AND DOWN THE LINE. HE BEAT TWO OLD STIFFS TO DEATH IN THE BASEMENT OF THE JUG LAST YEAR.

IF IT HAPPENED THE WAY YOU TELL IT, KID, IT WAS HIM OR YOU. BUT YOU'RE A HOT MAN, STAN. YOU'VE GOT TO MOVE QUIET AND FAST.

STANTON CARLISLE'S VOICE WAS GETTING BACK SOME OF ITS RESONANCE.

ZEENA, I'VE BEEN LIVING A GODDAMNED NIGHTMARE. I DON'T KNOW WHAT EVER GOT INTO ME. WHEN VAUDEVILLE CONKED OUT, WE COULD HAVE WORKED THE NIGHT CLUBS. I DON'T EXPECT MOLLY TO EVER FORGIVE ME. BUT I'M GLAD THE KID GOT HERSELF A GOOD SPOT. I HOPE HE'S A SWELL GUY. SHE DESERVES IT. DON'T TELL HER YOU EVER SAW ME. I WANT HER TO FORGET ME. I HAD MY CHANCE AND FLUFFED IT.

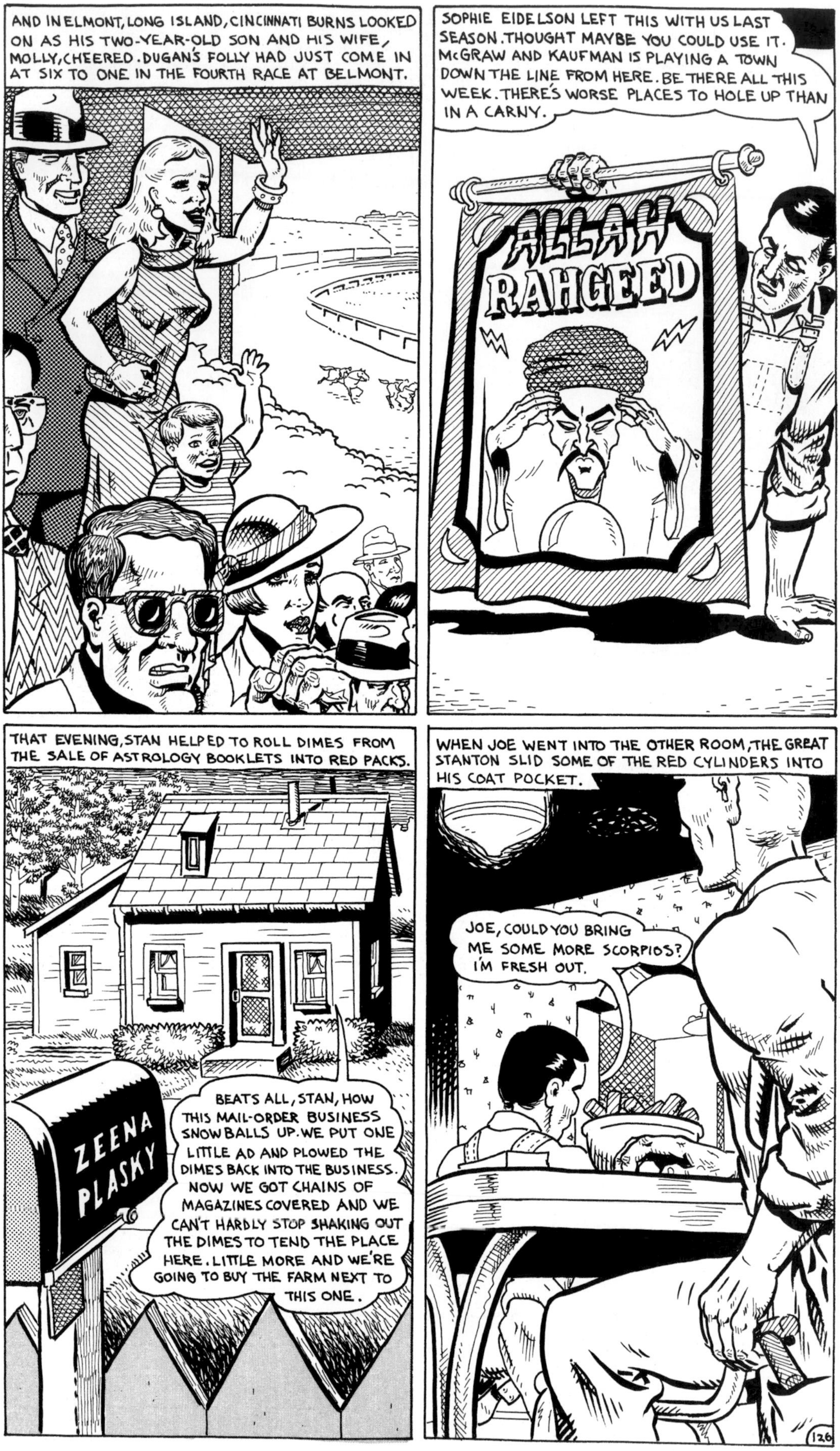
AND IN ELMONT, LONG ISLAND, CINCINNATI BURNS LOOKED ON AS HIS TWO-YEAR-OLD SON AND HIS WIFE, MOLLY, CHEERED. DUGAN'S FOLLY HAD JUST COME IN AT SIX TO ONE IN THE FOURTH RACE AT BELMONT.
SOPHIE EIDELSON LEFT THIS WITH US LAST SEASON. THOUGHT MAYBE YOU COULD USE IT. McGRAW AND KAUFMAN IS PLAYING A TOWN DOWN THE LINE FROM HERE. BE THERE ALL THIS WEEK. THERE'S WORSE PLACES TO HOLE UP THAN IN A CARNY.
ALLAH RAHGEED
THAT EVENING, STAN HELPED TO ROLL DIMES FROM THE SALE OF ASTROLOGY BOOKLETS INTO RED PACKS.
ZEENA PLASKY
BEATS ALL, STAN, HOW THIS MAIL-ORDER BUSINESS SNOWBALLS UP. WE PUT ONE LITTLE AD AND PLOWED THE DIMES BACK INTO THE BUSINESS. NOW WE GOT CHAINS OF MAGAZINES COVERED AND WE CAN'T HARDLY STOP SHAKING OUT THE DIMES TO TEND THE PLACE HERE. LITTLE MORE AND WE'RE GOING TO BUY THE FARM NEXT TO THIS ONE.
WHEN JOE WENT INTO THE OTHER ROOM, THE GREAT STANTON SLID SOME OF THE RED CYLINDERS INTO HIS COAT POCKET.
JOE, COULD YOU BRING ME SOME MORE SCORPIOS? I'M FRESH OUT.
126

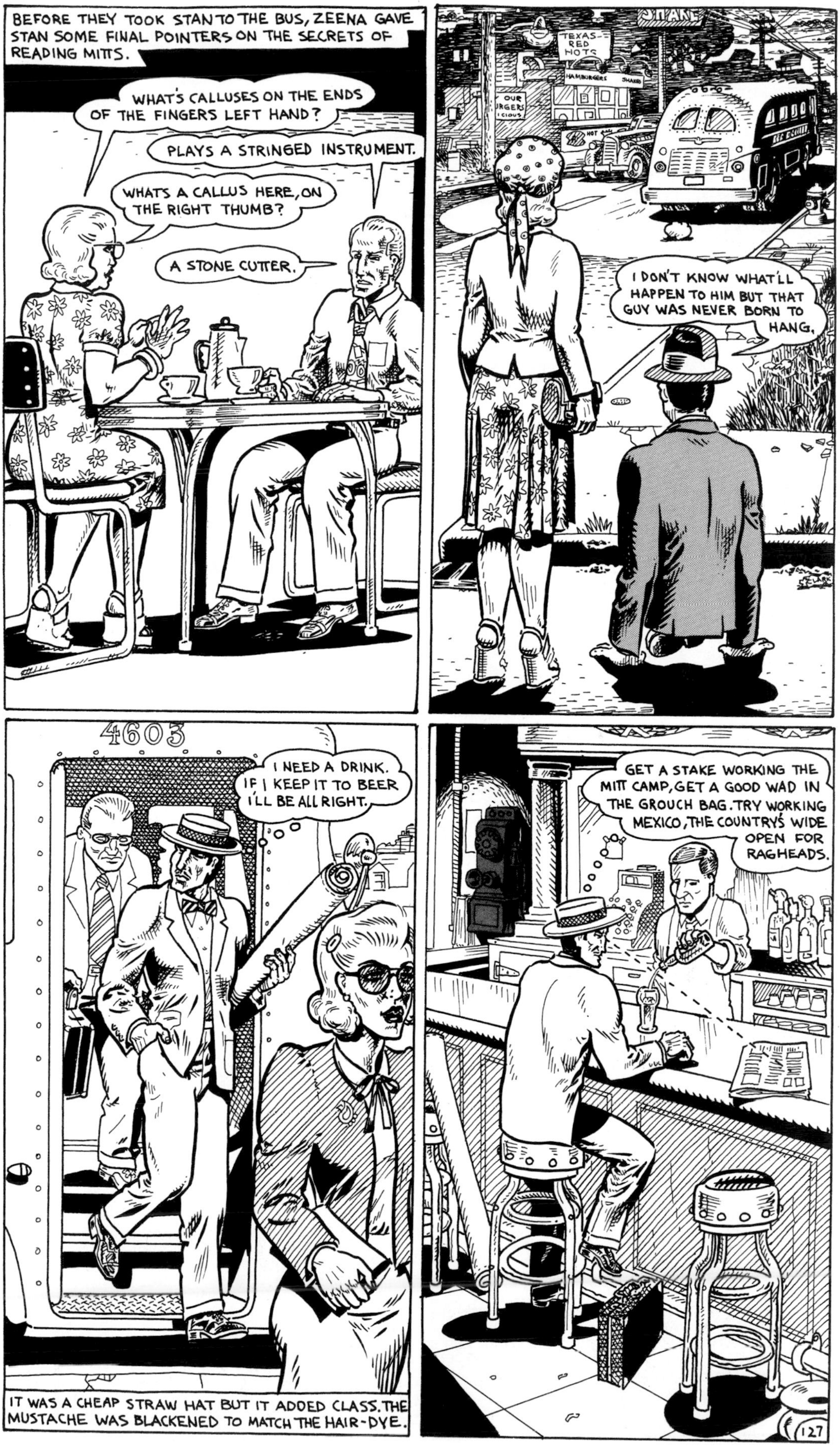
BEFORE THEY TOOK STAN TO THE BUS, ZEENA GAVE STAN SOME FINAL POINTERS ON THE SECRETS OF READING MITTS.
WHAT'S CALLUSES ON THE ENDS OF THE FINGERS LEFT HAND?
PLAYS A STRINGED INSTRUMENT.
WHATS A CALLUS HERE, ON THE RIGHT THUMB?
A STONE CUTTER.
TEXAS RED HOTS
HAMBURGERS
I DON'T KNOW WHAT'LL HAPPEN TO HIM BUT THAT GUY WAS NEVER BORN TO HANG.
4603
I NEED A DRINK. IF I KEEP IT TO BEER I'LL BE ALL RIGHT.
IT WAS A CHEAP STRAW HAT BUT IT ADDED CLASS. THE MUSTACHE WAS BLACKENED TO MATCH THE HAIR-DYE.
GET A STAKE WORKING THE MITT CAMP, GET A GOOD WAD IN THE GROUCH BAG. TRY WORKING MEXICO, THE COUNTRY'S WIDE OPEN FOR RAGHEADS.

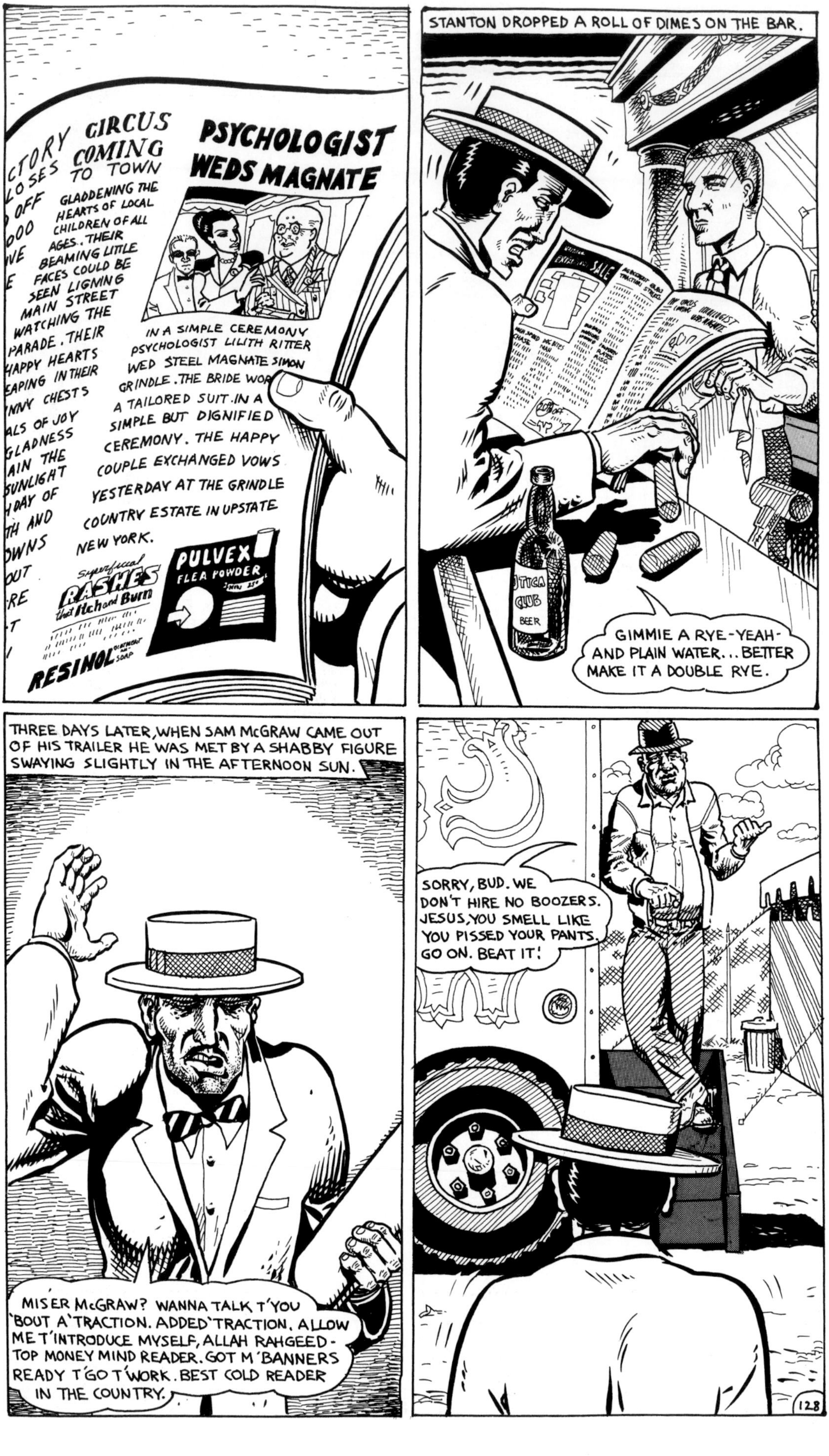
CIRCUS COMING TO TOWN
GLADDENING THE HEARTS OF LOCAL CHILDREN OF ALL AGES. THEIR BEAMING LITTLE FACES COULD BE SEEN LIGNING MAIN STREET WATCHING THE PARADE. THEIR HAPPY HEARTS
PSYCHOLOGIST WEDS MAGNATE
IN A SIMPLE CEREMONY PSYCHOLOGIST LILITH RITTER WED STEEL MAGNATE SIMON GRINDLE. THE BRIDE WOR A TAILORED SUIT. IN A SIMPLE BUT DIGNIFIED CEREMONY. THE HAPPY COUPLE EXCHANGED VOWS YESTERDAY AT THE GRINDLE COUNTRY ESTATE IN UPSTATE NEW YORK.
Superficial RASHES that Itch and Burn
RESINOL OINTMENT AND SOAP
PULVEX FLEA POWDER
STANTON DROPPED A ROLL OF DIMES ON THE BAR.
UTICA CLUB BEER
GIMMIE A RYE-YEAH-AND PLAIN WATER... BETTER MAKE IT A DOUBLE RYE.
THREE DAYS LATER, WHEN SAM McGRAW CAME OUT OF HIS TRAILER HE WAS MET BY A SHABBY FIGURE SWAYING SLIGHTLY IN THE AFTERNOON SUN.
MISER McGRAW? WANNA TALK T'YOU 'BOUT A'TRACTION. ADDED'TRACTION. ALLOW ME T'INTRODUCE MYSELF, ALLAH RAHGEED-TOP MONEY MIND READER. GOT M'BANNERS READY T'GO T'WORK. BEST COLD READER IN THE COUNTRY.
SORRY, BUD. WE DON'T HIRE NO BOOZERS. JESUS, YOU SMELL LIKE YOU PISSED YOUR PANTS. GO ON. BEAT IT!

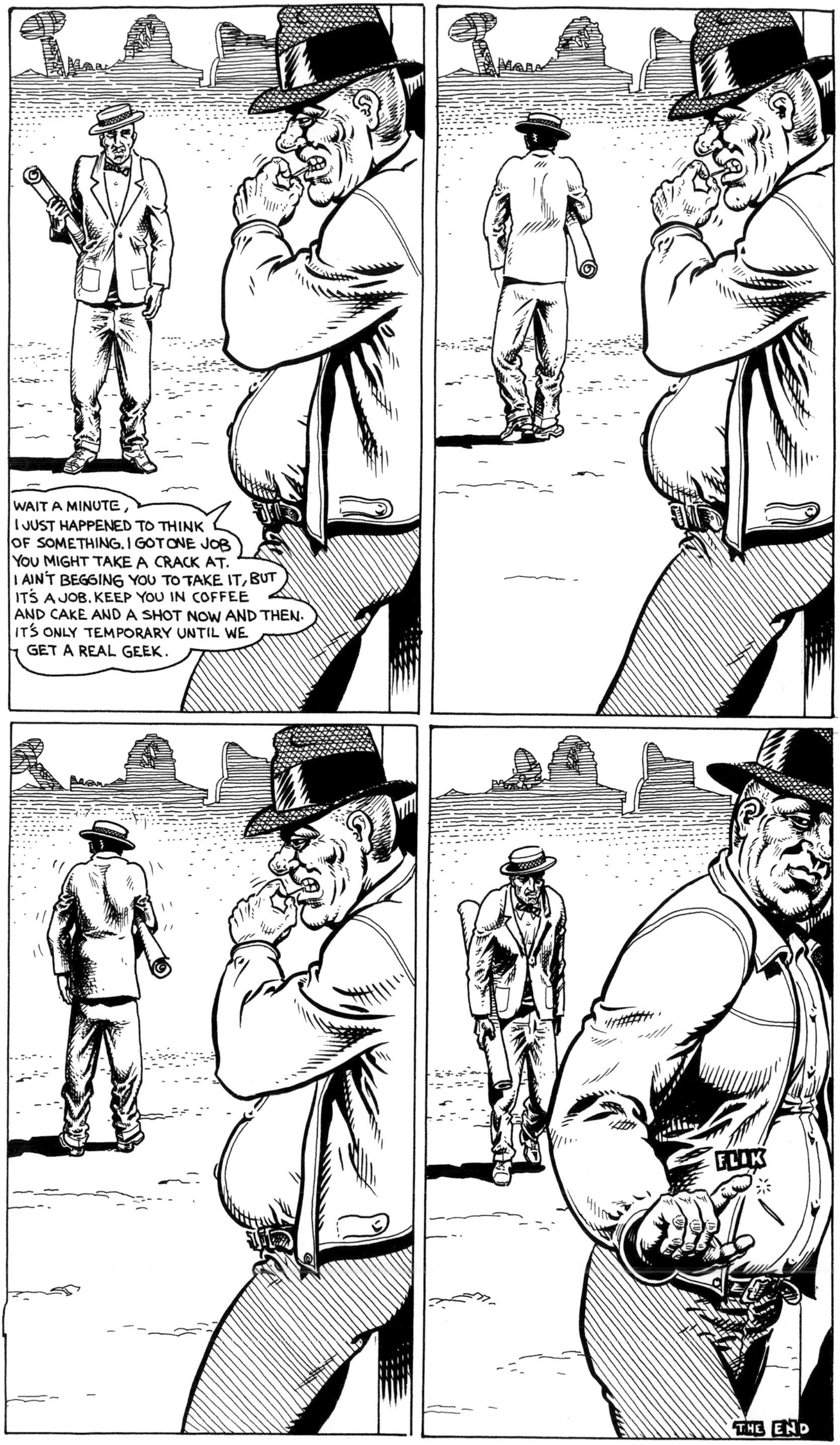
WAIT A MINUTE, I JUST HAPPENED TO THINK OF SOMETHING. I GOT ONE JOB YOU MIGHT TAKE A CRACK AT. I AIN'T BEGGING YOU TO TAKE IT, BUT IT'S A JOB. KEEP YOU IN COFFEE AND CAKE AND A SHOT NOW AND THEN. IT'S ONLY TEMPORARY UNTIL WE GET A REAL GEEK.
FLIK
THE END